INTOLERABLE

INTOLERABLE

Writings from Michel Foucault
and the Prisons Information Group
(1970–1980)

MICHEL FOUCAULT and THE PRISONS INFORMATION GROUP
EDITED by KEVIN THOMPSON and PERRY ZURN
TRANSLATED by PERRY ZURN and ERIK BERANEK

University of Minnesota Press
Minneapolis
London

Publication History on pages 444–60 gives original and previous publication history for the writings compiled in this book.

Texts from *Dits et écrits* by Michel Foucault copyright 1994 Éditions Gallimard, Paris

Published by the University of Minnesota Press
111 Third Avenue South, Suite 290
Minneapolis, MN 55401-2520
http://www.upress.umn.edu

ISBN 978-1-5179-0235-3 (pb)
ISBN 978-1-5179-0234-6 (hc)
Library of Congress record available at
https://lccn.loc.gov/2020026925

Printed in the United States of America on acid-free paper

The University of Minnesota is an equal-opportunity educator and employer.

27 26 25 24 23 22 21   10 9 8 7 6 5 4 3 2 1

Contents

Acknowledgments

Editors' Acknowledgments

Thanks to DePaul University's Humanities Center for its generous support of this project and its related symposium, "Foucault and the Legacy of the Prisons Information Group" (2015). Thanks also to DePaul University and American University for providing Kevin Thompson and Perry Zurn with travel grants for archival research at the Institut Mémoire de L'Édition Contemporaine (IMEC) and the Bibliothèque Nationale de France (BNF). Many thanks to IMEC and BNF for facilitating our consultation of the Groupe d'Information sur les Prisons (GIP) and Foucault archives.

Thanks to Daniel Defert for his support of the work and to Philippe Artières, Frédéric Gros, and, most especially, Henri-Paul Fruchaud for their aid in conceiving the project and securing rights to some of the material through the Foucault Estate. Thanks to our reviewers, especially Stuart Elden, for their recommendations as we finalized the collection. And special thanks to our editors at the University of Minnesota Press: Dani Kasprzak, for believing in the project and patiently seeing it through to completion, and Pieter Martin, for so deftly carrying it through production.

Thanks also to the Foucault Circle, where the idea for this project began, and for the recommendations of Richard Lynch, Corentin Durand, and Marcelo Hoffman regarding its contents. Finally, thanks to Joel Bock for his assistance in securing the photograph reprinted on the cover of the book.

Translators' Acknowledgments

Thanks to Michael Naas and Pascale-Anne Brault for bringing their unparalleled expertise to bear on a few sample pieces in this collection. Thanks to Eugene Sampson for comments on a significant portion of the early manuscript. Thanks also to the Foucault Circle of 2012, whose participants, especially Richard Lynch, Chloë Taylor, and Dianna Taylor, joined in a rich roundtable discussion of the earliest drafts of several pieces.

We are grateful to all the contributors to *Active Intolerance: Michel Foucault, the Prisons Information Group, and the Future of Abolition* (Palgrave, 2016) and *Carceral Notebooks* 12; their essays and conversations enhanced our understanding of these texts and their import, expanding what we could see and therefore make seeable in the process of translation.

Finally, we owe perhaps our deepest debt to Kevin Thompson, who meticulously and tirelessly combed through multiple drafts of the manuscript over the years and, without fail, offered invaluable feedback.

Notes on the Text

Editors' Notes

All of the material collected here has been previously edited and, in some cases, translated.

The introductory notes for each piece provide bibliographical information and historical contexts. They are based on the editorial notes of previous collections and elaborated on here wherever we deemed it appropriate. These notes also indicate if a previously translated text has been revised by the editors and translators of this volume.

Where important terms (e.g., people, places, events, magazines, groups) are repeated across the manuscript, an entry is provided in the Guide to Key Terms, People, and Organizations at the end of the book. If an important term is used only once, an explanatory footnote is provided.

We have also done our best to provide a clear attribution for each endnote. Whenever notes were produced by the author of the piece, the notes are unattributed. Notes provided by editors of the French collections *Archives d'une lutte, Dits et écrits,* or *Intolérable* are attributed as [AL Eds.], [DE Eds.], or [INT Ed.]. Notes provided by editors or translators of the previous English translation are flagged as [Orig. Eng. Ed.] or [Orig. Eng. Trans.]. In some cases, original editor notes were deleted in favor of an entry in the Guide to Key Terms, People, and Organizations. Finally, notes provided by the editors or translators of the current volume are attributed as [Eds.] or [Trans.]. Notes on terminology have been supplied by the translators, while biographical and historical notes have been supplied by the editors.

Following scholarly protocol, book titles have been, wherever possible, given in English (and, if helpful, their French counterpart has been provided in a note). All retained French terms have been placed in brackets (not parentheses) to distinguish them from parentheticals already within the text.

Translators' Notes

Because of their importance either in Michel Foucault's or the GIP's oeuvre, we have done our best to maintain, wherever possible, the use of the terms "carceral," "delinquency," "illegality," "intolerable," and "tolerable." We trust this will enrich future work done in both archives.

We have chosen not to introduce gender neutral language into the translation but have instead maintained the original texts' emphasis on men. Likewise, we have not ameliorated in translation the ableist language in the original texts (e.g., "paralyzed"). We very much hope feminist and disability analyses of Foucault and the GIP develop in critical dialogue with these texts.

As for specific translation decisions of important terms, their justifications are as follows.

Détenu: Prisoner. In the majority of instances, the GIP documents use the term *détenu* rather than *prisonnier*. Except in passages concerning pretrial detention, we have translated this common French term *détenu* by the similarly common English term "prisoner." Following consensus in critical prison studies, we have avoided the euphemistic term "inmate."

Enquête: Inquiry or investigation. Philologically, the term *enquête* can refer to the general movement of inquiry or to specific forms of investigation, such as surveys, polls, questionnaires, and so on. Historically, the term was used by GIP predecessor movements, such as the Maoist/Marxist workers inquiries that investigated egregious factory conditions, to refer to acts of investigation germane to political resistance. We have chosen to use both terms, inquiry and investigation, in different contexts to emphasize both the material and the conceptual elements of the *enquête*.

Maton: Screw. The French word employed here, *maton*, is slang for prison guard. Its root verb, *mater*, may be used in a number of senses: (1) to checkmate; (2) to put or pat down; or (3) to check out (voyeuristically). There are a number of English slang terms for prison guard—boss, bull, cop, copper, gov, hack, hog, pig, sally, snout, screw, and so on. Although some of these are far more common in a contemporary context, perhaps "screw" is most comparable to *maton*, because it carries several related, if not identical, connotations. To screw may mean (1) to lock up or lock in; (2) to cheat or take advantage of someone or something; or (3) to harass sexually. We have, with some reservations, chosen "screw" as the best marker by which to track the employment of this slang term in the GIP writings and pronouncements.

Prendre la parole: Take the floor. While this idiomatic phrase often means simply to "speak" or to "address," it also often carries the more militant or assertive sense of to "speak out" or to "speak up." Given the ubiquity of the latter sense in the GIP archives, we have chosen to use the colloquial English translation "take the floor," while maintaining the French in brackets so as to remind readers of the element of speech *[parole]*.

Note on the Cover Photograph

On January 17, 1972, Claude Liscia (left), Michel Foucault (center), and Fanny Deleuze (right), alongside other Prisons Information Group (GIP) activists, protested the French carceral system before the Ministry of Justice, Place Vendôme, Paris. Foucault was cofounder and coleader of the group. Fanny Deleuze, longtime translator of D. H. Lawrence and wife of Gilles Deleuze, was involved in the GIP, although to an unknown extent. Claude Liscia earned her master's in sociology in 1969 at Paris 8, an experimental university founded by Hélène Cixous. In 1970, her brother Bernard Liscia, a leader in the Gauche Proletarienne, was incarcerated and sentenced to five years in prison. At the time of this photograph, two years into his sentence, Claude Liscia was a doctoral candidate at EHESS. Upon graduating in 1976, she began a career as a sociologist whose work is concerned with poverty, confinement, and the liberatory power of theatre. Of particular relevance are her books *L'Enfermement des cités de transit* (1977) and *Familles hors de la loi* (1978), both of which utilize GIP-like methods, including investigations, collection and publication of original dossiers, and theoretical analyses rooted in histories of the present. While the former addresses the consignment of immigrant families to temporary housing centers, the latter details the development of the nineteenth-century family as an object of social policing, crafting its theoretical apparatus in express dialogue with the GIP's sister initiatives: *Le Journal du CAP* and GISTI, as well as Foucault's *Discipline and Punish* (1975) and "Society Must Be Defended" (1975–76) lectures. Credit: Élie Kagan in Michel Foucault, *Une Journée particulière,* 17 Janvier 1972, eds. Alain Jaubert and Philippe Artières (Lyon: Aedelsa Éditions, 2004), 85.

Abbreviations

The following abbreviations have been used in the text for frequently cited works.

AL   Philippe Artières, Laurent Quéro, and Michelle Zancarini-Fournel, eds., *Le Groupe d'information sur les prisons: Archives d'une lutte 1970–1972* (Paris: Éditions de l'IMEC, 2003).

DE   Michel Foucault, *Dits et écrits, 1954–1988,* ed. Daniel Defert and François Ewald, 4 vols. (Paris: Gallimard, 1994).

DEQ   Michel Foucault, *Dits et écrits, 1954–1988,* ed. Daniel Defert and François Ewald, 2 vols. (Paris: Quarto Gallimard, 2001).

INT   Groupe d'Information sur les Prisons, *Intolérable,* ed. Philippe Artières (Paris: Verticales, 2013).

Introduction
Legacies of Militancy and Theory

KEVIN THOMPSON AND PERRY ZURN

> Those who steal a piece of bread go to prison; those who steal
> millions go to the Palais Bourbon.
> —GROUPE D'INFORMATION SUR LES PRISONS (GIP)

> Information is a struggle.
> —DANIEL DEFERT

> The problem is not a model prison or the abolition of prisons. . . .
> The problem is the following: to offer a critique of the system that
> explains the process by which contemporary society pushes a
> portion of the population to the margins.
> —MICHEL FOUCAULT

The Prisons Information Group (Groupe d'Information sur les Prisons, GIP) was a radical prison activist group in France in the early
1970s. While instrumental in various prison reforms and aligned with
certain abolitionist perspectives, its primary goal was to amplify prisoners' voices—that is, to collect and circulate information about prisons from prisoners. These are its archives. This is its story.

Today's carceral system is a far cry from that of 1970s France. Then,
as now, incarceration targeted low-income, often immigrant, communities. It capitalized on a failed education system. And it served
as a political ploy more often than it honestly informed policy plat-
forms. As such, the prison entrenched systems of inequality, just as it
does today, and served as a continual locus of resistance movements.[1]
Nevertheless, many elements of the material structure of carcerality

1

have changed. In France, incarceration rates have doubled since 1973, while in the United States, they have nearly quintupled.[2] Prisons have been increasingly privatized and thereby have become subject to corporate interest.[3] The supermax prison is now the carceral architecture of choice and exported around the globe.[4] And most recently we have seen the rise of "e-carceration" and "digital prisons,"[5] where risk assessment algorithms and artificially intelligent (and biased) systems are used to project prison beds, determine bail, and monitor parole. With the coterminous and widespread advance of big data, corporate government, and the far right, moreover, there is every reason to believe we are entering a new era of differential criminalization and surveillance, an actuarial age of "screen and intervene."[6]

How is it, then, that a prison activist group in France, fifty years ago, has any bearing on prison issues today? How could the Prisons Information Group be anything more than a historical artifact? There are several ways of answering these questions. First, Michel Foucault's *Discipline and Punish: The Birth of the Modern Prison,* which was published in 1975 and is widely recognized as a cornerstone of critical prison studies, was the direct outgrowth of his deep involvement with the GIP and, in particular, its support of the prison revolts that occurred in France and the United States and elsewhere in the early 1970s. In retrospect, in fact, he remarked that the book "owes much to the GIP and . . . if it contains two or three good ideas, it gleaned them from there."[7] In the book itself, he famously notes its pivotal idea—that the soul is the prison of the body:

> [that] punishment in general and the prison in particular belong to a political technology of the body is a lesson that I have learnt not so much from history as from the present. In recent years, prison revolts have occurred throughout the world. . . . they were revolts at the level of the body, against the very body of the prison. What was at issue was not whether the prison environment was too harsh or too aseptic, too primitive or too efficient, but its very materiality insofar as it is an instrument and vector of power; it is this whole technology of power over the body that the technology of the "soul"—that of the educators, psychologists, and psychiatrists—fails either to conceal or to compensate for the very good reason that it is one of its tools. It is of this prison, with all the political investments of the body that

it assembles within its closed architecture, that I would like to write the history. By a sheer anachronism? No, if one understands by that writing the history of the past in the terms of the present. Yes, if one understands by that writing the history of the present.[8]

Insofar as critical prison studies concerns itself with a history of the present, the field thus owes a certain debt to the GIP.

Second, the GIP's support of the Black Panthers, especially in the cases of George Jackson and Angela Davis (later cofounder of the Critical Resistance Movement), places it squarely at the heart of U.S. prison resistance history. Acknowledging and appreciating the GIP's place in critical prison studies and the U.S. prison resistance movement importantly emphasizes the activist roots of theoretical texts and underscores the international cross-pollination of resistance efforts. Indeed, recovering this archive actively contests the confinement of theory to the ivory tower as well as the isolation of resistant geographies from one another—confinements themselves so easily effected by a carceral logic writ large.

But the GIP is also relevant for a simpler, much more fundamental reason. It is important to remember acts of human resistance. The work of memory honors the past, just as much as it has the capacity to challenge and transform the present. Whether innovative and course-changing or quotidian and banal, prison movements are a testament to the critical human capacity for identifying and fighting injustice even under the auspices of justice. Keeping the memory of prison resistance and unrest alive honors that capacity as much as it refuses the forces then and now built to silence and erase them. The GIP serves thus as a powerful model of political imagination and praxis. Itself an experiment in conceptual frameworks and activist strategies, the GIP provides unique insights into what is intolerable about the prison system, why participatory action and investigation matters, and how to work together across social differences, as thought-leaders and change-makers in and outside prison walls. As such, it serves as a resource for today.

The present volume is, at once, then, a historical archive, a conceptual challenge, and a tactical tool kit. It tracks the history and work of the GIP beginning with its genesis amid the aftermath of May '68, continuing with its major campaigns surrounding the conditions inside the prisons and the radicalism that arose out of that leading to its own dissolution, and concluding with the subsequent reflections that it provoked. It does so by presenting a number of different kinds of materials, from tracts, booklets, manifestos, and public statements to internal documents and interviews. Its aim is to afford access to the formation of the group, its development, and its legacies. Such a project is necessarily selective. We make no claim to have captured here all there was to the GIP. What we have sought to do is to document the GIP's life in a way that introduces this organization to those who are interested in the history of radical activism generally and struggles around prisons specifically and that also provides an entryway for those seeking resources for fostering diverse and genuinely new forms of resistance to penal society, what Foucault famously called the "carceral archipelago."

In this Introduction, we offer, in the first section, a brief sketch of events before turning to track the profound innovations in militancy and theory that the group and its work represent. In the second section, we explore the GIP's prisoner-centered and largely prisoner-led structure, predicated on the recognition that prisoners have the political knowledge and political agency most relevant to prison resistance movements. In the third section, we trace the GIP's concomitant reconceptualization of the prison and the intellectual, both of which it embeds in a shared social field of which the former is symptomatic and to which the latter is beholden. In the fourth section, we develop the GIP's anticarceral, even abolitionist, legacies implicit within these innovations of militancy and theory, as well as across its archive more generally. Finally, in the fifth section, we close by sketching the GIP archive's critical reception to date and then carve out new frontiers of interpretive debate in light of contemporary incarceration practices and developments in anticarceral theory.

A Brief Sketch of Events

The GIP appeared on the scene at a time when significant resistance movements and shifts in political consciousness defined the local and global landscape.[9] France was still living with the fallout of the Algerian War (1954–62), which left a large swath of Algerians incarcerated in French prisons. The Mouvement de Libération des Femmes (MLF), followed by the Front Homosexuel d'Action Révolutionnaire

(FHAR), was gaining strength. And the student and workers' revolt of May '68 had just rocked the very foundations of French culture and politics. It is in this milieu, so irrevocably marked by a deepening attention to race, immigration, gender, sexuality, and class, that the GIP is born and alongside which it develops. From this vantage point, the GIP's specific concern for the systemically oppressed and silenced, as well as its unique methods of jamming disciplinary machinery, are clearly the products of these intersecting currents.

The GIP grew out of the wave of government repression of radical activists, especially the antihierarchical Maoists of the Gauche Prolétarienne (Proletarian Left, GP), that took place in the early 1970s in France. Daniel Defert, already an experienced political activist and Foucault's partner, was a leading member of the Organisation des Prisonniers Politiques (Organization of Political Prisoners, OPP), a group created by the then-banned GP to support its political prisoners. He proposed that the group form a commission of public inquiry to study the general conditions of the prisons, conditions endured not only by the political prisoners of the GP, but by all those who were incarcerated. The commission was to be modeled on the public tribunals that radical groups had organized in the past in France to confront social and political issues, and Foucault was quickly recruited to serve as its director. A group of theorists, doctors, sociologists, and activists met at the apartment that Foucault and Defert shared at the end of December. Foucault urged that they reject the model of a public tribunal, charged with passing judgment on the prison system, as it simply replicated an element of the very system that he believed should be examined. Instead, he proposed that the group seek to collect and make public as much information as possible about prison conditions, information that would otherwise remain hidden. The group's original task was thus to expose the material conditions of prison life to the public. Foucault signaled the group's new direction by creating a distinctive name: the Groupe d'Information sur les Prisons (Prisons Information Group). In time, it came to see that doing this work required opening a space within which prisoners—both political and common-law prisoners—could speak and act for themselves. Foucault officially announced the formation of the GIP on February 8, 1971, at the Chapel of Saint Bernard, during a press conference held by the OPP's lawyers.

The GIP was thus a mobilization, a "relay," a "line of attack." Its target: the conditions inside French prisons. Its goal: information. Although it had no formal organizational structure and carried out its work largely anonymously, the group operated under the sponsorship and protection of three eminent intellectuals: Foucault; Jean-Marie Domenach, the former resistance fighter and editor of the journal *Esprit*; and Pierre Vidal-Naquet, a prominent historian and antiwar and antiracism activist. Over the course of its short life—strictly speaking, from late December 1970 through February 1973—its ranks included well-known academics, such as Gilles Deleuze, Hélène Cixous, Robert Castel, Jacques and Danièle Rancière, Jacques-Alain Miller, Jean-Claude Passeron, Jean Gattegno, and Jacques Donzelot; cultural icons like the writer Jean Genet, the director and founder of the avant-garde troupe Théâtre du Soleil Ariane Mnouchkine, the actors Hélène Châtelain and René Lefort, and the journalist Claude Mauriac; members of the legal community such as Louis Joinet, a well-known judge, and Christian Revon, Jean-Jacques de Felice, and Christine Martineau, all prominent attorneys at the time; radical political activists, among them Philippe Barret of the Gauche Prolétarienne; as well as a number of prison social workers and psychiatrists, together with current and former prisoners and their families, most famously Serge Livrozet, Michel Boraley, and Claude Vaudez, all of whom had played important roles in the prison uprisings that shook France in the early 1970s. And although the GIP was born in Paris, it quickly spawned regional affiliates in the provinces, all of which acted in a semiautonomous, but coordinated fashion.

The GIP employed many of the standard techniques of modern protest movements: hunger strikes, public demonstrations, leafleting, press conferences, street theater, even plays,[10] and documentaries,[11] but its most unique work consisted principally of two campaigns: (1) the publication of a series of distinctive information booklets, which were largely produced under the auspices of the Paris GIP, and (2) the organization of networks in support of the prison revolts that erupted throughout France in the winter of 1971–72, a project that arose from collaborations among the various GIP affiliates.

The Paris GIP carried out what Foucault called "*intolerance-investigations*." These formed the basis for a series of four booklets— published from May 1971 through February 1973—that the group titled the *Intolerable* series. They examined subjects as diverse as the overcrowding, unsanitary conditions, and arbitrary and inhumane treatment that formed the mundane conditions of prison life; the purported glories and realities of a "prison of the future"; analyses of a political assassination carried out in an effort to suppress the Black prison resistance movement in the United States; and the way in which prison suicides in France marked not only a symptom of these desperate conditions, but also a final form of protest and escape.

During the winter of 1971–72, a series of prison revolts rocked the French penitentiary system. The GIP affiliates, especially those in Toul and Nancy, worked with the Paris group and alongside the GP to organize support for these uprisings. The GIP created and distributed press releases, tracts, and pamphlets as ways of disseminating information about the prisoners' demands and alerting the public to various campaigns (e.g., hunger strikes) in support of the revolts. In collaboration with a legal organization, Défense Collective, the GIP also wrote and circulated manuals detailing the legal rights of those involved in the juridical proceedings following the revolts as well as of those taking part in the protests.

The final report in the *Intolerable* series, which was published in February 1973, was cosigned by the Comité d'Action des Prisonniers (CAP) and the Association pour la Défense des Droits des Détenus (ADDD). These organizations were developed by prisoners and their families and were inspired by the GIP. Their signatures signaled the GIP's official dissolution and, ultimately, the transferal of its work to these groups. The CAP and the ADDD had both been founded in November 1972. The organizers of the CAP were all former prisoners—among them Serge Livrozet, Michel Boraley, and Claude Vaudez—all of whom had been involved in the Melun Prison revolt. The goal of the group was to break down the barriers between common-law prisoners and political prisoners and to advocate for the complete abolition of incarceration. It distributed a widely popular newspaper, *Le CAP, journal des prisonniers,* which was created wholly for and by prisoners. The ADDD functioned as an officially registered support organization. It sought to foster the formation of a lawyers' association that provided legal counsel to prisoners and their families. It organized several public events with the GIP that assisted prisoners and their families in initiating legal action, fighting, in particular, for the right of prisoners to organize and join unions and, taking up an initiative central to the work of the GIP, having criminal records expunged so that former prisoners could pursue gainful means of employment. It also pursued greater means for the public to exercise direct control over penal institutions.

Across its short life span, the GIP was thus exemplary in its responsiveness to its historico-political milieu, its capacity to generate unexpected coalitions, its effectiveness in supporting prisoners' knowledge and political agency, and its flexibility in giving way to new leadership and new resistant formations. We turn now to explore in greater detail the innovations in thought and practice that subtend this exemplarity.

Experiments in Militancy

As we have noted, the GIP employed many of the standard techniques of modern protest movements. But, whereas other radical groups sought to speak on behalf of the marginalized and the oppressed against the ruling elite, what made the GIP truly experimental was its rejection of the trappings of representation and leadership in favor of a unique militancy that sought to link struggle, speech, and information around axes of resistance rooted in the concepts of intolerability, intolerance, and political agency.

Centering Prisoners' Political Knowledge

The GIP saw the disclosure of information about the otherwise largely hidden practices of incarceration as an integral part of the struggle to contest such techniques and the broader social framework of which they were a part. Its work of gathering this kind of information, however, was in service neither to disinterested study nor to the crafting of proposals for improved prisons. Rather, it sought to make the intolerable physical, mental, and emotional conditions of incarceration visible in ways that provoked and supported public intolerance of them. Its militancy was thus neither sociological, nor reformist, but what Foucault was to call, in an interview looking back on the group's efforts, an "enterprise of problematization": "an effort to render the evidences, practices, rules, institutions, and habits that had remained sedimented for decades and decades problematic and doubtful."[12]

At the very center of this work stood the struggle to publicize information directly from those living and working in the penal system and to do so in ways that enabled this speech to break through the encrusted discourse of conventional public debate, to become a true event. This is what the GIP meant by the phrase to which it so often returned: *prendre la parole* (literally, "to take up or take over speech"), whose crucial function within the GIP's discourse is best conveyed with the English idiomatic expression "to take the floor." To gather and publish this kind of information was thus to contest social repression in a variety of forms—not only the government censorship that sought to hide these conditions from the public, but also the inattention of the judiciary, the carelessness of the bar, the stalling of the guards' unions, and ultimately even the shame of the prisoners' families. Whether through questionnaires, on-site reports, critical analyses of the public record and media reports, tabulation of anecdotal evidence, direct testimony, and even the publication of personal correspondence and secret manuals, the GIP consistently sought to construct public spaces in which this information could reveal the most quotidian atrocities of prison life: from lack of adequate nourishment, heat, health and dental care, exercise, and visiting hours, to the profound exploitation of prison labor, the horrific practice of solitary confinement, the punishment of homosexuality, the gross mistreatment of mental illness, the suppression of familial and sexual relations, the death penalty, the debilitating shadow of a criminal record, and the way in which these brutalities, and so many others, often led prisoners to take their own lives when they saw this as their only way out. At each step, the GIP's concern was to forge spaces in which prisoners' own voices could be heard and the deeply mundane, yet radical nature of what they proclaimed could break through the boundaries of politics, academia, media, bureaucracy, and all the other predetermined domains of conventional public debate.

The GIP defined these spaces in a number of different ways, but most common throughout their work was the invocation of intolerability and intolerance. The back cover of the first Intolerable booklet proclaimed: "The goal of the G.I.P. is not reformist, we do not dream of an ideal prison: we hope that the prisoners will be able to say what is *intolerable* in the system of penal repression."[13] This same cover declared a host of social and political institutions to be intolerable:

"courts, cops, hospitals asylums, school, military service, the press, the tv, the state, and above all the prisons."[14] In an announcement regarding the GIP's first investigation, which he called an "intolerance-inquiry," Foucault pleaded: "let what is intolerable—imposed, as it is, by force and by silence—cease to be accepted. We do not conduct our inquiry in order to accumulate knowledge, but *to heighten our intolerance and make it an active intolerance.* Let us become people intolerant of prisons, the legal system, the hospital system, psychiatric practice, military service, etc."[15] But what exactly did they mean by intolerable conditions and by intolerance as a response to the existence of such conditions?

Although no systematic elaboration of these terms is to be found in the GIP materials (and the use of the composite term "active intolerance" appears only once), *intolerable* is consistently used as a pejorative to refer to the material conditions of incarceration and to certain social institutions and intolerance functions as a description of the response that these conditions provoke.[16] At their core, though, both terms derive from a common affective root: intolerable conditions and institutions are those that are felt to be oppressive by those living in them and intolerance is the passion that compels resistance to such oppression. For Foucault, in particular, at least during this still fairly early period in the development of his own thought about the operations of power, this clearly meant that such conditions and institutions are felt to be unbearable constraints and the shock that they provoke fuels a profound questioning of their acceptability. In a word, then, what is intolerable and thus what merits intolerance for the GIP is repression. The grievances set forth by the prisoners in response to the questionnaires, in their correspondence, and in the lists issued during the revolts all convey a profoundly similar and profoundly simple message: what is unbearable about incarceration is not being deprived of one's liberty, but being made to endure inadequate nutrition, hygiene, and medical care, restricted access to newspapers, isolation units, beatings and other forms of abuse at the hands of the guards, lack of adequate visitation from family, and the inequitable and arbitrary system of justice that pervades prison life. It is repression of the most mundane and ubiquitous sort, and, precisely because of that, it is a repression that is all the more insidious.

Now, although this is certainly where prisoners, and the GIP following their lead, began, their voices did not remain solely in this affective register. Prisoners, in particular, articulated what they called a "fundamental principle" to which they held themselves, the penal system, and society as a whole accountable: collective self-determination. Although the idea arises in various forms in different texts, the prisoners at Melun perhaps put it best in the postulate that they laid down as the prerequisite for any negotiations during their revolt in January 1972: "The reintegration of prisoners into society can only be the work of prisoners themselves."[17] Concretely, this meant, they said, that democratically elected committees of prisoners would need to be formed at each prison.[18] These committees would have the authority to speak as representatives of the entire prison population and to conduct negotiations with the administrative staff regarding the specific conditions of incarceration in each prison. Intolerability is thus, here, not just repression, but also whatever compromises personal and collective autonomy. In all this, the GIP saw its role, crucially, as supportive. GIP members—whether those formerly incarcerated, their families, lawyers, magistrates, activists, or academics—all worked alongside the prisoners, publicizing the conditions and the struggles, doing everything possible to garner public support and bring outrage to bear on the political system so as to call into question the practices of control, surveillance, normalization, and resocialization that formed the core of incarcerated life.

Facilitating Prisoners' Political Agency

Prisoners have historically not only been a disenfranchised population, but one that stood under moral condemnation and, as such, they have been excluded from the social and political system. As a result, they have fundamentally lacked any recognized form of political agency, any acknowledged forum for acting in concert with others. How, then, could they organize themselves into a genuinely collective movement? How could they, precisely as prisoners, speak and act as though they were no longer incarcerated?

Contributing to and supporting the creation of political agency for and by prisoners can be said, in one way or another, to be one of the fundamental aims of all the various and innovative techniques of protest that the GIP employed. However, political agency clearly takes center stage in its support for the wave of more than thirty prison revolts that took place in France in the winter of 1971–72. One of the most significant of these uprisings, and one of the first, occurred at the Ney Prison in Toul, a small town in the northeast of France.[19] The uprising began with a sit-in seeking the removal of the warden of the facility, but the protests quickly expanded to include demands for improvement of the most banal conditions of incarceration: food, showers, heat, access to dental services, pay, the removal of solitary confinement, and so on.[20] After initially announcing that the warden would be removed and agreeing to review the prisoners' demands, the administration failed to act and the protests became more aggressive, with prisoners destroying property and facilities and taking to the roofs to communicate their demands directly to the public. The revolt was put down by violent assault with numerous injuries, casualties, and punishments, both legal and otherwise.

The Toul GIP affiliate, together with the Paris group, worked closely with the banned Maoist organization, the Gauche Prolétarienne, during this time to mobilize support around the revolt.[21] They were, in fact, accused by the government of having even instigated the revolt, a charge they vehemently denied, insisting that it was, in all ways, a wholly homegrown rebellion. In a statement delivered at a joint press conference in January 1972, Foucault, speaking on behalf of the GIP, argued that a fundamentally new type of struggle—at least new to the French context—had arisen at Toul, one where the prisoners sought not to escape prison itself, but to barricade themselves in, becoming thereby masters of a fulcrum, in order to set forth their concrete demands and to assert their rights to, as Foucault put it, "get out of their status of being humiliated prisoners."[22] At its core, the revolt sought to take the forces by which the prisoners were ruled within the prison—money, prestige, and physical coercion—and redistribute them such that the prisoners, bound together as they were through their common conditions of being detained, humiliated, used, and exploited, "became a collective force opposite the [prison] administration. And it is in this way that they entered into a struggle."[23] In their objectives and their tactics the prisoners sought, fundamentally, to reallocate (even overturn) the administrative and material terms of their incarceration, to redistribute the day-to-day conduct of their imprisonment. In this way, Foucault contends, the rebels won a "double victory": (1) they exposed the administration, the supposed purveyors of morality, justice, and good and evil, engaging in the very act of lying to them and abusing their trust, and, perhaps most important, (2) they established themselves as a "collective force," with its own distinctive organization, objectives, and strategies, engaged in a unique form of struggle against an established regime of power. What occurred at Toul was nothing less than the creation of a distinctive form of political agency: "a political struggle was led against the entire penal system by the same social stratum that forms its primary victim."[24]

In its support of   the revolts, the GIP thus facilitated prisoners in forging their own spaces for genuine collaborative political struggle and, as such, the GIP devised new ways of nurturing the agency of excluded populations that did not co-opt that very agency. In so doing, they provided a model not only for how to enable the disenfranchised to speak about what only they knew best, but for how to enable the ones that society excludes to contest the terms of their exclusion and to do so as a genuinely shared endeavor.

Experiments in Thought

The innovative strategies and tactics that we have just reviewed served as models for the creation of a number of other organizations,[25] but they also had profound repercussions for two of the concepts that stand at the very center of so much of the history of social and political theory: the prison and the intellectual.[26]

The Prison

The GIP's militancy sought to challenge the conventional status of the prison as a distinctly social institution, an accepted pillar of modern life. Yet exactly how was this possible? How could the prison be moved from the social field, where it was widely accepted, and, as such, remained the concern mainly of specialists and charities, to the contested site of the political?

As we have noted, the GIP employed a variety of tactics and strategies over the course of its brief life and the fundamental goal of all of them was certainly to render the practice of incarceration problematic. But integral to achieving this aim was the GIP's exposure of the failures of reformism. The GIP was often criticized for never proposing full-scale alternatives to incarceration or even a concrete program for ameliorating the conditions that it publicized.[27] The GIP steadfastly refused this demand precisely because it sought to call into question the very validity of a penal regime itself, one that would grant a right to punish to particular individuals or groups and, from this, provide the grounds for a system of executing such a right. That is to say, the GIP saw its mission primarily as problematizing the penal system as such, not as devising a better, more humane form of extracting punishment.

The GIP's militancy was also clearly informed by a recognition— one that would bear fruit in the historical analyses of *Discipline and Punish*—that the penal regime as a whole, its practices and its institutions, were all elements of a broader system whereby power was diffused throughout the social fabric. Consequently, to call the prison into question was always necessarily bound up with challenging the other links in this chain: education, religion, the judicial system, health care, the military, the media, the government, as well as the racist and homophobic practices that undergird these. The diverse range of topics grappled with in the *Intolerable* series bears out this commitment to what Foucault would come to call the "diagram of power" that sustains and supports these institutions and practices.

But perhaps nowhere is the challenge to the penal system itself more evident than in the second booklet of the *Intolerable* series: *The GIP Investigates a Model Prison: Fleury-Mérogis*. This work, which was published in June 1971, is importantly unlike the other volumes in the series. Whereas the first and the fourth booklets sought to expose the repugnant conditions of the traditional French prison system by giving voice to those who inhabited these institutions, and the third sought to demonstrate the links between the French prison struggle and that of the Black prison resistance movement in the United States, the second booklet—whose principal authors/editors remained anonymous, but are now known to be Jacques-Alain Miller, a psychoanalyst, and François Regnault, a philosopher, both former students of Louis Althusser and Jacques Lacan—was a study of what was then considered to be the most advanced French prison, the "prison without bars," the "electronic prison," the "prison of the future." Functioning as a kind of reductio ad absurdum of the French government's propaganda about this facility at the time, which proclaimed Fleury-Mérogis to be a prison "different from all others," the

GIP authors culled from current prisoners' meticulous descriptions of the physical layout of the facility (both the yards and the cells), its intake procedures, its numerous technological innovations (e.g., having loudspeakers in each cell), and, especially, the extensive use of solitary confinement to show how even a prison designed to be the most sophisticated—at once humane and efficient—nonetheless still remained exploitative and humiliating, nothing less, they concluded, than a "concentration camp."

This unique type of investigation sought, then, to expose not simply the conditions within the historical prison system, but the specific ways in which even perhaps well-intentioned reformist projects still validated the central practices and historical norms of incarceration as a form of punishment. By exploring the layout, architecture, and practices of the most advanced penal facility, the GIP was thus able to expose how material conditions and techniques together create a machine that is able to render the body pliable to the demands of authority, even beyond the conventions of malnourishment, lack of heat, visitation, and so on. The problem is clearly not, then, a failure of the prison system to be sufficiently humane, sufficiently technologically advanced, the dream of reform; rather, the problem is incarceration itself precisely as a means of punishment. As such, the very legitimacy of the penal regime as a social institution is called into question and made an object of genuine political struggle.

The Intellectual

The GIP was keenly aware of the broader penal regime of which incarceration and the prison were but vectors and instruments. And it also knew that education and the academy were integral to this system. The intellectuals who populated the GIP's ranks thus came to acknowledge, precisely as a consequence of their work in the GIP, that they and their fellow academics could not feign a position outside the penal system that they sought to analyze, resist, and critique. Their work in the GIP thus provoked for them a reconsideration of the question of the social and political responsibility of intellectuals.

Broadly speaking, the modern concept of what it is to be an intellectual and what sorts of duties and obligations this entails originated in the nineteenth century in France: intellectuals were to be defenders of justice and ones who confront power with courage and personal integrity. The rationale for these responsibilities was rooted in the fact that because intellectuals are part of a privileged minority, granted special time, facilities, and training by society, they have a unique obligation to use the skills they acquire to expose political propaganda, to analyze the hidden motives and intentions of social institutions and agencies, and to examine the contexts within which historical events take place. Intellectuals are thus to use their abilities to uncover the true interests lying behind the distortive veils by which the ruling classes maintain their control of the social order. Both Jean-Paul Sartre, with his notion of "engaged literature," which he articulated in the late 1940s, claiming that all writing ultimately requires the author to take a stand on the issues of the day, and Noam Chomsky, in the late 1960s, sought to embody this kind of intellectual responsibility in their own activism and political analyses. It was a model of classical intellectual responsibility that Foucault was to come to call the "universal" intellectual: one who speaks with authority flowing from truth and justice as a "representative of the universal," as a "cantor of the eternal."[28]

The unique activism of the GIP taught the ad hoc collection of academics, professionals, and artists involved in the group—working beside former and current prisoners and their families—an important lesson about this canonical picture of what it meant to be a committed intellectual. Foucault offers an initial formulation of this insight in his discussion with Deleuze from March 1972, right in the midst of their collaboration in the GIP:

> The intellectual's role is no longer to place himself "somewhat ahead and to the side" in order to express the stifled truth of the collectivity; rather, it is to struggle against the forms of power that transform him into its object and instrument in the sphere of "knowledge," "truth," "consciousness," and "discourse." ... This is a struggle against power, a struggle aimed at revealing and undermining power where it is most invisible and insidious. It is not to "awaken consciousness" that we struggle (the masses have been aware for some time that consciousness is a form of knowledge; and consciousness as the basis of subjectivity is a prerogative of the bourgeoisie), but to sap power, to take power; it is an activity conducted alongside those who struggle for power, and not their illumination from a safe distance.[29]

Intellectuals are no longer, here, the bearers of the universal, the ones who speak in the name of justice and truth as such. They are no longer the leaders of the revolutionary masses. They have learned, as Deleuze famously put it, the "indignity of speaking for others." Those afforded the privileges of being intellectuals must speak precisely from their unique positions, as experts in their respective fields—as, at once, an object and an instrument of knowledge, truth, consciousness, and discourse—and they must engage the struggle with and against power precisely from and within these domains.[30] Each is thus what Foucault called, in his interview from June 1976 with Alessandro Fontana and Pasquale Pasquino, a "specific intellectual."[31]

But how exactly did what was clearly a small band of mostly "bourgeois intellectuals," who knew little to nothing of the world of incarceration (although much about the social policing of illegalities outside), find themselves at the center of such a profoundly new type of mobilization around prisons and a new conception of intellectual responsibility? There were, no doubt, several sources: from the various strands of anarchism and the legacies of the Resistance that were swirling around the universities to the student and worker uprisings of May '68. But what was decisive for the militant education of the majority of these academics, professionals, and artists was French Maoism and especially its emancipatory form of empiricism.[32]

As we noted, the GIP was born out of a project that began in the GP. This antihierarchical Maoist group, formed in late 1968, integrated many of the anarchists that had sparked the student uprisings fueling May '68. It was the product of a wave in French radicalism that had begun to incorporate Maoist principles and practices in opposition to the then Stalinist orthodoxy, defined as it was at the time by humanism and economism, that had been embraced by the official French Communist Party (the Parti Communiste Français). Maoism had inherited the Marxist tradition's conflicted relationship with intellectuals: on the one hand, it was suspicious of them as bourgeois ideologues and, on the other, it viewed them as potentially effective participants in revolutionary change. The model intellectual was to move dialectically, as it was said Marx himself did, between the concrete particularities of experience and the abstract theoretical lessons that such grounding offers. The Maoists used this model as a basis to recover the largely forgotten method of investigation, which

Marx himself had pioneered, as a central revolutionary technique.[33] Mao proclaimed in 1942: "Unless you have investigated a problem, you will be deprived of the right to speak on it." French Maoists followed this tradition, initially directing their investigations toward peasants in the countryside and workers in the factories, but they also began to move beyond these classical revolutionary figures to groups on the very margins of society itself: former psychiatric patients and prisoners.

The ad hoc collection of academics and artists in the GIP critically built on this legacy in their series of "*intolerance-investigations*" and doing so challenged them to rethink the responsibilities that their positions and privileges had bestowed upon them. But rather than simply researching prison conditions themselves and raising consciousness amongst the oppressed, the GIP understood the Maoist dialectical commitment to empiricism to mean that those living in these conditions who were already quite aware of their state must not only be allowed to speak for themselves, but facilitated in doing so.[34]

Hence, the very embodiment of the specific intellectual was not Foucault, Defert, Domenach, or any of the other academic and cultural icons with whom they collaborated in the GIP, but rather those like the staff psychiatrist at the Ney Prison in Toul, Doctor Édith Rose. Doctor Rose delivered a scathing exposé of the internal workings of the prison to the French authorities responsible for overseeing the penal system based on her own eyewitness testimony and reporting.[35] She spoke from a specific position *in* power—a position afforded her by her class, her training, and her official accreditation as a psychiatrist—and she spoke, in this position, from this position, resolutely, *of* power. She offered neither historical analysis, nor even moral judgment, but simply testimony, information. She plainly, but methodically, cataloged the practices that she witnessed, that she found troubling, and about which she wanted to alert her superiors and the public at large. But the "Rose Report" was not just a dossier of the violations of standard prison protocol, but a problematization, precisely in the critical sense of the word, of the engrained and calcified forms of thought and practice surrounding the art of punishment. The report displays a critical mind that senses the dangers that threaten in the habitual ways in which psychiatry and penalty have become entangled, and it renders doubtful the evidences and rules that have unreflectively been relied upon to draw these connections. It is the work of a specific intellectual as she intervenes in the battle to alter the conditions for what counts as well-formed truth claims and the authoritative practices that guide and mold action itself. The GIP, in collaboration with the GP, supported and publicized the report and its findings, and had it published on three separate occasions during December and January 1971–72.[36]

The GIP's militancy thus contributed to a decisive shift in France and beyond in the very conception of what it meant to be an intellectual and the responsibilities that come with this status.[37] Its centering of prisoners, their testimony, and actions in their work and its scholarly and even bodily commitment to forging spaces in which those voices and acts could begin to be heard displayed a fundamentally different way of being an intellectual. It was no longer to lead by being the spokesperson of the universal, but to make use precisely of one's specificity—one's expertise and the authority granted by one's position—to create various forums in which the voices and works of the oppressed could be heard and the broader carceral system problematized.

Anticarceral Legacies

The GIP's experiments in militancy and theory took a full swing at the root of the prison as a modern carceral institution. The twine of the GIP's thought and work, therefore, bears a distinct anticarceral, even abolitionist, legacy, a legacy only enriched in Foucault's later writings and the work of the CAP. As indicated in its Latinate roots, *ab-adolere*, the term "abolition" can mean either to cause not to grow—that is, to destroy—or to grow away from, in another direction. What we observe in these archives is a deep hope in real, systemic change and the creation of new social formations. These archives, however, also indicate an equally deep suspicion that existing institutions will co-opt that anticarceral energy to make merely cosmetic adjustments to the status quo.

Abolition and the GIP

The GIP developed in a climate of global prison resistance that toggled between prison reform and prison abolition. It was explicitly inspired by abolitionist efforts in Canada, Italy, Tanzania, and the

United States, where demands for the abolition of the "fascist penal record,"[38] "political and racial repression,"[39] and the full "abolition of prisons"[40] resounded. Within this milieu, the GIP focused its abolitionist energies both within the prison and beyond it.[41] First, it called for the "abolition" of various intolerable penal practices and policies: physical violence,[42] visiting rooms,[43] the "chicken coop,"[44] the travel ban,[45] labor exploitation,[46] censorship,[47] and good-conduct credits.[48] Asked what one thing—censorship, sexual repression, physical abuse, or legal corruption—was most important to fight, a prisoner at La Santé stated, "All of that put together. They are impossible to separate."[49] Insofar as intolerable prison realities form a tight network, abolition of any one node implicates abolition of the others. The GIP also trained its sights on the penal logics that extend beyond the prison. In this regard, it focused most heavily on the "abolition of the criminal record,"[50] a demand it expressly gave "first rank."[51] For the GIP, the criminal record was problematic for several reasons: (1) it belied the fact that the prison is not a place of reeducation, but rather of repression; (2) it limited prisoners' employment opportunities, often consigning them to the most exploitative employers and exploited work; and (3) it therefore extended carceral functions beyond the prisons into society itself.[52] "With the criminal record," the GIP wrote, "there is no release, there are only reprieves."[53] In calling for the abolition of the criminal record—or the travel ban, for that matter—the GIP thus suggested that an abolition of intolerable realities inside the prison extended to the abolition of penal logics outside it as well.

While the GIP focused on some pointed abolitionist efforts, there is also a sense in which it understood its general work as part and parcel of abolitionist praxis. "It is imperative that prisons be nowhere left in peace . . . ," it wrote. "Let us become people intolerant of prisons."[54] Such an abolitionist intolerance involved the act of gathering information from an inherently opaque institution (the prison),[55] giving the floor to a constitutively silenced group of people (prisoners),[56] and insisting upon the creature comforts of warmth, nourishment, and human touch in a penal system that presumes not only their disposability but the propriety of their weaponization.[57] And yet, the prison was never the GIP's only target or exclusive concern. As we have noted, "[t]hese are intolerable," it wrote: "courts, cops, hospitals, asylums, school, military service, the press, the tv, the state, and above all the prisons."[58] For an activist group seemingly focused exclusively on subjugated knowledges and creaturely politics, the work is inherently expansive and interconnected. It therefore must extend to and encompass any matrix of enforced silence and dehumanization. One prisoner at La Santé poignantly emphasized the ludicrousness of addressing the prison without also addressing the police, the courts, and so on; to do so, he wrote, is "to saw the tree into planks before cutting it down."[59] In the process of coming to know the extent of the carceral canopy and its root systems—a process in which prison scholar-activists are still involved today—the GIP became increasingly committed, as we have seen, to rethinking intellectual work, local struggle, and the revolutionary intimacy of being-in-relation. For the GIP, Stephen Dillon notes, "abolition was [always] a material and epistemological process."[60]

Abolition and Foucault

Following his work with the GIP, Foucault is most concerned about so-called successful abolitions that merely redirect punitive, carceral, or marginalizing forces in society. To "abolish" public executions in favor of prisons, Foucault argues in the opening of *Discipline and Punish,* is simply to mask corporeal punishment in noncorporeal garb, all the while extending the microphysics of power across penal, juridical, and academic institutions.[61] To "abolish" the death penalty in favor of life without parole, he further argues, is but to implement a cosmetic improvement, one that nevertheless solidifies the enmeshment of medical and psychological discourses in judicial decisions. It exchanges one form of death for another—"Prison is a death machine," he insists[62]—and maintains the core belief that some category of individuals is beyond redemption, fodder for "definitive elimination."[63] To "abolish" prisons themselves in favor of alternative penalties, he finally argues, could submerge the forces of marginalization in other institutions[64] and "liberate carceral functions" across society, diffusing the work of surveillance, control, and resocialization throughout the free world.[65] In each of these abolitionist efforts, the values and logics, affects and rationales of penality not only remain strong but grow more deeply entrenched. The real question for

Foucault is this: can abolition really turn social growth away from penal entrenchment and toward liberation?

Foucault can thus be read as recommending an abolitionist praxis of curiosity and vigilant reflection.[66] In an effort to address the pernicious subterranean logics of penality, he insists that we grapple with more basic, "prior" questions:[67] "What would a noncorporeal punishment be?"[68] "Can power exist that does not have a fondness for illegality?"[69] "Will there be a radical departure from a penal practice that maintains . . . certain individuals cannot be corrected?"[70] And how might we "offer a critique of the system" that "pushes a portion of the population to the margins"?[71] Pursuing these basic questions—and, indeed, looking for more—can steel us against the naive habit of hailing the changing facades of penal institutions as inherently ameliorative or delimiting of carceral power. But such questions do more than save us from a dangerous innocence. More fundamentally, they demystify the roots of carceral logic and inoculate their power. Abolition begins in the imagination, an imagination shot through with corporeal insight and intellectual experience. If the drive to punish is to be unseated anywhere, it must be there. It is perhaps for this reason that Foucault calls his readers "to remain on the alert,"[72] "to make penal practice a locus of constant reflection, research, and experience, of transformation,"[73] and "to question every aspect of punishment as it is practiced everywhere," from the prisons all the way through the schools.[74] And it is to this task that Foucault contributes his academic writing as "Molotov-cocktails" in an open field of sedimented power relations and ideational torpor.[75]

Abolition and the CAP

In comparison to the GIP and Foucault, the CAP is, unarguably, the most explicitly, unreservedly, and relentlessly abolitionist of the three. For the CAP, historian Christophe Soulié notes, the principle of abolition is unbreakable.[76] There is no conceivable circumstance in which incarceration would be warranted. As founder Serge Livrozet asserts, "The prison has no value . . . for anyone."[77] This abolitionist commitment is explicit in *Le Journal du CAP*'s header, where a pair of shackled fists break their chains.[78] The CAP's newspaper is rife with demands for abolition, oscillating—much as the GIP did—between demands for immediate reform and long-term social change.[79] CAP members call for the abolition of prisoner abuse (in all its physical, medical, and psychiatric forms),[80] as well as the guards' use of bullying and clubs.[81] They call for the abolition of censorship,[82] criminal records,[83] debtors' prison,[84] pretrial detention,[85] and travel bans.[86] They vehemently demand the abolition of the death penalty,[87] but also of life without parole[88] and long sentences,[89] noting that even after fifteen or sixteen years, "a being is broken."[90] They call for the abolition of the police[91] and immigration control.[92] Furthermore, recognizing the mundane ways in which prison violently breaks relational bonds, they demand the abolition of isolation, solitary, and arbitrary transfers.[93] Finally, they call for the abolition of sexual repression within prisons as well as outside, including the decriminalization of sex work.[94]

For the CAP, these targeted efforts to abolish nodes of punitive violence must necessarily extend not only to the carceral archipelago itself but to the whole network of social inequality. It must mean "the abolition pure and simple of this [very] form of [carceral] existence."[95] Such a project demands the abolition of alienation,[96] exploitation,[97] privileges,[98] domination,[99] social class,[100] and the capitalist spectacle.[101] "This struggle can end only in a radical change in society," CAP member Jean-Claude Deudon states; "Neither a reformist carceral society . . . nor a Marxist state society can abolish prisons."[102] Something else is necessary—a form of sociality as yet unimagined and unrealized. To undertake that work of abolition, beginning with a decarceration of imagination, the CAP insists, one must commit to unmasking social contradictions, where claims to liberalism coincide with constitutive violence.[103] The university is one such place: there, pretenses to a liberal education shroud an aggressive gatekeeping of knowledge itself. For this reason, the end of prison must also mean "the end of the university."[104] And yet, therein lies the promise of redemption. It is "the power of words," Livrozet reflects, "to abolish separation."[105] This is true in the visiting room as much as it is in an activist's circle. If the CAP is distinguished by its abolitionism, it is an abolitionism inseparable from *Le Journal du CAP*, where "action-reflection," strategy and theory, go hand in hand. [106]

The abolitionist legacy of the GIP makes it particularly prescient in an age of mass incarceration and a widespread recognition of the prison's failure. Its refusal to disengage theory from praxis and its equal loyalty to the demands of the now and to the promises of a different future, moreover, provide us with an exemplary model for anticarceral work today. Scholarship as a whole has really only begun to appreciate the wisdom of that legacy.

Critical Reception and Future Investigations

Today, the carceral archipelago is marked by the exponential increase in incarceration and immigrant detention, the exportation of maximum-security units and therefore of tortuous solitary confinement practices around the globe, the privatization of prisons, the rise of e-carceration, and the entrenchment of surveillance and control regimes well beyond prison walls. Across partisan lines and national borders, prisons are a recognized political problem. And prison resistance movements continue unabated, repeatedly reasserting the indignity of confinement itself and the systems of oppression in which it is implicated. In 2018, prisoners and immigrants staged the largest coordinated labor and hunger strike in U.S. history. This occurred on the heels of the 2010 prison strikes in Georgia, the 2013 Free Alabama Movement (documenting and broadcasting inhumane prison conditions with contraband cellphone cameras), the 2014 and 2015 hunger strikes in immigration detention centers (organized especially by mothers and other persons held in women's facilities), and the 2015 coordinated mass hunger strikes at Pelican Bay State Prison, to name only a few. Each of these movements involved forming prohibited coalitions between prisoners, immigrants, activists, journalists, scholars, and media personnel. And each of them centered on incarcerated people's own assessments of prisons or detention facilities themselves. Within this context, the GIP's model, methods, and principles remain, perhaps, as relevant as ever.

Many people involved in the contemporary prison resistance movement and critical prison studies are grappling with the role of history, discourse, and theory in the construction of the prison as a problem and in the concretization of resistance to it. They are reckoning with the power of public engagement, whether on the part of prisoners, activists, or scholars. They are exploring old strategies and generating new tactics. They are holding their work accountable to systems of inequality as never before, especially along the vectors of race, gender, sexuality, and disability. And they are centering prisoners' voices, through a proliferation of initiatives including blogs, podcasts, popular and academic press articles, Prison Radio, and the *Journal of Prisoners on Prisons*. It is perhaps no surprise, then, that the foci of scholarship on the GIP to date follow suit.[107] This growing body of literature addresses the GIP's relationship to historical figures and contexts, theories and practices of resistance, political systems of inequality, and prisoners' concerns and assessments.

On the historical front, scholars have investigated the GIP's relationship to its predecessors, its sister movements, and the key people involved. Several theorists, for example, have repeatedly reworked the GIP as an outgrowth of May '68, as well as the Maoist/Marxist worker inquiries and labor unions. Others have interrogated the collaborative and conceptual debts the GIP owes to the Black Panther Party (and therefore to George Jackson). More work could be done to link the GIP to other movements of its time, including the Mouvement de Libération des Femmes, the Front Homosexuel d'Action Révolutionnaire (and therefore Guy Hocquenghem), and Italy's Lotta Continua. A solid strand of work has considered the GIP in relation to Michel Foucault and even Gilles Deleuze, but more work could consider the GIP in relation to Daniel Defert, Jean Genet, and Jean-Paul Sartre. It is also important to note that little if any scholarship considers the role of women's prisons and women activists in the GIP, including Simone de Beauvoir, Catherine von Bülow, Hélène Châtelain, Hélène Cixous, Claude Liscia, Michèle Manceaux, Christine Martineau, Marianne Merleau-Ponty, Ariane Mnouchkine, Danièle Rancière, and others. Finally, the GIP consistently receives more attention than the CAP, despite the comparatively longer, more productive existence of the latter. A rich account of GIP member and CAP founder Serge Livrozet also remains absent in the literature.

Given the continued prescience of political unrest and political critique—whether of the prisons or of carceral society more generally—scholars have used the GIP's strategies and tactics as a springboard to retheorize issues germane to the material, discursive, and ideological nature of resistance. Noting the carceral function of surveillance and datafication, they have analyzed the GIP's anticarceral use of "counterveillance" and publicity as political tools. Within this context of silenced voices and subjugated knowledges, scholars also use the GIP as an impetus to elucidate the nature of speech itself, the difficulty of speaking for, and the necessity of speaking truth to power. Others have turned from the visual and verbal to gut-level resistance, analyzing the prisoners' use of hunger strikes and other creaturely demands to both catalyze and challenge the movement. Whatever the GIP's tools and strategies of resistance, one incontrovertible weapon is the public intellectual. In some sense, this figure is only made possible by the "abolition" of the solitary professional academic as we know it, an abolition that simultaneously creates the conditions for communities of publicly engaged, locally invested scholar-activists. Resistance catapults bodies, languages, and institutions into new relations.

Given the rapidly increasing salience of structural inequality and systemic oppression to any critical account of the prisons and prison resistance, moreover, scholars have also brought GIP insights to bear on the contemporary carceral terrain. Scholars analyze the convergences and important divergences between the GIP and Black feminism's critique of the prison, especially along lines of race, gender, and sexuality. Granting the complexity of the migratory context both in 1970s France and in the United States today, scholars also insist on the necessity of extending an anticarceral, antiracist critique to immigration detention centers and the weaponization of citizenship. In addition to addressing Black feminism, race theory, and immigration policy, some scholars have also taken up contemporary issues of sexuality and disability in the prison and beyond. Some analyze the GIP's account of H. M., highlighting the disruptive power of desire and anonymity, as well as the force of homophobic and transphobic dehumanization in carceral contexts. Others, revisiting the Toul Revolt, have placed disability, psychiatry, and care work in prison front and center. Across these projects, scholars and scholar-activists have culled rich resources from the GIP for rethinking marginalization, criminalization, and policing today.

Perhaps most important, outside of the typical confines of academic discourse, current prisoners themselves have reflected on the GIP's relevance. Given that prisoners are by and large cut off from their own histories—whether of the prison, of prisoners, or of prison resistance movements—more opportunities for them to engage with the GIP and similar archives need to be developed. Steve Champion (Adisa Kamara), incarcerated in San Quentin State Prison in California, has argued for the importance of GIP-like support networks for prison struggles such as the Pelican Bay Short Corridor Collective.[108] Janos Toevs, incarcerated in Arkansas Valley Correctional Facility in Colorado, has insisted on the GIP's commitment to "give the floor" to prisoners, who more intimately understand both the alienations and the solidarities of incarcerated life.[109] Abu-Ali Abdur'Rahman, Derrick Quintero, and Donald Middlebrooks, incarcerated at Riverbend Maximum Security Prison in Tennessee, have written their own Intolerable statements.[110] Marking everything from "rape" and "lack of honor and respect" to "people who should know their breath stinks, but still don't brush," they emphasize the creaturely politics of what is intolerable. Together, Champion, Toevs, Abdur'Rahman, Quintero, and Middlebrooks highlight a lacuna in the GIP scholarship, which ought to attend more closely to the relational violence of prisons, by which the bonds of families, lovers, friends, mentors, and allies are cruelly and gratuitously ruptured. They suggest that prison resistance recommit to honor interpersonal connection and collective relation across communities.

As both the Prisons Information Group and Foucault repeatedly make clear, archival work—specifically the work of de-subjugating knowledges as a way of writing/righting the history of the present—is always a critical component of political resistance and accountable scholarship. One might consider such work to engage in the project of abolitionist genealogy, whereby silenced archives—whether buried alive or long since lost—return to rewrite political imaginaries in the present.[111] The process is rarely easy and the results are often far from pleasant. But committing to this discomfort is precisely the precondition of thinking, doing, and being otherwise. It is by practicing this political curiosity that social change happens. By recovering the GIP archive and putting it back into conversation with contemporary prison resistance and theory, it is our hope that both scholarship and activism are renewed in ways heretofore unimaginable. In sum, we hope this book contributes to the larger project of generating that future.

Notes

1. Dan Berger and Toussant Losier, *Rethinking the American Prison Movement* (New York: Routledge, 2017).
2. See the "World Prison Brief" at https://www.prisonstudies.org/.
3. Lauren-Brooke Eisen, *Inside Private Prisons: An American Dilemma in the Age of Mass Incarceration* (New York: Columbia University Press, 2018).
4. Keramet Reiter, *23/7: Pelican Bay Prison and the Rise of Long-Term Solitary Confinement* (New Haven: Yale University Press, 2018).
5. Michelle Alexander, "The Newest Jim Crow," *New York Times,* November 9, 2018.
6. Bernard Harcourt, *Against Prediction: Profiling, Policing and Punishing in an Actuarial Age* (Chicago: University of Chicago Press, 2007), and Nikolas Rose and Joelle M. Abi-Rached, *Neuro: The New Brain Sciences and the Management of the Mind* (Princeton, N.J.: Princeton University Press, 2013), chap. 6.
7. Michel Foucault, "Still Prisons," this volume.
8. Michel Foucault, *Discipline and Punish* (New York: Vintage, 1979), 30–31 [translation modified]; originally published as *Surveiller et punir* (Paris: Gallimard, 1975), 39–40.
9. For a firsthand history of the group and its work, see Daniel Defert's invaluable "The Emergence of a New Front: The Prisons," this volume; in addition, see the introductions that preface each of the sections of this volume and the editorial notes that accompany each selection.
10. The GIP commissioned and performed a play about the trial of the leaders of the Nancy Prison revolt—*Le Procès de la mutinerie de Nancy*—that was written primarily by Hélène Cixous and staged by Ariane Mnouchkine and her famous ensemble, the Théâtre du Soleil.
11. *Les prisons aussi* (1972), directed by Hélène Châtelain and René Lefort, was a documentary that featured extended interviews with former prisoners detailing the conditions of their incarceration.
12. Michel Foucault, "Interview de Michel Foucault," DE IV, 688–89; "Interview with *Actes*," in *Power: Essential Works of Foucault, 1954–1984*, vol. 3, ed. James D. Faubion (New York: New Press, 2000), 394–95.
13. GIP, "Back Cover of *Intolerable 1*," this volume.
14. Ibid.
15. GIP, "On Prisons," this volume.
16. For a study of the intolerable, intolerance, and active intolerance across the GIP and Foucault archives, see Perry Zurn, "Toward an Account

of Intolerance: From Prison Resistance to Engaged Scholarship," *Carceral Notebooks* 12 (2017): 97–128. For a study of the intolerable specifically, see Kevin Thompson, "To Judge the Intolerable," *Philosophy Today* 54 (2010): 169–76. Cf. Michael Hames-García, "Are Prisons Tolerable?" *Carceral Notebooks* 12 (2017): 151–86, and Grégory Salle, "Mettre la prison à l'épreuve: Le GIP en guerre contre l'Intolérable,'" *Cultures & Conflits* 55 (2004): 71–96.

17. GIP, "Declaration to the Press and the Public Authorities Coming from the Prisoners of Melun," this volume.

18. They looked to the United States as a model for this. See Jean-Marie Domenach, "To Have Done with Prisons," this volume.

19. For the history of the Toul uprising, see the special issue of the journal *Négation*, "La Révolte de la prison de Toul: Délinquance sociale et justice gauchiste," avant-premier numéro (1971); the report published by the Comité Vérité Toul, *La Révolte de la centrale Ney* (Paris: Gallimard, 1973); and, for additional context and a broader perspective on the prison revolts, see Anne Guérin, *Prisonniers en révolte: Quotidien carcéral, mutineries et politique pénitentiaire en France (1970–1980)* (Marseille: Agone, 2013), chap. 6, and the documentary, *Sur les toits,* directed by Nicolas Drolc (2014; Les Mutins de Pangée, 2014, dvd).

20. Georges Galiana, the warden of the Toul facility, had previously served as the director of an Algerian prison during the War of Independence and he was the director of the prison at Nîmes during a revolt where a crackdown on the prisoners, a "bloody week," had occurred in 1967 (see Guérin, *Prisonniers en révolte,* 109n).

21. Among the first acts of their campaign, the GIP called for an independent commission of inquiry to be established, while the Gauche Prolétarienne created the Comité Vérité Toul to investigate the events of the uprising itself and to support this new "revolutionary front."

A GIP communiqué, from December 11, 1971, called for an independent commission of inquiry that would examine the bullying and abuse claims from throughout the prison system and for which many prisoners had already filed official complaints, research on the state of the medical care available through the French penitentiary system, and review of the treatment of the prisoners transferred out of Toul for being leaders of the uprising (see AL, 146).

Together the GP and the GIP collected extensive testimony, from both prisoners and guards, as to the intolerable conditions and practices under which they all operated within the prison. The collection, published twice in early 1972, was titled "Toul Hell." It was also included in the Comité Vérité Toul's *La Révolte de la centrale Ney,* 13–168. For a sample of some of the testimonies in the original collection, see Part III ("Prison Revolts") in this volume.

22. For an account of this press conference and its significance within the development of French intellectual history, see Julian Bourg, *From Revolution to Ethics: May 1968 and Contemporary French Thought* (Montreal: McGill-Queen's University Press, 2007), chap. 2.

23. See "To Escape Their Prison," this volume.

24. Ibid.

25. The Groupe Information Aisles, which worked on psychiatry, mental health, and the link between these and incarceration; the Groupe Information Santé, which examined the problem of health and sought to contest the health system; the Groupe d'Information des Travailleurs Sociaux, which was a social work advocacy organization; and, most famously, AIDeS, France's first AIDS advocacy organization, which was founded by Defert himself in honor of Foucault, who died of the disease in 1984.

26. In what follows, we consider two of the issues that, for Brigitte Robert, define the very crossroads at which the GIP was born: how to transform the prison from a social to a genuinely political, that is, contested, domain and how to change the role of intellectuals from being that of leaders to that of fostering forums in which others can speak. See her "Les luttes autour des prisons 1971–1972: Le Groupe d'information sur les prisons et la naissance du C.A.P.," Doctoral dissertation, Institut d'Études Politiques, 1981.

27. See the exchange around this issue in "Still Prisons," this volume.

28. On the history of the concept of the intellectual in France, see David Drake's studies: *French Intellectuals and Politics from the Dreyfus Affair to the Occupation* (New York: Palgrave, 2005), *Intellectuals and Politics in Post-War France* (London: Palgrave, 2002), and the meticulous study of this issue in François Dosse, *La saga des intellectuels français*, 2 vols. (Paris: Gallimard, 2018).

29. See "Intellectuals and Power," this volume. See also the interview from 1973 titled "L'intellectuel sert à rassembler les idées mais son savoir est partiel par rapport au savoir ouvrier," DE II, 421-23.

30. See also the interview with the Marxist journal *Quel corps?* from June 1975, published in DE II, 759, and in Foucault, *Power/Knowledge: Selected Interviews and Other Writings, 1972–1977*, ed. Colin Gordon (New York: Random House, 1988), 62.

31. See "Vérité et Pouvoir," DE III, 154, translated as, "Truth and Power," in *Ethics: Subjectivity and Truth*, ed. Paul Rabinow (New York: New Press, 1998), 126–27.

32. For studies of the unique form that French Maoism took, see Remi

Hess, *Les maoïstes français* (Paris: Éditions Anthropos, 1974), A. Belden Fields, *Trotskyism and Maoism* (New York: Praeger, 1988), chap. 3, Christophe Bourseiller, *Les maoïstes* (Paris: Plon, 1996), chaps. 4–6, Julian Bourg, "The Red Guards of Paris: French Student Maoism of the 1960s," *History of European Ideas* 31 (2005): 472–90, and "Principally Contradiction: The Flourishing of French Maoism," in *Mao's Little Red Book*, ed. Alexander C. Cook (New York: Cambridge University Press, 2014), 225–44.

33. See Marcelo Hoffman, *Militant Acts: Investigations in Radical Political Struggles and Theories* (Albany: State University of New York Press, 2019), chap. 2.

34. The GIP collaborated with others on producing such studies; e.g., Christine Martineau and Jean-Pierre Carasso, *Le travail dans les prisons. La misère, plus que la loi, condamne 20000 détenus au travail. Le capital veille sur l'ombre* (Paris: Champs Libre, 1972).

35. See "Report by Doctor Rose, Psychiatrist at Toul Prison," this volume.

36. The report was first published in December 1971, in the journal of the GP, *La Cause du peuple—J'accuse,* then, in the same month, as a full-page open letter in *Le Monde,* and finally, it appeared in a professional journal, *Psychiatrie d'aujourd'hui,* in January 1972.

37. See Dosse, *La saga des intellectuels français, II: L'avenir en miettes (1968–1989),* 101–7.

38. GIP, "The Prisoner Faces Segregation Every Day," this volume.

39. GIP, "A Movement of Struggle Is Developing Today," this volume.

40. Jean-Marie Domenach, "To Have Done with Prisons," this volume.

41. It should be noted that, to our knowledge, the earliest GIP reference to abolition appears in the following statement, penned on March 20, 1971, by a former prisoner: "I have had the occasion to read several articles concerning your movement of inquiry into the prisons. . . . I think the problem is poorly posed. . . . I believe your movement for amelioration ought to proceed by way of abolition" (Christophe Soulié, *Liberté sur paroles: Contribution à l'histoire du Comité d'action des prisonniers* [Bordeaux: Annalis, 1995], 58).

42. GIP, "La Santé: Questionnaire and Narratives," this volume.

43. GIP, "Dear Comrades, Here Are the Current Axes of the GIP's Development," this volume.

44. GIP, "Revendications de Loos," in INT, 226.

45. Ibid.

46. GIP, "Revendications de Nîmes," in INT, 277.

47. Ibid.

48. Ibid.

49. GIP, "La Santé: Questionnaire and Narratives," this volume.

50. Daniel Defert, "When Information Is a Struggle," this volume; GIP, "Preface," Intolerable 1, this volume; GIP, "Dear Comrades, Here Are the Current Axes of the GIP's Development," this volume; GIP, "Right to Information on the Prisons," this volume; GIP, "Declaration to the Press and the Public Authorities Coming from the Prisoners of Melun," this volume; Domenach, "To Have Done with Prisons," this volume; GIP, "Revendications de Loos," in INT, 226.

51. GIP, "Preface to Intolerable 1," this volume.

52. Ibid.

53. Ibid.

54. GIP, "On Prisons," this volume.

55. Perry Zurn and Andrew Dilts, "Active Intolerance—An Introduction," in Active Intolerance: Michel Foucault, the Prisons Information Group, and the Future of Abolition, ed. Perry Zurn and Andrew Dilts (New York: Palgrave, 2016), 8.

56. Ibid., 10.

57. Lisa Guenther, "Beyond Guilt and Innocence: The Creaturely Politics of Prison Resistance Movements," in Zurn and Dilts, Active Intolerance, 234, 237.

58. GIP, Back Cover of Intolerable 1, this volume.

59. GIP, "La Santé: Questionnaire and Narratives," this volume.

60. Stephen Dillon, "'Can They Ever Escape'? Foucault, Black Feminism, and the Intimacy of Abolition," in Zurn and Dilts, Active Intolerance, 271.

61. Michel Foucault, Discipline and Punish: The Birth of the Prison, trans. Alan Sheridan (New York: Vintage, 1977), 63, 263.

62. Foucault, "Pompidou's Two Deaths," this volume.

63. Michel Foucault, "Against Replacement Penalties" (1981), in Aesthetics, Method, and Epistemology, ed. James Faubion (New York: New Press, 1999), 461; cf. Michel Foucault, "To Punish Is the Most Difficult Thing There Is" (1981), in Aesthetics, Method, and Epistemology, 462.

64. Foucault, "The Great Confinement," this volume.

65. Michel Foucault, "Alternatives to the Prison: Dissemination or Decline of Social Control?" (1976), Theory, Culture, & Society 26.6 (2009): 17.

66. Zurn and Dilts, "Active Intolerance—An Introduction," 8.

67. Foucault, "Alternatives to the Prison," 24.

68. Foucault, Discipline and Punish, 16.

69. Foucault, "Alternatives to the Prison," 24.

70. Foucault, "Against Replacement Penalties," 461.

71. Foucault, "The Great Confinement," this volume.

72. Foucault, "Against Replacement Penalties," 461.

73. Ibid.

74. Foucault, "To Punish is the Most Difficult Thing There Is," 464.

75. Michel Foucault, "Sur la selette," *Les nouvelles littéraires* (March 17, 1975): 3. Cf. Rolf S. Folter, "On the Methodological Foundation of the Abolitionist Approach to the Criminal Justice System: A Comparison of the Ideas of Hulsmann, Mathiesen, and Foucault," *Contemporary Crises* 10 (1986): 55.

76. Soulié, *Liberté sur paroles,* 273, 119.

77. Serve Livrozet, "Interview de Claude Mauriac," *CAP* 36 (May 1975): 3.

78. For a partial online archive, see Fragments d'Histoire de la Gauche Radicale, http://archivesautonomies.org/spip.php?article116.

79. Soulié, *Liberté sur paroles,* 143.

80. Anonymous, "Communiqués," *CAP* 30 (November 1975): 8.

81. CAP, "Chambéry, une prison 'tranquille,'" *CAP* 30 (November 1975): 2.

82. Les 3 Étages du D3, "Une Prison-Modèle: Fleury," *CAP* 27 (July–August 1975): 7.

83. CAP, "Point 1 Du CAP," *CAP* 32 (December 1975): 5.

84. CAP, "Le Combat contre la contrainte par corps," *CAP* 45 (April 1977): 7.

85. CAP, "Un nouveau point du manifeste: Suppression de la garde à vue," *CAP* 13 (January 1974): 8.

86. CAP, "Non à interdiction de séjour!" Interview with André Rivereau, *CAP* 30 (November 1975): 8.

87. Un détenu, "Par-dessus les murs," *CAP* 31 (November 1975): 9; cf. Uriel, "Non à la peine de mort," *CAP* 42 (December 1976): 3.

88. Jean-Claude Deudon, "Mettre en fuite la perpétuité," *CAP* 47 (June 1977): 8.

89. Comité de liaison contre la peine de mort et les peines perpétuelles, "Peine de mort," *CAP* 62 (May 1979): 6.

90. Ibid.

91. Un détenu espagnol, "La vie de 'chateaux' en Espagne," *CAP* 44 (Mars 1977): 6.

92. Comité contre l'expulsion d'Arfaqui Bechir, "Notre Comité," *CAP* 32 (December 1975): 3.

93. CAP and Amis et familles de détenus, "Isoler les contagieux," *CAP* 40 (October 1976): 5.

94. Catherine, "Du Riffifi chez les femmes," *CAP* 66 (February 1980): 4.

95. CAP, "Suppression de la prison," *CAP* 9 (September 1973): 8.

96. Mot d'Ordre 68, "Au Café de la jeunesse perdue," *CAP* 61 (March/April 1979): 7.

97. Serge Livrozet, "Le CAP: Journal des détenus," *CAP* 9 (September 1973): 2.

98. Jean Lapeyrie, "Se défendre face à la justice," *CAP* 43 (January 1977): 6.

99. Serge Livrozet, "J'ai lu: 'Simple Militant,' de Maurice Jaquier," *CAP* 14 (February 1974): 4.

100. Mot d'Ordre 68, "Au Café de la jeunesse perdue," 7.

101. Ibid.

102. Deudon, "Mettre en fuite la perpétuité," 8.

103. CAP, "Justice pénitentiare," *CAP* 61 (March/April 1979): 5.

104. Mot d'Ordre 68, "Au Café de la jeunesse perdue," 7.

105. Serge Livrozet, "Répression, Frustration," *CAP* 38 (July 1975): 5.

106. Soulié, *Liberté sur paroles*, 274.

107. See "Further Reading" at the end of this book for an authoritative bibliography.

108. Steve Champion, "Breaking the Conditioning: The Relevance of the Prisons Information Group," in Zurn and Dilts, *Active Intolerance*, 95–104.

109. Janos Toevs, "Giving the Floor to Whom?" *Carceral Notebooks* 12 (2017): 131–49.

110. Abu-Ali Abdur'Rahman, "Intolerable 1," in Zurn and Dilts, *Active Intolerance*, 92; Derrick Quintero, "Intolerable 2," in Zurn and Dilts, *Active Intolerance*, 141; Donald Middlebrooks, "Intolerable 3," in Zurn and Dilts, *Active Intolerance*, 222.

111. Andrew Dilts, "Toward Abolitionist Genealogy," *Southern Journal of Philosophy* 55 (2017): 51–77.

The Emergence of a New Front
The Prisons

DANIEL DEFERT

*Daniel Defert wrote this reflection, "L'émergence d'un nouveau
front: les prisons," for the publication of the first collection of GIP
documents,* Le Groupe d'information sur les prisons: Archives
d'une lutte, 1970–1972, *edited by Philippe Artières, Laurent Quéro,
and Michelle Zancarini-Fournel (Paris: Éditions de l'IMEC, 2003),
315–26.*

As part of the Gauche Prolétarienne's (GP) defensive strategies—to
"broaden resistance"[1]—the Groupe d'Information sur les Prisons
(GIP) was created in late 1970, but the GIP very quickly became au-
tonomous. When the GP was dissolved by Georges Pompidou's administration on May 27, 1970, all its militant activities, including the
circulation of its journal, *La Cause du peuple,* were branded illegal.
Reconstituting a dissolved association was punishable with a heavy
prison sentence and acts of violence, such as assault or assault with
intent, and landed one before the State Security Court, a special
tribunal that was originally created to prosecute the Organisation
Armée Secrète (OAS). The leaders of the GP, which had gone underground, appealed to a strategy that was traditional in the history of
communist movements: an alliance with public figures or organizations engaged in the defense of civil rights and considered "democrats" in the pejorative sense afforded by those, in this same tradition,
who considered themselves "revolutionaries." Thus, Jean-Paul Sartre
assumed the editorship of the banned *La Cause du peuple* (following the imprisonment of its two previous editors, Michel Le Bris and
Jean-Pierre Le Dantec), while a new journal, *J'accuse,* took over its

35

public role.[2] Simone de Beauvoir sponsored the new Association of the Friends of *La Cause du peuple,* which endeavored to maintain the paper's unrestricted circulation. It is in this context that the Secours Rouge, that once-famous acronym,[3] was reestablished, bringing together representatives from three generations of the French Left, which is to say, from the entire Left since the Dreyfus Affair: Mrs. Halbwachs-Basch, daughter of Victor Basch and widow of Maurice Halbwachs; Pierre Halbwachs; their son, Charles Tillon, founder of the FTP;[4] Jean Chaintron; Bernard Lambert, head of the Paysans Travailleurs;[5] Jeanette Colombel; and Sartre, to name just a few of the founders. Left-wing Gaullists also joined the movement. It was during this process of reconfigurations that Maurice Clavel introduced Michel Foucault and Claude Mauriac. The mobilization grew widespread all the more easily owing to the fact that the GP's dissolution had been preceded, in April 1970, by the "antiwreckers" *[anticasseur]* law, which put the freedom to protest back into question by establishing the collective responsibility of political organizations for everything that might happen during a demonstration—and since May '68, much had happened.

During the summer of 1970, a cell of the underground Gauche Prolétarienne was created in order to maintain political ties with its imprisoned militants, prepare their defense, make their trial a political platform, in accordance with the Leninist tradition, and affirm, to the "masses," the political meaning of the acts for which they were charged. At the time, nearly two hundred people were affected, sent off to a dozen prisons across France. My friend Jacques Rancière invited me to join this cell, called the Organisation des Prisonniers Politiques (OPP). The step was probably intended as a means of approaching Foucault, who, having been away from France in 1968, seemed to be devoid of partisan affiliations. Several months later, I anticipated the GP's wishes by proposing that he direct a commission of inquiry into the prisons.

In September 1970, the OPP, then headed by Serge July, carried out the preparations and logistics for a first hunger strike by imprisoned militants with the aim of obtaining the status of political prisoners. The goal was not to obtain special privileges, as the propaganda circulated by other *groupuscules* made it seem, but rather to secure the right to assemble, to communicate with their organization, and to access news media, which was still forbidden in prisons (all rights the FLN had secured in its time).[6] Above all, the goal was to exert some political force in order to keep these new and very harsh forms of repression at bay. No government admits that it detains political prisoners. Despite the notoriety of certain figures among the imprisoned (e.g., Michel Le Bris, Jean-Pierre Le Dantec, Alain Geismar), the strike did not garner considerable support on the outside and fizzled out. Someone new took over the OPP. He was ascetic, sufficiently magnetic to inspire his troops, and bedecked with pseudonyms and aliases, from Pierre Victor to Jean Tsétoung. I later learned it was Benny Lévy. A second hunger strike was planned for mid-January 1971, after the Christmas packages stopped coming in, because, in the French prisons, Christmas was the only opportunity for prisoners to receive supplies from their families.

From the beginning of December 1970, the OPP prepared to mobilize the "democrats" who were supposed to provide external endorsement for this new strike. Following the model of the people's tribunal the GP had just held at Lens (it had called in doctors as expert witnesses to report on unhealthy and precarious conditions in the mines),[7] I proposed the formation of a commission of inquiry to look into the general situation of prisons, an inquiry to be conducted by experts and directed by Michel Foucault. The leadership of the GP seized upon the project, immediately envisioning a spectacular operation where public figures present themselves at prison gates in the name of the people, but are driven back by the police or even bludgeoned in front of cameras. Yet that was precisely the kind of manipulation Foucault detested the most, understanding it to be just a form of French anti-intellectualism.

I had put Foucault's name forward unbeknownst to him. But the fear that this would divert him from his Benedictine labors paralyzed me at the time. The leadership of the GP sensed my reticence and dispatched several militants to bypass it, including Foucault's assistants at Vincennes, Jacques-Alain and Judith Miller. Jacques-Alain advocated for a certain model of public investigation: the American judicial committees on prisons.[8] Ultimately, Foucault agreed and said that it fell in line with his work.

At the end of December, he brought together, in his home, those he deemed capable of either forming or planning a commission of inquiry on the prisons. On the advice of his friend Casamayor (a judge who excluded himself from the commission for the sake of professional confidentiality), Foucault invited Jean-Marie Domenach; Louis Joinet, who had just founded the Syndicat de la Magistrature; several doctors from the penitentiary administration; Frédéric Pottecher, the judicial columnist; several lawyers, Christian Revon, Jean-Jacques de Felice, and Christine Martineau, who would later form the "Défense active" collective; and my friends the philosopher Danièle Rancière and the sociologist Jacques Donzelot. The GP was also represented by Philippe Barret, who was close to the organization's leaders, and I was never quite certain whether he was or was not our political superintendent *[commissaire]* so to speak. In all, some twenty people were present. Each one expounded on both the necessity and the impracticality of such an investigation. Some held that only prisoners possessed the competence to deal with these issues, while others hypothesized that prisoner testimony is unreliable. Danièle Rancière and Christine Martineau—the latter was preparing a book on prison labor[9]—had already drafted the basic outlines of a questionnaire that we wanted to hand out to prisoners. Danièle Rancière was well versed in conducting inquiries at factory gates using the "Maoist" method, which consisted in jotting down in a notebook the questions and answers that arose over the course of conversations with workers. But in this case, the questionnaire was necessary, given both the difficulty of communicating with prisoners and the need to standardize our questions in order to construct a comparative approach to the conditions of incarceration. We thought that attending, from the outset, to material conditions would convince the prisoners that we were with them and invested in them. Our model was Marx's worker inquiry *[enquête ouvrière].*

This first gathering of, for the most part, "specific" intellectuals—in the sense Foucault would soon give to that term, which is to say, intellectuals bent on subverting their position of knowledge and of power in knowledge—was a failure. The only person who was ultimately going to fulfill this political role of the specific intellectual was Dr. Rose, psychiatrist at the Ney Prison in Toul, author of the famous "Rose Report," which would cost her her job following the prisoners' double revolt and partial destruction of the prison in December 1971. Nevertheless, that evening in December 1970, Louis Joinet, examining the questionnaire, admitted that "at least it was sound." Immediately upon opening the meeting, Foucault had rejected the project of a people's commission of inquiry into the prisons (the whole reason we had been called in) and argued instead for the production of various kinds of information, the channels for which could be subterranean and multifaceted. It was then that he proposed the name "Groupe d'Information sur les Prisons" (Prisons Information Group) or GIP. The group was to be an anonymous network, protected by three public figures, who were respected particularly in the domain of truth and inquiry: Jean-Marie Domenach, former resistance fighter and editor of the journal *Esprit,* which became, among other things, a reference point for social workers,[10] a social group that was in the process of professionalization and that had already distanced itself from its origins in charity work; the historian Pierre Vidal-Naquet, whose well-documented denunciation of the torture utilized by the French army during the Algerian War had been of considerable importance in the 1960s; and finally, Michel Foucault, who declared this work on prisons to be an extension of his history of psychiatric confinement. Having learned the advantages of an informal network from the clandestine nature of the GP, we knew the GIP could not have the formalized structure of an association. No one could know who our informants were. The "names" representing the group had to protect its informants and to guarantee the veracity of what was said.

By the end of that meeting in December 1970, all we had left to do was develop an underground network for circulating the questionnaires. We only had three modes of access: former prisoners or political prisoners, whose assistance had been essential in drafting the questionnaire; penitentiary personnel, with whom we began making discreet contact; and the queues of visitors at the prison doors—the administration still being wont to humiliate the prisoners' families with long waits outside the doors on visiting days. The GIP was organized on the basis of one group per prison. At first active only in Paris, this model was rapidly implemented wherever there were imprisoned militants: Toulouse, Besançon, Nancy, Lille, and so on. With the formation of the groups, the printing of questionnaires using the Vietnamese Roneo[11] (with stencils and handmade silk-screen plates), and transporting them to the provinces, we were totally ready when the political prisoners' hunger strike, which began in January 1971, came to an end on February 8, 1971. This time, it had been well publicized on the outside: the hunger strikes staged in solidarity, especially by the Friends of *La Cause du peuple* in the Saint-Bernard chapel in Montparnasse, and the visit paid to them by Simone Signoret and Yves Montand, which was followed by the press, compelled Minister of Justice René Pleven to give in. On February 8, 1971, the strikers' lawyers, Georges Kiejman, Henri Leclerc, and Jean-Jacques de Felice, announced in that same chapel that a "special status" had been obtained, which granted the imprisoned militants the prerogatives of "political" standing, but without granting them the name of political prisoners. Concerned about the health of Alain Geismar, who had undertaken the two successive hunger strikes, the militants compromised over the wording, all the more so given that Foucault publicly announced the formation of the GIP, thereby indicating that the struggle would continue. Now public, the GIP was able to function autonomously, irrespective of the GP's initial strategy, while also benefiting from the social mobilization around the question of prisons incited on the outside. Foucault, who had always refused to play the "fellow traveler," was not unhappy to generalize the issue to the problem of detention itself and the justice system's responsibility, rather than simply support the demands of an organization [like the GP] to which he lent his friendly support while keeping a critical distance. Sometime later, Foucault said to me—and I don't know whether this struck him in the moment or after the fact—that the acronym GIP evoked the GP, but with one iota of difference that intellectuals owed it to themselves to introduce. When I created an association for the struggle against AIDS after Foucault's death in 1984, I wanted to transcribe this remark and filiation into its name: to introduce, into the English acronym for an illness, AIDS, the difference that solidarity makes, whence "AIDeS."[12]

May '68 had passed the prisons by—and parliament, too, for that matter—as if these sites didn't symbolize forms of power. I recall having later read the journal of a prisoner at La Santé who, on one of the most turbulent days of May '68, had simply noted: "Today I saw a rat." What's more, some prisoners reported to us that they had been afraid, and even that the guards—"the screws *[matons]*" as the GIP had begun to call them in the media—had made them afraid of a revolutionaries' victory, confirming an old Marxist mistrust of the

THE EMERGENCE OF A NEW FRONT | 41

"lumpenproletariat" that still organized certain political discourses. This mistrust sometimes arose—in the name of the masses—at our GP meetings. Jean Genet recalled to us a moment, which had really wounded him, when a communist member of the resistance refused to be shackled to him at La Santé under the Occupation. So, Foucault was not unhappy to situate himself outside that divide by having the GIP investigation extend to so-called common-law prisoners. We very quickly received signs of support from the anarchist faction of prisoners—the self-taught elite of the prisons.[13] Serge Livrozet, who founded the Comité d'Action des Prisonniers (CAP) in the autumn of 1972, came from that ideological family. In turn, the anarchists expected us to organize violent actions on the outside, while the Maoists expected a show of violence on the inside, as a sign of the politicization of the prisoners. Certain GP leaders seemed to me to become truly interested in the GIP only when revolts broke out. For me, the objective of our group was, in the first place, to render prison inoperative as an instrument of political repression. But we soon learned how savagely and silently prison revolts were suppressed, and that dissuaded us from provoking actions we ourselves could not safeguard.

Our allies at *Esprit,* who fell within the philanthropic Christian tradition, founded on a faith in the role of prison rehabilitation, expected GIP actions to produce reforms. Paul Thibaud, for example, later reproached Michel Foucault on these grounds. Even the Syndicat de la Magistrature, which sought to assemble the guards in one giant political-syndicalist group, was opposed to the antagonism between the prisoners and the "screws" that we were in the process of exacerbating and that served as a springboard for our action. All this is to say that even if prisons were absent from the political field, they did not function within an ideological void. The decisive element in Foucault's proposal to form a simple information group was its dismissal of ideological frameworks and obstructions. By refusing the idea of a commission of inquiry, which necessarily would have had the power of the state as its only interlocutor and sole target, and by advocating instead for a description of the material and anonymous functioning of penitentiary control, as reported by its targets, the prisoners, the GIP displaced the whole notion of power so traditional in politics. Both the Marxist mistrust of and the philanthropic interest in prisoners equally obfuscated the very materiality of punishment, its violence, and the lawlessness that surrounded it under the pretense of justice. To provide information about these problems was to struggle against the censorship of the administration, the inattention of the judges, the carelessness of the lawyers, the stalling of the guard unions (these unions being the true administrators of the penitentiary), and the ignorance and shame of the families. It is this material aspect of punishment that was soon to appear in the press and, before long, in political debates. Newly elected in 1974, Valéry Giscard d'Estaing visited a prison and created a Secretary of State on Prison Conditions. But these measures had only a temporary effect, as Foucault would observe in *Surveiller et punir* (1975; *Discipline and Punish*, 1977), recalling the ineffective succession of reforms since 1822, that is, just after the creation of the penitentiary system.

In the spring of 1971, journalists began to mingle with GIP militants in the waiting lines outside prison gates. Reports on the penitentiary system began to appear. The GIP's questionnaires framed this new perception of incarceration. Former prisoners and families of so-called common-law prisoners began to distribute leaflets, to take the floor in meetings, to sign petitions, and to demonstrate in front of the Chancellery; in short, they liberated themselves from moral stigma in order to adopt the traditional repertoire of political action.

At the beginning of summer, René Pleven gave in regarding newspapers in prisons and admitted them into the general population, a privilege once restricted to prisoners with special status. As a result, the GIP's work became even better known among prisoners, and it seemed as though popular oversight of punishments pronounced in the name of the French people was finally taking shape.

The taking of hostages at Clairvaux in September 1971 radicalized the situation. Imprisoned for violent crimes, Buffet and Bontems capitalized on unrest in the prison, which was slowly developing into a collective movement, to attempt an escape, taking a nurse and a guard hostage and then executing them. The guard unions blamed the situation on the press, who had just been authorized to enter the prisons and, several days earlier, had extensively covered the revolt at Attica, a prison in New York. At the same time, death penalty advocates, whose position had been weakened by the growing critical attention to all forms of penalization, took action, launching a new campaign in favor of the death penalty in October 1971.

In order to defuse the situation and appease the guard union, René Pleven imposed a collective sanction on all the prisoners: the elimi-nation of that year's Christmas packages. In point of fact, the system-atic search of these packages (for fear of the nail file hidden in the sausage) was additional work hardly popular among the personnel. The disciplinary action was announced quietly in November. I can still hear my friends from the GP, especially [André] Glucksmann, say-ing to me, "Let's move on this!" and me saying that I didn't see how we could possibly mobilize the public around Christmas packages. Yet that was the spark that set off thirty-two revolts in the winter of 1971–72—some of which were accompanied by the systematic de-struction of cells, as was the case at Toul and Nancy.

It began in Poissy just as the GIP was organizing a families' protest in Place Vendôme. We were credited with a coordination that never existed, but, with the revolts under way, mobilization against vio-lent suppression became possible. The mobilization of high-school students, of the Secours Rouge, of the GIP movement, as well as the interest of the press made it such that everything unfolded under the watchful eye of the public. First, the rebels occupied the roof-tops, from which they communicated with the people. At Nancy, they threw leaflets from the rooftops, which the Nancy GIP hurried to re-produce and then circulate throughout the city. During the winter of 1971–72, the prisons became a front of violent and predominantly working-class struggles.

The analysis of prison, no longer in terms of reform or rehabilita-tion, but from the point of view of the materiality of incarceration, of the inhumanity of punishments more than of the inhumanity of the law, of the relations of violence that structure all the internal rela-tions in prison, problematized the question of prison differently. The daily management of prisons operationalized all the hierarchies of the outside world: the moral hierarchy among crimes, the economic hierarchy among prisoners, the hierarchy of sexes and sexualities.

The situation in women's prisons was radically different from that in men's prisons, as the GIP group at La Roquette, led by Claude

Rouault, observed: there was a difference in the number and nature of the crimes committed, a difference in prisoners' relations with the screws, and a difference in their relations with the outside. The group at La Roquette, therefore, inscribed its efforts within the problematic of feminist struggles just beginning to be organized. We were also called upon for specific action by a group of transvestites housed together at Fresnes, where they were mistreated, brought in dressed as women and released bearded, hairy, and in miniskirts. In this way, the prison struggles that we had tried to integrate into the proletarian struggles[14] rapidly became more and more aligned with the new feminist, homosexual,[15] and immigrant movements, in which the social control of the body and the desecration of identities was the structuring concern.

The booklets produced by the GIP display the evolving transformation of the penitentiary system between 1971 and 1972.

Their objective was to make knowledge of incarceration, and of the daily experience of prisoners themselves, truly become a part of the public domain. We had no discourse of our own; the heterogeneity of what the GIP produced testifies to that. The first booklet, *Enquête dans 20 prisons,* released in June 1971, consists of questionnaires that were filled out anonymously by prisoners and came to us from some twenty different institutions over the course of less than three months. We did not have extensive means of verifying our information, nor, especially, of identifying our informants; for instance, the story of the restraint beds used at Toul seemed so monstrous and so incredible that at first we hesitated to publish it, before finally getting behind it. The Toul Revolt in December 1971 exposed the scandal of its isolation units—prisoners could remain there, bound to a prison bed, for several days. We then learned that this unbelievable questionnaire, filled out by a prisoner who had been the victim of such treatment, had been mailed in by Toul's prison chaplain. Did the personnel and chaplains really have no other recourse than an anonymous group, legitimated by the names of respected intellectuals, by which to denounce what they knew to be unacceptable? Mrs. d'Escrivan, the social worker at Fresnes, and Dr. Rose, the psychiatrist at Toul, actually lost their jobs for acting in accordance with their consciences and indignation. The Minister of Justice filed a libel suit against the GIP, which had spread the news of a work accident at the Caen Prison, news that was then picked up by the newspaper *Le Monde*. The proof came from several of that prison's former prisoners: there was no trial over the veracity of the facts reported by the GIP. Not one prisoner had lied.

Information is a struggle. That also meant that to obtain information from prisoners—and from the place where law, discipline, and secrecy most forbid it—was to give credence to the veracity of their speech *[parole]* and ultimately to give their speech the status of an event. When a prison suicide made the front page of *France-Soir* on November 3, 1972, after years of suicides being hidden from sight and appearing only in penitentiary statistics, society's way of looking at the prison had changed.

The second booklet, put together by Jacques-Alain Miller and François Regnault, was titled *Le GIP enquête dans une prison-modèle: Fleury-Mérogis* and it focuses on an institution typical of 1960s penitentiary reformism. This booklet collected texts that highlighted the penitentiary technology organizing the new prisons, among which Stammheim in Germany was the most extreme version, rationalizing even sensory deprivation.

L'Assassinat de George Jackson is a reminder that the difficulty of politicizing the question of prisons in France led the GIP to become interested, on the one hand, in the struggles in Italian prisons led by Lotta Continua and, on the other hand, in the American Black Panthers. Genet had proposed to Foucault—and this was why they met— the drafting of a text in favor of George Jackson's liberation (which had been postponed indefinitely) when suddenly Jackson was assassinated. With Genet's help, we then dissected the American press coverage to uncover the truth about this concealed political assassination. A little later, the Attica revolt explicitly used the overimprisonment of American Blacks to ground their demands for civil rights.

The *Cahiers de revendications sortis des prisons lors des récentes révoltes*, organized by Hélène Cixous and Jean Gattegno, showed the rapid evolution of prisoners' speech *[parole]*. At first fragmented, gathered only randomly and with difficulty from networks of secret informants, this speech—starting in 1972 and with the help of our questionnaires—became collective, political, dissenting, and even reformist speech. And it emerged from the prisons where prisoners labored in workshops, notably from Melun, where Serge Livrozet was held.

Suicides de prison (1972), a booklet that I created with Gilles Deleuze, showed the movement of collective prison revolts falling back, and its violence turning back on itself, a violence that the new context no longer allowed to be collectivized. It was the end of the post-May situation for the prisons, given that Toul (December 1971) was really the May '68 of prisons. Two successive revolts there illustrated this transformation: the first, organized by the oldest prisoners, ended with a return to order, once certain improvements were secured; the second, led by youths facing broken promises, provoked the vandalization of cells and the turmoil of an open forum one long night in the courtyard, much like at the Sorbonne in 1968. Foucault noted that this change influenced the rebellions to follow. The revolt at Toul divided the leaders of the GP: Robert Linhart, managing editor of *J'accuse,* founded a Comité Vérité Toul (CVT) made up of GP militants, this time antagonists of the GIP, and prevailed upon Sartre to declare that the prisoners fought in the name of all, as if it were a disgrace to fight for oneself, as if it were necessary to oppose all divisions in the course of these struggles.

Following the "divine surprise" of '68—as spontaneous and multifaceted as it was, liberating the speech *[parole]* of innumerable groups and generating a general *suspension,* rather than a general strike, of the country—came, in 1969–70, with the electoral victory of the right, an attempt to regenerate a social movement through Marxist, Marxist-Leninist, Maoist, and Trotskyist organizations, which were more or less authoritarian and appealed to rather traditional modes of analysis and intervention. The Trotskyists emphasized party building in milieus that were already well structured, while the GP immersed itself in the heart of the so-called masses, that is, the mobilizable factions of the working class, the marginalized, and the rural poor.

The GIP probably played the transitional role between this second period of post-May and the emergence of movements called liberation movements (of women and of homosexuals in particular),[16] which, in their recruitment, in their mode of analysis, and in their objectives, differed greatly from the political movements that claimed to prolong '68, on a forced march, in an assertive and, abroad, really a terrorist fashion. I would actually characterize these new liberation movements as being not only political, but as also socio-ethical to the degree that, for them, it was a matter of the subversion of the relations of power, of hierarchies, and of values.

Notes

1. [Orig. Eds.] For example, the GP initiated the movement of "installing" militants as factory workers.

2. [Eds.] Historical accounts state that *La Cause du peuple* was never banned, though the group was. See Julian Bourg, *From Revolution to Ethics: May 1968 and French Thought* (McGill-Queen's University Press, 2017), 65–66.

3. [Eds.] The original Secours Rouge Internationale (1922–32) was often referred to by the acronym of its Soviet antecedent: MOPR (Mazurskie Ochotnicze Pogotowie Ratunkowe).

4. [Eds.] The Francs-Tireurs Partisans (FTP), active from 1941 to 1944, was a network of armed militants, established under the direction of the French Communist Party.

5. [Eds.] The Paysans Travailleurs (PT) was a French farmers' union established by Bernard Lambert in 1970 with his book *Les Paysans dans la lutte des classes.*

6. [Eds.] The Front de Libération Nationale (FLN) was an Algerian socialist party established in 1954. It played a significant role in the Algerian War for Independence and remains a leading political party in Algeria today.

7. [Orig. Eds.] A response organized by Serge July—in which Sartre, with his famed voice, took on the role of prosecutor—to the trial of the GP militants (on December 12, 1970), who had attacked the headquarters of the Collieries that had been deemed responsible for the terrible accident that took place at the Fouquières-lès-Lens mine. (Cf. Secours Rouge du Nord, *Les Mineurs accusent* [Paris: François Maspero, 1970]).

8. [Eds.] Defert may be referring, here, to efforts in the United States such as the Commission on Law Enforcement and the Administration of Justice (1967) and the National Commission on the Reform of Federal Criminal Laws (1967–69). For more information, see Naomi Murakawa, *The First Civil Right: How Liberals Built Prison America* (Oxford: Oxford University Press, 2014).

9. [Orig. Eds.] Christine Martineau and Jean-Pierre Carasso, *Le Travail dans les prisons* (Paris: Champ Libre, coll. "Symptômes," 1972).

10. [Orig. Eds.] Cf. *Esprit*, no. 413, April–May 1972; special issue "Pourquoi le travail social?" (the issue was reprinted three times).

11. [Eds.] The Vietnamese Roneo was a stencil duplicator or mimeograph machine, commonly used by activist and subculture groups at this time.

12. [Eds.] The French noun *aide* (pl. *aides*) means help or helper, assistance or assistant. For more information on Defert's role in the founding of AIDeS, see his account in *Une vie politique. Entretiens avec Philippe Artières et Eric Favereau avec la collaboration de Joséphine Gross* (Paris: Seuil, 2014), 100–149.

13. Our first publisher, Champ libre, close with the anarchists and to whom Deleuze had introduced us, chased us off when it learned of the part that Maoists played in the birth of the GIP.

14. [Orig. Eds.] At the behest of Hélène Cixous and Adriane Mnouchkine, the Théâtre du Soleil went with the GIP to perform several comedy sketches on detention at the gates of the Renault-Billancourt factory, that sacrosanct temple of worker culture, and was warmly welcomed by the workers, who were mostly immigrants.

15. [Eds.] This is in part a reference to the Mouvement de Libération des Femmes (MLF), the Front Homosexuel d'Action Révolutionnaire (FHAR), the Groupe Information Asiles (GIA), and Groupe d'Information et de Soutien des Immigrés (GISTI). [Orig. Eds.] For certain leaders of the GP, the new movements were representative of the typically petit-bourgeois society.

16. [Orig. Eds.] The GIP, the FHAR, and the MLF shared the same local street, rue Buffon.

Charles-III Prison in Nancy, France, and site of a major GIP prison revolt in 1972. Demolished in 2010. Photograph by Gérard Drolc.

Part I
Genesis (1970-1971)

This part documents the genesis of the Prisons Information Group. It includes declarations, reports, and manifestos that track its emergence out of the wave of government repression against radical activists in the aftermath of the uprisings that had taken place in May 1968 in France.

Numerous radical groups formed in France and collaborated during this period: the short-lived Maoist group, Vive la Révolution; the feminist organization, Mouvement de Libération des Femmes; and the early gay liberation group, Front Homosexuel d'Action Révolutionnaire. But the most prominent of these organizations was the Gauche Prolétarienne (Proletarian Left, the GP). This antihierarchical Maoist organization had quickly become home to a significant part of the radical student movement and, by the beginning of 1969, it had evolved into an important independent political force all its own. As GP protests grew more and more intense, however, the government reacted by officially dissolving the organization in early 1970 and they arrested, tried, and eventually convicted the editors of its newspaper, *La Cause du peuple*, of "inciting crimes against the security of the state and condoning murder, theft, pillage, and fire." They were sentenced to eight months to one year of incarceration.

Several members of the banned GP continued its work during this period by creating a new group, the Organisation des Prisonniers

Politiques (the Organization of Political Prisoners, OPP). This group sought to maintain ties between the ex-GP members and its imprisoned leaders and to assist their lawyers in preparing their defense. But its mission was also to transform the coming trial into a political forum and to argue publicly for the political significance of the acts for which the former editors were charged.

It was at this point, in June 1970, that Daniel Defert, already a longtime political activist and professor of sociology, joined the OPP at the behest of his friend Jacques Rancière. On September 1, 1970, the OPP began a hunger strike along with the imprisoned activists demanding political status for their editors. The OPP eventually came to see advocating for this status for its leaders as a mistake and began to pursue a strategy of protesting the conditions of all prisoners.

In early December, Defert proposed to the OPP that a commission of public inquiry be formed, one that would be modeled on the public tribunals that various radical groups had organized in the past to confront other social and political issues, but this one would study and assess the general conditions of the French prison system. Defert suggested that his partner, Michel Foucault, be the director of the group (the suggestion was unbeknownst, at the time, to Foucault himself). The OPP approved the proposal and Foucault was eventually persuaded to serve as the commission's director.

At the end of December, Foucault invited a group of theorists, doctors, sociologists, and activists to meet to discuss the proposed study. At this session, Foucault rejected the public tribunal model for the group, arguing instead that they should seek to collect and make public, in various forms, information about prison conditions that would otherwise remain hidden, drawing upon subterranean and diverse sources. The group agreed. Its original charge was thus to expose the material conditions of prison life to the public. In time, as we shall see, the GIP came to realize that doing this required opening a space within which prisoners could speak for themselves.

Foucault signaled the group's distinctive direction by proposing a rather unique, if unpretentious, name: the Groupe d'Information sur les Prisons (Prisons Information Group). It was to be an anonymous alliance protected by three public figures, whose impeccable reputations in the domains of truth speaking and political resistance served to validate its work: Jean-Marie Domenach, the former resistance fighter and editor of *Esprit,* Pierre Vidal-Naquet, a prominent historian and antiwar, antitorture, and antiracism activist, and Foucault.

On February 8, 1971, at the Chapel of Saint Bernard, lawyers for the imprisoned GP leaders held a press conference to announce the end of a second hunger strike. Foucault followed and, for the first time, publicly announced the formation of the GIP. Several further announcements, statements, a true manifesto, and interviews followed, all devoted to defining and elaborating the group's original vision.

The group quickly spawned regional affiliates in the provinces; each acted, however, autonomously. The GIP was thus forged to be a decidedly horizontal form of social and political mobilization, a "line of attack."

Declaration of Political Prisoners on Hunger Strike

ANONYMOUS

This declaration, dated September 1, 1970, marked the beginning of the first hunger strike of "political prisoners"—of which there were a total of thirty-seven in the prisons of La Santé, La Petite Roquette, Fresnes, Rennes, Saint-Nazaire, and Rouen. The hunger strike lasted twenty-five days, at the end of which the prisoners brought their action to an end; however, only the prisoners subject to the State Security Court obtained special (i.e., officially political) status, while "common-law" prisoners received no improvement in their lot.

We insist upon the real recognition of our standing as political prisoners. We do not, for all that, demand privileges over those labeled "common-law" prisoners: in our eyes, they are victims of a social system, which, after producing them, refuses to rehabilitate them and contents itself with demeaning and rejecting them. Much more important to us is that our fight, which denounces the scandalous contemporary regime of prisons, be in the service of all prisoners.

In demanding this recognition of our standing as political prisoners, we need only to insist that a tradition, secured through the struggles and sacrifices of the past, be upheld.

It must be noted that the present regime has not ceased to cut back on the rights recognized by this tradition under the pretext of not wanting to recognize the very existence of political prisoners in the state prisons. Examples of this cutback could be multiplied ad infinitum.

Let it be remembered, for example, that in May 1920 revolutionary militants, imprisoned for conspiring against the security of the state, received, in the first week of their incarceration, eighteen visits from political friends.

We demand:

1. that all those who are or will be incarcerated, in Paris or in the provinces, for actions whose motives are political be recognized as political prisoners and that they therefore be able to obtain, immediately and without delay, the benefits of the special status currently denied them.

   In particular, we demand that this measure be applied to Michel Julien, who has been imprisoned for more than three months in solitary confinement in La Santé Prison, for having written a political slogan on a wall;

2. that the isolation of all political prisoners be brought to an end and that they be able to communicate among themselves. That, to this end, those who are currently isolated, like Alain Geismar in Fresnes, be immediately transferred;

3. that common areas, in which political prisoners are able to gather, be opened without delay, common areas that, not so long ago, were available to all political prisoners;

4. that the visitation system be improved as regards the number of visitors allowed, the duration of visits, and the conditions in which they take place;

5. that the general conditions of incarceration be improved and that harassment be ceased immediately. In no way does such a step indicate an acceptance of even the principle of our incarceration. We affirm that we continue and that we will continue to fight on the side of the people, against this regime that claims to represent participation, but practices repression and oppression.

Written in the prisons of France, September 1, 1970

Report on the Prisons

ORGANISATION DES PRISONNIERS POLITIQUES (OPP)

This report was most likely drafted in September 1970 by the Organization of Political Prisoners (OPP). Formed in the summer of 1970 following the dissolution of the Maoist organization the Gauche Prolétarianne (GP), the OPP was established by, most notably, Nicole Linhart, Bernard Schiavo, Philippe Barret, Daniel Defert, Redith Geismar, and Jacques Rancière—to whom the writing of this text is attributed.

. . . What stands out most clearly from the experience of comrades who have passed through the French prisons, and from the discussions and connections that they (on the inside) or their families (on the outside) have been able to have with "common-law" prisoners is that the penitentiary regime marshals all the conditions necessary to break the individual completely, physically as much as morally.

Examples abound. In everyday life:

1. HYGIENE: In La Santé Prison, the cells on the lower level have walls covered in grime, the straw mattresses (canvas filled with straw) are darkened with filth. On the upper level (it is there, in general, that the North African prisoners and the recidivists are confined, six to a cell), only the pit toilet is supplied with water: there is no drinking fountain. In most provincial prisons (e.g., Dunkerque), there is no sanitary facility: in communal cells, the prisoners have to use sanitary buckets. Most often, the windows are truly deadly: the sun doesn't make it through to the cells when it is cold, nor does the air when it is hot. At La Santé, fleas, cockroaches, and other bugs overrun the cells. From time to time, a product is

sprayed, whose sole effect is to grease the cells, and families are prevented from bringing in disinfectants, DDT . . . or anything for cleaning the toilets . . .

2. FOOD: Prisons are state establishments, subject, in principle, to medical inspections: who is capable of saying that at the Loos Prison (Lille), for example, these inspections are really or seriously made? The prisoners have on average one piece of fruit and one hunk of cheese each month. Meat is eaten once or twice a week, sometimes rotten (spoiled meals are common currency in prison). In other cases, worms are found in the salad, pieces of steel wool in the purée. That is why the courtyard of La Santé is littered with meals thrown from the windows. The prisoners' "diet" is generally composed of potatoes, pasta, and rice, all of which is bathed in a revolting sauce. At Loos, all the women start losing their hair, developing dental cavities, and broken nails as early as the eighth day of this regimen. Intestinal diseases are almost inevitable; the prisoners are sick and often remain so after their release. Health monitoring consists of weight measurement. Yet few prisoners grow thinner because of both their lack of movement and the fact that their unhealthy food makes them gain weight: so all's well . . .

3. EXERCISE: In theory, exercise lasts for one hour each day (before the decree of 1969 it was half an hour).[1] In reality: at Dunkerque, it lasts ten minutes; at La Santé, transit time (ten to fifteen minutes) is subtracted from that allotted for exercise. Most of the imprisoned militants go to Courtyard 4. Their only horizon: four cement walls with grating on the fourth side. Dimensions of the courtyard: 8m x 3m; water drains poorly and stagnates on the ground. The courtyard is apparently never cleaned despite the cigarette butts, spit, etc.

Two hundred prisoners, those in maximum security, have only two hours of exercise on Sundays.

Everything is done to make it impossible for the prisoners to maintain good health over the course of months and years: considered to be beasts, they must live like beasts.

But worse than these conditions of physical life is the total and irreversible crushing of the prisoner's sense of self [personnalité] (it is nothing less than naive to be surprised by the number of suicides in prison, failed or not; inside, the prisoners are pushed to the brink and often it is after their release that they kill themselves, branded by their incarceration, the police keeping tabs on them, etc.).

This crushing takes numerous forms:

A) ISOLATION: Utilized in the prison first of all for "dangerous" prisoners and in every case for the political ones. *No contact* with other prisoners is allowed. (It is important to note that "special" status [e.g., right to books, to radio, etc.] has an important underbelly: the isolation of the prisoner.)

For common-law prisoners, it is either total isolation or overcrowding and the impossibility of being alone at any moment whatsoever.

The separation from the outside is expressed essentially through the visitation system. For the upper levels (which consist of the most overpopulated sections), the two and a half hours of visitation each week are very often reduced to ten or fifteen minutes. At Loos, families are often made to wait for four hours and there are no visits on Saturdays; during the visit, the prisoner is separated from the visitor by two metal grates and a glass partition.[2] For unmarried couples, the partner can visit provided s/he has a good police report.

Restrictions concerning the mail also contribute to the torment and isolation of the prisoner: letters must not contain more than sixty lines, thirty when the letter is in a foreign language (which is not enough for Arabs). The amount of time it takes to receive a letter is currently up to fifteen days. The regulations say: "correspondence must only concern subjects pertaining to family affairs or private interests." That is why a prisoner's letter to his family was intercepted for the following phrase: "Here, like outside, you have to fight against yourself in order to pull through." The prison administration did not fail to see a political allusion in it.

B) HARASSMENT: Personal effects (watch, etc.) are confiscated from the prisoner upon entry into the prison; the prisoner is searched and stripped of everything, often including clothes (especially in the case of women). An in-depth search is performed for each visit from a lawyer, each class session, etc....

When in transit through the prison, prisoners must have closed jackets with their hands out of their pockets; they have to walk straight and in single file.

There is also the *prétoire,* a sort of tribunal internal to the prison: fifty to one hundred prisoners pass through it each day before the warden and two ultradecorated guards: the cases are handled in one minute in a large-scale mise-en-scène; a guard continuously pokes the prisoner's back and legs so that s/he remains at attention. A write-up filed by a "screw" is enough to get one sent to the *prétoire,* where it is generally impossible to explain oneself. The most common sentence is four, sometimes six days in "the hole"; otherwise, it is a shaved head. One example of a *prétoire* judgment should really be mentioned: a prisoner who caught birds with a string and some bread was tossed in the hole for four days by the warden with the following remark: "Are you not ashamed of wanting to imprison these little creatures?"

The hole: it is a cell plunged in partial darkness. The prisoners there wear prison garb and are nourished on two half-meals a day. The few pieces of furniture are fastened to the walls, there are often rats, and the beatings are frequent … At Loos, a girl sent to the hole for two days for having talked back to a guard was stripped of all her undergarments and her shoes, as is usual, and dressed only in a prison smock.

The young prisoner, who is released after having served a sentence of six months to four years, finds himself jobless, sometimes abandoned by his wife facing pressure from social workers. More than 45 percent of prisoners become repeat offenders after their release. Prison is a place of harassment, of the debasement of the individual, not of rehabilitation.

Appendix on Prison Labor

Let us first note that the possibility of working in prison is considered by most people to be a *good opportunity.* Really, in prisons where such a possibility does not even exist, there is nothing to break up the boredom. Work is also a good opportunity because, for many, it is the only source of money, which allows them "to canteen" (which is to say, to buy food, a comb, some paper, etc.). Different companies call upon this prison workforce, exploiting the prisoners' state of mind. The salaries are derisory; the deposited sum is distributed as follows:

¼ for the prison, ¼ for the legal fees, ¼ for savings, and ¼ remains at the disposal of the prisoner, for the canteen.

The salary: it is always calculated as a function of production; in the best of cases, the hourly salary is 1.50 francs (this calculation was made by an imprisoned militant *worker*). The labor is always tedious: gluing, folding, sewing tags, etc. The prisoners employed in "general service" at Loos serve food, sew, etc. for 75 centimes a day!

This is only a sketch of an investigation, *still to be carried out,* into prison labor; still to be addressed are the working conditions (chains, the pace in the workshops, harassment by the bosses), the work of maintaining the prison that is done by prisoners for practically nothing, and the excessive exploitation and constant oppression to which the prisoners are subjected.

Notes

1. [Eds.] The legislation referred to here is Décret n. 69–189 (May 14, 1969), which regulates penitentiary establishments and determines the ways in which deprivations of liberty are to be executed.

2. [Eds.] In some cases, two circular metal grates, maybe ten inches across, were set within the glass pane. Prisoner and visitor would take turns speaking into the grates or turning their ear to the grates to listen.

Letter Addressed to the Families of Common-Law Prisoners

GROUPE D'INFORMATION SUR LES PRISONS (GIP)

A Maoist circular written in January 1971 before the public announcement of the GIP's formation. The text links the struggle of political prisoners to those of common-law prisoners.

Dear Friends,

Our comrades, fellow workers, and students who, like Alain Geismar, are in prison today because they fought against a society that condemns and rejects the poor, have decided to continue the fight behind bars so that the authorities might grant them political status.

By initiating an open-ended hunger strike on January 14, the hunger strikers of La Santé, Fresnes, prisons in Epinal, Montbéliard, Toulouse, Nantes . . . are drawing the public's attention to the horrendous conditions of detention to which common-law prisoners are subjected.

People still do not think about what prisoners are subjected to by the penitentiary regime: from the lack of hygiene to severe malnourishment, from underpaid work to bogus medicine, from inhumane visiting rooms where prisoners cannot even hug their children, to a broad lack of information and humiliating censorship, not to mention the ceaseless and senseless bullying by the screws, all of this will one day come to light; so will the disapproval, even the contempt weighing on the families of common-law prisoners who are often ashamed of their relatives "because they are in prison"; the public will eventually learn that these are the victims of a society that prefers to condemn its poor and allow the real thieves and murderers, those crooks who are the bosses, the exploiters, and their lackeys, to get off scot-free.

Moreover, prisoners did not wait for backup before revolting against and resisting this degrading regime day after day (hunger strikes, spontaneous riots, organized strikes . . .). Up until now, however, everything has been done to keep their movement of anger from being known or explained on the outside.

Today, thanks to the hunger strike, all these outrages are coming to light. Henceforth, prisoners are no longer alone. Outside, a large support system is being organized (through Secours Rouge in particular), bent on breaking down the wall of silence and everywhere making the voice of their revolt known.

Common-law prisoners, take advantage of this movement to enter the struggle. Democrats and intellectuals are mobilized. Help us in this denunciation campaign by sending us detailed accounts of detention (with place, dates, and the name of the prison). A commission of inquiry on prisons is being formed. Send all your information to us at:

Mr. Foucault
285 Rue de Vaugirard,
Paris XV[1]

Political prisoners support common-law prisoners through their fight.

Prisoners and the families of prisoners, Secours Rouge supports you.

The comrades of political prisoners.

Note

1. [Eds.] The address, 285 Rue de Vaugirard, was Foucault's residence at the time.

GIP Manifesto

GROUPE D'INFORMATION SUR LES PRISONS (GIP)

The text of a press conference statement read aloud by Michel Foucault on February 8, 1971, upon the cessation of the second hunger strike by the imprisoned Gauche Prolétarienne leaders and their support committee.

None of us is sure to escape prison. Today less than ever. Police control *[quadrillage]*[1] is tightening its grip around day-to-day life: in the street and on the highways; around foreigners and youths; the criminalization of free speech has resurfaced; and antidrug measures only increase arbitrary constraints. We are consigned to "close supervision" *[garde à vue]*.[2] They tell us the justice system is overwhelmed. We certainly see that. But what if the police have overwhelmed it? They tell us prisons are overpopulated. But what if the population has been overimprisoned?

Little information is published on prisons; it is one of the hidden regions of our social system, one of the black boxes of our life. We have the right to know, and we want to know. That is why, with magistrates, lawyers, journalists, doctors, and psychologists, we have formed a Prisons Information Group.

We plan to make known what the prison is: who goes there; how and why they go there; what happens; what life is like for the prisoners and, equally, for the supervisory staff; what the buildings, diet, and hygiene are like; how internal regulation, medical supervision, and the workshops function; how one gets out and what it is, in our society, to be one of those who has gotten out.

We do not find this information in the official reports. We seek it from those who, in whatever capacity, have an experience of prison or a connection with it. We urge such persons to contact us and to convey what they know. We have drafted a questionnaire that is available upon request. As soon as enough of them are completed, the results will be published.

It is not for us to suggest a reform. We wish only to make the reality known. And to make it known immediately, almost on a day-to-day basis, because time is running out. It is a matter of alerting public opinion and of keeping it on the alert. We will try to utilize every mode of information: daily, weekly, monthly. We therefore appeal to all possible forums.

Finally, it is good to know what threatens us; but it is also good to know how to defend ourselves. One of our first tasks will be to publish a little *Manual for the Perfect Arrestee [arrêté],* which would of course double as a *Notice to Arrestors [arrêteurs].*

All those who wish to inform, be informed, or participate in the work can write to the Prisons Information Group: 285 Rue de Vaugirard Paris-XV.

On behalf of the Prisons Information Group,
Jean-Marie Domenach
Michel Foucault
Pierre Vidal-Naquet[3]

Notes

1. [Trans.] *Quadrillage* is a grid-like systematic control and division of an area.

2. [Trans.] Technically, *garde à vue* refers to a common police practice of keeping suspects in custody without charge for up to twenty-four hours. Here the sense is generalized.

3. [Eds.] Although this signature does not appear in DE and DEQ, it is retained in AL.

On Prisons

GROUPE D'INFORMATION SUR LES PRISONS (GIP)

*A public announcement written by Michel Foucault originally
published in* J'accuse, *no. 3 (March 15, 1971): 26.*

The Prisons Information Group just launched its first inquiry. It is not
a sociological inquiry. Rather, it aims to let those who have an experience of prison speak. Not that they need us to help "*raise consciousness*": awareness *[conscience]* of oppression is crystal clear there; they
know the enemy well. But the present system denies them the means
to express and organize themselves.

We want to break down the double isolation in which prisoners
find themselves confined: we want to enable them, through our inquiry, to communicate among themselves, to transmit what they
know, and to speak from prison to prison, from cell to cell. We want
them to address the population and we want the population to speak
to them. These experiences, these isolated revolts must be transformed into common knowledge and coordinated practice.

Groups are being formed, bringing together ex-prisoners, prisoners' families, lawyers, doctors, and activists—all those who decided
to stop tolerating the present prison system. It is for them to launch
new inquiries (inside and outside of Paris), to receive and diffuse information, to imagine new modes of action. It is imperative that prisons be nowhere left in peace.

Last January's hunger strike forced the press to speak. Let us profit
from that breach: let what is intolerable—imposed, as it is, by force
and by silence—cease to be accepted. We do not conduct our inquiry
in order to accumulate knowledge, but *to heighten our intolerance
and make it an active intolerance.*[1] Let us become people intolerant

of prisons, the legal system, the hospital system, psychiatric practice, military service, etc.

As the first act of this "*intolerance-inquiry*," we duly distributed a questionnaire at prison doors and to all those who are in a position to know and want to act.

Prisons Information Group
285, Rue de Vaugirard
Paris-15e

Note

1. [Eds.] While italics do not appear in DE, they are retained in AL.

The Prison Is Everywhere

MICHEL FOUCAULT

A statement written by Michel Foucault and published in Combat, *no. 8335 (May 5, 1971): 1, following his and other GIP activists' arrest at a demonstration outside the gates of La Santé.*

Over the past three months, the Prisons Information Group has been conducting its inquiry. It has asked its questions of prisoners, ex-prisoners, and their families, all those who pass through prison gates. After all, none of us is exempt from the possibility of going to prison; by what right, then, are we kept from knowing what prison really is? It is an instrument of power, and one of the most excessive at that. By what right does power shroud it in secrecy?

On the first of May, we went to the gates of Fresnes and La Santé. Much like every other Saturday, the visitors would wait there for a half hour, forty-five minutes, before being allowed to enter. Jean-Marie Domenach, along with several others, went to Fresnes; I was with another group at La Santé. We spoke with folks, primarily, about the criminal record. We delivered a statement and distributed sprigs of lily of the valley.[1]

Shortly thereafter, the police arrived and we were taken to the station. They must not have really known why. At Fresnes, it was for "breach of legal deposit";[2] at La Santé, for "hawking without a license." Not by chance: neither of these two charges had any bearing on the case. Incidental? No. The street is in the process of becoming a domain reserved for the police; here, police caprice becomes law: keep moving, don't stop; walk, don't speak; whatever you've written, keep it to yourself; and don't congregate. The prison begins well in advance of its gates. The minute you leave your house.

68

But what followed was yet more enlightening. At the station, one, asked us for our names, those of our relatives, etc. "But there are . . . how many of you have an authentic Gallic name?" One student remarked that in fact she was not carrying a Gallic name; that she knew it well since it had been remarked upon during the war; and following such remarks it had been deportation and the crematorium for her family. The cop approached her, he asked her what went wrong and if, by chance, she had taken hash. Then, he silenced her. After fifteen minutes had transpired, gesturing as if to aim and fire an imaginary pistol, he shouted, "Heil Hitler!" The ranking officer, I think, was ill at ease. He quickly processed and released us.

But there was still a cop—another cop—shadowing us on the sidewalk; I was already quite far from the police station when he struck me in the back and insulted me. His "colleagues" came looking for him; he kept yelling; they got a hold of him, and I had the impression that he struggled. Assaulting an officer? The law is severe, I believe, for this sort of offense. Let's hope.

For our part, certainly, we are pressing charges, because it must be made known that in the minute and everyday arbitrariness of the street, in the apparently simple case of distributed tracts, even the lowest-ranking police officer is perfectly aware of the role he's made to play; he embodies the whole system that gradually establishes itself through his rough, heavy-handed gestures; he welcomes his new function and proudly hails the commander in chief he deserves.

Notes

1. [Eds.] May Day, which is observed annually on May 1, is the French national labor holiday. It is customary to give sprigs of lily of the valley to loved ones in celebration.

2. [Eds.] Breach of copyright law; failure to deposit copies of publications.

When Information Is a Struggle

DANIEL DEFERT

A manifesto, written by Daniel Defert, that originally appeared as "La Prison, enjeu d'un combat" in a combined issue of La Cause du peuple—J'accuse *(May 25, 1971): 6–7. The text was flanked by reports on the prisons at Clairvaux and Fleury-Mérogis, and by an account of the feature of* L'Express *on the French prison system.*

Apparently, everyone in the press is talking about it, saying the same thing and in the same way: the French prisons are among the worst in the world—filthy and overpopulated. Upon investigation, *L'Express* says it again and then hands it back over to Pleven. Now, when the Prisons Information Group goes to prison doors to distribute its questionnaires and talks to the families of prisoners, they are arrested, taken to the police station, and fined. Further: a prisoner has absolutely no right to speak about prison. Neither in the visiting room (for the guard interrupts him), nor in his letters (for the censor suppresses them). Not even to mention the cold or the food. To pass "pieces of information" on to the outside world, the sort of information the GIP solicits in its questionnaires, is to risk being written up and sent to solitary; it may even risk criminal court. Some information about prisons is certainly accepted and solicited by power. The sort of information that allows power to hide another kind of information, which comes from prisoners, and to hide the movement that, since the hunger strike in January, has been resounding on both sides of the prison walls. The GIP inscribes its action in this movement.

To Inquire and to Fight

(a) The GIP never asked to visit any prison, it did not address the administration, nor did it seek out the administration's point of view.

The prisoners are the ones who give information. They give it by responding to questions they themselves have posed. The first questionnaire was drafted, initially, with the help of former prisoners; it was modified after responses were received. Several thousand copies are now in circulation.

This means that the questions are not neutral, external, or impartial. What matters is whatever prisoners want to make known, by saying it themselves. The point is to transfer to them the right and the possibility to speak about prisons. To say what only they have the power to say.

We offered this questionnaire to those who should have "known everything there is to know about prisons": lawyers who go there every week, magistrates who send prisoners there every day, penitentiary officers who spend their whole lives there. They were unable to respond. This is conclusive proof: the questions were really addressed by prisoners to prisoners. And responding to the questionnaire is an act of solidarity, of struggle against the censorship and silence imposed by punishment.

(b) These questions speak less to the experience or misery of prisoners than to their rights. The right to defend themselves against the courts. The right to information, visits, and mail. The right to hygiene and nourishment. The right to a decent salary for their work and the right to be able to work after they get out. The right to maintain a family. Of these rights, some have been recognized, with difficulty, after many struggles (e.g., the Algerian struggle at La Santé from 1957 to 1961), but they are called into question, again and again. Many have yet to be won: they are struggles still to come. The questionnaire is a way of declaring these rights and affirming our will to advance them.

(c) The responses demonstrate that the prisoners' struggle is not fundamentally different from those undertaken within the society from which detainees are "excluded."

— They work 8 to 10 hours a day for a pittance (less than a franc a day sometimes). From which the administration deducts more than half. They are exposed to[1]

— The prison uses money to maintain, sometimes exacerbate, divisions among prisoners.

— The prisoner is trapped—hands and feet bound—inside a pecking order that tortures him around the clock. He is both the reason for and the victim of conflicts that set managers and supervisors, screws and officers against one another.

— The prison multiplies all the ideological constraints of the outside world. Absolute respect for superiors, perfect obedience, the redemptive value of work; blackmail in reward and in punishment; the double repression of sexuality because the other sex is forbidden and homosexuality is punished.

(d) Ultimately the inquiry itself is a struggle. Prisoners perceive it as such when, despite threats or punishments, they circulate questionnaire sheets throughout the cells as if they were political tracts. They understand it as such when they take great risks to pass the questionnaires in and out of prison. Take a single anecdote: the mother of a young man, imprisoned near Paris, got the questionnaire: it was impossible to give it to him directly and she was forbidden to speak of it during visitation. She copied it in fragments, on bits of paper. In the visiting room, while the screw had his back turned, she quickly read a question. Upon leaving, she wrote down his answer. The screw caught them at it recently; the young man was written up and had to go to the *prétoire*. He wanted to continue anyway; in two months' time, the questionnaire was complete.

Groups of Struggle

The struggle against the penitentiary system ought to destroy, before anything else, the divisions that the system establishes and that permit it to subsist: the hierarchical divisions inside the prison and the isolation of families outside.

(a) Against this isolation, the GIP has formed groups that go to prison doors and make contact with the families waiting in line for visiting hours.

To join the line, enter into conversation, hand out questionnaires, and not talk about oneself—this is not sociological work. The police are there, tightening up the line; young people are quickly perceived as leftists, and the memory of the hunger strike is still fresh. Conversely, to accept the questionnaire, to speak out about prison, before or after visitation, to participate in meetings—this is not a simple act for the prisoners' families. For them, it is to agree to gather together with people who do not have loved ones in prison; it is to agree to this despite police barricades and threats; it is to agree to this on a political basis, it is a political act. From there, larger gatherings formed: families proposed to establish an association for the abolition of criminal records; others decided to form a group concerned with the problems detention poses for imprisoned women and the wives of those imprisoned.

(b) Other groups struggle against the divisions inside the prisons. For example: one group was formed by prison doctors, or others who had already left the penitentiary, disgusted, and even former prisoners—some of whom served as aides in the infirmaries. From the first meeting, these doctors said: "We cannot offer care, and not only because the administration keeps us from doing our job, but because this job puts us in collusion with the administration. Compensating for nutritional deficiencies, giving a sedative to a 'bull-headed' patient, putting a hunger striker on an IV drip, giving valium to someone who has been preventatively detained for three years—this is done not to 'save a man,' but to ensure that detention functions smoothly, to enable it to continue. We cannot offer care without siding with the cops."

We see a group being formed around this precise point—medical care in prison.[2]

Lawyer–prisoner groups are also meeting. The walls are beginning to crack.

Against the Penal System

We must not believe prison is an isolated "black hole." In fact, the penal system, lying at the disposal of the ruling class, includes three interdependent pieces: the police, the legal system, and the prison.

And prison is not the least important.

It is the privileged instrument of a biased legal system.

(a) By the type of offense it sanctions, it especially threatens certain strata of the population (young people, the unemployed, immigrants).

(b) Its effects are especially felt by the proletariat: the revocation of salary and social security, the costs of visits and the canteen.

(c) Preventative imprisonment takes away part of the detainee's means of defense (his financial resources are reduced, his contacts with a lawyer and the outside world are limited, he is physically and morally exhausted by preparing for a case that has lasted years). Hence, the less resources and support he has, the more the pretrial detainee risks going into preventative detention and experiencing its disastrous effects.

(d) When he gets out of prison with a criminal record, the prisoner is condemned to unemployment, to overexploited and unstable employment.[3]

There is not one part of prison so outdated it must be replaced, while others are so advanced and effective they should be multiplied. There is PRISON, as a function, as a major piece of the penal system, and as an instrument of class oppression. It is against this entire system that the GIP calls us to unite.

Notes

1. [Trans.] The end of this sentence is indecipherable in the original. In fact, all reference to this final sentence of the paragraph is removed from the reprinted version in Daniel Defert, *Une vie politique* (Paris: Seuil, 2014), 227–37; the line here in question appears at 229.

2. [Trans.] This line ends with an illegible sentence, beginning with "*Il renve.*" All reference to it has been removed from the reprinted version in Defert's *Une vie politique*, 231.

3. [Trans.] This line ends with an illegible sentence, beginning with "*Ne s'en tirent.*" Again, all reference to it has been removed from the reprinted version in Defert's *Une vie politique*, 232.

I Perceive the Intolerable

MICHEL FOUCAULT

An interview with Michel Foucault conducted by Geneviève Armleder. It originally appeared in Journal de Genève: Samedi littéraire *("cahier 135"), no. 170 (July 24–25, 1971).*

GENEVIÈVE ARMLEDER: Michel Foucault, you asked me not to pose questions related to literature, linguistics, or semiology. Nevertheless, I would like you to piece together briefly the connection between your past preoccupations and the initiative in which you are currently engaged.

MICHEL FOUCAULT: I noticed that the majority of theorists who try to leave metaphysics, literature, idealism, or bourgeois society behind don't manage to do so at all and that nothing is more metaphysical, literary, idealistic, or bourgeois than the way in which they try to liberate themselves from theories.

In years past, I myself preferred subjects as abstract and distant from us as the history of the sciences. Today, I would really like to leave all that behind. Due to particular circumstances and events, my interest has moved to the problem of prisons, and this new preoccupation appeared to me to be a real issue in light of the weariness I felt at the hands of the literary thing.[1] However, I am rediscovering here a continuity I would have liked to disrupt. For, in the past, I did try to analyze the system of internment at work in our society in the seventeenth and eighteenth centuries.

From a general point of view, one can occupy oneself with classifying societies into different types. There are exiling societies: when a group or social body cannot stand an individual, it rejects him—not unlike the Greek solution; at one time, the Greeks preferred exile to every other punishment.

There are also killing, torturing, or purifying societies, which submit the accused to a kind of punitive or purifying ritual, and, finally, confining societies, such as ours has become since the sixteenth and seventeenth centuries.

In this epoch, social and economic norms were imposed on the population simultaneously by the development of the state apparatus and by that of the economy. Our society began to practice a system of exclusion and inclusion—internment or imprisonment—against every individual who did not correspond to these norms. Since then, men have been excluded from the population circuit and at the same time included in prisons, those privileged places that are in some way the real utopias of a society.[2] The aim of internment is not only to punish, but also to impose by constraint a certain model of behavior and acquiescence *[acceptations]*: the values and the agreements *[acceptations]* of society.

G. A.: Don't you think that internment also triggers a phenomenon of "deculpabilization"?

M. F.: Yes. Internment is probably linked to a certain form of de-Christianization or the attenuation of Christian conscience. After all, the entire world participates in the sin of one. But, from the moment the prison world exists, those who are on the outside must be just or widely thought to be such; while those in prison, and they alone, must be culpable. That in fact prompts a kind of rift between one side and the other, and those who are on the outside have the impression of no longer being responsible for those who are on the inside.

G. A.: Today, you are at the head of the Prisons Information Group, alongside Gilles Deleuze, Jean-Marie Domenach, and Pierre Vidal-Naquet. What are the events that led you to this point?

M. F.: Last December, political prisoners, leftists and Maoists, went on a hunger strike to fight against the general conditions of detention, whether for political or common-law detainees. This movement started with prisons and has since developed beyond them. It was at that moment that I began to take an interest in it.

G. A.: What is the intended objective of the Prisons Information Group?

M. F.: We literally would like to give the floor *[à donner la parole]* to prisoners. Our intention is not to do sociological or reformist work. It is not to propose an ideal prison. I believe that by definition the prison is an instrument of repression. Its function was defined by the Napoleonic code, almost 170 years ago, and it has evolved relatively little since.

G. A.: What then are the means you employ?

M. F.: We have, for example, drafted a fairly precise questionnaire on the conditions of detention. We are sending it to prisoners and asking them to recount their life in prison with as much detail as possible. Thus, numerous contacts have been made; by these means, we have received autobiographies, private journals, and narrative fragments. Some pieces are written by people who hardly know how to hold a pencil. There are some shocking things. I would not say these texts are very beautiful because that would be to inscribe them within the horror of the literary institution. Be that as it may, we are going to try hereafter to publish this material in its raw state.

G. A.: In your opinion, what will the attitude of authorities be when faced with this political action?

M. F.: One of two things: either the penitentiary administration and the Minister of Justice will say nothing and will recognize the well-founded character of this action, or they will turn against us; then voila! Jean-Marie Domenach, Gilles Deleuze, Pierre Vidal-Naquet, and Foucault are in prison!

G. A.: What are your personal opinions on the problem created by the existence of prisons?

M. F.: I have none. I am here to receive, to disseminate, and, if need be, to elicit documents. Simply put, I perceive the intolerable. The blandness of the soup or the coldness of winter is relatively bearable. But to imprison an individual just because he has a run-in with the legal system, that is not acceptable!

Notes

1. [Eds.] This is the only appearance of the term "chose littéraire" in DE. For a Lacanian interpretation of "the literary thing" in relation to Foucault and other writers of madness, see Shoshana Felman, *La Folie et la chose littéraire* (Paris: Seuil, 1978) and "The Literary Thing," in *Writing and*

Madness: (Literature/Philosophy/Psychoanalysis) (Palo Alto, Calif.: Stanford University Press, 2003), 259–62.

2. [Eds.] This line might well be read in conjunction with Foucault's theory of heterotopias. See "Des espaces autres" (1967), originally published in *Architecture, mouvement, continuité* 5 (1984): 46-49, and then in English translation as "Different Spaces," in *Aesthetics, Method, and Epistemology* (New York; Penguin, 1998), 175–85, as well as two radio addresses from December 7 and 21, 1966, eventually transcribed and published with an introduction by Daniel Defert as *Le Corps utopique—Les Hétérotopies* (Paris: Éditions Lignes, 2009).

The Penal System Is a Problem That Has Interested Me for Some Time

MICHEL FOUCAULT

An interview with Michel Foucault conducted by Jalila Hafsia and published in La Presse de Tunisie *(August 12, 1971), 3.*

JALILA HAFSIA: Professor, would you please speak with us about your oeuvre? About your current projects? And about your work at the Collège de France?

MICHEL FOUCAULT: Well, I don't speak about my oeuvre for the very good reason that I don't feel myself to be the bearer of a potential oeuvre. I tried to say what I wanted to say a certain number of years ago. That said, it exists or it doesn't exist, it is read or it isn't; I have to say that, right now, I'm not looking back at what I have done. But if you ask me where I'm looking right now, I'll tell you that it isn't really toward things to be written. A problem that has interested me for some time is that of the penal system, the way in which a society defines good and evil, what is permitted and what isn't, legality and illegality, the way in which it articulates all the offenses and transgressions committed against its laws.

I already encountered this problem in the context of madness, for madness is also a form of transgression. It was very difficult for our civilizations to distinguish the deviation that is madness from the transgressions that are misdeeds or crimes. My concern, then, is the problem of the transgression of the law and of the repression of illegality. So, I will undoubtedly devote a series of courses to that during the twenty-seven years I have left at the Collège de France. I'm not saying that I'm going to devote all twenty-seven years to that, but undoubtedly a certain number of them. Some friends of

mine—in particular, Jean-Marie Domenach, the editor of the journal *Esprit*—and I have formed a sort of little group. What to say
about it? It is an intervention and action group concerned with
the justice system, the penal system, and penitentiary institutions
in France, and we have launched an inquiry into the conditions
of prisoners in France. French prisons are actually extraordinarily
archaic institutions, even medieval: among the oldest and also the
harshest in the world. We have undertaken this inquiry in a rather
peculiar manner: instead of addressing ourselves to the penitentiary administration, in order to find out how things were going
from their point of view, we addressed ourselves directly to ex-
prisoners, to those who had been released from prison, and, operating illegally ourselves, we addressed current prisoners by covert
means and received their responses the same way. We learned exactly what life in prison is. We are going to publish the preliminary
results of this inquiry in the coming weeks. Truth be told, the preliminary result is already known, namely the tremendous irritation
of the French administration and the government. Jean-Marie Domenach and I even spent several hours at the police station having been arrested by the police. That's what I'm currently devoting
my energies to and maybe will be for months and years to come.

J. H.: Are you preparing a book at the moment?

M. F.: No. For the moment, my activities are essentially practical. Perhaps one day I will attempt to take stock of the movement that is
just now taking shape. What strikes me is that the penal system,
the system of repression at work in a society such as ours, actually dates back to 160 years ago, since it's the Penal Code of 1810,
hardly modified since Napoleon, that determines what is permitted and what is illicit in our current system, though it was certainly adapted to the organization of the bourgeois state at the
moment of its formation at the beginning of the nineteenth century. I believe that the code now needs to be completely reformed,
profoundly reformed. We need a new Beccaria,[1] a new Bertin,[2] and
I don't at all have the pretention of being a new Beccaria or Bertin,
for it isn't up to a theoretician to undertake the reform of states.
It is up to those on whom this undoubtedly unjust justice system
weighs, it is up to them to reform and reforge *[refonte]* it.

J. H.: Until now, then, you have dealt with the sayable and now you want to deal with the doable. Your primary concern is practice. But practice only garners meaning when it is expressed in one way or another. There, too, it is a question of the statement *[énoncé]*: isn't the doing connected to the saying?

M. F.: Yes. Your question is very important. I don't want to tell my own story (there would be no interest in that), but the first thing in which I was interested was the phenomenon of the exclusion of the mad in Western society since the end of the sixteenth century. The phenomenon has two sides: on the one hand, you have institutions, practices, types of customs—the way, for example, in which the police, families, or the justice system classified and sorted the mad, and pushed them into the shadows; it is a practice that was hardly ever articulated and it is extremely difficult to uncover the forms and rules of these customs with any precision, since, having not been formulated, they left no traces. They were without utterance *[énoncé]*. And, on the other hand, despite all that, these institutions and practices of madness were, to a certain extent, bound to and supported by a philosophical, religious, juridical, and above all medical discourse. And it is this ensemble of "practices and discourses" that constitutes what I called the experience of madness—which, incidentally, is a bad turn of phrase, since, in reality, it isn't an experience. Nevertheless, I tried to clarify the system from this practice of the exclusion of the mad. Now, however, I find myself oscillating between the two poles, discourse and practice. In *The Order of Things,* I primarily studied layers, ensembles of discourse. The same goes for *The Archaeology of Knowledge.* Now, with a new swing of the pendulum, I am interested in institutions and practices, in these things that are in some way beneath the sayable.

J. H.: All the same, one cannot act in that manner without having an idea of what is doable and what isn't, of what is, in short, good or evil. It comes back to moral discourse, even if one disagrees with the division between good and evil. How do you escape this in your concrete practice? Won't your decisions need to rely upon a discourse all the same?

M. F.: Yes, they rest upon a discourse in a sense, but what we are currently trying to do, you see, finds no place in a certain theory of good and evil or of what can and can't be done. That is not at all

what interests me. One thing is certain: that the current penitentiary system and, in a general manner, the repressive system, or
even the penal system, is no longer supported by the people. Thus,
with respect to prison and the justice system, there is in France
a de facto discontentment, a discontentment that evidently belongs to the poorest and most exploited classes. Now, my problem
isn't that of knowing what would be the ideal penal system, the
ideal repressive system. I am simply trying to see, to reveal, and
to transform into a discourse graspable by everyone what can be
unbearable for the least favored classes in the current justice system. A lawyer is bought, which is ultimately to say that the right
to justice is bought. I am picking a simple example, but it is clear
that one obtains justice according to the class to which one belongs, according to the possibilities bestowed by chance, according to one's social position. Justice is not allocated to you in the
same way. The inequality in the face of justice, which was felt quite
distinctly in the eighteenth century, and against which Beccaria
and Bertin and the great Napoleonic codes rightly reacted, this
inequality has been reestablished, if indeed it was ever abolished.
It has been reestablished and the people are currently suffering
from it quite violently. This inequality is felt almost daily before the
courts and before the police. That, if you like, is what we are trying
to bring to light: to grasp the impetus of the revolt and to show it.

J. H.: In sum, if I regard all of that as a philosophical activity, I could
say that, from the beginning, you have subordinated logical discourse to a moral discourse and that, at bottom, this moral discourse dominates all of your works, and this will lead not to a
metaphysics but to a morality?

M. F.: Perhaps! . . . Well, I won't say no! . . . Instead, let's say: I once
wrote a book on the history of madness. It was rather poorly received except for a few people like Blanchot and Barthes. More
recently, in the universities, whenever this book was brought up
with students it was pointed out that it hadn't been written by a
doctor and that it should therefore be avoided like the plague. Yet
one thing struck me: several years ago in Italy, around Basaglia,
and in England a movement called antipsychiatry developed. The
people involved obviously developed their movement on the basis
of their own ideas and their own experiences with psychiatrists,

but they saw in the book that I had written a sort of historical justification and, in a certain way, they took it up, took it into account,
to a certain extent they found themselves in it, and so this history
book is currently having a practical outcome. Let's say, then, that
I'm a little jealous and that now I'd really like to do things myself. Instead of writing a book on the history of the justice system,
which would then be taken up by people who would call the justice system into question practically, I'd like to begin by calling
the justice system into question practically, and then, well, if I'm
still alive and I haven't been thrown in prison, I suppose I'll write
the book . . .

Notes

1. [Eds.] Cesare Beccaria (1738–94), an Italian criminologist, authored
the classic text *Dei Delitti e Delle Pene* (1764), which was later translated as
On Crimes and Punishments. As a founding work in the field of penology,
Beccaria's treatise argues against torture and the death penalty.

2. [Eds.] Henri-Léonard-Jean-Baptiste Bertin (1720–92) was a remark-
able French statesman who served as Lieutenant General of the Paris police from 1757 until 1759.

GIP flyer announcing a meeting at Toulouse on December 16, 1971.

Part II
The *Intolerable* Series (1971–1973)

The GIP conducted various types of protests over the course of its brief existence: leafleting; street theater; public demonstrations and meetings; press conferences; a play with the writer Hélène Cixous, the director Ariane Mnouchkine, and her ensemble, Théâtre du Soleil; and it produced a documentary with extensive interviews with former prisoners, *Les prisons aussi,* directed by Hélène Châtelain and René Lefort. Its principal work, however, consisted of two innovative campaigns: (1) the creation and publication of a series of unique information booklets, what the group called the *Intolerable* series, which was overseen by the Paris GIP, and (2) the organization of support networks for the prison revolts that erupted throughout France in the winter of 1971–72, a project that arose from collaborations among the various regional GIP affiliates. This section documents the *Intolerable* series by presenting representative samples from each of the booklets together with supporting materials that provide some context for each investigation. The following section is devoted to the GIP's support of the prison revolts.

The first booklet in the series, *Investigation into Twenty Prisons* (Enquête dans 20 prisons), was published in May 1971 by the anarchist press Champ Libre. The Paris GIP had begun its work by launching what Foucault called "*intolerance-investigations*." Their goal was to collect and reveal what was intolerable about French prison life at the time and to rouse public intolerance against these conditions. The group created a detailed questionnaire about life in incarceration that was clandestinely circulated to prisoners and detention staffs through prisoners' families from February through April 1971. The responses poured in from prisons all across France. And though they certainly came from prisoners who were almost exclusively literate, politicized French nationals, and thus not representative of the whole prison population at the time, the responses all told a similar alarming story of overcrowding, unsanitary conditions, and arbitrary and cruel treatment. The ensuing booklet—which was officially anonymous, but is acknowledged to be the work of an editorial team that included Daniel Defert, Michel Foucault, Christine Martineau, and Danièle Rancière—contained the original questionnaire, several samples of the narratives that had been received, and tabulated responses to the inquiries.

Intolerable 2. The GIP Investigates A Model Prison: Fleury-Mérogis (Le GIP enquête dans une prison modèle: Fleury-Mérogis), published by Champ Libre in June 1971, was a study of what was then considered to be the most sophisticated French prison, the "prison of the future." Although the editors and authors remained anonymous, it is believed to have been compiled and produced by Jacques-Alain Miller and François Regnault. Through a meticulous reconstruction of the experience of living in this prison and careful descriptions of its architecture and layout, the GIP was able to expose the intolerable conditions that prevailed even in this most advanced and supposedly most humane form of incarceration. Assessing the "superior" system of cells, isolation units, loudspeakers, and ventilation, which supported an expanded capacity for sanctioned violence, humiliation, and repression (especially of prisoner communications), the GIP found Fleury-Mérogis to be exemplary of penal bankruptcy.

Intolerable 3. The Assassination of George Jackson (L'assassinat de George Jackson), was published by Gallimard in November 1971. It included a preface by Jean Genet, the famous French writer and fervent supporter of the Black Panthers; translations of interviews with Jackson, one of the imprisoned members of the Panthers and a co-founder of the Black Guerrilla Family (an African American Marxist prisoner organization); and several texts, unattributed but believed to be by Catherine von Bülow (Genet's assistant and an important intermediary between the GIP and the Black Panthers), Defert, Gilles Deleuze, and Foucault. The group argued that the killing of Jackson in August 1971, as he was supposedly trying to escape from San Quentin, was actually a "political assassination," an "act of war," that sought to undermine the growing alliance between various racial groups within the prison system.

Finally, *Intolerable 4. Prison Suicides* (Suicides de prison), was edited in the fall of 1972 but published by Gallimard in February 1973. The volume, again anonymous but believed to be the work primarily of Defert and Deleuze, contained a list of thirty-seven known suicides that had occurred in French prisons in 1972, a set of case histories, and reproductions of a series of prison letters by "H. M.," a young man repeatedly incarcerated on charges of petty theft who later hanged himself in solitary. The letters detailed his early life, his time in incarceration, his struggles with drug addiction and mental illness, and the criminalization of his homosexuality. They were accompanied by a brief introduction, an unsigned commentary, and a report on an interview with the Medical Inspector for penitentiary medicine regarding the rash of suicides plaguing the prison system, almost a quarter of which, the GIP noted, were effectuated by immigrant detainees.

Early on, the GIP announced further booklets that were to appear in the series—Against the Criminal Record (Contre le casier judiciaire), Revolts in the Prisons (Révoltes dans les prisons), and an Arrest Manual (Manuel de l'arrêté)—but none of these were ever published.

Preface to *Intolerable 1*

GROUPE D'INFORMATION SUR LES PRISONS (GIP)

The preface to the GIP's first booklet, Intolérable 1: Enquête dans 20 prisons *(Paris: Éditions Champs Libre, May 28, 1971). The text, though unsigned, was overseen by Michel Foucault.*

Courts, prisons, hospitals, psychiatric hospitals, occupational medicine, universities, press organizations, and information centers: through all these institutions and beneath different masks, an oppression is exercised that is, at its root, a political oppression.

The exploited class has always known how to recognize this oppression; it has never ceased to resist it; but it has still been forced to submit to it. That oppression is now becoming intolerable to new social strata—intellectuals, technicians, jurists, doctors, journalists, etc. It always claims to exercise itself through them, with their aid or complicity, but without thereby taking their interests or, above all, their political beliefs *[idéologie]* into account. Those responsible for the distribution of justice, health, knowledge, and information are beginning to sense the oppression of a political power in what they themselves do. This new intolerance converges with the fights and struggles led for so long by the proletariat. And these two joint intolerances are rediscovering instruments the proletariat formed in the nineteenth century: in the first place, inquiries made into working conditions by workers themselves. This situates the "*intolerance-investigations*" we now undertake.

1. These inquiries are not designed to ameliorate, to soften, or to render an oppressive power more bearable. They are designed to

89

attack it wherever it is exercised under another name—that of justice, technique, knowledge, objectivity. Each inquiry must therefore be *a political act.*

2. They aim at specific targets, institutions that have a name and a place, administrators, officials, and directors—who victimize and also incite revolts, even among those in charge. Each inquiry must therefore be *the first episode of a struggle.*

3. Around these targets, these inquiries gather diverse social strata that have been segregated by the ruling class through the play of social hierarchies and divergent economic interests. They have to break down these barriers that are indispensable to power by assembling prisoners, lawyers, and magistrates—or even doctors, the sick, and hospital personnel. Each inquiry must constitute, at each strategically important point, *a front,* and *an attack front.*

4. These inquiries are not made from the outside by a group of specialists: the inquirers, here, are the inquirees themselves. It is for them to take the floor *[prendre la parole],* to dismantle this stratification, to formulate what is intolerable, and to no longer tolerate it. *It is for them to take charge of the struggle that will frustrate the exercise of oppression.*

Prisons are the first target. Why?

Since May '68, the judicial apparatus—an instrument relatively quiet and docile up to that point—has been "overused": to repress French workers and immigrants, to repress students, to repress shopkeepers and farmers. CRS trucks,[1] street raids, clubs and teargas, police custody, police abuse, *flagrants délits,* preventative detentions, subjective verdicts (made on the basis of class, political opinion, and skin color), arbitrary discharges—all of this has made the classist legal system intolerable. But this system is beginning to lose the support of the very institutions and men it had itself appointed. Many lawyers, judges, and penitentiary employees no longer tolerate the job required of them. What is more, state power no longer supports its own judges: it declares them *cowardly.*

By going on hunger strike last winter, incarcerated political activists gave new form to what was still but a voiceless discontent. They marshaled many prisoners around their action; outside, they instigated a movement against the conditions of detention; and on both sides of the prison walls, they made it possible for people to gather together, people who wanted to struggle against the same intolerable reality: a justice system indentured to the ruling class. It is here that the inquiry on prisons takes place.

This booklet is not a report: it forms an integral part of the inquiry's unfolding. It aims to give prisoners from different prisons the means of taking the floor *[prendre la parole]* together regarding conditions of detention, incarceration, and release.

It aims also to penetrate prisons and reveal what is happening there right now—abuses, suicides, hunger strikes, agitation, revolts.

The questionnaire was drafted with former prisoners and modified beginning with the first responses. Presently, almost a thousand questionnaires are in circulation.

It has permitted the formation of inquiry groups, gathering former prisoners, their families, various penitentiary employees appalled by their work, lawyers, magistrates, students, and intellectuals around a number of prisons.

It has been distributed by these groups at prison doors and in visitors' queues. Despite the censorship of visiting rooms, some families have become inquirers themselves, thus making known within prison the action undertaken outside.

In order to distribute information as quickly as possible, we drafted this booklet starting with the first questionnaires:

1. As an example, two completed questionnaires have been reproduced in full;
2. Two narratives, which follow the order of questions posed by the questionnaire, have also been transcribed;
3. The most characteristic responses have been gathered under the questionnaire's principal categories.

Starting with these documents and others still to be published, different campaigns will be organized to denounce the appalling conditions of detention and the entire judicial system that produces and sustains them. Among the immediate demands of prisoners and their families, the abolition of criminal records assumes first rank.

1. From the outset, a criminal record discredits the hypocritical pretention that prison is a place of reeducation;

2. Every day, the state judges the value of its own penitentiary system by banning civil-service access to those holding a criminal record;

3. The judicial system contravenes the right to work: it condemns former prisoners to unemployment, to the arbitrariness of employers, and to the most exploited work;

4. With a criminal record, there is no release, there are only reprieves. The abolition of criminal records will be the theme of our next campaign.

The Prisons Information Group[2]

Notes

1. [Eds.] Compagnies Républicaines de Sécurité (CRS), special mobile French police force.

2. [Eds.] While this signature does not appear in DE/DEQ, it is retained in AL and INT.

Back Cover of *Intolerable 1*

GROUPE D'INFORMATION SUR LES PRISONS (GIP)

A statement from the back cover of Intolérable 1: Enquête dans 20 prisons.

intolerable:
courts
cops
hospitals asylums
school
military service
the press the tv
the state
and above all the prisons

the G.I.P. (Prisons Information Group)
does not propose to speak
for the detainees of different prisons:
it proposes on the contrary
to allow them the possibility
of speaking for themselves,
and to say what happens in the prisons.
The goal of the G.I.P. is not reformist,
we do not dream of an ideal prison:
we hope that the prisoners will be able to say
what is *intolerable*
in the system of penal repression.
We must spread the revelations

made by these prisoners
as quickly and as widely as possible.
This is the only way to unite the interior and exterior of the prison
in the same struggle.

La Santé

Questionnaire and Narratives

GROUPE D'INFORMATION SUR LES PRISONS (GIP)

This is a selection from the GIP questionnaire, distributed early in 1971, the findings of which composed the primary content of the Intolerable 1 *booklet. The selections are taken from responses provided by prisoners at La Santé Prison.*

I. Questionnaire

La Santé

VISITS

QUESTION: Do you get visits?

ANSWER: Yes.

Q.: How many per month, on average?

A.: Eight.

Q.: How long do folks wait in line outside?

A.: It varies. Sometimes 45 minutes, sometimes just 10.

Q.: Does your family have to miss work for it?

A.: My wife had to take a job that, while it pays poorly, leaves her some days off for visitation; but, for the majority of prisoners, freedom to come to the visiting room is limited because work gets in the way.

Q.: What is the exact length of a visit?

A.: 30 minutes.

Q.: Can you describe the conditions of a visit (and what appears to you to be the most intolerable)?

A.: No. You cannot describe the conditions of a visit. They must be lived *[vécu]*. You can, nevertheless, mention the noise, the filth of the visiting rooms, and above all the constant tension created by awaiting the thirtieth and last minute of the visit. The line outside is also traumatizing for the families. For those who love one another, there is also the torture of being present to one another and nevertheless aware of living in two different universes.

Q.: Does your lawyer come to the prison?

A.: From time to time.

LETTERS

Q.: Do you receive all the letters addressed to you?

A.: In theory.

Q.: Do all the letters that you send arrive?

A.: No. Some have been confiscated by the investigating officer.

Q.: Can you recount examples of your mail to family and friends being censored?

A.: All the letters are censored. Not only has the mail reached me all of forty-six days after it left. But my wife keeps getting my letters with the same delay. Eleven days is really the minimum. At the same time, I did not have the right to visitation. Such conditions render all correspondence absolutely ridiculous!!!

Q.: With your lawyer?

A.: Yes. Some letters from my lawyer were opened several times "by mistake." Given the high number of these "errors," it's clear that this is a matter of consciously established censorship.

Q.: With the judge?

A.: I do not write to the judge.

YOUR RIGHTS

Q.: Do you know the prison rules?

A.: The ones routinely posted inside the cells. It is worth noting that prisoners pay them no mind. The guards often don't know them any better. One time, in solitary, a prisoner appealed to the rules and succeeded in changing the meal system. The guards, who were reasonable, had never really read that particular article of the rules of punishment concerning meals in its strict sense.

Q.: Were you told what your rights were in prison?

A.: Never! They spoke to me only of my duties. If anything, they consistently hid themselves behind a relatively obscure rule to oppose all my requests, or at least most of them.

Q.: Do you have any comments to make concerning the rules?

A.: A good deal. On the sheet I am sending you, I go into greater detail about some specific examples.

Q.: Did preventive detention deprive you of the means of preparing your defense?

A.: Absolutely. If only for the money I couldn't earn.

Q.: Did you choose your lawyer?

A.: Yes.

Q.: Was he court appointed?

A.: No. But, incidentally, the result is very nearly the same.

Q.: Do you know that, if your lawyer has never visited you or showed up at hearings, you can write to the President of the Bar?

A.: Yes. But I also know that doing so is rarely recommended. The bar mafia harbors a tenacious grudge.

Q.: And do you know whether doing so has any effect?

A.: None. I saw some examples. On the other hand, there is a not inconsiderable "return to sender" effect.

CELL

Q.: Are you in a cell?

A.: Yes.

Q.: Are there still chicken coops?

A.: Yes. At Poissy, for example.

Q.: Toilets?

A.: Yes.

Q.: Washbasin in the cell?

A.: Yes.

Q.: How many showers can you take per week?

A.: One.

Q.: Are there bugs?

A.: A matchbox full every week.

Q.: How often are the cells fumigated?

A.: By request, but that changes nothing: there is just a reprieve of several days. Not all the cells are infested.

Q.: How often are your linens changed?

A.: The sheets, every month. For those issued clothing—those within the penal population—this laundry is changed every week. The underwear service is good.

Q.: Do you know how much the laundering of your personal laundry costs your family (tips to intermediaries, etc.)?

A.: My laundry is washed by my family. The tip for a sack of laundry deposited at the café is 5 francs on top of the intake cost.

WALKS

Q.: How are the walks?

A.: One hour of walking in the morning. 60 guys milling around in a space of 300 to 400 square meters. In the high-security quarters, 12 to 15 dudes in a courtyard of 4 meters by 8 meters.

FOOD

Q.: How many times a week do you eat meat?

A.: Four times, and fish two times.

Q.: Fruits?

A.: Three times. An apple or orange, pear, banana, depending on the season.

Q.: Portions?

A.: About 100 grams of meat, an average-size whiting, or a 100- to 150-gram cut or slice of a big fish such as a young pollock.

Q.: Quality of the food you receive?

A.: Good for the meat in general. Bad for the vegetables, pasta, or starchy foods.
Above all, the vegetables are poorly prepared.

Q.: Have you had illnesses due to the food (hair loss, tooth decay, stomachaches, intestinal troubles, etc.)?

A.: Yes. Hair loss and ailing eyes.

CANTEEN

Q.: Do you have the means to buy items at the canteen?

A.: Yes, but discounted stuff.

Q.: How much does it cost you per month?

A.: 100 francs.

Q.: What do you buy at the canteen?

A.: Fruits, milk, butter, stamps, toiletries, books.

Q.: What non-food items do you find at the canteen, and can you give us some prices?

A.: I believe that the prices are nearly the same as those on the outside.

LEISURE TIME

Q.: How do you spend your time outside of work?

A.: Reading. Courses of study permitted at La Santé. The same courses are not available in all the prisons. We have the assistants and the CNTE to thank.

Q.: Can you engage in sports regularly?

A.: Absolutely not. Outside of the physical training done on one's own.

Q.: Can you listen to the radio?

A.: No.

Q.: TV?

A.: Ah, that's a good joke! The dithering of the Minister and different wardens indicates more a willful refusal to capitulate to prisoners' demands than a real desire to ban the radio!!!

Q.: Do you have film screenings?

A.: No. There are presentations with slides given by various people. These social events are extremely recent. Only about a hundred prisoners, out of two thousand, have attended.

Q.: What newspapers do you have the right to read?

A.: No dailies: *Paris-Match, Jours de France,* and magazines of that sort. *Le Chasseur français* is, I believe, the most sophisticated magazine allowed. *L'Express* in the carceral universe is considered explosive. As for Marx or anything Marxist, you won't find it!!! They purely and simply prohibit such things. The current warden seems to be more liberal in matters of reading without, however, changing fundamental policies. With the exception of detective series books, paperbacks are sold at the canteen.

Q.: Have you met with an instructor or a schoolteacher?

A.: Yes, both.

Q.: Did they provide you with a tutor?

A.: No. I know, however, that the schoolteachers are full of goodwill and that they provide enormous services to certain students. From the moment of his arrival, the instructor is set on his course by the warden, but then seems to have found a path all his own.

Q.: Do you know how many instructors or schoolteachers are in the prison?

A.: Two schoolteachers, maybe three. One instructor. For the work of teachers and instructors to be useful, both their rights and their duties must be clearly established. Their working conditions are unusual. The supervision of the warden is too strict and blocks all initiative. In spite of the warden's theoretical agreement with declarations made by the Minister of Justice and various other wardens, any generalized access to studies is blocked. A deputy does not dare to get involved because he does not know if his superiors will disavow him the next day. If a prisoner—at the level of a primary-school boy, as most of them are—studies, even out of self-interest (whether seeking pardon, or parole), he will never be the same afterward. I am not speaking on the basis of statistics, but from experience.

Q.: Do you know that you have the right to vocational training?

A.: No. Who would have told me about it?

Q.: To take correspondence courses?

A.: Yes.

Q.: To sit exams?

A.: Yes.

Q.: Have you been able to take advantage of them?

A.: No. Because I refused for personal reasons.

Q.: How much does that cost you per year (enrollment, books)?

A.: 75F for enrollment in the CNTE. You have to allow for 250F total, on average. Social services does its best to help the most needy. Nevertheless, some can't afford this amount and go through AUXILIA, another correspondence course provider that sends books but doesn't require enrollment fees most of the time. The CNTE sometimes waives the 75F upon request.

WORK

Q.: Do you work?

A.: No. Besides, it's not really a matter of work so much as unadulterated, mind-numbing tedium.

Q.: Are you assigned [classé] to General Services?

A.: No. But I am designated [classé] "by" General Services as "someone to monitor very closely."

MEDICAL CARE

Q.: How does a medical visit go?

A.: Chaplinesque. 30 seconds in front of the cell door. Despite the statements made and the papers written by penitentiary doctors, medical services in the penitentiary system are of a much lower quality than those outside. That says a lot.

Q.: In case of illness, can you see the doctor immediately?

A.: Theoretically, and assuming he is here. The doctor is much more difficult to see than the warden.

Q.: When one is still awaiting trial, there is a charge for medical treatments. Has that kept you from taking care of yourself?

A.: Actually, there is a charge for dental care and glasses, in addition to prosthetics, but medical care, including surgery, is free.

Q.: Under what conditions do you have a right to the infirmary?

A.: Being very well regarded by the head nurse, or having leprosy, cholera, or metastasized cancer.

Q.: With what medications are you treated most often?

A.: Aspirin. If it's very serious, you might get Aspro or Valium.

Q.: Did you have to complain about medical care yourself?

A.: Yes.

Q.: Are your teeth decayed?

A.: No.

Q.: Is your vision looked after?

A.: No. Ever since I was a pretrial detainee, my eyes have been constantly fatigued.

Q.: Has the social worker been of any help to you?

A.: Yes, but social services as a whole seems to be stuck in the medieval period. The social workers are basically "charity ladies," barely tolerated by the warden. As it is currently designed, social services is useless. Do-gooders [dames patronesses] would do just as well. Rights and duties here also need to be clarified.

Q.: Can you tell us about the battery of psychological tests?

A.: I took an intelligence test and a personality test. They never shared the results with me. The results were, however, sent to an expert. The experts appointed by the investigating officer are a huge joke. Some see prisoners for only a few minutes, often less than 10. And, on the basis of these sessions, they construct a 20-page court report. The experts have access to prisoners' files and build their report according to the content of those files. Everything is completely misrepresented and formulaic, a mere playacting of sympathy between the expert and the evaluated [expertisés].

DISCIPLINE

Q.: What do you have to say about discipline?

A.: Nothing. Discipline varies depending on the personality of each prisoner. Moreover, there is a split among the guards: those who miss the good old days and those who treat the prisoners as men. The latter are more and more numerous. Nevertheless, it is instructive to note it is always the former who carry the day.

Q.: Guards?

A.: They are men much like those who work at Simca[1] or somewhere similar. What is infinitely more serious is that a guy who is vindictive and cruel always finds a way to channel that in here, and the effect is far worse than on the outside because the average prisoner has no defense.

Q.: About the strip search?

A.: It's an infamous formality. One must go through it to describe it. A mechanical apparatus would be 100 times more effective, and less humiliating. The guards conducting the search would be the first to say so. In prison, the strip search is the means of transforming man into object.

Q.: Have you been to the *prétoire*?

A.: Yes, often.

Q.: On what grounds?

A.: Coffee secured by families, being caught at the window (prohibited), etc. . . .

Q.: Are there fines?

A.: Yes. Personally, no one could make me pay them. I would refuse categorically.

Q.: Have you been in solitary?

A.: Yes.

Q.: How long?

A.: In total, 90 days.

Q.: In a strip cell?

A.: No.

Q.: Can you explain how that goes?

A.: Yes, but not in three lines.

Q.: Have you been a victim of physical violence?

A.: Never. However, I know of many cases, indexed by reference number, name, and date.

Q.: What abuses are you keen to denounce?

A.: The beatings, first of all. Then the straitjacket, applied in an isolation cell, to make you absolutely immobile . . . and used despite the sentencing judge's formal ban.

Q.: Have you gotten word of hunger strikes?

A.: I participated in all of them. I did one on my own, too. They're not over, I think.

Q.: Of suicides?

A.: Many. A boy disemboweled himself with a knife. Another hanged himself. One committed suicide by hunger strike (111 days).

Q.: Of revolts?

A.: Yes, I witnessed two of them.

Q.: What are the most scandalous aspects of penitentiary life that you wish to see the outside involve, first and foremost, in the struggle: means of assuring one's defense once in prison, the right to information, elimination *[abolition]* of physical violence, right to a sex life?

A.: All of that put together. They are impossible to separate. Also, the reform of the visiting rooms: the condemned have a right to just 30 minutes each week. This restriction should be promptly abolished.

Q.: What observations do you have about this investigation and about this questionnaire?

A.: Only one: you've come to the wrong place. Reforms in the prisons cannot be carried out alone. They depend entirely on reforms of the police and the justice system. To act otherwise is to saw the tree into planks before cutting it down. The penitentiary system is not independent like the P&T or the SNCF.[2] It's part of a much bigger system that we call justice. Moreover, the injustices committed by the penitentiary administration appear almost benign compared to those perpetrated by police and magistrates of all stripes. With the powers available to them, a prison warden or a head guard could render carceral conditions absolutely untenable. They do not do so. For example, I never heard anyone speak of men hung by their feet and beaten in their most sensitive areas, nor of those plunged into ice baths, nor of men whose testicles have been hooked up to an electrical current, No woman, I believe, has miscarried her child because of kicks to the belly. All of these methods, however, are presently being used by various police forces. If magistrates, steeped in humanism, do not employ physical violence, they nevertheless use a still more objectionable violence: the conditioning of witnesses and the orientation of their depositions, threats of incarceration, the will to make an investigation fit not the truth but the presumption of guilt by the police, preventive detention, rigging cases, etc. Of course, outside of their contexts, these facts appear benign. They are, however, tragic for those who live through them. Gold-plated cell bars and chicken at every meal would change nothing about the underlying condition of the prisoner. For reform of the offender to be effective, justice must present to him an unbroken face. The magistrate should ceaselessly question the legality of these methods. When an offender commits an act of violence, a theft, even a murder, he involves [engager] only himself. But when a magistrate uses similar methods, deceitfulness, the cover-up of police violence, the refusal of objectivity, he involves [engager] a whole system, a whole civilization. If the justice system employs the same methods as the man that it judges, in what name does it do so? The offender will harden and develop the conviction that he is the noble man, the righteous man because he struggles alone, without the apparatus of the law, without the immunity of magistrates. The imprisoned man, more than any other, needs justice. He must see before him the face of a social order that is the essence of civilization and not a group of bandits hiding beneath their magic robe to assuage the hatreds and hang-ups of their education. In attacking the prisons, the problem is inverted. One takes the effect for the cause. Now, despite what I have just told you, the necessity of an inquiry such as yours was urgent. I thank you. I am available to confirm my statements wherever and whenever you wish.

2. Narratives

La Santé

From the moment you walk through the door, everything is set in motion to humiliate you, debase you, make you understand that you have to "walk straight" and that you are no longer a man but a number, and a number should be quiet and above all expect nothing. "You're going to shut up over there," "Hurry your ass up," "You're starting to piss me off," "Fucking shit!," and all of that in a tone that ꞇes the bark of a local police sergeant sound like a soft and tender murmur. Upon arrival, at the strip search, you must be stripped naked "to be searched," but under the pretext of saving time … "You will get dressed again in just a bit, come sign here … take your package and go to the other room to get dressed."

MATERIAL CONDITIONS

They are often very harsh.

Heating in winter that works badly and, in any case, even at its best, could not suffice to adequately heat the cell. This winter, in certain cells of the division, the oil congealed to the point of being stuck in the bottle, but one still had to wash and shave with ice water. Admittedly, in the winter a supplementary blanket is distributed, although it has no use except at night because during the day it is strictly forbidden to lie down under the blankets. The food is foul, though some efforts to improve it have been made for some time now. Here is the menu, which has remained largely the same for the past several years.

Every evening: a ladle of soup and vegetables. The soup is "drinkable," but the vegetables (almost always on rice or pasta) are absolutely inedible, and prisoners without money almost always prefer to eat dry bread.

At noon, they distribute salad, which is hardly washed or seasoned. Thus, whoever can't buy oil and vinegar doesn't eat it. Along with the salad, the following things are also served at noon:

Monday: a ladle of vegetables, a slice of black pudding pate
Tuesday: a ladle of vegetables, a cut of meat (50–100 g)
Wednesday: a ladle of vegetables, a poorly cooked and very small fish
Thursday: a ladle of vegetables, a cut of meat (50–100 g)
Friday: a ladle of vegetables, a poorly cooked and very small fish
Saturday: a ladle of vegetables, a hard-boiled egg. So, not being spoiled by "great cuisine," a prisoner who cannot buy supplementary food from the canteen will go hungry on Saturday, for example, when he eats only a hardboiled egg and some vegetables, with a ladle of soup in the evening. The warden cannot be held responsible because there are still some days, if very rarely, when the vegetables are almost well prepared and edible. Given that we find ourselves in prison and can't ask for refined food, it is unthinkable in France,

in 1971, that men, having broken the law, are nevertheless men (although that might remain a question for the administration) who cannot eat their fill.

WORK

It is sometimes very difficult to be able to work at La Santé and, while it is possible, one must do it for an absurdly low salary: around 3 francs for the making of 1,000 labels. An average worker working 8 hours makes 2,500. If he is convicted, the administration will deduct half of the 7.50F he would have made, that is, 3.75F. Out of his 3.75F, he will only be able to spend 1.87F and the 1.88F that are left will be divided in two: 94 centimes for legal costs and 94 centimes for earnings paid on release. One must therefore not be surprised if many folks do not want to work and be exploited by the slave drivers [négriers] who are the agents of prisons and by the bloodsucker that is the Administration.

If the material conditions of work are often foul (dirty visiting rooms, a stool and a table of 80 by 60 cm in a cell of 3.80 m by 3.80 m for 4, sometimes 5 prisoners in high security at La Santé), they aren't the worst.

WHAT IS INTOLERABLE

To feel subjected and to be subjected to the arbitrariness of the guards, frustrated beings often of little intelligence, some of whom go so far as to provoke the prisoners to fly off the handle. Others, drunk from morning to night, indulge in the rudest of remarks, but one must bear them, and be quiet, because at La Santé, and in all of the prisons in general, the guard is king. Whether he is stupid, drunk, narrow-minded, or dishonest, he is always right. And his word alone is enough to get you sent to "solitary." He will write a report indicating what he wants (he functions with complete autonomy), and the next day you will appear in the "*prétoire.*" Right or wrong, that does not matter. You will be wrong. "But, warden, sir, I was at the window, but I was not talking." "It is forbidden to be at the window and if the guard says you were talking, it's because it's true." "Warden, sir, if I tell the guard to leave me alone, it's because he was drunk and went around my cell looking for contraband and found fault with a poorly folded blanket or a dirty washbasin." "You are a liar. The guards don't drink." And then it's solitary and, if you're not complacent, the "beat down"[3] (although this sort of beating has become increasingly rare over the last several years, it unfortunately still happens).

In solitary, the prison within prison, there is a "light diet": one day, normal meals served with a wooden spoon, which forces you to eat meat (if there is any) with your hands (although the piece is often so small you can eat it in one mouthful). The day after this sumptuous fare, there is only a bowl of soup at noon and then again in the evening. Add to this diet the prohibition of receiving letters from and writing to your family (just one letter to inform them of your transfer), the winter cold (the heating pipes are in the ceiling), boredom and nothing else to do but to pace back and forth; for, even if textbooks are left there, pencils and pens are forbidden. And the filth: you have to sleep without sheets, on a mattress whose cover is shiny with residue (of sperm in particular, because a lot of prisoners use masturbation as a sleeping pill). But this diet is not enough for the tough ones, so there are warnings of head shaves and dry bread with water in the rules posted on the door. Of course, rights to the visiting room and canteen orders are taken away, otherwise that would be funny. In 1971, in a civilized country, one can dream.

Solitary in itself is still not the worst of it. The worst is the following. I write these lines while watching my door so as not to be caught, which would cost me 8 or 15 days of solitary plus a disciplinary report. For being at the window, you get written up; for throwing a few punches with a fellow prisoner, you get written up; and when you request parole, it is denied for bad behavior. "Think about it. He's a hothead. Parole is not made for people like him." (At any rate, it's not made for anyone and when you win 6 months out of 4 or 5 years, you must be happy because it's very rare). We will not consider the facile motives for these reports. Just their numbers will suffice. As for those who write them, it doesn't matter; a guard is a guard and a guard is never wrong. It also doesn't matter if, in leaving, I truly intend to get back on my feet or if, returning to the prison without a primary-school certificate, I plan on getting a professional certificate next year. The only thing that matters is that I am a hothead and parole is not made for people like me. So, in the first place, what is most intolerable is being subjected to the arbitrariness not only of the guards but also of the whole administrative personnel. The censor sends back whichever letters they want to, whenever they want to, and under any pretext. "Only speak of family affairs," or more simply "Prohibited." Do you have something to complain about? The warden doesn't follow up on complaints. Do you write to the Minister of Justice? The prosecutor? They send the letters to the warden, who, of course, doesn't follow up on them and sometimes even punishes people for unjustified complaints. As for the rules, it's difficult to know what they are exactly and to know what our rights are. Anyway, it doesn't matter because all of the rules in prison do but one thing: secure the administration over and above the prisoner.

MEDICAL SERVICE

This is completely ineffective. The nurses and doctors are in general very nice and understanding. It's nonetheless true that, whether their fault or no, it is difficult to receive appropriate treatment.

As for the dentist, if you aren't yet convicted, you have to pay out of pocket. And again, if you are convicted but have some money, even a little, the services are no longer free. And the least you could say is that fees for the prison dentist are not the kindest. And even before treating a tooth he checks to see if the prisoner has money in his account and how much.

There is so much more to say about the abuses of prisons: reading restrictions. It isn't possible to read the books you want. Mail restrictions and a lot of other things, but all of that would exceed the confines of a letter.

Notes

1. [Eds.] SIMCA (Société Industrielle de Mécanique et Carrosserie Automobile) was a French automaker, founded in November 1934 and merged with Chrysler in 1970.

2. [Eds.] The Société Nationale des Chemins de Fer Français (SNCF) is the French National Railway Corporation.

3. [Trans.] The phrase used here, *machine á bosseler*, is a euphemism for a fist beating. The verb *bosseler* refers to the act of denting, indenting, stamping, or pitting. Officers would use their fists (rather than batons, boots, etc.) so as to ensure significant pain but avoid permanent or expensive damage to the prisoner.

Inquiry on Prisons
Let Us Break Down the Bars of Silence

MICHEL FOUCAULT AND PIERRE VIDAL-NAQUET

Claude Angeli's interview with Michel Foucault and Pierre Vidal-Naquet originally appeared in Politique-Hebdo, *no. 24 (March 18, 1971): 4–6.*

CLAUDE ANGELI: Much has already been written about prisons, in general, and on the conditions of life in prison. There have also been several films and too many people think they know what happens behind bars. Could this make your work difficult?

MICHEL FOUCAULT/PIERRE VIDAL-NAQUET: No. You really have to understand who we are. We do not pretend to be the commission of inquiry; that is not our role. What we want to be is this: an information group that searches for, provokes, and distributes information, and marks targets for possible action.

This idea is fairly recent. You remember, back in February, the political prisoners' second hunger strike? At that time, people said: "Well, there they go—those bourgeois youths, those leftists! They want to be dealt with separately, they demand special treatment!" Well, in general, that didn't work. Neither in public opinion—the press took a long time to react, but in the end . . .— nor above all among the families of common-law prisoners. We still see this today. When those political prisoners who demanded special treatment said: "We have to call the whole penitentiary system, the function of prison, etc., into question," the feedback *[l'écho]* finally proved very strong. Among common-law prisoners and even in the press. People suddenly understood that the prison regime was intolerable.

C. A.: And, from where you're standing, what's been the feedback [*l'écho*]?

M. F./P. V.: For our first meeting, we called a magistrate: several came. We called a prison chaplain: several came. We called a psychologist: same thing. A real brush fire. To tell you the truth, we were surprised. Even very surprised.

Then, we had to publicize it. Several newspapers, *Politique-Hebdo* among them, announced our existence, and we began to receive letters. Letters from doctors, prisoners, and their relatives; letters from lawyers, prison visitors . . . People put themselves at our disposal, asked us what needed to be done, and sent us a little money.

Now, after five weeks of work, we no longer receive just individual letters: high-school committees, student groups, and Secours Rouge committees write to us.

That all happened very quickly. It was astonishing even for those who, like us, believed so much in the necessity of this inquiry. You see, it isn't we who lead but already hundreds of other people . . . They simply needed a catalyst. From now on, we are the relay station for groups formed in and outside of Paris.

C. A.: In terms of the inquiry, what will you do—publish a book of testimonies?

M. F./P. V.: Perhaps, but that's not the question. We don't claim to raise consciousness [*prendre conscience*], among prisoners and their families, of the conditions to which they are subjected. They have had this awareness [*conscience*] for a long time, but it hasn't had the means to express itself. Knowledge, reactions, indignations, reflections on the penitentiary situation—that all exists on an individual level but still isn't coming to light. From here on out, information must circulate, from mouth to ear, from group to group. It might be a surprising method, but it's still the best one. Information must reverberate [*rebondir*]. Individual experience must be transformed into collective knowledge. That is to say, into political knowledge.

Here's an example: every Saturday, we go to the door of La Santé where the families of prisoners wait in line for visiting hours. There, we pass out our questionnaire. The first week, we received a very cold reception. The second, people were still mistrustful.

The third, someone said to us: "That's all just idle talk. Something would have had to have been done a long time ago." And then abruptly, this woman started telling us everything. She burst out in anger, spoke of the visits, of the money she gave to prisoners, of the rich who are not in prison, and of the filth. Everyone noticed the plainclothes cops pricking up their ears . . .

The fourth Saturday was yet more extraordinary. Even before we got there, people in the queue were talking about the questionnaire and the scandal of the prisons . . . That day, instead of making people wait in the street until the usual 1:30 p.m., La Santé opened its doors forty-five minutes early . . .

C. A.: How will you use the responses to your questionnaire?

M. F./P. V.: We're going to put them in a booklet that we'll then distribute, at the doors of La Santé, to the families of prisoners. We'll also send it to our correspondents outside of Paris who ask us for information, and we'll tell them: "Do the same and collect information yourself."

You see, we want there to be little difference between the inquirers and the inquirees. For us, it would be ideal for families to communicate with prisoners. For prisoners to communicate with each other. For prisoners to communicate with the public. This would mean breaking open the ghetto. Let them define their demands for themselves and let them define the necessary actions as well.

C. A.: You don't make any distinction, of course, between political and common-law prisoners, do you?

M. F./P. V.: Absolutely no distinction. If it all got started with political prisoners, that's because the authorities—the government and its Minister of Justice—made the mistake (from their point of view) of mixing the two types of prisoners.

Political prisoners have means that common-law prisoners do not. They have the means to express themselves. They have knowledges, social relations, outside contacts that permit them to make known what they say, what they do, and above all they have the political support to make their action reverberate. Several dozen common-law prisoners would not be able, like political prisoners, to react together, or write and make their demands known to the outside world.

C. A.: Given the initiatives you have taken on, is their isolation sure to diminish?

M. F./P. V.: That is what we want. The prison institution is largely an iceberg. The visible part is its justification: "Prisons are necessary because there are criminals." But the hidden part, the most important and formidable of the two, is this: prison is an instrument of social repression.

Serious offenders, serious criminals do not represent even 5 percent of the prison population. The rest are average offenders and petty criminals. Mainly from poor classes. Here are two thought-provoking statistics: 40 percent of prisoners are charged in a case yet to be judged and about 16 percent are immigrants. Most people are unaware of that because the existence of prisons is always justified by the existence of serious criminals.

C. A.: So that's the theory. But in everyday life, how do prisoners react? And their families?

M. F./P. V.: The questionnaire is only interested in living conditions. Prisoners speak of their work, their visits, the crammed cells, the books they are refused, the hunger, and the cold.

This winter, in Nantes, the bed covers were frosted over in the morning. In Draguignan, the temperature was consistently below freezing in certain cells. In Clairvaux, fifty-eight chicken coops (cells composed entirely of bars) are never heated. At Loos, during the winter of 1969, the heat was out for a month. Add to that the most egregious harassment. They forbid prisoners to lie beneath the covers during the day. The warden said: "You want to get warm? Run in your cells!" or "You shouldn't have come here in the first place!"

Many prisoners, however, report: "Material conditions in prison aren't the worst of it." And thus we discovered a whole series of repressions still harder to endure than overcrowding, boredom, or hunger.

The most important, perhaps, is the total absence of real law *[droit]*. The judicial system sends a man to prison and that man can't defend his rights against it. He is completely disarmed. The length of preventative detention and the living conditions all depend on the judicial system. Now, when he writes to the prosecutor to complain, his letter can be intercepted or partially rewritten by the court clerk. Sometimes he is even thrown into solitary confinement, just to stop his complaints. Judges know well that the penitentiary administration functions as a screen between them and the prisoners. This is actually one of the functions of prison that judges appreciate most.

Here is another example of a right *[droit]* refused: a prisoner enrolled in a correspondence course directed by the Faculty of Arts. He wrote to his warden: "For some time now, when my homework returns corrected, I have the great displeasure of seeing the censor stamp right in the middle of annotations by the professor. I happen to know this isn't done on account of your orders, since the measure isn't generalized. Clearly, the stamp's insertion ruins my work and deprives me of the instructions that annotated homework can afford, and I can't retain such marks in the documents I aim to save."

Written in the margin was: "Censorship did its job."

Here's another letter from a prisoner. He wrote to the warden: "I would be obliged if you kindly authorized me to receive various textbooks—on mathematics and mechanics—from outside." Written in the margin was: "No, it's one or the other."

Here's another common case. A man condemned, for example, to three years in prison often has the right—depending on the nature of his offense—to request his conditional release after eighteen months of detention. Now, everything depends on the number of punishments and the opinion of the judge responsible for the application of penalties. Punishments are allocated by the *prétoire*—which is to say, by a committee that knows the warden, the deputy warden, and the chief of the guard. A guard complains and a punishment falls. Some arbitrary punishments suffice to ensure that conditional release is refused.

One prisoner wrote to us: "The prisoner is the object of perpetual social aggression." The tone of this remark might be surprising, because it doesn't concern a political prisoner—but that would be a shame, because the remark is terribly true.

C. A.: What else is intolerable in prison?

M. F./P. V.: Many things. Sexual repression, for instance. Prisoners sometimes avoid talking about it. But some do anyway. One of them said: "In the visiting room, the screw checks to see if my wife

stays fully dressed." This is common, it seems. Prisoners mastur-
bate in the visiting room after having asked their wife to show a
breast, and this situation—with the constant possibility of intervention by the guard—is always difficult to bear.

Also difficult to bear is the lack of money. Several families tell
us they give their imprisoned relative between 100 and 150 francs
a month. But not every family has the means necessary to do so.

In the best of cases, the prisoner works. For nothing or almost
nothing. We did the calculation: when a prisoner works 8 hours a
day, 22 days a month, he gets, on average, 15–20 francs. We found
the highest "salaries"—if we must talk about "salaries" in this context—in La Petite Roquette: 40 francs a month to make the bags
for Dior stockings. When you know that a prisoner has to pay for
his stamps, that an escalope in the canteen costs 6 francs, that the
mere enrollment in a correspondence course costs 35–50 francs
a year, without counting the required books, you see what this
means.

C. A.: Businesses have an interest in supplying work to prisoners, but
doesn't the state take a good part of the salary all the same?

M. F./P. V.: Yes. Five-tenths of the salary is retained for housing costs;
two-tenths more for court costs; one-tenth for savings remitted
upon release. The prisoner gets only the crumbs: two-tenths of
his salary.

Draw up a balance sheet. A man condemned to six months or
two years no longer has any rights, so to speak. As a citizen, he is
naked before the law. As a prisoner, he is unable to have his remaining rights recognized. As a worker, he is overexploited; he
rarely gets the chance to study. And all prisoners, whether male
or female, have no rights at their disposal with respect to their
sexuality.

Add further the permanent threat of solitary confinement and
beatings, and there you have what prison is today. Sometimes with
other scandals like the following: in a *maison centrale,* in 1970, six
prisoners tried to escape through the pipes. The alarm went off
and the order was given to open the waterworks. At the risk of
drowning them! Fortunately, the six were able to get out in time,
but they were beaten in the yard by the guards. The penitentiary
administration knows this but has taken no disciplinary action.

One magistrate told us: "If you were to conduct an investigation, the case would fall back on the guards. They too are victims ..."

Here, again, there is a problem: 73 percent of all the extended sick leaves obtained by prison guards are for mental illnesses (see the declaration of Mr. Petit, in 1969, before the Superior Council of Penitentiary Administration and the Minister of Justice).[1]

C. A.: Prisoners essentially belong to the poorest classes. Isn't that ultimately the most important thing?

M. F./P. V.: Perhaps. One thing struck us, if one recalls recent political history. No one or nearly no one talks anymore about the Algerian demonstration on October 17, 1961. That day and the days following, about two hundred Algerians were killed by police in the streets and thrown to drown in the Seine. On the other hand, people are always talking about the nine dead at Charonne where, on February 8, 1962, a demonstration against the OAS was stamped out.

In our opinion, this means that there is always one group of human beings, the boundaries of which may vary, at the mercy of others. In the nineteenth century, they called this group "*les classes dangereuses.*"[2] Today, it's still the same.

There is the slum population, the overcrowded projects, the immigrants and the marginalized, whether youths or adults. There's nothing astonishing about finding them, especially them, before the courts of justice or behind bars.

Notes

1. [Eds.] See "Procès verbal da la réunion du conseil supérieur de l'administration pénitentiare du 5 décembre 1969," in *Rapport général sur l'exercice,* présenté à Monsieur Le Garde Des Sceaux, Ministre de la Justice, par Henri Le Corno, Directeur de l'Administration Pénitentiare (Conseil Supérieur de l'Administration Pénitentiaire, 1969), 317–68.

2. [Eds.] See Honoré A. Frégier's *Des Classes dangereuses de la population dans les grandes villes, et des moyens de les rendre meilleurs* (Paris, 1840). Frégier was particularly concerned with the urban poor who, succumbing to idleness, quickly fell into depravity and perversity, thereby constituting a "criminal class."

No, This Is Not an Official Inquiry . . .

MICHEL FOUCAULT

The second part of an interview with Michel Foucault, broadcast on April 21, 1971, by the "Format France" program of Radio-Canada. Foucault had traveled to Quebec to meet with those seeking independence and to visit one of their most prominent leaders, Pierre Vallières, author of Nègres blancs d'Amérique *(1967), who was in prison for his alleged part in what was called the October Crisis, one of Canada's most significant terrorist events. While the first part of the interview addresses the relations between power and the right to speak, the second part concerns the problem of prisons and the GIP's initiative.*

FORMAT FRANCE: ... The philosopher of structuralism, Michel Foucault, professor at the Collège de France, author of, among other things, *History of Madness* and *The Order of Things,* both published by Gallimard, is at this moment conducting an inquiry that might surprise us coming from a philosopher, coming from a thinker of structuralism: it is an inquiry into French prisons and their prisoners. There is something very peculiar about this inquiry, for it is not entirely official.

MICHEL FOUCAULT: No, it is not an official inquiry, it is an inquiry whose point of departure is linked to the imprisonment of a number of students and intellectuals we in France call "leftists"— perhaps they are also called that in Canada?

F. F.: Not just in France (laughs); since 1968?

M. F.: Since 1968 and especially since 1970, quite a large number of people belonging to a former movement of the Gauche Prolétarienne found themselves in prison and, within these prisons, went on a hunger strike. They launched a protest movement, not at all to obtain some privileged status: nowhere did they argue the political character of their offense or, in any case, of their action, in order to demand a certain number of advantages for their own profit or benefit. In fact, they initiated the strike to attract public attention to the conditions of detention in France, conditions that are incredibly medieval and archaic.

F. F.: So, they aren't complaining about the conditions to which they are subjected, but about the conditions to which all prisoners are subjected?

M. F.: The general conditions for all prisoners, and these conditions are extraordinarily harsh and severe, and I believe that they can all be summarized in one word: detention. Detention is in principle the privation of the freedom to leave, the freedom to act ordinarily within one's family and work environment, and that's it. But why is it that prison must furthermore lead to the privation of a certain number of other fundamental freedoms? Yet, this is precisely what is happening in France: under the pretext of confining people, one deprives them of a certain number of other freedoms, or a certain number of other fundamental rights, for example the right to information, or the right to work, in any case, the right to legitimate compensation for work, the right also to a sex life, etc. In this vein, I take a certain number of fairly curious examples: in France, a prisoner doesn't have the right to receive even the slightest bit of political information.

F. F.: This means that they can't read newspapers?

M. F.: They can certainly read newspapers; they are given *Paris-Match* or even *Jours de France.* You know these publications; they are really not very dangerous.

F. F.: There are pictures.

M. F.: There are pictures and, when there is political news, the prison administration takes scissors and cuts out the page, the half page, or the quarter page on which this information is found.

F. F.: And radio and television?

M. F.: In the two or three French prisons where there are radios, there isn't a single television. The very minute the news came on, they would cut the radio, so that, in 1968, there were prisoners who had heard nothing; the events of May fell, for them, into complete silence.

F. F.: Prisoners accused of being wreckers [*casseurs*], or at least of having committed certain acts . . . are they considered political prisoners?

M. F.: No, they don't have political status, they are treated as common-law prisoners. You know, when there were political convicts, we might say of right-wing origins, during the time of the OAS, they had a fairly comfortable political status, relatively speaking. Now that political prisoners are from the left, they no longer have political status. They have, instead, a status that is fairly distinctive because it keeps them from having the least contact with the rest of the prisoners. They can't speak with other prisoners, go on walks with other prisoners, and, when by chance in the corridor a political prisoner comes across a group of common-law prisoners, the political prisoner is turned to face the wall so as not to exchange even a contagious wink with the common-law prisoners.

F. F.: Do they fear contagion?

M. F.: Ah yes, they fear contagion even at a glance, even in the silence of a wink.

F. F.: That means these prisoners can no longer know what happens outside prison walls?

M. F.: That's it; the campaign we led is a campaign that consists essentially in alerting public opinion to this refusal of rights to detainees in general. For example, this goes for the right to compensated work: there are prisoners who work 8 hours a day, 22 days a month; they earn almost the equivalent of 15 dollars; 15 dollars for a month's work, 8 hours a day, 22 days a month, and the prison still retains a supplementary sum for a certain number of costs. So, there are prisoners who, after having done this work, find themselves with 3 dollars in their pocket.

F. F.: Your inquiry is almost clandestine, I believe?

M. F.: It isn't exactly clandestine; it is in fact completely unofficial, for our problem isn't so much to have objective data—one can obtain that perfectly well through the official documents provided. Our problem is, as it were, to get prisoners to speak, to give prisoners, for the first time, I think, the right to speak.

F. F.: But to do that, don't you necessarily have to collaborate with prison authorities?

M. F.: No, and that's where our enterprise is a little clandestine. With the aid of a number of families of prisoners, with the aid of lawyers, and of people who work in prisons—doctors, psychologists, prison employees, who are absolutely scandalized by the situation in the prisons, etc.—we have had questionnaires passed to prisoners who then convey their experience and their current demands. They're beginning to send us texts, narratives, fragments of autobiographies, and newspaper clippings spontaneously. Thus, we intend, within several days, or in any case within several weeks, to launch a small paper in France, slightly *underground*,[1] in which we'll publish, in their raw state, so to speak, these texts on detention, this discourse of imprisonment that has remained voiceless, that has remained suppressed and censured for centuries.

F. F.: Do you intend to compete with that other French philosopher, Sartre, who also distributes a paper on street corners?

M. F.: No. It does so happen that he distributes a paper on street corners, but he distributes political newspapers written by specific political groups. Yes, it's an experiment we're trying and which, as you see, is not so far from my former preoccupations, when I studied confinement and the techniques of confinement in the classical era. The problem is to give the right to speak to all people that have in one way or another been excluded from discourse, excluded from speech.

F. F.: And with all these documents you currently have in your possession, are you coming to the conclusion that the prisons in France are extremely archaic?

M. F.: Yes, they are archaic, medieval. Moreover, I don't know if there can be good prisons. I hold in principle that all repression is bad, I also hold in principle that every state is repressive, and from there I conclude that every state is bad (laughs).

F. F.: We should really talk for the next century but we have less than a minute. By coming to the conclusion that every state is bad, are you an anarchist?

M. F.: Perhaps not absolutely, I simply ask myself if the forms of state that we've known up to this point, if the forms of state that have developed in history, let's say, since Greece, are the only forms of social organization to which we can refer. We probably must think of another type of social organization . . .

Note

1. [Trans.] The English word *underground* appears here in the French original.

Intolerable 2. The GIP Investigates a Model Prison: Fleury-Mérogis

They Build New Prisons!

GROUPE D'INFORMATION SUR LES PRISONS (GIP)

A text excerpted from Intolérable 2. Le GIP enquête dans une prison-modèle: Fleury-Mérogis, *published with Éditions Champ Libre on June 7–8, 1971. This text, like the entire booklet, was written by the Fleury-Mérogis Information Group, principally led by Jacques-Alain Miller and François Regnault.*

Fleury-Mérogis, the most modern prison in France.

Fleury-Mérogis, the biggest prison in France.

Big enough for all the young people living in Paris or the *banlieue*[1] since '68 to march right into it. Big enough for the judges to steer more and more youth there. It whetted their appetite, it cannot satiate their craving for justice. In summer, the numbers wane, the police are away on vacation.

If you are between eighteen and twenty-one years old, if you are from the *banlieue* or Paris, you are headed to Fleury, Building D2 or Building D4.

At intake, the newcomers are already crammed by twos and threes into cells intended for one. It is the model prison, which Pleven toured when his prisons were disparaged. The model prison, but it is also the suicide prison, the prison where people kill themselves the most. In one year, in D2, out of 1,500 youths, there were seventy-five attempted suicides. One is alone for twenty-three of twenty-four hours there. The administration congratulates itself for thereby preventing "bad influences."

The clean and orderly prison, the silent prison. But this is because the most Valium is distributed there, and if you don't agree to take it, you are injected with it.

The prison without bars. But we are reminded of them every day.

The electronic prison. But they bark orders at you over the loudspeaker, and listen to you even while you sleep.

The prison of the future, the one that should be built all over France in dozens of copies.

Originally, Fleury-Mérogis was going to replace La Santé. The old prison had to be demolished, its site sold, its prisoners transferred to the new prison. But La Santé is still standing and Fleury is filling up.

Originally, La Santé was made for one thousand prisoners. There are now three thousand. Fleury was made for three thousand. One day, if nothing changes, there will be nine thousand.

A prison for women is now being built in Fleury. It is supposed to replace La Roquette. But we can be sure that they will both remain.

They are building new prisons and they are not destroying the old ones. This is because more and more youths are going to prison in France today. The mean age in prison has gone from forty to twenty-five. And meanwhile, the good souls are demanding new loans for the Minister of Justice, more prisons, more screws, more judges. New loans?

Visit Fleury-Mérogis. Listen to what those inside have to say. Learn about the future they are preparing for us. See the great plot being hatched against our liberty.

At Fleury, at this very moment, four of our brothers are in solitary for having thrown papers into the exercise yard on which they had written:

"THE MORE WE ARE IMPRISONED, THE MORE WE WILL REVOLT!"

We say it with them.

Groupe d'Information sur Fleury-Mérogis, May 10, 1971

Note

1. [Eds.] *Banlieue* refers to the severely depressed outskirts of a major city or town. It is commonly associated with urban decay and violence.

The Model Prison
Alone Twenty-Three out of Twenty-Four Hours

GROUPE D'INFORMATION SUR LES PRISONS (GIP)

An excerpt from Intolérable 2. Le GIP enquête dans une prison-modèle: Fleury-Mérogis, *which appeared in* La Cause du peuple *on June 7, 1971.*

ALL THE GUYS WHO ARE RELEASED FROM FLEURY will tell you: alone 23 out of 24 hours, anything but that. I went to Fresnes. With two guys, with several, you can help each other out, talk, work. There are only two educators for the whole prison and you don't always have the screws on your back and you can travel freely between the floors, go down to the barber all by yourself. It isn't clean like it is in Fleury, it's true, but I prefer the filth to being all alone. And the others are like me. To be absolutely alone, that is the worst suffering.

You're always waiting for something to happen, you spend your time waiting for food, for your walk, for bedtime, for someone to come. The screw, the prisoner on duty *[auxiliaire],* sometimes you're quite happy to see them, even if it's only for a few seconds. The rest of the time ... the rest of the time you move around your cell, you listen to your own heart beat all day long. The solitude has strange effects: you examine yourself all the time, you interrogate yourself, you feel yourself grow older; since you eat a lot, you see yourself grow fatter. You end up knowing your cell down to the smallest nook and still you can't keep yourself from looking it over again. There are those who wash their cells three times a day. As for me, I multiplied the floor tiles and checked my answers by counting them. Or else I would count the number of days I had left in the slammer, the number of days Jojo had left, the number of days that all my buddies had left, and I would total

123

them up and change that into months or years—and every day the total would change, so I'd start all over again. All the guys are either depressive or overexcited, since they have all this energy that they can't let out. Everyone talks, at some point, of slashing his wrists or of tearing the screws to pieces.

People don't realize that this prison is really the worst, that it's a concentration camp. You have bouts of depression that strike without warning, you feel as though you're rotting, guys jerk off four, sometimes five times a day, there are those who cut holes in their foam mattress, and I knew one guy who stuck it in a piece of meat. What is certain is that in the beginning, at night, you dream of what you used to do. And then later on, you no longer dream of anything but the prison, the screw, the gate, the bars, the courtyard. Your entire life is the prison.

In the morning, when you wake up, you need to get it back into your head that you're really in prison. All of a sudden, the loudspeaker starts blaring: "Time to wake up, it is 6:45!" You get up, you wash: at 7:00 the doors automatically open, you put your trash can out in the corridor, you grab the pants hanging outside. At 7:30 they pass out coffee, a bowl of barley grain mixed with a little bit of water, milk, and sugar, and two pieces of stale bread, bread to be found nowhere else, prison bread. Then your day really begins when you get your mail and your goods from the canteen. With the censorship, you never know if the mail will arrive, you're always afraid that your letter will be censored without you knowing it, which isolates you all the more—and in Fleury, that's unbearable.

The visiting room is your oxygen; when they take that away from you, it kills you. And those who find out that their daughter has let them down, you see that here . . . It's like that in all the prisons, but in Fleury it's worse because you find yourself all alone again in your cell.

You mustn't forget that Fleury is 25 km from Paris. If they live in the city center, it could take those who come to visit you five hours to get there and it costs money. Then there are the lawyers, you mustn't count too much on them. You're lucky if they make it to the sentencing; sometimes they don't—but if they do, you have to pay. There are guys whose families make sacrifices to get a lawyer. All the guys say: the more cash you have, the better your chances of getting out: they all dream of securing Floriot.[1]

It's the worst during preventive detention, when you don't know what's going to become of you, and in Fleury you can't talk to anyone about it.

You shouldn't be surprised, then, that so many guys in Fleury think about killing themselves. I remember one afternoon when the guards were running from cell to cell because guys were trying to kill themselves left and right. There are times like that. When you learn about someone trying to kill himself, there are often seven, eight, ten, twelve, fifteen others who have also tried. There is an indescribable panic among the screws, like during a revolt. Disciplinary actions grow milder overnight, there is much more consideration for everyone, and then, of course, everything gradually tightens up again.

To cut your bread and your meat, you get a little penknife. You can't sharpen your spoon or fork because the metal breaks. But it's possible to sharpen the penknife on the edge of your washbasin or on the bars, and that can work for slashing your wrists, as well as for jumping the screws. In February of this year, there was a guy who carved up two screws like that. And a little later, there was another who did the same thing, to only one screw this time, and he almost sank his penknife into his throat.

You need to realize that in Fleury you don't even have the right to talk or to sing in your cell. You'll be humming softly, like in any other prison, and daydreaming, and then you're rudely awakened by the voice on the loudspeaker: "That's enough, down there!" And you can get up to 8 days in solitary for it.

Note

1. [Eds.] René Floriot (1902–1975) was a famous French criminal lawyer who defended several high-profile clients, including Otto Abetz, Pierre Jaccoud, and Gustave Mentre.

Dear Comrades, Here Are the Current Axes of the GIP's Development

GROUPE D'INFORMATION SUR LES PRISONS (GIP)

A GIP circular, dating from the spring of 1971.

Dear Comrades,

Here are the current axes of the GIP's development:

(a) A progressive group of people united on the basis of their social practice: it would be ideal to involve penitentiary doctors, magistrates, lawyers, etc., chaplains, etc., more and more, on a day-to-day basis, in the work of information.

(b) A group of prisoners' wives: wives of prisoners at Toulouse are leading an initiative for the abolition of visiting rooms, those in Fresnes are working to lengthen the visit from 20 to 30 minutes (there are tracts, refusals to leave the visiting rooms; a nascent women's collective in Paris is writing a leaflet on the rights of authorized families, cohabitation, marriage in prison . . .). Let us know all the problems *[Pb]* of this type with which you are familiar.

(c) A group of former and current prisoners, with the former as intermediaries, through which tracts have circulated in certain prisons. The themes of the tracts: decent grub, the right to control it; the right to choose cellmates (let's organize this); the right to visitation and correspondence with people outside of one's own family, the right to apprentice for a job (let's organize this). There is a discussion going on between the outside and certain prisoners: is it right to introduce a tract from the outside? We want your opinion on this.

It is obvious that political activists, objectors, and dissenters have an important role in developing the idea of the organization, whether it be modeled after an internal commission (like the OAS) or like either the trade unions or the clubs: several years ago in Caen, prisoners organized various clubs (music, sports, world knowledge, do-it-yourself).

We welcome all proposals concerning organizational possibilities. Former prisoners could organize into an association for the abolition of criminal records. At the moment, that presents difficulties for them (law on the association of malefactors, conditional freedom, etc.).

(d) Expected attacks: the administration is inquiring into which of its personnel informs us; there are threats of sanctions. So we have to multiply the sources of information. Suggestions. Multiply the individual targets: names of screws, etc. One screw attacked in the tracts at FM [Fleury-Mérogis] is looking into whether or not he should press charges. Go after targets like this.

We want your opinion on the axes that we present here and your own proposals for the GIP.

> Fraternal salute from your
> comrades.

Right to Information on the Prisons

GROUPE D'INFORMATION SUR LES PRISONS (GIP)

A GIP leaflet drafted after several of its members (including Michel Foucault and Jean-Marie Domenach) were picked up for questioning on May 1, 1971, outside the prison gates at Fresnes and La Santé, where they were launching the campaign for the abolition of criminal records. Michel Foucault wrote a text about this arrest, "The Prison Is Everywhere" (also collected in the present volume) on May 5, 1971 (cf. DE II, no. 90, 193–94 / DEQ I, no. 90, 1061–62), which was published in Combat *(no. 8335).*

For three months, now, we have forced the press to reveal the scandal of the prisons:

1. Hunger strike by the political prisoners.
2. Circulation, by the GIP, of a thousand questionnaires at the gates and inside the prisons of Paris and the provinces.
3. Constitution of prison information groups in some twenty cities.

All of this has allowed the prisoners and their families to take the floor *[prendre la parole]*. In this way, prison came to be recognized as a place where unemployment or underpaid work (40 francs per month is a maximum) numbs the mind, a place of physical violence, a place where everything is bought: the canteen, the lawyer, the screws. One finds the worst forms of exploitation and oppression in prisons. They need to stop talking to us about rehabilitation.

Those in power want to stop this campaign.

Since the first of May, the police have arrested the groups from Fresnes, from La Santé, from Douai, from La Roquette. Those in power are afraid and are trying to silence the prisoners, their families,

128

and those who unite together to make a common voice heard. Those in power already control the radio, the television, certain newspapers, and they are afraid of the street and its liberty.

The police crackdown on the first of May is also explained by the fact that we are beginning a CAMPAIGN FOR THE ABOLITION OF CRIMINAL RECORDS.

The criminal record is a means of blackmail and pressure, brandished by the police and employers over those who have, nevertheless, "served" their time. The criminal record condemns one, on the whims of employers, to unemployment or to the most exploited occupations. The criminal record contradicts the right to work; with a criminal record, there is no liberation, there is only reprieve.

To retaliate:

Let us expand our action to all the prisons.

Circulate this leaflet to all those who may be concerned.

Gather information on the problem of criminal records and send it to the GIP, 176, rue de Grenelle, Paris VIIe.

Several families have suggested that they organize and create an ASSOCIATION OF PRISONERS' FAMILIES: for the abolition of the criminal record, for the recognition of their rights, for the denunciation of the conditions under which justice is exercised, and for the public control of prison operations.

If you would like to participate in this movement, write to the GIP: 176, rue de Grenelle, Paris VIIe.

The Death of George Jackson Is Not a Prison Accident

GROUPE D'INFORMATION SUR LES PRISONS (GIP)

A statement from the back cover of Intolérable 3. L'assassinat de George Jackson, *which was published by Gallimard on November 10, 1971.*

The death of George Jackson is not a prison[1] accident.

It is a political assassination.

In America, assassination was and today remains a mode of political action.

This booklet does not claim to shed light on the events of August 21, 1971, at San Quentin prison: for the moment, at least, they are beyond our reach. We merely want to address two questions:

1. So, what was this living being they wanted to kill? What threat did he pose *[portait]*, he who wore *[portait]* only chains?

2. And why did they want to kill this death, to suffocate it under lies? What more did they have to fear from it?

In order to address the first question, we have chosen to present some of the most recent interviews in which Jackson analyzes the revolutionary function of the prison movement.

To address the second, we have analyzed a number of news reports and documents published immediately after Jackson's death.

THE G.I.P.[2]

Notes

1. [Eds.] The term "prison" here appears in the original booklet, as well as in AL, but is not retained in INT.

2. [Eds.] This original signature does not appear in AL, but it is retained in INT, albeit sans periods.

Preface to *Intolérable 3*

The preface to Intolérable 3. L'assassinat de George Jackson *has since been republished in Jean Genet,* L'Ennemi déclaré, *ed. Albert Dichy (Paris: Gallimard, 1991), 111–17, and translated in Jean Genet,* The Declared Enemy: Texts and Interviews, *ed. Albert Dichy (Palo Alto, Calif.: Stanford University Press, 2003), 91–97.*

It has become more and more rare in Europe for a man to accept being killed for the ideas he defends. Black people in America do it every day. For them, "liberty or death" is not a clichéd slogan. When they join the Black Panther Party, black people know they will be killed or will die in prison. I shall speak of a man who is now famous, George Jackson; but if the quake his death unleashed in us has not ceased, we ought also to know that every day young anonymous blacks are struck down in the streets by the police or by whites, while others are tortured in American prisons. Dead, they will survive among us—which isn't much—but they will live among the peoples who have been crushed by the white world, thanks to the resounding voice of George Jackson.

Unlike the Americans who, from a lack of ideas, victoriously set out to fight in Vietnam only to return broken men, many blacks, already broken, moved in the opposite direction, entering into prison or into death only to reemerge victorious. Out of the repeated slaughter of blacks—from Soledad Prison to Attica[1]—George Jackson, assassinated by elite sharpshooters—that is, gunmen for the elite[2]—rises up, shakes himself off, and is now illustrious, that is, luminous, the bearer of a light so intense that it shines on him and on all black Americans.

Who was George Jackson? An eighteen-year-old black man imprisoned for eleven years for being an accomplice in a theft of seventy dollars. A magnificent writer, one of the greatest black writers, the author of widely dispersed letters which, when brought together, make up a revolutionary book. A brother to his brother, Jonathan Jackson, who at seventeen years old entered a courtroom in San Rafael, freeing three blacks and taking one hostage: the presiding judge. Finally, a resolute, that is, conscious, martyr, assassinated on August 21 in the courtyard—or in a cell—of San Quentin Prison, on the eve of his trial.

"An eighteen-year-old black man imprisoned for eleven years for being the accomplice in a theft." George was given this strange sentence: one year to life. It's an odd statement. It means that Jackson was sentenced to one year of prison, but that at the end of this year he would have to appear before a parole board which decides whether he will be released or retained. The parole board retained him eleven times in eleven years. It is obvious that the guards of Soledad saw in him, almost every day, and almost at every moment, the force of an independence and a pride intolerable to whites, a pride that they call arrogance because it comes from a black man. Finally, in solitude, with the help of his lawyer, Fay Stender, and with the help of Huey P. Newton, a leader in the Black Panther Parry with whom he was in contact, Jackson very quickly became politicized: too quickly and too much so, for the guards of Soledad laid an ambush for him. On January 13, 1970, Miller—another sharpshooter—standing atop a watchtower, shoulders his rifle, aims, fires, nicks a white prisoner but kills three blacks who were fighting. Miller is not prosecuted, neither for murder nor for manslaughter. Three days later, in another section of Soledad, the guard John Mills is found almost dead at the foot of a high wall, having fallen from the third floor. George Jackson—along with two other black prisoners—is charged with murder. All three are transferred to a California state prison in San Francisco.

"The author of a revolutionary book." It is difficult to know whether Jackson and his book would have been possible without the creation of the Black Panther Party, or whether the BPP would have been possible without Malcolm X, or whether Malcolm himself would have been possible without the rebel slaves: Nat Turner, Harriet Tubman, Frederick Douglass. Without going into any detail here, it is necessary to invoke their names and their dedication, their achievements.

As for the style of the letters, Jackson brings a new tone into black literature: he does not refer to the Old Testament. He does not quote from the Prophets or the Apostles. He goes straight into sarcasm:

"If there were a god or anyone else reading some of my thoughts I would be uncomfortable in the extreme" [152].[3]

"So, if they would reach me now, across my many barricades, it must be with a bullet and it must be final" [153].

"I hope I have trained all of the slave out of me" [154–55].

"Right here in Soledad, a white (nameless and faceless now) stabbed a brother with my surname. . . . In an honest case of mistaken identity, the Mexicans were supposed to be out to get me for it" [162].

"So most of these inmates are sick, my friend, but who created the monster in them?" [163].

"United States prisons are the last refuge of the brainless. If the inmates are failures, at least they were reaching . . ." [163].

"But the restraints come off when they [the guards] walk through the compound gates.[4] Their whole posture goes through a total metamorphosis. Inflict pain, satisfy the power complex, get a check" [164].

"This is one nigger who is positively displeased. I'll never forgive, I'll never forget, and if I'm guilty of anything at all it's of not leaning on them hard enough. War without terms" [165].

"How do you deal with the perverted, disease-bearing, voracious bastard who wants to cast his image over all things, eat from every plate at every table, police the world with racist shibboleths and a dying doctrine of marketplaces peopled by monopolies, top-heavy bureaus, and scum-swilling pigs to gun down any who would object?" [165].

"People's war, class struggle, war of liberation means *armed* struggle. Men like Hoover, Reagan, Hunt, Agnew, Johnson, Helms, Westmoreland, Abrams, Campbell, Carswell, are dangerous men who believe that they are the rightful führers of all the world's people.[5] They must be dealt with now. Can men like these be converted? Will they allow anyone to maneuver them out of their positions of power while they still live? Would Nixon accept a people's government, a people's economy?" [169].

"The thing that fixes me best is how the revolution is gauged to operate on the family plan, children with a role, women in the same roles as men, education standardized" [170].

"The family, the nuns, the pigs, I resisted them all. I know my mother likes to tell everyone that I was a good boy, but that isn't true. I've been a brigand all my life. It was these years in prison with the time and the opportunity available to me for research and thought that motivated a desire to remold my character. I think that if I had been on the street from age eighteen to twenty-four, I would probably be a dope fiend or a small-stakes gambler, or a hump in the ground. ['They' don't know it and certainly didn't foresee it, but they're responsible for my present attitude."] [172–73].[6]

"Down here we hear relaxed, matter-of-fact conversations centering around how best to kill all the nation's niggers and in what order. It's not the fact that they consider killing me that upsets. They've been 'killing all the niggers' for nearly half a millennium now, but I am still alive. I might be the most resilient dead man in the universe. The upsetting thing is that they never take into consideration the fact that I am going to resist. Do they honestly believe that shit?" [174].

"The fascists, it seems, have a standard M.O. for dealing with the lower classes.[7] Actually, oppressive power throughout history has used it. They turn a man against himself—think of all the innocent things that make us feel good, but that make some of us also feel guilty.[8] Consider the con going through the courts on a capital offense who supports capital punishment. I swear I heard something just like that today.[9] After the Civil War, the form of slavery changed from chattel to economic slavery, and we were thrown onto the labor market to compete at a disadvantage with poor whites. Ever since that time, our principal enemy must be isolated and identified as capitalism. The slaver was and is the factory owner, the businessman of capitalist Amerika, the man responsible for employment, wages, prices, control of the nation's institutions and culture. It was the capitalist infrastructure of Europe and the U.S. which was responsible for the rape of Africa and Asia. Capitalism murdered those thirty million in the Congo. Believe me, the European and Anglo-Amerikan capitalist would never have wasted the ball and powder were it not for the profit principle. The men, all the men who went into Africa and Asia, the fleas who climbed on that elephant's back with rape on their minds, richly deserve all that they are called. Every one of them deserved to die for their crimes. So do the ones who are still in Vietnam, Angola, Union of South Africa (USA!!). But we must not allow the emotional aspects of these issues, the scum at the surface, to obstruct our view of the big picture, the whole rotten hunk. It was capitalism that armed the ships, free enterprise that launched them, private ownership of property that fed the troops. Imperialism took up where the slave trade left off. It wasn't until after the slave trade ended that Amerika, England, France, and the Netherlands invaded and settled in on Afro-Asian soil in earnest. As the European industrial revolution took hold, new economic attractions replaced the older ones; chattel slavery was replaced by neoslavery. Capitalism, 'free' enterprise, private ownership of public property armed and launched the ships and fed the troops; it should be clear that it was the profit motive that kept them there.

"It was the profit motive that built the tenement house and the city project. Profit and loss prevents repairs and maintenance. Free enterprise brought the monopolistic chain store into the neighborhood. The concept of private ownership of facilities that the people need to exist brought the legions of hip-shooting, brainless pigs down upon our heads, our homes, our streets. They're there to protect the entrepreneur!! His chain store, and his property that you are renting, his bank.

"If the entrepreneur decides that he no longer wants to sell you food, let's say, because the Yankee dollar that we value *so* dearly has suddenly lost its last thirty cents of purchasing power, private ownership means that the only way many of the people will eat is to break the law.[10]

"Black capitalism, black against itself. The silliest contradiction in a long train of spineless, mindless contradictions. Another painless, ultimate remedy: be a better fascist than the fascist. ["Sylvester Brown is ready to die, or to *see* our sons die, for the sake of a street sweeper's contract."][11] Bill Cosby, acting out the establishment agent—what message was this soul brother conveying to our children?[12] This running dog in the company of a fascist with a cause, a flunky's flunky, was transmitting the credo of the slave to our youth, the mod version of the old house nigger. We can never learn to trust as long as we have them. They are as much a part of the repression, more even than the real live rat-informer-pig. Aren't they telling our kids that it is romantic to be a running dog? The kids are *so* hungry to see the black male do some shooting and throw some hands that they can't help themselves from identifying with the quislings.[13] So first they turn *us* against ourselves, precluding all possibility of trust, then fascism takes any latent divisible forces and develops them into divisions in fact: racism, nationalism, religions" [175–77].

"I was born with terminal cancer, a suppurating, malignant sore that attacked me in the region just behind the eyes and moves outward to destroy my peace.

"It has robbed me of these twenty-eight years. It has robbed us all for nearly half a millennium. The greatest bandit of all time, you'll stop him now" [186].

"Black Mama, you're going to have to stop making cowards: 'Be a good *boy*'; 'You're going to worry me to death, *boy*'; 'Don't trust those niggers'; 'Stop letting those bad niggers lead you around, *boy*'; 'Make you a dollar, *boy*.' Black Mama, your overriding concern with the survival of our sons is mistaken if it is survival at the cost of their manhood" [189].

"A brother to his brother Jonathan." The affection that bound George to Jonathan was, for the former, woven from many long hours of solitude. George had left behind a seven-year-old brother, a child in whom he took a constant interest, but a great distance separated the house where Jonathan lived from George's cell. One may wonder whether George really knew who his brother was, but he grew close to Jonathan very quickly when he found out that he had become a friend of Angela Davis, and then almost completely melded with him when he learned of the incredible act he had carried out: the truly heroic attempt to rescue three black comrades from a San Rafael courtroom on August 7, 1970.

I think that we must not deny this sort of magnificence of reverie and of action to revolutionaries, when it becomes necessary for them, especially when the action ought to become exemplary, that is, when it serves to reveal with spectacular brilliance the meaning of a life devoted entirely to opposing a false fatality.

"All right, gentlemen, I'm taking over now." These words were spoken by Jonathan in the San Rafael courtroom, and George, while leaving them to Jonathan, seems to make them his own.[14] It was not a question of identifying with Jonathan, on the contrary: if Jonathan's admiration for George pushed him to imitate him, with Jonathan dead, and dying in freedom—in a "revolutionary suicide," to use Newton's expression—George in turn admired Jonathan to the point, it seems, of wanting to imitate him as well. Perhaps then we can see the intertwined admiration binding Georgia Jackson's two sons, as they helped each other become a defining moment of black consciousness and revolution.

One year apart, history gave birth, covered with the blood of two black Gemini.

"A resolute martyr, assassinated by whites." The penal authorities at San Quentin have not yet allowed anyone to learn the details of the real death—I mean the one that happens when the heart stops and the temperature goes down, that moment when a man becomes a corpse—of Jackson's real death. In his book, in his letters, in conversations, he had announced it, one might almost say he foresaw it, so great was the guards' hatred of him, and so powerful, "born within me from the blows inflicted by this society of haves and have-nots, this flame that will not go out"; when the warden of San Quentin speaks of escape, this does not square with the "logic of the living."[15]

It is difficult to believe that, so soon before his trial, resolved to use it for the purposes of a political forum in which he could, in turn, judge America, Jackson would have planned an escape attempt that had so little chance of success—we know, for example, that Clutchette and Drumgo, who were also accused, refused to leave their cells, as did Magee—but his attitude might make sense if, caught in a plot hatched against him—whether in Reagan's consulting rooms or somewhere closer, in the prison warden's offices—Jackson saw that he was surrounded, and, perhaps with a revolver in hand, decided not to bet all or nothing, as the papers wrote, but to rush into the courtyard where he knew he would be shot down by the "sharpshooters" (them again) perched atop two watchtowers. Thus, like

Jonathan—but trapped—he freely decided on a death in the light of day, a sacrifice, or better, a "revolutionary suicide."

These few notes fall far short of capturing or depicting Jackson, who lived on for weeks after his death, from the uprising in Attica to the one in Baltimore, and yesterday, Tuesday, September 22, another in New Orleans.

The goal of Jackson's book, *Soledad Brother,* and of the one that will soon appear, is not to speak only of Jackson but of all the anonymous blacks trapped in prison and in the ghetto.[16] Let us keep this in mind: the word *criminal* applied to blacks by whites has no meaning. For whites, all blacks are criminals because they are black, which amounts to saying: in a white society, no black can be a criminal.

Notes

1. [Orig. Eng. Ed.] On September 13, 1971, police stormed Attica Prison (in New York State) to put down an uprising of black prisoners who had taken their guards hostage. Thirty black prisoners and ten white guards were killed.

2. [Orig. Eng. Trans.] Genet is playing on the French term for sharpshooter, *tireur d'élite,* literally "elite shooter."

3. [Orig. Eng. Trans.] All quotes are from *Soledad Brother: The Prison Letters of George Jackson* (New York: Bantam Books, 1970). Page numbers, which Genet did not include but which I have added, are given in square brackets.

4. [Orig. Eng. Trans.] Genet's interpolation.

5. [Orig. Eng. Ed.] American politicians and military men implicated in the Vietnam War or in the repression of black revolutionary movements.

6. [Orig. Eng. Trans.] The sentence in brackets is not in the text of Jackson's letter (as published in the 1970 edition). I have translated it from Genet's French.

7. [Orig. Eng. Trans.] Beginning with this sentence, and ending with ". . . racism, nationalism, religions," Genet quotes a long passage from one of Jackson's letters in its entirety, except for four sentences that I have indicated in the notes.

8. [Orig. Eng. Trans.] The following sentence was omitted from Genet's quotation: "Think of how the people of the lower classes weigh themselves against the men who rule."

9. [Orig. Eng. Trans.] The following sentence was omitted from Genet's quotation: "Look how long Hershey ran Selective Service. Blacks embrace

capitalism, the most unnatural and outstanding example of man against himself that history can offer."

10. [Orig. Eng. Trans.] The following sentence was omitted from Genet's quotation: "Fat Rat Daley has ordered all looters shot."

11. [Orig. Eng. Trans.] This sentence is not in Jackson's published letter.

12. [Orig. Eng. Ed.] The editors of the original booklet added the following note identifying Bill Cosby: "Black actor and comedian who played a secret agent working with another white agent in a television series. It is usually the white who wins the day, and it is always the white who wins the heart of the white woman at the end of the episode." [The following sentence was omitted from Genet's quotation: "I Spy was certainly programmed to a child's mentality."—Orig. Eng. Trans.]

13. [Orig. Eng. Trans.] Collaborator or traitor; the word comes from the name of Major Vidkun Quisling (1887–1945), a Norwegian army officer and diplomat who collaborated with the German occupying force in Norway.

14. [Orig. Eng. Trans.] George Jackson's book ends by quoting these words of his brother.

15. [Orig. Eng. Ed.] An indirect reference to the work by François Jacob, *La Logique du vivant,* published in January 1971 by Éditions Gallimard (English trans. *The Logic of Life,* trans. Berry E. Spillman [Princeton, N.J.: Princeton University Press, 1993]).

16. [Orig. Eng. Ed.] George Jackson was working on a second book when he was killed. It was never completed. It was published in 1972 by Random House under the title *Blood in My Eye.*

The Assassination Coverup, After the Assassination, and Jackson's Place in the Prison Movement

GROUPE D'INFORMATION SUR LES PRISONS (GIP)

Part II of Intolérable 3. L'assassinat de George Jackson. *Though unsigned, this section of the booklet is attributed to Michel Foucault, Catherine von Bülow, Gilles Deleuze, and Daniel Defert. The original translation, "The Masked Assassin," and notes by Sirene Harb with editorial notes by Joy James appears in* Warfare in the American Homeland: Policing and Prison in a Penal Democracy, *ed. Joy James (Durham, N.C.: Duke University Press, 2007), 140–60. The translation has been revised for this volume.*

The Assassination Coverup

For a number of weeks, American newspapers have published articles about Jackson's death. Many discrepancies exist between all, or almost all, of these articles. Impossibilities and contradictions appear at every stage. Sometimes the events start at 3:10 p.m., other times at 2:25 p.m. Sometimes the revolver is a 9 mm; other times a .38 caliber. Sometimes Jackson wore a wig; other times he did not. On Saturday, the whole event was described as a thirty-second blaze; on Monday, it became a long massacre of thirty minutes.

Most of this information comes directly from the penitentiary administration. A man whose account of his neighbor's death was half as incongruous as the one of Jackson's death given by the warden of San Quentin would be immediately accused of the crime. But this won't happen to the warden of San Quentin.

Jackson has already said it: What is happening in the prisons is war, a war having other fronts in the black ghettos, the army, and the courts. There was a time when a combatant in prison was a soldier outside of combat. For the ruling power, prison was, after murder, the most effective weapon against its adversaries. Today, the imprisoned revolutionary militants and the common-law prisoners, who became revolutionaries specifically during their detention, paved the way for the war front to extend inside prisons. This combat is terribly mismatched since all of the weapons (as can be noted from the recent events in Attica) are in the hands of one party. Despite this fact, such a combat worries the American administration, since it has become clear that court sentences will not be able to stop it. Scandalous verdicts have transformed the prisoners into combatants and, in turn, the combat in prisons has rendered court sentences derisory, whatever they might be. At this stage, the ruling power is left with one resort: murder.

Jackson's murder will never be prosecuted by the American justice system. No court will actually try to find out what happened: It was an act of war. And what the ruling power, the administration of the penitentiary, and the reactionary newspapers have published must be considered as "war communiqués."

This means that they fulfill some tactical exigencies; they serve a specific purpose; and they outwardly extend the battle being waged on the internal front.

It is therefore pointless to try to find out what is more or less accurate in the communiqués of the administration. Rather, it is sufficient to know the purpose this or that statement would serve and what the administration sought to achieve and gain through its use.

A few hours after Jackson's death, Jim Park, associate warden of the prison, gave the first version of the events:

—Everything happened in thirty seconds. It was 3:10 in the afternoon—that is, "a little more than an hour after the end of visiting time."

—The incident took place in the maximum-security cellblock of the prison, where the "worst of the incorrigibles" are locked up. Seventeen to twenty prisoners were involved in it; among them were Jackson, the other two Soledad Brothers ([Fleeta] Drumgo and [John] Clutchette), and [Ruchell] Magee (implicated, along with Angela Davis, in the events of August 7, 1970).[1]

—"What exactly was Jackson's role? Was he the leader?" Jim Park was asked. "He was the first to leave his prison cell, and he had a revolver in his hand. You can draw your own conclusions."

—This revolver was a .38 caliber. We don't know if he used it or not. Anyway, the five victims (three guards, two white prisoners) were stabbed with knives, which were either smuggled in or fabricated on-site. Two other guards were injured in the same way.

—Less than one minute after the beginning of the riot, Jackson fled the maximum-security cellblock, running. [Johnny] Spain, another prisoner, was with him. Jackson was immediately shot down, Spain was slightly wounded.

—The guards only fired one or two shots. The remaining ones (some thirty or so) were intended to warn the prisoners and force them to go out and lie down in the yard.

What are the purposes that this first version serves?

To depict an abrupt, violent, and absurd riot, without cause or precise goal, and a prompt and flawless response by the police.

But this was merely a hasty first operation, designed to address the most pressing issues. Other operations were necessary, and they were enacted over the subsequent days. Undoubtedly, the American administration needed Jackson's death: he was the principal figure of the revolutionary movement in the prisons; thus, it was necessary to eliminate him. But this administration feared that his assassination would only provoke an explosion, which would, in turn, reinforce the revolutionaries. Consequently, there was a series of operations, which took the form of communiqués, news reports, and disclosures. Their goal was the manipulation of public opinion—at least, that of the people who were still "undecided"—and to prepare a certain number of repressive measures. This counteroffensive tactic aimed to achieve five goals:

1. Compromise those black and white lawyers who provide legal and political assistance to the prisoners.
2. Plant the seeds of suspicion about the complicity of the entire black community.
3. Present the guards, whose reputation had been sullied, in a more positive light.
4. Destroy the unified front of resistance formed by black and white prisoners.

5. Detract from the prestige of the black figures who led the struggle in the prisons, along with common-law prisoners and political prisoners.

First Operation: "The Suspect Lawyer"

The plan is obvious: Jackson's death must be directly linked to a visit, a lawyer's visit—a lawyer who had ties with blacks and radicals and who, acting as an illegal courier, must have provided the instruments of the drama.

1. The Timetable

According to the first version, the riot started at 3:10 p.m., an hour after the end of visiting time. This is also the chronology reported by *The Oregonian* of August 23.

But:

—The events "started immediately after the end of visiting time" (*New York Times*, August 23).

—The events took place at 3:10 p.m., "at the time when the visits were over" (*San Francisco Examiner*,[2] August 24).

—At 2:35 p.m., Jackson was led back to the maximum-security cellblock, and the events started at that specific moment (*San Francisco Chronicle*, August 24).

—At 2:27 p.m., Guard De Leon signed the log confirming that Jackson had just been led back to the maximum-security cellblock. Jackson pulled out his revolver a few seconds later (*New York Times*, September 3).

2. The Revolver Smuggled In

—Park declares: "Apparently a gun was introduced" (*San Francisco Chronicle* and *San Francisco Examiner*, August 22).

—Nelson, warden of San Quentin State Prison, revealed that Jackson had received a visit on Saturday, August 21, at the beginning of the afternoon. Nelson did not want to reveal the identity or the profession of the visitor, but in a "slip of the tongue," he spoke of the table that separated Jackson from the "attorney." Nelson "supposed" that the visitor smuggled the revolver in. "But how was it possible," Nelson was asked, "for the visitor carrying a gun to go through the metal detector?" He replied, "In life, anything is possible" (*New York Times*, August 23).

—The officials disclose the name of the lawyer: Stephen Bingham. He is young, white, and progressive; he participated in a number of sit-ins at Berkeley, collaborated with Martin Luther King Jr., and, in March 1970, defended three men accused of violence against an agent during a court session in the trial of the Soledad Brothers (*San Francisco Chronicle,* August 23, and *San Francisco Examiner,* August 24).

—Bingham arrived at San Quentin at two in the afternoon, with a young woman who registered under the name Anderson. The young woman had a briefcase. Since she was denied access to the visiting area, she gave the briefcase to Bingham. When he entered the visiting area with the briefcase, the metal detector went off. The briefcase was opened, and it contained an apparently functional tape recorder. Some working parts had been taken out of the machine to conceal a gun (*San Francisco Chronicle,* August 24).

—Bingham and the young woman entered the visiting area together and spoke with Jackson. It is noted that the young woman is in communication with a female lawyer from the East Bay (*San Francisco Examiner,* August 24).

—The address given by the young woman is that of the Oakland chapter of the Black Panthers (*San Francisco Chronicle,* August 24).

—The address of the young woman is 2230 10th Street, Berkeley (*San Francisco Examiner,* August 25).

—The revolver had been purchased by the Black Panthers in Reno (*San Francisco Examiner,* August 23).

—Bingham and his companion had arrived at San Quentin at 10:15 in the morning. Since Bingham was not Jackson's official defense attorney, he had to get a visit permit, but Miss Anderson was denied one. Bingham met with Jackson in the visiting area at 1:25 p.m. (*New York Times,* September 3).

—During this meeting, Bingham gave Jackson not only the revolver but also two ammunition clips and a wig (*New York Times,* September 3).

—Bingham completely disappeared; Bales, the prosecutor, officially charged him with five murders on the basis of a California state law that does not discriminate between perpetrators of crimes and their accomplices (*New York Times,* September 3).

Second Operation: "The Black Conspiracy"

This time, it is a matter of demonstrating that, in this war waged in prisons, the entire black community must be considered suspect; the women and children are combatants disguised as civilians.

—The authorities reported an escape plan that they had "discovered." A former prisoner [James E. Carr] who was Jackson's cellmate sent Jackson a letter through a lawyer. Jackson had written a response on the back of the letter. The former prisoner slipped the letter in his pocket. At the cleaners, an employee found the letter and gave it to the officials, who, "to avoid raising his [Carr's] suspicion," made a copy of it and then put it back in the pocket (*San Francisco Examiner,* August 24).

—In this letter, Jackson asked his sisters to "hide pistols in the heels of their shoes"; he enclosed a "diagram to show them how to get past the metal detector." Furthermore, the women must have hidden tubes of explosives in their vaginas. Jackson also indicated how they could interrupt the prison's electrical current and he requested that he be picked up in "a four-wheel drive vehicle."

On August 1, Jackson had actually received a visit from two of his sisters with three children. Park, the associate warden of San Quentin, thinks that this was a "trial balloon"; it was done to "test the effectiveness of the metal detector." In fact, one of the children was discovered to have metal buckles on his shoes and his belt. All three carried concealed toy pistols.

The authorities did not at that point report the escape plan and the suspicious visit of the family because, as they said, "they did not want to cause problems for Jackson," whose trial was due to take place soon in a San Francisco court (*San Francisco Chronicle,* August 24).

—In fact, next to Jackson's body in the San Quentin yard, they found not only a gun and two ammunition clips, but also a Molotov cocktail (*San Francisco Chronicle,* August 24).

Third Operation: "The Nonviolent Guards"

On the one side, the prisoners, all the weapons, all the tricks, all the violence; on the other, the guards, unarmed, powerless, and easygoing. The blacks are waging permanent war; the whites seek to maintain a lenient order. If the guards don't want to be the first and only victims, they will have to resort, as Jim Park said, "to old corrective methods." One day, *they, too,* will have to be armed.

1. The Revolver Exchanged during the Visits

—Usually, Jackson was taken to the visiting area in chains. But "because, lately, he had been cooperative," they had recently decided to remove his chains during visits (*New York Times,* September 3).
—Often, in the visiting room, prisoners and visitors are separated. That day, there was only a table between Jackson and the lawyer (*New York Times*, August 23).
—In principle, a guard is supposed to continuously supervise *[surveiller]* the small visiting room where Jackson met Bingham. It is the visiting room usually reserved for those visiting prisoners condemned to death. On August 21, only one guard was assigned to supervise the main and the small visiting rooms. He wasn't able to keep his eyes fixed on Jackson the whole time (*San Francisco Chronicle,* August 24).

2. The Arsenal in the Hair

(a) What Was Jackson's Hair Like?
—Towering African-style hair (*Oakland Tribune,* August 24).
—An African hairstyle of average length (*San Francisco Chronicle,* August 24).
—For some time, Jackson had regularly worn a small cap on the back of his head. It is under this cap, and not under his hair—or probably "a combination of both"—that Jackson concealed and transported the weapon (*San Francisco Chronicle*, August 24).
—The officials reported a wig that was later found jammed in a cell toilet. They maintained that it could be connected to the events of August 21, but they did not indicate how (*San Francisco Examiner,* August 24).
—One of the guards had had the impression that Jackson wore a wig, but he had never said anything. He only revealed this when the wig was discovered (*San Francisco Chronicle,* August 25).

(b) What was the Arsenal?
—A .38 caliber revolver (*San Francisco Chronicle* and *San Francisco Examiner,* August 22).
—A 9 mm revolver of foreign origin (*New York Times,* August 23).

—A 9 mm Spanish-made Llama (*San Francisco Examiner,* August 23).

—An Astro M600 (*San Francisco Chronicle,* August 24).

—A short 9 mm Llama [Llama Corto], five inches long; not a standard Llama, which is eight inches long (*San Francisco Examiner,* August 29).

—A revolver eight inches long, five inches tall, and 1.5 inches wide. In addition, under his wig, Jackson carried two full ammunition clips (*New York Times,* September 3).

3. The Discovery of the Revolver

—After his return to the maximum-security cellblock, Jackson pulled out his revolver and shot the man who was frisking him (*San Francisco Examiner,* August 23).

—The guard who was frisking Jackson noticed something in his hair, something that resembled the point of a pencil. The guard asked him what it was and, instead of responding, Jackson pulled out the revolver. According to some sources, the revolver was not loaded, so Jackson loaded it and then overpowered the "dumbfounded" guards, who stood helpless (*San Francisco Chronicle,* August 24).

—When the incident was taking place, there was a total of six guards on the ground floor of the cellblock, one of whom was noncommissioned. Three guards were in the corridor leading to the cells (*New York Times,* August 23; *San Francisco Chronicle,* August 23).

—Jackson had just been brought to the cellblock by Guard De Leon. Rubiaco is in front of Jackson, frisking him. Behind Jackson, Sergeant McCray is supervising. Rubiaco notices something in Jackson's hair and tries to grab it, but Jackson jumps aside, whips off his wig, grabs the revolver and the two ammunition clips, slides one of the clips in the revolver, and turns toward the guards, whom he neutralizes (*New York Times,* September 3).

Fourth Operation: The Black Massacre

The American administration has constantly used racism against the revolutionary movement in the prisons. Now, the war front no longer lies between black prisoners and white prisoners but, rather, between all the revolutionary prisoners, on the one side, and the administration (and all those who serve it, be they guards or prisoners), on the other. Jackson played a determining role in this evolution of the struggle.

For the authorities, it is crucial to break this new front at all costs and to reestablish as soon as possible virulent antiblack racism in the prisons. They therefore have to show that the events at San Quentin did not belong to a *new* stage in the political struggle, but rather constitute a return to the *old* practices of savage massacre.

(a) Jackson's Participation

—Jackson left the cellblock thirty seconds after having brandished his revolver (Five men had their throats slashed by "other prisoners.") (*San Francisco Examiner* and *San Francisco Chronicle*, August 22).

—Jackson pulled out his revolver and forced the guards to open all the cells on the ground floor. Right after that, he left the building and he was killed. Everything happened within thirty seconds, but the guards were not able to regain control of the cellblock for another 15 minutes. They found five bodies. When he was asked "why these murders," the Associate Warden replied: "Doubtless to avenge Jackson's death" (*New York Times*, August 23).

—Using an automatic lever, Jackson opened all the cells on the ground floor. It was shortly after 2:35 p.m. "For nearly a half hour," Jackson and a companion carried out the massacre. It wasn't until 3:10 p.m. that Jackson left the building and tried to escape (*San Francisco Chronicle*, August 23).

—In Jackson's cell were found, piled on top of each other, four dead bodies and one wounded guard whom the throat-slashers had left for dead.

—To prevent them from recognizing their murderers, the victims had been blindfolded (*San Francisco Examiner*, August 27).

(b) The Savagery of the Massacre

—All the victims had their throats slashed within thirty seconds (*San Francisco Chronicle* and *San Francisco Examiner*, August 22).

—The massacre lasted 30 minutes. Using half a razor blade, Jackson and the other prisoners attempted to slash the throats of their hostages. However, since the blade was dull, they were forced to use it like a saw. A number of shots fired forced them to retreat to the back of the building; they dragged their victims with them, all while continuing to saw at their throats (*San Francisco Chronicle*, August 23).

—Since the razor blade was spent, a fingernail clipper was used to sever the jugular artery of a guard.

—Autopsies of the victims. Jere Graham: two stab wounds to the chest, another two to the abdomen, a bullet to the back of the head. Frank De Leon: throat slashed on both sides, a bullet to the back of the head, a facial wound caused by a blunt instrument, strangled with an electrical wire. Paul Kravenes: three razor blade slashes to the throat, another to the right side of the torso, strangled with an electrical wire. John Lynn: four wounds on the right side of the neck, two on the left side. Ronald Rane:[3] severed artery on the right side of the throat (*San Francisco Chronicle*, August 24).

(c) The Death of White Prisoners

—The insurgent blacks killed, in addition to the three guards, two white prisoners because "they didn't like them" (*San Francisco Chronicle* and *San Francisco Examiner*, August 23).

—There were four white prisoners on the ground floor of the cellblock. When Jackson forced the cell doors open, two of the prisoners, realizing the blacks were going to kill them, reclosed their cell door, thereby saving their lives (*San Francisco Chronicle*, August 24).

—The blacks killed two white prisoners because they were employed as prison personnel [*auxiliaires*],[4] and the blacks could never become personnel (*San Francisco Chronicle*, August 24).

—The two prisoners employed as personnel had just finished their shift in the kitchen. They remained in their cells. The rebels asked them: "We're breaking out. Are you with us?—We're not against you, but we're not walking out.—Then you're against us." They were killed (*San Francisco Chronicle*, August 25).

—The two white prisoners employed as prison personnel were killed while they were still at work in the kitchen (*New York Times*, September 3).

Fifth Operation: "The Irresponsible Leader"

Jackson was perceived to be the leader of the revolutionary movement in the prisons. For the administration, it was crucial to destroy his body. But it was also necessary to destroy his image (so that he did not live on) and his function (so that no one would take his place): consequently, a narrative had to be constructed that Jackson had dragged the other prisoners into a plan without an exit strategy; that this plan aimed to achieve his own, personal goals; and that he abandoned his comrades in the midst of the combat and attempted, on his own, to escape.

> —A collective escape attempt of which Jackson appears to have been the leader (*San Francisco Chronicle* and *San Francisco Examiner,* August 22).
> —Jackson intended to escape before the Soledad Brothers' trial, which was to take place shortly thereafter. By discovering the revolver in his hair, the guards frustrated his plot. It is precisely at that moment that Jackson triggers the riot (*San Francisco Chronicle,* August 24).
> —For the upcoming trial, Jackson and his accomplices had prepared a plan of action, somewhat similar to that of August 1970. He wanted to use a revolver in court. When he saw that his plan was discovered, he dragged in his comrades (*San Francisco Chronicle,* August 24).
> —From the outset of the riot, Jackson is trying to escape (*New York Times,* August 23).
> —When the alarm sounded, Jackson tries to escape. He flees the cellblock and runs toward the outer wall (seven meters high). He is killed by two bullets: one to the head, the other to the heel (*San Francisco Chronicle,* August 24).

After the Assassination

On August 23, the preliminary hearing for the events at Soledad took place. A bulletproof sheet of glass separated the public, including the journalists, from the court. Regarding the attitude of the judges, the public was so outraged that they pounded on the glass, yelling, "Pigs," "Pigs." Two days later, Cluchette's mother was expelled from the court after a crisis that the authorities described as hysterical; blacks and police clashed in the courtroom. On August 23, Cluchette submitted to the lawyers a petition signed by twenty-six prisoners of San Quentin who had witnessed the drama on Saturday. The petition was written on the back of a greeting card sent to one of them and bearing the inscription, "I live to love you." On several occasions, the petition was rejected by the judges, who considered it inadmissible. Lawyers read it to the public and the press outside the courtroom. The petition reported Jackson's assassination:

> We, the undersigned, are all held in solitary due to the suffering and injury, both physical and moral, inflicted upon us by the agents of the prison warden, Louis S. Nelson. Warden Nelson and Deputy Warden James L. Park, by means of their agents, killed a man named George Jackson and plotted the murder of the undersigned who refused to take part in the state officials' conspiracy.

The text continues, recounting instances of physical cruelty and torture. It calls for investigation and protection. Lawyers who were able to see some of the prisoners in the maximum-security cellblock confirmed that Ruchell Magee was also in a very bad state.

The prisoners also succeeded in leaking a longer text to the outside:

> We, the twenty-seven prisoner-slaves—black, brown, and white all together—of the maximum-security cellblock at San Quentin, are the victims of an assassination conspiracy, just as our comrade G. L. Jackson was assassinated on August 21.
>
> The scene had been staged to suggest an escape attempt, but it was a conspiracy to assassinate the Soledad Brothers, and with them Ruchell Magee and the rest of the freedom fighters . . . Since August 21, the twenty-seven of us have experienced fascism in its cruelest form. We have been subjected to all sorts of brutality; we have been kicked and beaten with clubs, tortured with lit cigarettes and needles; we have been abused, spat on, dragged on the ground, etc. All of this while we are chained up like animals, spread naked on the grass . . . Our lives are threatened every day: we will be poisoned, asphyxiated; we will never leave the maximum-security cellblock alive; we will never receive a trial; and our lawyers will not be able to come to our aid because they too will be killed, etc. Here there are

comrades—black, brown, and white—who don't belong to any particular political organization. All that we are asking for is the support of the people in our daily struggle. Among us, there are men who don't read Marx, Lenin, Engels, or Mao; there are some who cannot even read a single sentence. What we are saying is that we need everyone's help, whether they be an outlaw, a pimp, a prostitute, a priest, or a doctor of philosophy . . . We are not grieving, we are not crying over the death of our beloved comrade George Jackson. He brought courage to our hearts and spirits, and he taught us how to pursue his ideals. He made the ultimate sacrifice, and his black blood is the nourishment that gives us the resolution to fight against the crushing forces of oppression. We will avenge him, because we are the ones who knew him best and loved him the most.

It is clear that there was no escape attempt but, rather, an assassination, the premeditated murder, of Jackson. For some time, the director of the California Department of Corrections, R. K. Procunier, had been spreading rumors that trouble might break out at San Quentin. The guards wanted to kill Jackson *along with*[5] other "dangerous" prisoners to make people believe that there was a collective escape attempt. Jackson, who knew very well that the guards wanted his hide above all, succeeded in reaching the yard, where he was killed: he thereby rendered impossible the "prepackaged" official version and prevented the massacre of the other prisoners. This is what led lawyers and other prisoners to say: George Jackson sacrificed his life. It is possible, then, that the guards and the two prisoners were killed in a brief fight following Jackson's assassination. It fell to Park himself, the warden[6] of the prison, to say: "Perhaps in retaliation for Jackson's death."

Jackson had known for some time that he was perpetually on the brink of death: whether at the hand of a prisoner put up to it *[dressé]* by the racism as well as the promises or threats of the guards, or directly by the guards themselves. And this threat grew in step with Jackson's political sense and prestige. The Soledad case was less and less likely to go to court while Jackson was still living. There were numerous attempts to eliminate Jackson, as his prison letters testify. And as does Allan Mancino's statement of March 19, 1971 (Mancino was held at Soledad): one night in January 1970, Spoon, a guard, and

Moody, a captain, pulled him from his cell and suggested that he kill Jackson.[7] *(Moody then asked me directly if I was willing to kill George Jackson. He said that he didn't need another Eldridge Cleaver.)*

It is within this atmosphere of death that Jackson chose his most challenging path:

"I may flee *[fuie]*, but all the while I'll be looking for a weapon *[une arme]*! A defensive position!"[8]

And always, within that same atmosphere, he seeks after and leads the political education of his parents:

> With each attempt the pigs made on my life in San Quentin, I would send an SOS to my family. They would always respond by listening and writing letters to the joint pigs and Sacramento rats, but they didn't entirely accept that I was telling them the truth about the pig mentality. I would get dubious stares when I told them the lieutenants and the others who propositioned some of the most vicious white convicts in the state: "Kill Jackson, we'll do you some good." You understand, my father wanted to know why. And all I could tell him was that I related to Mao and couldn't kowtow. His mind couldn't deal with it. I would use every device, every historical and current example I could reach to explain to him that there were no good pigs. But the task was too big, I was fighting his mind first, and his fear of admitting the existence of an identifiable enemy element that was oppressing us because that would either commit him to attack that enemy or force him to admit his cowardice . . .
>
> I was leading up to the obvious fact that black women in this country are far more aggressive than black males. But this is qualified by the fact that their aggression has, until very recently, been within the system—that "get a diploma boy" stuff, or "earn you some money." Where it should have been the gun. Development of the ability for serious fighting and organized violence was surely not encouraged in the black female, but neither was it discouraged, as it was in the case of the black male.[9]

This is the point, after the assassination of her son, that brought Jackson's mother to say: "Both of his legs looked like they'd been cut. He just looked so mangled, it's pitiful . . . He said they were trying to kill him. They wanted to kill George, they wanted to kill George years ago. . . ."[10]

Jackson said:

> It's no coincidence that Malcolm X and M. L. King died *when* they
> did. Malcolm X had just put it together (two and three *[sic]*). I se-
> riously believe, they knew all along but were holding out and pre-
> senting the truth in such a way that it would affect the most people
> situationally—without getting them damaged by gunfire. You re-
> member what was on his lips when he died. Vietnam and econom-
> ics, political economy. The professional killers could have murdered
> him long before they did. They let Malcolm rage on about muslim
> *[sic]* nationalism for a number of years because they knew it was an
> empty ideal, but the second he got his feet on the ground, they mur-
> dered him.[11]

The same thing can be said about Jackson: He was killed exactly
when the time came that he had announced and for which he had
worked, when "blacks, browns, and whites" were becoming less and
less mystified by the trappings of organized racism and were instead
beginning to present a front of collective resistance within the prisons themselves. There is something inside us that often pushes us to
believe that the interventions of power, when they aren't just, are at
least diabolical and well calculated. This is not true. Everything escapes power, beginning with what it does, what it conspires to do,
and yet fails to dominate. The assassination of Jackson is one of those
things, a line of escape *[une ligne de fuite]*,[12] as Jackson would say,
where revolutionaries are engaged.

Jackson's Place in the Prison Movement

In the black revolutionary movement, Jackson wanted to be perceived as a military figure. But the heart of his reflection focused on
the links between military action and political action.

This is the fundamental issue over which Cleaver broke with Newton. Cleaver reproached Newton for what he called his "pacifism," his
"legalism," in short, his "revisionism." By contrast, Cleaver advocated
the immediate transition to armed struggle, which he considered to
be the supreme form of political struggle.

Hence, Jackson, the military figure, condemned the militarism of
the weathermen,[13] whose actions lacked preparation and political
support in the masses, and he gave his support to Newton and to his

popular action programs, such as the distribution of snack-meals to black children in the ghettos. Because these programs enabled the black community to organize itself, they would find themselves increasingly threatened by fascist repression. Soon, Jackson said, these programs could no longer even be conceived without military leadership.

For at least two years, Jackson was in charge of the preparation of this military protection, and, in particular, he was in charge of the preparation in the prisons, there where men burdened with chains and without weapons train themselves for war. This is Jackson's grand initiative. It is made possible by two profoundly connected facts: on the one hand, the entire black avant-garde lives under the threat of prison, and many of its leaders are held there for long periods of time; on the other hand, under the influence of this presence, the prisoners, in turn, become politicized. One of these prisoners, for example, when asked about his plans for after his release, answered, "To help my people." Hence, it is not only in the ghettos, in the factories, in the rebellions in the military, but also in the prisons that the hard core, the armed revolutionary leadership, will form.

This is an anticipation that upsets many commonly accepted ideas, in the history of the labor movement, about the prison population.

In the prisons, Jackson was preparing the military protection necessary for political work. Such preparation was still fragile and threatened by an administration that practices systematic murder. This is why, outside the prisons, political organizations launch, in their turn, military operations to rescue and to liberate the most threatened prisoners. In this context, Angela Davis became a heroic figure for black people when she was accused—despite belonging to a pacifist, legalist communist party—of having contributed to the audacious action of support, undertaken from the outside on August 7, 1970, to rescue Soledad prisoners. From both sides of the walls, the prisons' army and the people's army are preparing themselves for the same war of liberation.

In this movement, Jackson occupies a decisive position. He is one of the first revolutionary leaders to acquire his political education entirely in prison ("I have all the theory . . . and I've put my books aside now"),[14] but he is also the first whose political action has been wholly framed by the prison. He is the first to make a class-based analysis of prisoners and to assign them a specific role in the revolutionary process:

> You would be very surprised to see how these particular lumpen in here accept class war and revolutionary scientific socialism, once they understand [that] our real historical contribution was not the African feudalism of the US and other government stooges, but the agricultural community described by [W. E. B.] Du Bois, [Earl] Ofari [Huchinson], and others.[15] All these cats in here are lumpen, that's all I've ever been—it has not damaged my capacity to love. . . . Then all these brothers are similar. Violent, yes, but ninety percent tenderness. It can be seen in the intense longing for community. Even out there, the unconscious one looks for parties and gatherings with a passion, that's a reaction to the absence of community, no family or clan or national ties; so they search for parties, dances, etc., in their love for and longing for community, commune-ity. That's what helps define us as a class.[16]
>
> I have spent eleven years—from the age of eighteen to twenty-nine—caged like an animal for a crime that would have earned anyone else six months or a suspended sentence.[17]

Ten years in prison for seventy dollars is a political experience, a hostage experience, a concentration camp experience, a class warfare experience, a colonized experience.

In prison, Jackson put his theory of communism into everyday practice. He shared money and books; he taught his brothers how to read and write; he helped to develop their political consciousness; and he organized them so that they could resist, by all means, fascist methods of repression and dehumanization.

Daily violence and the permanent threat of death constitute the most rigorous apprenticeship in vigilance, the cunning of war, and class hatred. It's an experience of guerrilla warfare. The people's liberation army will find its He Long[18] and its "revolutionary outlaws" not in the mountains, but in the prisons. The place that Jackson assigned to the incarcerated in the revolution was the place of protection for political work: a military supervision, a place of sacrifice. It was by supporting Jackson, Drumgo, Clutchette, and the three Soledad Brothers that Jonathan Jackson and Angela Davis enabled a decisive step in the support movement behind prisoners.

This support, traditionally, is one of the forms of democratic struggle, which is carried out through marches, demonstrations, and meetings. By kidnapping a judge in a full courtroom, Jonathan Jackson designated the justice system as the indubitable instrument of fascist repression in the USA. This same system, with its white judges and its white jurors, consigned hundreds of thousands of black prisoners to the bloodthirsty screws of concentration camps. He demonstrated that supporting prisoners is a form of war.

Jackson's death ignited the prisons, from Attica to Ashkelon.[19] Prison struggle has become a new front of the revolution.

Notes

1. [Orig. Eng. Ed.] Ruchell Magee, who was serving a life sentence in San Quentin State Prison, was present at the August 7, 1970, trial of James McClain when Jonathan Jackson entered the Marin County Courthouse. Magee assisted Jonathan Jackson, along with the prisoners James McClain and William Christmas, in taking Judge Harold Haley, the district attorney, and members of the jury hostage. As the only prisoner who survived the guards' gunfire, Magee was indicted by a Marin County Grand Jury, along with Angela Davis, in a joint charge of first-degree murder (of Judge Harold Haley), kidnapping, and conspiracy. Magee and Davis filed to have their cases severed because Magee, acting as his own counsel, needed to seek judicial recognition that he had been falsely imprisoned in the state penitentiary for almost eight years. By establishing that his original conviction was illegal, Magee planned to demonstrate just cause for his participation in the August 7 events at the Marin County Courthouse. See Bettina Aptheker, *The Morning Breaks* (New York: International Publishers Co., 1975), and Angela Davis, *Angela Davis: An Autobiography* (New York: Random House, 1974).

2. [Eds.] Between 1965 and 2000, the *San Francisco Examiner* and the *San Francisco Chronicle* shared a Sunday edition, while the *Chronicle* published daily in the morning and the *Examiner* published daily in the afternoon.

3. [Orig. Eng. Trans.] The fourth victim's name was actually Ronald Kane.

4. [Orig. Eng. Trans.] Sometimes referred to as "tier tenders," these are prisoners "who serve food and pick up laundry in the adjustment center [maximum-security cellblock] and thus have some degree of freedom":

"The Quentin Violence-First Inside Account," *San Francisco Chronicle*, August 24, 1971, 18.

5. [Eds.] The term *avec* here translated as "along with" is italicized in the original, but not in INT.

6. [Orig. Eng. Trans.] As stated correctly earlier, Park was the associate warden of the prison.

7. [Eds.] The statement, actually dated March 1, 1971, appears in *San Quentin to Attica: The Sound before the Fury* (New York: National Lawyers Guild, 1972), 10.

8. [Eds.] This famous and oft-quoted line appears in the English original as "I may run, but all the while that I am, I'll be looking for a stick. A defensible position!" (George Jackson, *Soledad Brother: The Prison Letters of George Jackson* [New York: Lawrence Hill Books, 1994], 328).

9. [Eds.] Ibid., 29, 298–99; cf. *Les Frères de Soledad,* trans. Catherine Roux (Paris: Gallimard, 1971), 219–20, 208.

10. [Orig. Eng. Trans.] This quotation comes from an interview with Georgia Jackson, George Jackson's mother, titled "I Bought the Plot a Year Ago, I Knew They Would Kill Him" (*Sun Reporter* [San Francisco], August 28, 1971, 24).

11. [Eds.] Jackson, *Soledad Brother,* 310; cf. *Les Frères de Soledad,* 216.

12. [Eds.] Jackson's phrase here, "a line of escape," takes on significant importance and theoretical depth in the collaborative work of Gilles Deleuze and Félix Guattari.

13. [Trans.] In English in the original. [Eds.] The Weathermen, later the Weather Underground Organization, was an American left-wing organization that came to align itself with the Black Panther Party and carried out a series of bombings, jailbreaks, and revolts from 1969 through the 1970s.

14. [Orig. Eng. Trans.] The quote is from Pat Gallyot, "George Jackson, a Beautiful Black Warrior," *Sun Reporter* (San Francisco), August 28, 1971, 2.

15. [Orig. Eng. Ed.] Earl Ofari Hutchinson's publications include *The Myth of Black Capitalism* (New York: Monthly Review Press, 1970) and *Let Your Motto Be Resistance* (Boston: Beacon Press, 1972).

16. [INT Ed.] Excerpt from a letter written shortly after the death of Jonathan Jackson (cited in *Sun Reporter,* August 28, 1971).

17. [Orig. Eng. Trans.] One part of this quote is from Gallyot, "George Jackson, a Beautiful Black Warrior," 2.

18. [Eds.] He Long (1896–1967) was a Communist Chinese general who, after years of leading a guerrilla army, was named one of ten marshals of the People's Liberation Army (1955).

19. [Orig. Eng. Ed.] In September 1971, responding to George Jackson's killing by San Quentin State Prison guards, administrators, and dehumanizing and racist prison conditions, 1,500 African American, Puerto Rican, and white prisoners seized control of Attica, a maximum-security prison in New York. Eight days after the events in the maximum-security prison of Attica, Palestinian inmates began revolting in the Israeli prison of Ashkelon.

Intolerable 4. Prison Suicides

(There Have Always Been Suicides)

GROUPE D'INFORMATION SUR LES PRISONS (GIP),
COMITÉ D'ACTION DES PRISONNIERS (CAP), AND ASSOCIATION
POUR LA DÉFENSE DES DROITS DES DÉTENUS (ADDD)

A prefatory tract in Intolérable 4. Suicides de Prison.

There have always been suicides in prisons, "self-harm" as the official reports have it. This year [1972], they have been more numerous than ever, and they have an added significance, an additional impact.

1. Until very recently, prisoners killed themselves for personal reasons (depression, health, family concerns) that, when exacerbated by prison conditions, rendered their lives impossible. Many current suicides, however, are incorporated into the life of the prison itself and express the struggle against the penitentiary system; they are part of the revolt among these men who have only their bodies with which to fight and to resist.

2. Until very recently, prisoners responded to suicides with silence and dejection; for them, it was a personal affair. Today, they give their fallen comrades new life *[ils prolongent la mort]* by their collective movements (at Dijon, at Grenoble, at Fleury, at Fresnes).

3. The pathetic promises of reform—which, moreover, have not been kept—are one of the principal causes of current suicides. Such promises work to obscure a more immediate repression: at the smallest protest, there is payback from the Garde Mobile;[1] indifference collects around traditional forms of struggle like the hunger strike. Suicide becomes a necessary escalation. One must not think, however, that these suicides mark an end to the revolts. They

161

form another aspect of the prisoners' collective intolerance and their appeal to public opinion. Each suicide today is already taken up in the modes of combat developed for tomorrow.

The GIP
(Prisons Information Group)

The CAP
(Prisoners Action Committee)

The ADDD
(Association for the Defense of Detainee Rights)

Note

1. [Eds.] The Garde Mobile (or Gendarme Mobile or Gendarmerie Mobile) is a special police unit charged with maintaining public order and general security; it is often deployed for crowd control or riot control.

Letters from "H. M."

GROUPE D'INFORMATION SUR LES PRISONS (GIP)

A presentation of the letters of the prisoner "H. M." (Gérard Grandmontagne), which form the centerpiece of the GIP booklet Intolérable 4. Suicides de Prison, *published in 1972.*

H. M.

Born in 1940.

Placed at an early age in the IMP[1] of Montesson: "anxious."

Then his family is dispersed, the ten brothers and sisters are separated. H. lives first with an uncle, then with a sister. Feels at home nowhere.

First sentencing at the age of sixteen for stealing some candy. Arrested at La Roch-sur-Yon, sentenced in Paris, 15th Chamber, in December 1959. In January 1961, sentenced in Paris, 15th Chamber, for stealing a scooter and two burglaries: sentenced to three consecutive two-year sentences. Confusion over a two-year suspended sentence. Suspension revoked in October 1961 following a new six-month sentence for attempted burglary.

A tour of the prisons: May 1962, Oermingen for a month, then Sarreguemines, then Limoges (hunger strike for twenty-eight days), then transferred to the Poissy Prison. Expected to be released in August–September 1963; forty-five days of confinement (failure to pay legal fees) are added to the main sentence. Ten days before his release, "a fight with a guard." Which is to say that one night, for some forgotten reason, he was violently torn from his chicken coop and beaten with batons in the courtyard. Fractured jawbone, from which he retains the scar. The next day, the warden comes to find him: "the guard you assaulted last night has pressed charges against you." He wants to get out ahead of them. Manages to pay the debt that led to his confinement. Debt cleared, he is going to be released. Spends the morning being searched, getting back his belongings, at the Registry, finalizing his discharge . . . "Hold on a second, there's something for you . . . Come in, gentlemen. . . ." Two police inspectors then notify him of the detention warrant resulting from the guard's charges. . . .

He stands trial, never opens his mouth, doesn't ask for a lawyer.

The administration, however, is represented. It takes six months. He appeals. That takes eight. Transferred to Privas, immediately put in solitary (forty-five days?). Upon his release, he spends several months sharing in the life and work of a foster family in the Ardèche, who remain very attached to him. Then, always remaining in touch with the family, he settles into the Protestant Social Center in Valence. Worker in an ink factory: suffers an attack of pulmonary emphysema (he's long been consumptive). Station café waiter first in Valence, then in Montrouge. He then returns to live with his sister. Homosexual fling with T. Découverte of Saint-Germain, and drugs. Soon picked up by the narcs. A new series of convictions.

1971: 16th Chamber, two years + a five-year travel ban, which was reduced to twenty months + five years of travel ban at the 10th Court of Appeals. Transferred from Fresnes to Mauzac, brought back to Fresnes and released from Fresnes last February.

Hospitalized one month later at La-Queue-en-Brie, Henri-Mondor, and Albert-Chenevier. Psychotherapy, aftercare treatment following rehab.

Arrested again in the summer of 1972 by entrapment. Sent back to prison, as expected. Sentenced in the *prétoire* to six days of solitary for homosexuality. He hangs himself.

H. M. had been in fifteen or so prisons.

The letters that follow are reproduced in full (except for names), the orthography and punctuation are respected, as can be seen. These letters, having most often been written under the adverse effects of a soporific, display not only variations in orthography, but, more profoundly, a difference in handwriting, which progressively devolves into a scrawl. They were written just before his suicide.

94 FRESNES 260
(stamp "censored mail")

Dear S.,

I'm in prison again for drugs. I'm going totally insane. I thought I wouldn't touch that crap but once my psychiatrist left for vacation I was lost also I started taking opium again. Please I'd like you to write to me because I want to die I can't take prison anymore. If you don't want to respond to me I won't bother you anymore with my letters. Life won't be very long for me anymore also I'd like to be able to remember that I had brothers and sisters and that I'm not alone in the world. in any case if I died I'll donate my body to science so no one will be bothered by it.

I'm looking forward to hearing from you, though. Your brother who thinks you haven't forgotten.

Fraternally,

H.

Hello to M.

• • •

(drawing)

A day, an evening
sad, sad and to die for!

Hello my brother!

My one failing (among so many others!) is that I'm stubborn: I love being told yes otherwise fuck it! I wrote you a letter but silence! I keep on hoping that you'll respond to me. Well if you don't respond I won't write a third time because it's my cell mates who buy the stamps and I don't want to waste them.

But when we last met I thought (oh how gullible I am!) we understood each other. Of course you had it right you had a feeling you were talking to a moron. They had requested the village idiot story for a laugh. Don't forget that you'd told me that your door was always open to me. Maybe for me, but not for my letters. You know that of all our brothers I like you the best: I'm not just trying to flatter you, I'm in no position to do that! Maybe it's your beatnik or anarchist side that makes me like you. But I realize that you're an ego like the others. You're seeking your path, too, but despite your anarchist tendencies you lead a bourgeois little life. You're also seeking your path it isn't one that leads to Kathmandu. But I don't have to make predictions about your life. Your life is your life, I don't especially want to make things hard for you. I really loved your house: I think of it as the gypsy caravan from Cocteau's *Les Parents terribles.*[2] I felt good there, too bad we didn't have the chance to talk one on one. I don't know if you read the fascist newspapers that made deceptive and defamatory claims about my case. But the only thing I can be reproached for is for having tried to sell ten slabs of opium to a cop who passed himself off as a Junky.

I'm going to end my letter here since the effects of the soporifics are beginning to make everything funny and I can't see what I'm writing anymore.

Amicably and Fraternally,

H.

Hello to M. and to Tarzan. Make an effort write to me! . . . FREEDOM!

• • •

Thursday the 6th

Dear S.,

I just received your letter this evening and I'm responding to it immediately.

I'm glad that *you* aren't dropping me because, besides my psychiatrist and the nurse who takes care of me in the hospital, I have no mail.

I'm going to respond to your most pressing questions first. To get a visitation permit you don't have to write but go see Judge Roussel in office 76 of the Paris Palais de Justice; that's the judge in charge of investigating my case and only he can give you the permit (you need to bring 2 kinds of photo ID). Mr. Tuffery is also a judge for "junk" but he has nothing to do with my case.

If you want to send me a little money you have to do it with a regular money order.

Monday I was visited by my psychiatrist Doc Trolonge and the nurse in charge of my "psychotherapy." They were both very nice and I was happy to see them. Doc Trolonge brought me a book by David

Cooper: *Psychiatry and Anti-psychiatry*.[3] I think I've already told you about Antipsychiatry. Experiment conducted at Kinsethall[4] in London and that had rather surprising results . . . and rather unexpected for its promoters: Cooper, Laing, and Esterson. They were so far into their identification with their patients labeled "schizophrenics" that they all went on an incredible "trip"[5] (trip means *voyage* in English, but for junkies (or druggies) it's a voyage outside of time and space!).

The Doc has to come back on Monday the 18th and I asked for Laing's book *The Divided Self*.[6] Maybe it would be interesting for you to meet him (no, not for you!) because you could discuss me and the image the family had of me during my childhood. That could be of importance. Because what I tell him myself is just what I grasped of my experience while you are external to my own life but still a witness of my familial context (even for how little we lived together). Well if you want to see him you can call him at the A. Chenevier hospital in the morning between 10 and 12 o'clock. Ask the operator for the first floor of the Pavillon Rist and ask for doc Trolonge or Mrs. Landrieux. Well do as you like. You know the doc is a very nice guy and you'll be surprised when you see him because he seems more like a hippie than a psychiatrist.

I write like a slob it's because of one of my fingers on my right hand, which was operated on two months ago for a ruptured tendon. I was given a "pin" in other words a steel wire with hooks and sinkers (some real fishing equipment!). I had a cast but the narcs broke it to see if I had any junk inside. I still have the pin in there and I write letter after letter to the doctor to get him to send me to surgery to have it removed, apparently it doesn't seem urgent.

You know when you say "you don't like yourself, then change yourself" I could respond to you like R. Devos: "what bad luck I'm still in luck!"[7] To change yourself isn't as simple as all that. If you've read even a little about psychology you must know that there are things that get into your head that are hard to get back out. Sometimes it is a person who takes hold inside you and you want to get rid of it but you don't know how this person came into existence like you don't know how (or are afraid) to chase it off, and that can seem complex and irrational but in matters of psychology nothing is rational.

I know that there are good people in this world, I've met some of them. But maybe it's those good people who have done me the most harm ... But that's another story too long to tell! Well I've had a friend for the last 5 years and that was my "trip." It's with him that I wanted to leave for the Indies and it's certainly with him that I would've left myself behind. I left him in Amsterdam two days before my arrest; he knows that I'm here but apparently he doesn't want to write me. Well he sent his greetings through a girlfriend and apologized for having "lost" my address. Five years with him and 5 years of junk. A mad Junky's life! You see it's stupid to love someone and ever more stupid to feel ashamed and to make yourself cling to the needle in order to forget yourself, in order to create a new dependence that makes you suffer less than the first. Maybe you're able to understand this battle between me and that unknown who is in me and whose presence I can't chase off ... it's the beginning of the problem and it's there that all the guilty feelings join together and that disidentification begins.

I'm going to leave you for the evening because I just took my medication and in a few minutes I'm going to be delirious.

A big kiss and I hope to see you soon.

H.

P.S. The visiting room isn't very cheerful but it would make me very happy to see you. You have to show up at 1:00 o'clock on Monday, Thursday, or Saturday.

P.P.S. Kiss M. for me and say hello to T. and N. if you see them.

•　•　•

Fresnes, 9.15.72

Dear S.,

I just received your money order, thank you. It's not that you need lots of money here since the grub has seriously improved these last ten years. But then there's a drug you can't live without which is tobacco and there's a heap of little things you have to buy to prepare the grub: oil, vinegar, margarine, etc ... So your money order was a welcome sight.

I'm sorry I didn't have the pleasure of hearing from you this week. Anyway I really wasn't spoiled with letters this week. Other than a letter from Dr. Olievenstein (high priest of psychiatry in drug-related matters). A letter of four lines in response to a letter of four pages I had sent to him. No news from the Doc, but he should finally be coming to the visiting room on Monday.

I hoped to see you in the visiting room today because I know it's the only day you're free, but I think you have a lot to do around the house on your days off also I understand full well that you can't come see me. And then you know the visiting room isn't very cheerful! First there is a bad sound system and you have to shout through perforated plastic slabs to be heard. Well I have to believe it's something you get used to because the boys here tell me that they manage to be heard . . .

I had to interrupt my letter because the Magic Potion was just brought to me. Also I have to hurry up if I don't want to start babbling incoherently in half an hour. Yesterday I managed to write to Doc Trolonge but I was so messed up I needed three envelopes to write the address. And this morning, oh! surprise I thought I'd written a letter in hieroglyphics . . . This morning I saw the defense's psychiatrist. He was much nicer than the first and told me that my prison stay would not resolve my psychotic problems. Well I hope that he's going to give me a favorable report because he told me that I wasn't crazy and that my questions and responses were very pertinent, but that . . . well . . . I suffered from psycho-something-or-other-what's-it-called due to an unhappy childhood and a constant feeling of isolation. We discussed Anti-psychiatry but he's old school and doesn't believe their results. How are you and M.? You know I wanted to make leather bags and various other things in order to earn my living because being in the hospital it was impossible to work not being registered with social security but unfortunately the guys with whom I'd undertaken this work made off with my dough which I'd had a hard time getting together and the work that I'd done which was itself a little work of art. But I forgive them because they are junkies and among junkies it isn't uncommon for someone to pull a fast one. The junk made me cool[8] and maybe cowardly. I decided to do Hatha Yoga and Zen Buddhism to make myself even cooler *[plus cool]*. Can you get me Sartre's book *Saint Genet, Actor and Martyr*[9] you will leave it in the visiting room in the Director's office in your visiting room (if there is one). Write me: a word, a sentence but write me from time to time. I'm so alone. Of course I have a cell mate I've known for five years but I'm better at keeping up his morale than he is at giving me any comfort. Of course we like each other a lot and I console him in this moment of despair. He has a fiancée and is all worked up again wanting to know if he is the father of the kid he thinks is his. We count the months to see if it isn't a bastard. But in any case whether the kid is red, yellow, or black he'll accept it because he needs to give meaning to his life. I wish him happiness although his fiancée being an old junkie I doubt it'll stick (or that his relationship because he decided to get married will last long). Well I hope his life will be cool[10] after all the unfortunate experiences he's lived through.

I hope the developers haven't yet built their crappy HLM in front of your garden because it was wild and lovely and it made me happy.

I'll leave off because I can't really see the lines. Kiss N., M., and all N's kids and send all my love to T. who was always a good friend to me and who always intuitively knew how to understand me.

Kisses to you and also M. Your brother who often thinks of you.

H.

P.S. i'm sorry for using the 0.30 fr stamp but it really bothers me giving cash to P&T. Do the same: being a day late is worth being stingy with them.

I had a load of things to tell you but I'm heading for the Kingdom of Dreams: "Dream is not over."[11]

† PSU,[12] CGT, PC = shit shit shit

Cheers

—But who do you love mysterious strange.
—I love the clouds down there ... down there ... The marvelous clouds.
C. Baudelaire[13]

•   •   •

Monday

Dear S.,

I just received your letter with great pleasure. I wrote to Mom, D., and you and I was sure you'd be the one to respond first (anyway maybe you'll be the only one!). You know I write like a slob because I have a broken tendon in my right hand. I was operated on one or two months ago but the police broke my cast during my arrest and ever since then I've had a "pin" in my finger.

You know that I went to dinner at T.'s the next week. He was very kind to me, but, as you say, I always feel like a pariah, a stranger. It's no accident I had your address: I'd asked Mom for it so that I could go see you. But in the meantime I met up with my "junky" friends and tried my own psychotherapy with opium, therapy which led me to this sad place.

You knew that my life was a trap: travel ban and stuck in a psychiatric hospital, it was hard for me to put my life back together. I'd decided to leave, to go far, very far away, to the Indies. I'd written to a Protestant mission to go to the Indies to evangelize. I abandoned this project later when I discovered the Hare Krishna Shivaist sect and I flipped my shit on that trip.

I'm writing quickly because I took my medicine; sacrosanct medication that makes us forget all the misery of the World! Soon I won't see the lines anymore and it'll take me five minutes to write one word. But I need it: it's the only way for me to unwind and to have the courage of words. You know junk makes you weak and cowardly toward yourself.

You tell me that we are brothers yes you I've always considered you to be my brother because you may be the only one who has felt my soul's malaise and who has been able to understand me.

Don't think that I consider your life to be my ideal. Me I completely missed the boat. And then society has the power to regard me as marginal [and] made me marginal. You know now there's a big black hole in my head. I didn't want (like D. said to me) to have money in order to impress others. No, I just want to be allowed to live without constantly feeling a billy club over my head. Did you know that while I was in the hospital some cops from Nevers visited me in order to confront me with some kid who was maybe ten years old? I never knew why because they didn't tell me anything. How can I not be distressed in this world where a host of problems can come my way thanks to the word of a kid (because I judged by the look of the cops that they were ready to give me a good thrashing at the slightest instigation). You don't know the effect it has to be living in a psychiatric asylum and to only feel safe in that place. As soon as I set foot outside the anguish began to tie my guts in a knot.

I have news from my psychiatrist. He wrote to me and said that he'll come to see me as soon as possible. You know he isn't what you would imagine when you think of a psychiatrist: white smock and a somewhat dazed air! No he's a guy about thirty years old with long hair and dressed like a bum. Very nice and we're on the same wavelength. Okay I'm three sheets to the wind. You must find my letter a little freaky and my language a little sibylline. It's the slang of the "junkies" in other words the druggies. Shit I had a load of things to say but I can't see much anymore also I'm going to try to get back to my bed.

I hope to hear from you soon.

Your brother who often thinks of you. Kisses.

H.

All my love to M. The sun is going down it's almost night and I'm afraid of tomorrow! . . .

Freedom dear freedom[14]

HARE KRISHNA

P.S. If you can send me a little money because I'm bereft of everything especially tobacco and that's tough . . .[15]

· · ·

9.20.72
(Give me your department
number and postal code!)

Dear S.,

Another day gone by with no mail! I write a lot but I get the impression that I'm a voice crying in the wilderness![16]

In the last 10 days I only received one letter from my psychiatrist and yet I write one, and sometimes two, letters a day. You'll admit that it's disappointing.

I know that you have your job and that in the evening you must be exhausted and that you're more in the mood to crash on the couch to watch TV than to pick up a pen to write to your jailbird brother. Well when you have a moment write a word, a sentence, and put it in an envelope with a stamp worth 30 (Because[17] there's no reason to give our cash to P&T!). You know that it isn't the length of the letter that makes you happy but knowing from time to time that you aren't all alone.

I just interrupted my letter to give some legal information to a new arrival in the cell. Talking to him is no walk in the park since he's Colombian and he speaks English with a Spanish accent and I speak English with the accent of a Montélimard. Well it's a distraction because there were two of us in the cell for a month and since we knew each other for 7 years we didn't have much to tell each other.

Tomorrow the Doc is coming to see me and that makes me really happy. It isn't really great seeing someone in those plastic cages but at least it gives me the feeling of taking in a breath of fresh air.

I don't know if I told you (I repeat myself a lot because I'm losing my memory with the Manix!)[18] but I saw the psychiatric expert witness. We had an interview that was a little longer than the one I had with the first. Well he told me to be optimistic that he'll do what he can to make sure the court isn't too hard on me because he doesn't think prison would be a solution to my problem.

S. you don't have to be angry with me. I've admitted to you what I've hidden from everyone for years. maybe it's good to have told you about it you can't just put on an act your whole life and there are moments when you have to get something off your chest. Maybe you have moral biases and that's why I asked you to buy me Sartre's book *Jean Genet: Actor and Martyr*[19] maybe in reading it you'll understand what a hell my life has been. The greasers, the violence, then the drugs and the peace and love.[20] I want to make peace with myself. Try to live despite my flaws and adapt myself to life. Of course I know that if I get out everything will be complicated for me but I'd get rid of the idea that I was "born to lose."[21] I want to live healthily and freely. Do you remember your plan with T. to buy a small farmhouse? That's what I'm thinking of now: "a goat and a few sheep, one year good, the next not."

I want to go back to the old dream of phalansterian communities[22] and not the Hippie microsocieties that simply imitate our fascist society. Society has rejected me but I'll survive without it. It can't harm me anymore. Its institutional system has smothered me and I've reached the depths of despair. I won't ask for the leniency of the court but will howl injustice, I'll proclaim the corruption of the police and their barbaric and arbitrary methods. Whatever it costs me I'll speak the Truth, they won't believe me because they're sure of being perfect and upright[23] (it's only practical!). I'll leave off because delirium is just around the corner and they'll use these letters to bury me...

Kisses

H.

• • •

9.21.72

Dear S.,

I don't know if you receive all my letters but I think I've responded to you since I received your money order. But you know my head is a bit in the clouds and I'm not sure of anything. In any case thank you very much for your money order which allows me to smoke (one drug I don't need to give up!). Thank you also for the letter I received today which made me very happy.

Regarding my psychiatrist I no longer think it's necessary for you to see him: I had a little bit of a freak-out over schizophrenia and I thought I was having schizophrenic trips, but these "absences" were only due to the drug. I saw him today and he didn't say anything about it, also I think he doesn't deem this "confrontation" with the familial environment useful.

Where am I? I don't have a darn clue! I told you yesterday that I'd seen the psychiatric expert witness and now I'm waiting for the expert toxicology and psychiatric report.

Why am I here? A drug offense. It's a legal term that doesn't mean anything and is applied to drug addicts and drug dealers alike. Here's what happened. My friend T. had returned from Amsterdam to have his identification papers updated. Naturally he came directly to the hospital to see me. He had a little bit of savings and I had to pick up a check for 850F, a court restitution payment (money they'd seized from me during the incident in '70). With that money we intended to leave for the Indies (a trip we'd wanted to make for 5 years!). In Amsterdam there's a bus called the Magic Bus[24] which shuttles between Amsterdam and Kabul and it costs 180 guldens (270F). So on July 22 we left T. me and another friend I'd met in a psychiatric hospital and who had fits of epilepsy, also I'd had to drive his car. I stayed in Amsterdam for a week then I had to return to France to return my friend's car because his wife needed it to go on vacation and then had to pick up for him 10,000F from his insurance for an accident that made him epileptic. The money was going to be useful for our journey to the Indies because he had to go with us.

For my part I had to collect the check for 850F and get my "pin" and my cast removed on August 3 (I've explained that a finger on my right hand had been operated on?).

So I returned from Amsterdam on July 30. Of course down there I came across junky friends who gave me a taste for opium again and I started to get hooked again because I had some problems with my friend and I sought refuge in drugs.

Well we'd always been set on leaving for the Indies and after having collected my things from the hospital and talked to my psychiatrist I meant to leave for Amsterdam again and then for the Indies.

Two days after my return from Amsterdam a guy called me in the hospital and told me a weird story about a girl in need who'd given him my phone number because she knew that I was an old Junky and that I'd always managed to find her opium. Well I walked right into it because I know how withdrawal feels and I felt pity for her. I'd heard in Amsterdam that one of my old sweethearts had bought some opium for himself also I had been seeing him to ask him to do to sell me 10 slabs of opium (sorry but I'm messed up and having a hard time writing!) to help out a sick girl. Of course this was only entrapment by the cops and the guy he sent me was either a rat or a cop. The fact is that when I showed the opium to the guy three cops jumped me. As for the guy he'd disappeared (and for good reason!). So I'm in here for intent to sell since the sale never actually happened. Well my head is in the clouds and I don't know where I am anymore. I'll leave off because I can't write anymore. I'm SORRY[25]!

Kisses for you and M.

H.

P.S.: No news from D. = Fascist!

· · ·

Thursday

Hello X.,

Another day gone! and one of the hardest because brother F. was rather frightening today. After his little excursion to the Palais yesterday he'd come back a little freaked out and they had to knock him out with a dose of Mandrax. This morning more of the same: he wanted to go on a hunger strike and it took me all day to dissuade him (of course the visit from his Mother and Stonette helped me some). But you know when something's in your head it's no walk in the park getting it out again.

I wonder why they refused to give you my clothes at the hospital: in your letter to F. you aren't very explicit. Let it be for now because I have to see my psychiatrist in the visiting room on Monday the 4th and I'll ask him to have them give them to you if of course it doesn't bother you to go back down there. Maybe I'll have the chance to see you in the visiting room since F. tells me that you may be coming on Monday.

Here I'm sending you my membership card for KOSMOS in Amsterdam. If you go to take a tour over there before October 26, you'll save 5 florins if you want to eat or listen to some good music it's great and not very expensive (it seems you're a little tightfisted!?).

At the same time (always if you go up there to the north) drop by . . . where my friends S. and T. live. I can't write to them because the house is supposed to be abandoned so the mail won't go there. Have to explain to you where they sleep because it's a real tower of Babel where you find Italian, American, Chinese, English. Well they're the only French you can't get mixed up. If you go in two months don't look for it because the government has to destroy the whole neighborhood to build the Metro there. But if you do see one of the brothers, whether S. or T., give them my address and tell them that a word or two now and then would be welcome.

F. tells me that you aren't sending me money, since Stonette needs to send me some. Anyway, my morale is up. I had my preliminary hearing and the guy who was with me during the incident admitted that the slabs of opium belonged to him. What's more I said to the judge that I was the victim of entrapment, since if that cop hadn't called me and sold me that spiel to get me to get opium for him, I never would have dealt it.

Yesterday I wrote to the journalist from Aurore[26] to tell him that I filed a complaint against him for defamation and false statements (that fascist's going to look like an idiot!).

Okay I'm leaving off for the evening. I'm going to try to write a quick letter to P. before my medicine takes effect and I blabber on incoherently.

Amicably,

H.

Cheers

P.S. I write to you using the name X., jr. because[27] I learned yesterday that your father was called X! Is the mail much faster with stamps worth 50 instead of 30?

• • •

Fresnes, 9.23.72

Hello X.,

Why am I writing to you? Because[28] it makes me happy to write and it lets me unwind. Don't think I'm waiting for you to respond. No it's free it's great for my ego!

I'm very happy you managed to escape the army. We're not the sort to go play the puppet in uniform. Me I was lucky I never saw a uniform: they exempted me from service while I was in the slammer saying I was psycho-neuro-parano-something-or-other, anyway not wanted in the army. On the other hand, I didn't want the army at all, either!

F. had your letter today and he saw T. and P. in the visiting room. Anyway he seems less paranoid these last few days: that makes a full week that he hasn't sharpened his knife or prepared a rope to hang himself with, which means he still has a little hope. Of course in the evening he wakes me up because I take my medications with him and I notice he's unhappy. But I too have my problems and still I try to comfort him the best I can, but sadly I can't do much . . . That's it I'm starting to get messed up also don't be surprised if I become il-legible and incoherent. You told me that I wasn't as well-built as you but you should see me now I'm a real athlete I do an hour of yoga every morning and I've lifted 64 kg weights and I've I've lifted 76 kg a meter 82. F . . . does his exercises every morning. he's totally narcissistic and takes care of his body he's the women's idol and he is a real rascal at heart at least that's what he professes. I'll leave off so not not too delirious or I would finish my letter finiletter for today short . . .[29]

Sunday

As you can see I'm doing a stint in rehab! . . . I didn't want to cross out those last lines from yesterday evening they give you an idea of the drugs they give me to break my addiction. I'm sure that I was far more lucid on opium: in any case less incoherent.

F. is dozing this afternoon because Sunday is the most boring day of the week: no mail, no movement.

I'm at the same point in my case as F. I saw the psychiatric expert witness and am awaiting the results of some assessments. Afterward I'll try to request a provisional release (come what may!) or I'll await my sentence unless life becomes too difficult for me to bear and I decide not to wait anymore. It's something I catch a glimpse of each day, but it's as hard to live as it's hard to die.

Okay I'm going to lie down and keep reading my book by [R. D.] Laing, because I'm decidedly not in high spirits today.

Cheers Amicably

H.

P.S.: Could you tell your mother to order me *Jean Genet Actor Martyr*[30] and *Critique of Dialectical Reason*[31] by J. P. Sartre. She can send the bill to Madame Landrieux or to Dr Trolonge Albert Chenevier Hospital.

Pavillon Rist.

Rue Mesly

94—Créteil

She'll get them to the Visiting Room with T. or P. in the name of F. Don't worry I had 600F in my savings at the hospital and I don't mean to confuse you!

• • •

Fresnes, 9.8.72

Dear P.,

I received your letter at midday and am hurrying to respond to it hoping that you'll have my letter before you depart for Aude.

You're right to leave for the countryside because Paris isn't very nice in autumn.

I'm still with F. and I am really happy that he has his provisional release because he's becoming antsy and there are days when you just have to do it. Anyway I don't hold it against him, prison isn't good for morale. Those endless waits make you a nervous wreck: you're always waiting for something: the mail, a visit, and especially freedom.

Well for me morale is higher than last time I wrote to you. My psychiatrist is taking care of me and just saw me in the visiting room. And, something unexpected, one of my brothers (there are 8 in the family!) remembered my existence after 15 years of separation from my family. He wrote to me and promised to help me and to come see me.

Forgive me for writing like a slob but I had a finger in my right hand operated on and I still have a "pin" in the finger; in other words a steel wire with hooks that hold the broken tendon in place and anchoring fixtures coming out of each side of the finger. When I was arrested I had a cast over my whole right hand but the cops busted it to see if I hadn't stashed some junk inside. Ever since I've had my little fishing gear in my finger and apparently, despite all my letters to the doctor, nobody's worried about it.

Tell X. that I'm sorry about his useless trips to Créteil but I'm having problems recovering my clothes. The miser at the hospital doesn't want to give them up without a directive signed by my hand and here I'm not allowed to send the directive without the judge's authorization. He gave me this authorization at my last hearing. What became of it? I don't know[32]?

You tell me that you don't know the Doors but you had their two best records at your place: "When a Music over" and "Strange day."[33] They're the first records I listened to the night of my departure. Do you remember? We had gone to the movies with D., S., and J. to see the most frightening film I've ever seen: *Night of the Living Dead.* That evening when we returned we listened to those excellent records by the Doors. Shit I feel like that happened a century ago when it was only 7 months and 4 days! If you like Rock you should like the Doors because they're one of the best hard rock groups. Sadly after Jim Morrisson *[sic]* died in 71 the group fell off a bit. We'll talk about it again.

Cheers! Fraternally

H.

• • •

9.20.72

Hello[34] P.!

So you haven't left for the grape harvest but that hasn't stopped you from drinking the juice of the vine!

I'm not worried for a second that you're becoming a drunk but watch out because at the moment you seem to be hitting the bottle pretty hard. Believe me in this game you quickly come to seek oblivion or a mirage at the bottom of the bottle. I know what I'm talking about being a junky with a drunk for a father and a grandfather . . . well a whole ancestry of alcoholism . . .

F. read your letter of course because I make him read all of my letters and he does the same. He isn't mad at you though: a little binge now and then sometimes it avoids a bout of depression that could have much more serious consequences . . .

You know F.'s morale was way low and your visit on Monday did him good. He had the feeling that his whole family abandoned him. And then that evening he got the letter from your mother and now I don't think he doubts his family's loyalty anymore.

You know he had me read the letter from your mother and I really I had tears in my eyes. I was messed up on Manix and I told him that he was a bastard and that he was unworthy of such a mother. I didn't think about it at all the next day, but it pained me to imagine your mother so unhappy. You know that if I had had a mother like yours maybe I would never have become what I am (though we never know what life holds in store for us!). I don't want to keep harping on this rather melodramatic theme . . . I'd just like to tell you to give your mother lots of love because she deserves it and because she needs her sons to show her a little affection. I don't doubt for a second that you love your mother! But you see at the moment she isn't having the easiest of times with her sons (F. told me about what had happened to S. and about X.'s problems) and on top of that you have to add F. in the slammer. Okay, I said no more melodrama!...

F. told me that you want to come see me. That's very nice of you, but you've seen that the visiting rooms aren't all that fun. First you can't hear anything and then it's a pain in the ass to see your buddy through that yellow, plastic haze. Well if you still want to you can do it. But then you'll need parental authorization, since you're a minor. Then you go to see Judge Roussel to ask him for a permit.

You must have been really messed up when you wrote your letter because you asked me if I can get permission to see you? I can't really do anything to see you except be released to freedom (which is my deepest desire!).

I'm trying to keep my spirits up but you know it's hard for me to find myself behind bars again and for nothing at that; only to confirm the statistics concerning the arrest of drug addicts. And to get this done the cops use any means necessary. In other words, they had me leave the hospital and sent me a "rat" who sweet-talked me into finding opium for him. And I, like an idiot, all to help a girl who was sick (well that's what he led me to believe), I walked right into it . . . and that's it . . . and here I am . . .

You say that it's worth it to live and to overcome! To overcome you have to struggle, and to struggle against society and its corruption isn't something a guy who's all alone like me can do. But don't worry, I'll struggle even if they have to make me pay dearly for the Truth, I'll tell them the Truth . . .

I have no lawyer and I don't know if I'll get one because I don't want a lawyer who'll come to cry and beg for the clemency of the court. I want a lawyer who'll come to bellow, storm, and howl Injustice . . . Sadly I don't know if that breed exists!

amicably your pal

H.

. . .

Thursday

Hey P.! Kisses from F.

I just wrote a letter to X. and I'm hurrying to write to you because I took my little narcotic made in Fresnes[35] and I'm worried I won't be able to finish my note before the Mandrax's effects kick in.

I learned from F. that you used to cycle which is really great because you'll have a sense of balance and soon I'll be able (what's-his-name willing) to see you fly by at 180 Km/h on a 750 Norton. It's amazing don't you think? you know the first motorbike that I bought was a 125 Motobécane with spring-based shock absorbers. One day I took off the wheel and I didn't notice that I'd forgotten to put back the ball bearings so I broke the hub with each acceleration. ah here it is I'm beginning to[36]

F. is finishing the letter because I can't write anymore. Do you do Vietnamese boxing and do you go to the stadium. I hope so. I like you a lot and if you want to make me happy talk to me about music especially the Doors.

You know I do a lot here to help F. cope because he's quite distressed and he's too impulsive would do something stupid if I weren't here.

Monday I had visiting room with my psychiatrist and I'm very happy about it. i'd like him to continue my psychotherapeutic treatment.

I know that you have records by the Doors so send me songs. Strange day by Gilles Morrisson is my idol.

I'm ending the letter because I'm messed up. The letter from X. arrived. It's to see the difference between stamps worth 30 and stamps worth 50.

Goodnight little ones I'm getting into bed.

With all my friendship.

H.

I have lots of [[37]] for you.

Cheers.

I'm writing a quick little note to ask a small favor of you. You know that I have no one taking care of me and I'd like you to do something for me.

A few days before getting arrested I received a check from a court restitution for a sum of money that had been taken from me back in

70. The check is for deposit only but I signed my name to the back, so it will be enough for you to write: pay to the order of . . . for you to get it.

If you could endorse this check for 850F and send me the cash you would be really nice because you know that other than this money I'm not counting on getting anything else and I really need to smoke.

You know I'm completely flipping out right now also I don't tell you too much about what's going on in my head. Anyway things are going much better since F. is here with me.

I read an article in *Aurore* today. They said that I sold opium to drug addicts in the 20th. I'm going to file a defamation suit because it's absolutely false that I sold opium to anyone at all.

I'll write more to you next time.

Amicably

H.

P.S.: The check is in my passport at the Albert Chennevier Hospital, Rue Mesly in Créteil—This letter will be enough for you to get it. As for my other things I'll have my aide get them when she gets back from vacation.

Cheers!

• • •

Fresnes, 9.5.72

Dear A.,

Thanks for your letter which I was awaiting since yesterday. F. tells me that I shouldn't call you A., but G. Personally I like A. more it's funnier.

F. received your papers and I made him something to put them in. Around it I wrote John Lennon's words: Love is free, free is love; Love is wanting, wanting love: Love is needing, to be loved.[38] If you understand a little English you'll find it quite nice.

F. has the flu and being my cell mate he's passing it on to me.

Yesterday I had a visit from my psychiatrist and a nurse who looked after me. They were really kind to me. They sent me a book by David Cooper on Anti-psychiatry and the stationery on which I'm writing to you. F. and me have visitation at the same time and I was able to see his mother when I met my psychiatrist. Because[39] I want to buy some books and I'd prefer him [F.] to buy them through his mom.

Other than that it isn't so great always being between these four walls. Well being with F. it's a little more bearable. Even if he isn't always the most fun to be around! When he's down in the dumps he always finds an excuse to give me hell and to treat me like a dirty fascist, reactionary, paranoiac, schizo, or some other lovely name of that sort. Me, always stoic (yeah right!) I wait for the storm to pass. Well I hope with all my heart, for him and for you, that all goes well on the 15th. It would make for a great life in the cell (that guy sure can talk!) but I'll be really happy for you.

I wrote four pages of incoherent babbling to Olivenstein and I don't really remember what I wrote to him anymore. But you know I didn't know Olivenstein, at Marmottant my case was always handled by another psychiatrist and I usually went to Orcel and I was his first patient who was a junkie.

F. tells me: M. is writing more then . . . No it isn't a joke he worries himself sick if he doesn't get two letters a day; so make an effort: you write to him more often that does him good and also me, because[40] then he's a little more relaxed.

We still haven't received the money orders you sent . . . worth keeping a lookout.

Kisses, your friend

H.

P.S.: I'm ba . . . ored so I'll stay with you for another moment.

F. is taking his Spanish course and Mandrax the Magnificent hasn't yet arrived. As regards suicide attempts don't worry I'm on the lookout. In any case it's funny he won't be able to jump from the 4th anymore because they installed nets today and it really wouldn't be so serious to jump from the 4th floor only to fall like a sack into a net. Now he'll have to have more imagination if he wants to go airborne.

L. tells me that you need to bone up on your English and your shorthand . . .

I don't know what else to tell you because he interrupts me every other moment.

More kisses but from him this time.

H.

Be brave for 9 more days . . .

. . .

Fresnes, 9.10.72

Dear A.,

F. is taking a siesta also I'm taking the moment of tranquillity to write you a word.

Yesterday evening I had a welcome surprise: a letter from R.! I didn't think it was still possible. I thought that he'd dropped me like the other times. Anyway I was really happy to read his letter. He promised to write to me regularly, well we'll see . . .

F. is calming down. He's starting to get over this sad reality. You can't fight against windmills like Don Quixote!

Today Sunday is the longest day: no mail, no movement. That's why F. is dozing because he hates Sundays. I can't sleep I'm too conditioned by the soporifics and only they can put me to sleep.

I'm not at all mad at you about the money orders I know that life is hard for you. In any case I'm temporarily in the clear because my nurse sent me 100F. I'm not mad at you for what happened with the cops either, they made you do a job and you're only a young girl and you went along with it not realizing what the consequences of your words would be. You know B. who I like a lot (and that's putting it lightly!) was also a victim of this kind of extortion and he also went along with it. When I heard that I didn't want to believe it. But when I was released and made him admit the truth I couldn't be mad at him.

Don't worry F. loves you too and since I've known him I've never seen him as hung up on a girl as on you. Above all take care of yourself if you want to give F. a beautiful baby. You know he talks to me about that future kid as though it was already born. Just yesterday he told me that his kid would want for nothing which proves that he wants to start over and to start out on the right foot. Besides he wants to get clean and that's really serious. But with that you'll have to help because (whatever he says) he's very weak and often lets himself fall into one of his own traps or back into the role he plays in his family. We're no longer in the time when the wife was the husband's slave. Today the wife is her husband's equal and sometimes to make a happy household the wife has to take over his responsibilities. Anyway it isn't my problem and I'm only talking to you as a friend who'd like to see the two of you happy. Like Lennon says: "Dream is over yesterday."[41] When he gets out I hope you'll start a new life. But to catch sight of that new life you have to break with your entire past. I know a thing or two after trying to leave that circle of junkies with T. for five years. But for T. it's impossible! Well I'm going to leave off now and ask you to be brave and to wait. He's also waiting and believe me his wait is more nerve-racking.

Amicably

H.

•   •   •

9.15.72

Dear A.,

I'm responding a bit late to your letter but I admit that I didn't really know what to write to you. Of course your last letter was addressed to me but it was really meant for F. What's more he read it before me!

Of course I'm taking care of him: he's my friend forever and I believe he really needs me around. I'm his confidant and the only one who can comfort him during the rough patch he's going through. It's not always fun because sometimes he lets his fear and anger out on me. I try to be understanding but there are days when I want to run away from him and go to a cell with calmer guys. Then I put in a request for an appointment to change my cell but then I tear it up because he asks me not to leave him.

Sometime in the evening, after taking his medicine, he begins crying and shouting that he's unhappy. I try to console him but it's hard to do because I too have my problems and when I see him unhappy his anguish is contagious. What is there to do or to say at such moments? Phrases like: "happiness isn't everything!" He knows that he isn't alone though! You love him, you really love him with an impossible love!

At the moment his major problem is his family. He has the feeling that everyone in his family (except for B.!) have banded together against him and cut him out. J's letters really are rare and

O.'s nonexistent. He also has problems regarding his *contrainte par corps*[42] which hasn't been paid and risks standing in the way of his provisional release. As for his lawyer, whose fees his mother pays, it seems he hasn't been paid. You know how these sharks are as long as they haven't been paid they don't go to much trouble for their client.

Anyway there you have the problems that are torturing him, in broad strokes. We saw the second psychiatric expert yesterday. He was really much nicer than the first and for my part he said that the slammer wasn't a solution for me and let me see that his report on me would be favorable. For L. I don't know what the result of his interview was but I think that he must've been cool[43] with him too.

That's the basic news. Go take a look over at his place to see what exactly is going on. I'm doing all I can to lift his spirits but alas I can't do much!

Friendly kisses

H.

P.S.: Write to him; write to him as often as you can. You can't know how much your letters lift his spirits.

• • •

Tuesday

Dear A.,

A quick word to give you some news about me and my troubles (and F.'s!). There's no getting used to this prison for me. Despite F.'s presence, it's not all sunshine and rainbows in my brain. I had news from my psychiatrist. He obtained a visitation permit and is coming to see me next Monday. It seems rather strange because it'll be the first visit I'll have in six years of the slammer.

Anyway if I'm writing to you it's mainly for F. because you know he adores you and impatiently awaits your letters all day long. Also the days he doesn't receive one of your letters he worries himself sick. So be kind and write to him, it doesn't matter what, but write to him every day! Because[44] when his spirits are low he sends me bad vibes and I also get down in the dumps for the whole day.

I had my preliminary hearing and my witness confrontation with M. I think that once the experts' reports are finished his preliminary will be done.

I never get any news from T. I wrote to him in Amsterdam, but either he ignored it or he didn't receive my mail because he lives in an abandoned house. If you have any news of him (three lines crossed out)

I didn't have a chance to write to P. also tell him not to bother with my things at the hospital. Given that I'm going to see my psychiatrist I'll ask him if he'll take care of endorsing my check and then I'll let P. know what day he can meet my psychiatrist who'll give him my clothes. I'm sorry I made him make all those trips for nothing and I don't understand why they refused to give him my bags.

I'm not asking you to write me because I prefer you to write more often to F. but anyway if you still have a few minutes you don't know what to do with a quick word from you would always make me happy.

Kisses

Your friend H.

P.S. Send me Y.'s address (the guy I met with you near the university). Quickly

Notes

1. [Eds.] The Institut Médico-Pédagogique (IMP) provides specialized education to children between the ages of four and fifteen who present with learning disorders and/or communication difficulties.

2. [Eds.] Jean Cocteau, *Les Parents terribles* (Paris: Gallimard, 1938).

3. [Eds.] David Cooper, *Psychiatry and Anti-Psychiatry* (London: Tavistock Publishers, 1967), republished in French as *Psychiatrie et anti-psychiatrie* (Paris: Seuil, 1970).

4. [Eds.] Kinsethall appears to be a mistaken reference to Kingsley Hall, which was famously the home of a radical experiment in the mid-1960s that invited schizophrenics to explore, rather than quell, their trancelike states.

5. [Trans.] In English in the original.

6. [Eds.] R. D. Laing, *The Divided Self: An Existential Study of Sanity and Madness* (Harmondsworth: Penguin, 1960), republished in French as *Le Moi divisé* (Paris: Stock, 1970).

7. [Eds.] Raymond Devos (1922–2006) was a Belgian–French humorist famous for his puns.

8. [Trans.] In English in the original.

9. [Eds.] Jean-Paul Sartre, *Saint Genet: Actor and Martyr,* trans.

Bernard Frechtman (Minneapolis: University of Minnesota Press, 2012), originally published as *Saint Genet comédien martyre* (Paris: Gallimard, 1963).

10. [Trans.] In English in the original.

11. [Trans.] In English in the original. This appears to be an implicit reference to John Lennon's 1970 song "God," which includes the refrain "the dream is over."

12. [Eds.] The Parti Socialiste Unifié (PSU), or Unified Socialist Party, formed in 1960 with the fusion of the Parti Socialiste Autonome (PSA), the Union de la Gauche Socialiste (UGS), and the editorial collective of the *Tribune du communisme*; it dissolved in 1990.

13. [Eds.] H. M. here roughly recalls lines from Charles Baudelaire's poem "L'Étranger": "Eh! Qu'aimes-tu donc, extraordinaire étranger? / J'aime les nuages . . . les nuages qui passent . . . là-bas . . . là-bas . . . les merveilleux nuages!"

14. [Trans.] In English in the original. This appears to be an implicit reference to the national anthem of France, "La Marseillaise," which includes the line "Liberté, Liberté chérie."

15. [INT Ed.] The P.S. was on the first page, probably added the next day.

16. [Eds.] H. M.'s locution, "je suis la voix qui crie dans le désert," refers to John the Baptist, who also "crie dans le désert" (John 1:23; Isaiah 40:3).

17. [Trans.] In English in the original.

18. [Eds.] This may refer to methaqualone, a sedative, which is sold under the brand name of Mandrax or Quaalude (cf. the letter to X. below).

19. [Eds.] Referring to *Jean Genet comédien martyre* here, H. M. misremembers the title of Jean-Paul Sartre's book, *Saint Genet comédien martyre*.

20. [Trans.] The phrase "the peace and love" is in English in the original.

21. [Trans.] In English in the original. This may be an implicit reference to Ray Charles's 1962 song "Born to Lose."

22. [Eds.] Charles Fourier (1772–1837), a French philosopher credited with "utopian socialism," proposed phalansteries or cooperative, self-sustaining, although hierarchical communities.

23. [Eds.] H. M.'s locution, "intègre et droit," refers to Job, who was "un homme intègre et droit" (Job 1:1).

24. [Trans.] In English in the original.

25. [Trans.] In English in the original.

26. [Eds.] *L'Aurore* was a leftist newspaper established in 1943 and absorbed into *Le Figaro* in 1985.

27. [Trans.] In English in the original.

28. [Trans.] In English in the original.

29. [Eds.] As indicated in the original *Intolérable 4* booklet, "two illegible words" follow.

30. [Eds.] Here again, H. M. misremembers the title of Jean-Paul Sartre's book, *Saint Genet comédien martyre.*

31. [Eds.] Jean-Paul Sartre, *Critique of Dialectical Reason,* trans. Quintin Hoare (New York: Verso, 2006), originally published as *Critique de la raison dialectique* (Paris: Éditions Gallimard, 1960).

32. [Trans.] In English in the original.

33. [Eds.] H. M. here misremembers the song titles, which are "Strange Days" and "When the Music's Over."

34. [Trans.] In English in the original.

35. [Trans.] The phrase "made in Fresnes" appears in English in the original.

36. [Eds.] As indicated in the original *Intolérable 4* booklet, what follows is "illegible."

37. [Eds.] As indicated in the original *Intolérable 4* booklet, the word here is "illegible."

38. [Trans.] These lines from John Lennon's 1970 song "Love" are in English in the original.

39. [Trans.] In English in the original.

40. [Trans.] In English in the original.

41. [Trans.] In English in the original. This is a reference to John Lennon's 1972 song "God."

42. [Eds.] The enforcement by committal *(contrainte par corps)* is a policy that permits the detention of a person for up to one year because of unpaid debts.

43. [Trans.] In English in the original.

44. [Trans.] In English in the original.

On the Letters of "H. M."

GILLES DELEUZE AND DANIEL DEFERT

*Although unsigned, this text is attributed to Gilles Deleuze and
Daniel Defert. It has been translated by Michael Taormina as "H.
M.'s Letters," in Gilles Deleuze,* Desert Islands and Other Texts,
1953–1974, *ed. David Lapoujade (New York: Semiotext(e), 2004),
244–46. The translation has been revised for this volume.*

Our prisons are filled primarily with young men, "minor delinquents,"
with or without work, the unemployed, social outcasts of all sorts.
As many officials privately admit, these young people have no business being in prison; the Arpaillange Report, still classified, confirms
as much. An expert witness will dare say to H. M.: "Prison is not the
solution to your problem." We would like to ask this expert witness
for whom and for which problem is prison a "solution." Very shortly
after release, these young men are led back to prison by a very precise system of police, criminal records, and control, which forecloses
every chance of escaping the consequences of a first conviction. One
conviction follows another, getting them labeled "irrecoverable."

Young people today walk a fine line between a persistent temptation to commit suicide and the birth of a certain form of political
consciousness, which develops in prison itself. It's not about vaguely
incriminating society, or fate, any more than it is about making good
resolutions; rather, it's about making lived analysis of the personified mechanisms that ceaselessly push them into reform school, the
hospital, the barracks, into prison. Born from solitude, the need to
write to family and friends nourishes this new type of political reflection that tends to erase traditional distinctions between public

191

and private, the sexual and the social, collective demands and one's own way of life.

In many of H. M.'s letters, the writing progressively changes, under the influence of Mandrax, "Mandrax the Magnificent," and it bears witness to the complementary or opposed personalities that were restlessly stirring in the prisoner, all of them participating in the same effort of reflection. The suicidal one won out; it could have been different if penitentiary medicine were not just a simple extension of policing. This correspondence is exemplary because, at once heartfelt and reflective, it says exactly what a prisoner thinks. And it is not what we usually believe.

These letters keep turning over all kinds of obsessions: write me, if you only knew what a word from you means . . . , include a 30 franc stamp, no use giving your money to P. and T., my writing is chicken scratch, my hand is ruined, they broke my cast and won't replace it, "it's perhaps good people who have done me the most harm," Mandrax, I'm losing my mind . . . , FREEDOM, send me books, *Anti-Psychiatry, Saint Genet* by Sartre . . . These letters talk about all kinds of desires to flee, and to live *[envies de fuir, comme de vivre]*. Not an impossible escape. But fleeing the traps of the police which landed him back in prison. Fleeing to India, where he wanted to go before his last arrest. Spiritual flight to Krishna. Or even in the prison itself fleeing in place *[sur place]*, fleeing himself by ridding himself of certain personalities that inhabit him, fleeing like the schizophrenics and antipsychiatry. Flights like Genet, where it is a matter of "staying cool" about the feeling of persecution that he feels rising in him and that he knows is provoked by persecutions all too real. Communitarian flights where the "community" is defined in opposition to the "hippy micro-societies that do nothing but imitate our fascist society." Or, again, active flights, in the political sense, like [George] Jackson, where one doesn't flee without looking for weapons, without attacking: "I have no lawyer and I don't know if I'll get one because I don't want a lawyer who'll come to cry and beg for the clemency of the court. I want a lawyer who'll come to bellow and storm . . ." "I've reached the depths of despair. I won't ask for the leniency of the court but will howl injustice, I'll proclaim the corruption of the police . . . , I'll leave off because delirium is just around the corner and they'll use these letters to bury me." And if nothing else is possible, to flee by committing suicide: "I'll await my sentence unless life becomes too difficult for me to bear and I decide not to wait anymore. It's something I catch a glimpse of each day, but it's as hard to live as it's hard to die. Okay I'm going to lie down and keep reading my book by Laing, because I'm decidedly not in high spirits today" (suicide watch). There is every chance that the warden and the guards said: blackmail, bad reading material, or simply playacting.

H. M. was homosexual. There are some who think that a homosexual has it easier in prison, since everybody becomes homosexual in prison. The opposite is true; prison is the last place where one can be "naturally" homosexual without being caught in a system of harassment and prostitution in which *the Administration voluntarily plays a part in order to divide the prisoners against one another.* H. M., however, was appreciated and loved by the other prisoners without having to hide his homosexuality. And it is precisely due to a report by a guard, following an incident, that H. M. was sent to solitary confinement for being "caught in the act *[flagrant délit]*." We have to ask ourselves what right the prison has to judge and punish homosexuality.

The prisoner thinks he is never given a moment's peace; indeed, it's all laid on thick, with an unfailing relentlessness. Yet even the prison has a prison still more secret, more grotesque, and more severe—solitary confinement—which the Pleven "reform" is careful not to touch. During a previous conviction for attempted burglary, H. M's sentence already complete, forty-five more days of confinement were added on (for nonpayment of his court fees), and then, as he was leaving, he was taken back into custody on a complaint from a screw who, having beaten him, swore he had been attacked by him. Or this: having taken drugs, and begun psychotherapy, and being in the hospital for a completely different reason (viral hepatitis), he was pursued into the hospital itself by a plant who calls him, begs him to cop a few slabs of opium, keeps insisting, and then reports him to the police. This is how they turn a drug user, current or former, into a "major dealer" for police statistics and the editorials of reactionary newspapers such as *Aurore*. Arrested immediately, sentenced to a new preventative detention, a new entrapment, "being caught in the act" of homosexuality lands him in solitary confinement where he kills himself. What is at stake here is not only a social system in general, with its exclusions and condemnations, but the set of deliberate and personified entrapments by which the system functions and ensures its order, by which it constructs its excluded and its condemned, conforming to a politics of power, the police, and the administration. A certain number of people are directly and personally responsible for the death of this prisoner.

Report on an Interview with Doctor Fully

GROUPE D'INFORMATION SUR LES PRISONS (GIP)

On Monday, November 6, 1972, three members of the Association for the Defense of Detainees' Rights (ADDD), Gilles Deleuze, Daniel Defert, and Jean-Marie Domenach, posed a series of questions to Doctor Georges Fully, Medical Inspector of Penitentiary Medicine, concerning the circumstances of twenty-two suicides that had been brought to the attention of the Association. Doctor Fully is later violently killed (and his assistant seriously injured) in his home on June 20, 1973; the murder remains unsolved. This text was published in Intolerable 4. Prison Suicides.

General disclaimer at the outset: "You know, I don't agree with everyone at the Ministry."

QUESTION: Did the directors at Fresnes know the psychiatric record of Gérard Grandmontagne?

GEORGES FULLY: Of course he had a psychiatric record, he had been monitored by Dr. Bourguignon for several years. The psychiatric record would have to be consulted in order to determine if a certain sanction was appropriate for the prisoner. That is the protocol that Brun, the former warden at La Santé, set up in collaboration with Dr. Hyvert.

Q: Is the warden at Fresnes liable then?

G. F.: Yes.

Q.: Was an expert assessment of G. Grandmontagne ordered? Who made it? To whom does the doctor charged with making the expert assessment report?

G. F.: I don't know if an expert assessment took place. But if a death is suspect, an expert assessment is made.

Q.: Who determines that a death is suspect?

G. F.: The prison doctor, of course. The family can request a second opinion, as the family of Goaguer did, which revealed that his death resulted from a complication related to the hunger strike.

Q.: The warden at Fresnes should have been prepared [un homme averti], since the Grandmontagne affair is a repetition of the Cicurel affair, for which Mrs. d'Escrivan was fired.[1] Now, it strikes us that the Cicurel affair proves that attempted suicides are punished with solitary confinement, contrary to the ministry's recent statements?

G. F.: Yes, this is hypocrisy on the part of the prison administration. There is no punishment for the act itself, no one is formally punished for attempting suicide, but after an attempted suicide, for a broken window pane, for having torn a sheet, yes, it is possible, as you say, that a prisoner at Fresnes would be penalized for the dish towel that he ripped in trying to hang himself. I remember a German camp where one was hanged for stealing public property [effets civils], but never for attempted escape. In the case of suicide, there is always damaged material. You can confiscate shoelaces, ties, matches, but you cannot physically prevent suicide; prevention is of the psychological order.

Q.: There was a lawsuit against a psychiatrist, Dr. Pomelle, two of whose former patients killed themselves upon being released from the hospital. Who in the prison is responsible?

G. F.: The carceral system is responsible, it is not the same thing inside as it is outside: suicides inside cannot be compared to suicides outside. When it comes to the responsibility of the penitentiary administration, it's hard to tell, really. It's necessary to find fault— the absence of surveillance, for instance—but it's always difficult.

Q.: In the Grandmontagne case, someone was at fault: the psychiatric record, even though it was known, had no effect on the decision made.

G. F.: If there was a Nuremberg of prisons, I would plead guilty. But are doctors to be put on trial?

Q.: In any case, we should be surprised by the difference in treatment between a prison psychiatrist and a warden, who is never called into question.

G. F.: The prison is not a health-care facility. But I recognize that someone who speaks of suicide should be monitored more closely by the psychiatrist than someone else.

Q.: The cell mate of J.-P. Motto, who hanged himself at Nice on October 15, was depicted in the press as suicidal (two attempts). What preventative measures were taken in his case?

G. F.: At Nice, there is a volunteer psychiatrist. There is no psychiatric monitoring. There are only placards saying, in such and such a prison, there is a psychiatrist. In this specific case, I don't know what happened. At bottom, there is an irreconcilable difference between medical conduct and the administration. The psychiatrist is the outside expert called in to address troublesome *[conflictuelles]* situations; I myself ask that the psychiatrist be concerned with the causes of the trouble *[conflict]*.

Q.: Dr. Rose demonstrated her concern for the causes of the trouble. In what way have you shown her your support?

G. F.: Mrs. Rose did not act like a doctor. I was the only doctor on the Schmelck Commission and I therefore interviewed her: "Did you see this? When was it?"—"No, I didn't see it, but everyone here knows it." A doctor does not make assessments on the basis of hearsay. Mr. Schmelck has not made a favorable impression. The climate was such that the decision made could not be satisfying. But Dr. Girardin was also sacked. He signed blank prescriptions to cover the restraint beds. But, as you know, we are told here that it is the suppression of restraint beds that caused this wave of suicides! Yet these suicides are not significant: in 1960 there were 28; 183 in ten years. The record is in '45, the year of reform![2]

Q.: Do you mean the year reform was put into practice or the year reform was promised?

G. F.: The year reform was promised. But can that be linked to reform? A prisoner just hanged himself after learning of his conditional release. No, it is the intolerance in prisons that is increasing. *L'Express* reports that I said drug addicts rarely commit suicide. I never said that. The magistrates are worse than the cops when it comes to drug addicts. They harass the petty dealers. Their "offense," however, is only the epiphenomenon of an addiction.

Q.: Do you ask for a detailed report of each suicide case?

G. F.: Those reports are on record at the Detention Bureau. As for the measures taken? That is not exactly known.

Q.: A doctor is usually responsible for people in danger. If a doctor here doesn't have responsibilities toward people in a dangerous situation, that's deplorable.

G. F.: The doctor doesn't have authority. He can have someone released from solitary, but nothing specifies that the warden needs to take the psychiatrist's advice. It's up to the psychiatrist to make the first move.

Q.: Do you have the right, as Medical Inspector, to request sanctions?

G. F.: Yes.

Q.: Have you done so?

G. F.: Once. Eight years ago at Beaune for a death by hemorrhage. But there was a whole host of delays; it didn't succeed. But bring me facts and I will file a complaint.

Q.: After a suicide, do you ask for a psychiatric evaluation of the guard?

G. F.: No. There is only a psychiatric evaluation at the time of recruitment.

Q.: The model prisons have a record number of suicides: La Talaudière takes first place; Fleury, second. The mere prospect of a transfer to Varces[3] produced two suicide attempts at Grenoble, both in recent memory. What model prevention measures exist?

G. F.: When you envision the construction of a correctional facility, you really have to know its function. But at Fleury-Mérogis, for instance, the only concern was escapes. The angles were calculated for the sake of visibility.

Q.: We have doubts about the reality of the suicides at Riom.

G. F.: Yes, there was a series of incidents.

Q.: According to our sources, there was the beginning of a revolt. Now, in the most traditional prison revolts, they first set fire to straw mattresses in order to bust through *[venir à bout de]* the gates. What idiot *[ignorant]* had inflammable synthetic mattresses, which release dangerous heat and gases, put into the prisons? Have you at least found a fireproof textile for the police?

G. F.: Yes, one doesn't kill oneself with fire in prison. In the case of Pontoise, the emergency services were very slow. The purchasing department is under the responsibility of an engineer who had weighed these risks. But after a certain period of usage those mattresses become combustible. That was not foreseen. The administration considered suing.

Q.: Many of those who have committed suicide are Algerian. Given their disproportionate solitary confinement and the general difficulties faced by Algerians, what specific measures are taken in their regard?

G. F.: It is true of the immigrant population as a whole. Take, for example, the Spanish worker who hanged himself at La Rochesur-Yon. Nothing in particular is done for them. There is no general circular for them to read. For the North Africans, there is a visitor, special teachers, food.

Q.: Are the Investigating Officers putting together a report on the suicides?

G. F.: The report is by the administration, not by the JAP.[4] According to the Code, Article D 280, the prison must inform either the Investigating Officer or the JAP of every incident.

Q.: What are the regulations concerning the announcement of suicides?

G. F.: The administration does not inform the outside. Newspapers are informed by leaks or by conducting district audits where prisons are located.

Q.: There is not only an increase in the number of suicides, but a qualitative change in [the nature of] the suicides, as well.

G. F.: Yes. The intolerance in prison is growing. You, you speak of an absence of reform, but I don't know about that. I myself am a former jailbird, back in Lyon during the war. I did eighteen years. The basic rules from back then, I'm coming across them again now. Heating, food, it has been possible to make changes there. But not in the basic rules. That's because the general public is very repressive. I see two explanations for suicides today. There was a period of relative calm after Clairvaux and Toul.[5] At that point, there were no suicides. The Minister said to me, "Even so, I can't hold sessions *[séances]* for them on the rooftops!" There is a difficult situation with the administration, out of which often arises both a deflected aggression and a self-directed aggressivity. Reforms were announced. Maybe the reforms will be late or will not be put into practice. I don't know about all that. The reforms concern the *maisons centrales* more than the *maisons d'arrêt*. But people kill themselves more in the *maisons d'arrêt,* these are the folks with shorter sentences.

They are youths. They are the same youths as are in the factories, in the universities, which is to say, they have the same reactions. In the army, certain things are no longer accepted. A great evolution in discipline has taken place. You can't speak of penitentiary reform without penal reform. 50 percent of the people in prison shouldn't be there. Just because those people were sent to prison doesn't make it the prisons' fault.

At the end of the interview:
—Yes, it is the same young people who are in prison, in school, in the universities, in the factories, in the army. No doubt, they put up with less and less. No doubt, the majority of young people in prison don't belong there. No doubt, the warden's power should be limited. I do everything I can, but the support from the outside is invaluable to me. You intend to file a complaint concerning the suicide cases alongside the families? Well, that's good, that's constructive.[6]

Notes

1. [Eds.] Mr. Cicurel, incarcerated in Fresnes prison, was a suicidal prisoner held under abusive conditions. Josette d'Escrivan, a social worker at the prison, protested in a formal letter, which was published in the GIP's booklet, *Lists of Demands*.

2. [Eds.] For information on the 1945 commission, including its fourteen basic principles, see Charles Germain, "Postwar Prison Reform in France," *Annals of the American Academy of Political and Social Sciences* 293 (1954): 139–51.

3. [Eds.] Varces Prison opened on October 25, 1972, and was constructed on the model of Fleury-Mérogis.

4. [Eds.] The Juge de l'Application des Peines (JAP) is the judge responsible for enforcing sentences.

5. [Eds.] Dr. Fully here refers to the prison revolts at Clairvaux and Toul prisons; see Part III, "Prison Revolts (1971–1972)," in this volume.

6. The ADDD has filed several complaints following observations obtained concerning several different suicides.

Prisoners display ON.A.FAIM banner [WE.ARE.HUNGRY] during the revolt at Charles-III Prison in Nancy, France, on January 15, 1972. Photograph by Gérard Drolc.

Part III
Prison Revolts (1971–1972)

Besides the creation and publication of the *Intolérable* booklets, the other major campaign that the GIP mounted was the organization of support networks for the prison revolts that broke out across France in the winter of 1971–72. This was done through collaboration between the GIP's various regional affiliates. This section tracks the GIP's work in support of two of the largest revolts, the ones at the prisons in Toul and Nancy, but it also includes materials documenting some of the broader context in which these rebellions arose and what they left behind in their wake.

The revolts began in response to events at Clairvaux Prison and the government crackdown that followed. On September 21, 1971, two prisoners, Claude Buffet and Roger Bontems, took a nurse, Nicole Comte, and a guard, Guy Girardot, hostage. The prisoners barricaded themselves and their hostages inside the prison hospital and demanded weapons and a car for their escape. The hospital was stormed by prison authorities the next morning and both hostages were found dead. Now, similar hostage takings had occurred earlier in the year (at Aix-en-Provence in February and at Saint-Paul in July) and, as a result, mainly for fear of reprisals, the climate inside the prison system as a whole, but especially between the guards and the prisoners, became exceedingly tense.

The government's crackdown was swift. In October, a general

increase in prisoner surveillance was instituted. On November 11, the Paris GIP responded by holding a large public meeting. The event was devoted to the situation in French and American prisons and featured a film about the Attica revolt, which had taken place in September, and San Quentin, the site of the August killing of George Jackson (his suspicious death was one of the contributing factors that had ignited the revolt at Attica). The event also included testimony about prison conditions by former prisoners and their families, as well as a brief address by its principal organizer, Daniel Defert.

The government crackdown reached its peak when, in a circular dated November 12, the Minister of Justice, René Pleven, announced that the long-standing practice of allowing prisoners to receive Christmas packages from their families—what one prisoner called "the last thing that made us men like other men"—was being rescinded.

A series of hunger strikes in protest of Pleven's edict ensued at numerous prisons throughout the French system (Draguignan, Lyon, Poissy, Fresnes, etc.). In support, the Paris GIP organized a demonstration at the Ministry of Justice in Place Vendôme. The event, which took place on the night of December 4, was the first public protest to include both activists and families of the so-called common-law prisoners and it featured giant reproductions of Christmas parcels with signs proclaiming them to be "piss packages [colis de colère]."

A succession of major prison revolts followed. Two of the most prominent occurred at the Centrale Ney Prison in Toul (December 5–13) and at the Charles-III Prison in Nancy (January 13–16).

Both uprisings followed a similar trajectory: they began as resistance movements—with nonviolent strikes and work stoppages, demands for dialogue with prison officials concerning improvement of the material conditions of incarceration (food, showers, heat, access to dental services, pay, the end of solitary confinement, etc.), and, in Nancy in particular, a call for a general critique of the rehabilitative possibilities of the current penal and legal structures themselves. But, after a determined refusal by the prison authorities even to acknowledge these movements, they quickly became violent rebellions, with prisoners destroying property and facilities, taking, in the case of Nancy, to the roofs to communicate their demands directly to the public, in some instances even wrapping them around stones and throwing them over the prison walls. In both cases, the revolts were put down by violent assault with numerous injuries, casualties, and punishments, both legal and otherwise.

The Toul and Nancy GIP affiliates, together with the Paris group, worked closely with the GP to mobilize around these uprisings. Their campaigns, which were clearly essential as they marshaled support beyond the prison walls, took two basic forms. The GIP created and distributed press releases, tracts, and pamphlets as ways of disseminating information about the prisoners' demands and alerting the public to various campaigns (e.g., hunger strikes) in support of the revolts. The most important of these, *Lists of Demands from the Prisons during the Recent Revolts (Cahiers de revendications sortis des prisons lors des récentes révoltes),* which was organized by GIP activists Hélène Cixous and Jean Gattegno, was published in April 1972. It collected the lists of various prisoner grievances from the prison revolts. The GIP, in collaboration with a legal organization, Défense Collective, also wrote and circulated manuals detailing the legal rights of those involved in the legal proceedings following the revolts, as well as for those taking part in the protests.

Especially noteworthy in the context of the revolt at the Ney Prison in Toul was the contribution of its staff psychiatrist, Doctor Édith Rose. Doctor Rose, acting as pivotal example of what Foucault would come to call a "specific intellectual," produced a scathing exposé of the internal workings of the prison, which she submitted to the French authorities responsible for overseeing the penal system, and for which she was later fired. Her report is included in this section ("Report by Doctor Rose, Psychiatrist at Toul Prison"), as well as Michel Foucault's commentary on this important document ("The Toul Speech").

Growing Discontent

The Prisoner Faces Segregation Every Day

GROUPE D'INFORMATION SUR LES PRISONS (GIP)

This GIP text was published in La Cause du peuple *(an issue in which Jean Genet also published an article on Attica) several days after the Attica revolt in September 1971. Illustrated with a photograph of the Attica revolt, with the caption "Prison is the school of the revolution," this is one of the few published texts in which the GIP evokes the internationalization of the struggles surrounding prisons (Italy, the United States, England, and France).*

The prisoner faces segregation, debasement, physical and mental degradation every day. All of this is racism. Racism is the ready-made *[tout prêt]* instrument of fascist terror. The prisoners' struggle is part of the general struggle against racism and fascism. The life and death of Jackson and the Attica massacre have shown that the Amerikkkan prisons are also sites for the formation of revolutionary militants.

The revolution is also beginning in Italian prisons, which are populated, like the shantytowns of Turin's industrial suburbs, with southern Italians who have emigrated inward. In two years, Italian prisoners have passed from mutiny to prolonged struggle: struggle for the abolition of the fascist penal code that has been in effect since Mussolini (one doesn't know why one is in prison, one doesn't know when one will be tried), refusal to stand trial, demand for an internal assembly of prisoners, decision to participate in the general workers' strike. Easter Monday saw the systematic destruction of the Turin prison, "Le Nuove."[1]

In France, prisons are systematically used for the repression of young people and immigrants. The struggle they are leading on the outside against the racism and fascism of the cops and officers is taking over on the inside (Grenoble). The judicial system has suffered serious assaults this year: the grotesque and always overturned *[cassé]* trials of the State Security Court, the Guiot affair,[2] the Tomasini affair,[3] the first popular tribunals. The political prisoners' hunger strike in January and February triggered the first mass protests, supported by all prisoners, against the entire penitentiary system. August 9: there was a general hunger strike staged by the prisoners at Grenoble and support in the streets. September 1 and 2: there were strikes and threats of sabotage at the prison workshops in Melun.

First victory: Pleven had to grant all prisoners this right, which goes without saying in Attica: the right to read a newspaper!

Notes

1. [Eds.] For an account of the tumultuous history of Le Nuove, including its significant role in a wave of prison revolts in Italy in the 1970s, see Eleanor Canright Chiari, *Undoing Time: The Cultural Memory of an Italian Prison* (New York: Peter Lang, 2012).

2. [Eds.] In February 1971, a student, Gilles Guiot, was arrested leaving the Lycée Chaptal in the midst of a protest. His arrest launched the first significant student mobilization to occur after May '68.

3. [Eds.] Elected secretary-general of the Gaullist party in February 1971, René Tomasini, a previously obscure politician, publicly defended the French police as "the representative of liberty" and insisted that they were never to blame for breakdowns in law and order. *Combat,* a liberal newspaper, dubbed him "Mussolini Tomasini." Magistrates from all over France suspended court in protest and French students, who were currently protesting the Guiot affair, were furious. See "Agnew à la Mode," *Time* (March 1, 1971): 24.

Violence at Fleury-Mérogis

GROUPE D'INFORMATION SUR LES PRISONS (GIP)

A GIP report on the events of September 26, 1971, at the Fleury-Mérogis prison, where young prisoners were victims of violence at the hands of the guards, published in a special bulletin of the Agence de presse Libération (APL) on October 16, 1971. This GIP inquiry is similar to that conducted by the committee of inquiry into the Jaubert affair[1] in June 1971 (cf. DE II, no. 93, 199–203 / DEQ I, no. 93, 1067–71). The aim here was to produce a counternarrative.

Friday, September 24

A day of mourning for the prison guards following the tragic events at Clairvaux. There will be no visitations, no exercise, no activities for the prisoners of most prisons.

Toward midday: the young people of Fleury-Mérogis are rather irritable; exercise is the only activity the administration is providing for them. In *groupe scolaire no. 1* (GS 1),[2] some of them have been deprived of it for forty-eight hours. When the turnkey opens the cell of a young prisoner for meal distribution, the latter makes as if to leave, expecting his exercise. He receives a violent blow to the head with the ladle and a dozen guards overpower him.

Normally, there is one guard per corridor.

"The cries of the victim were unbearable" (another prisoner). All the youths of the corridor immediately protest, banging on the doors to their cells.

The uproar lasts the whole afternoon, spreads to other buildings, some windowpanes are broken, some bits of mattress are set ablaze and soar through the windows.

At 7:30 p.m.: a joint union meeting brings guards and [prison] teachers together in the prison mess hall.

At that moment, the prisoners demand that the radio be reinstated. Some fifty guards, most off duty and wearing civilian clothes, enter the detention blocks *[bâtiments de detention]* against all regulations. Some of them have billy clubs.

They open the cell doors of GS 1 one after another and in fives or sixes pummel the majority of the young prisoners. After a half hour, they leave comparing the state of their fists, some of them covered in blood.

Saturday 25, in the Morning

The prison teachers try to see the wounded. Mr. Negre, the manager of Building D2, denies them entry but states, reassuringly, "There was no other solution, it was done swiftly and cleanly."

Seven or eight of the wounded are transported to the disciplinary ward, Building D3, to the "big hole" *[grand mitard]*. The big hole had been closed as the result of an extremely high number of attempted suicides. Other prisoners, beaten in other buildings, were taken to the "small holes" *[petits mitards]*. Fifteen prisoners were demoted (lost their employment).

Tuesday, September 28

Le Monde reports on a statement from the Teachers Union, which confirms these facts.

To the hole: the youths of GS 1 are sentenced to eleven days of the punishment cell—or the hole (a completely empty cell, illuminated night and day, in which a pallet is set down for the night).

In order to justify this punishment, the guards have to submit a report.

According to what the guards said to other prisoners, the following reports were submitted in order to cover up the brutalities in case a complaint was made:

—attempt to take a hostage (if this were true, you can be sure that the administration would have publicized it);
—nervous breakdown (which would have been treated with eleven days in solitary confinement without medical monitoring);
—political work in the prison.

In the hole, the prisoners were beaten daily. Especially in the evening, when they went down the corridor in order to get out their pallets (tripped and hit with billy clubs). One of them was strapped to his bed for three days.

To protest this treatment, the prisoners staged a hunger strike for the duration of their punishment.

Wednesday, September 29

The hunger strikers are authorized to sit down on a chair during the day, given their weakness.

Friday, October 2

Numerous transfers to prisons in the east take place: Toul and Écrouves. Attempted revolt on a bus, quickly suppressed.

Tuesday, October 5

Most of the beaten prisoners are released from the holes.

The surveillance of visiting rooms is heightened. The families of the beaten youths are systematically sent to the visiting rooms where the administration can listen in (the door to a visiting room had been open while a young man recounted everything to his parents, and someone reminded him that conversations had to pertain to familial subjects).

The prisoners who no longer dared to speak with their families had to be threatened.

The student groups are broken up. Students are dispersed throughout the buildings. They slowly retrieve several study books, but they no longer have the right to group lessons.

These facts call for the following comments:

1. The victims were not chosen at random. They had student status (after BEPC), which was regarded especially poorly by the guards.
2. Some of them, during the political prisoners' hunger strike of the previous winter, had also staged a hunger strike to protest the length of preventive detention (some of them are in preventive for more than thirty months).
3. They had secured permission to put on a play by Jean-Paul Sartre: *Morts sans sépulture*.[3] The rehearsals irritated the guards, who got their revenge by humiliating them in various ways. They had to

perform the play soon and thought they would be prevented from doing so.

4. Fifteen days earlier, the students had been reassembled well before the resumption of courses and the bullying intensified.

5. The first to be beaten was very popular with his comrades, who said, "The guards knew that by beating him, they would enrage us all. It was a provocation."

6. Clairvaux served as a pretext for the guards to settle their scores, just as it had served as a pretext for those in power to unleash a press campaign against the prisoners, which would make them unpopular and authorize any means of suppressing them.

The families judge that, according to the law, their children have been put in prison by judges "in order to punish and improve them," and that this climate of hate and brutality, this constant inactivity, and the occasional mind-numbing, underpaid jobs do not constitute rehabilitation. They ask that a democratic check be established over the prisons.

They have prevailed upon the investigating officers concerned in this matter and demanded that their children be removed from prison and that the judges who incarcerated them hear them out.

The families want to know if the Ministry of Justice [la justice] carries out checks on the guards' brutalities or if it conceals them. They ask for a judicial inquiry into the prison administration.

They are relying on the statements made by the Director of Criminal Affairs, which appeared in *Le Monde* on September 28:

"It is impossible to allow the idea that events of this nature can go on without legal consequences to gain credence in the minds of the guards."

They make use of the inquiry into punishment at Troyes by the examining magistrate, who, after the bloody crackdown that followed an attempted escape at Clairvaux in May 1970, wrote:

"This seed of hate appears to me to be an act that is oblivious to its worst potential consequences."

In fact, we just saw these consequences, after a silent revolt, in the tragedy at Clairvaux.

Are those the only penalties that Pleven will allow?

Will Mr. Rousseau, the assistant warden at Fleury-Mérogis, become the new warden, just as the former assistant warden at Clairvaux became warden after that violent crackdown, or will it be Mr. Negre or Mr. Gomez?

The families and the GIP pose the question.

Those in power have already given a partial answer: the executive magistrate of Corbeil, who went to account for these sites, at Fleury-Mérogis, has already been punished.

The GIP has decided not to let this affair stay shrouded in the general silence.

Notes

1. [Eds.] On May 29, 1971, Alain Jaubert, as a journalist for the *Nouvel observateur,* witnessed police violence during a French West Indian protest and then was himself subject to a beating by the police responsible for crowd control. Michel Foucault, among others, was involved in the subsequent investigation into the event.

2. [Eds.] In juvenile detention facilities, youths are housed by age group and educational level.

3. [Eds.] Jean-Paul Sartre's *Morts sans sépulture* (1946), translated in 1949 by Kitty Black as *Men without Shadows* (New York: Penguin Books, 1960), is set in 1944 and concerns the torture of French resistance fighters.

A Movement of Struggle Is Developing Today . . .

GROUPE D'INFORMATION SUR LES PRISONS (GIP)

A GIP leaflet announcing a "Prisons Meeting" at La Mutualité on November 11, 1971, and presenting an assessment of actions conducted since the first two Intolérable *booklets. During the meeting, two films about American prisons were screened, one about San Quentin and the other about Soledad, where George Jackson had been incarcerated.*

A movement of struggle is developing in the prisons today. Unevenly, but everywhere.

Those in power are trying to conceal it with a vast campaign of indoctrination:

—A press campaign regarding several serious criminals. But they hide the fact that in reality 100,000 people pass through prison every year; they hide the fact that the penal system essentially suppresses the working class: unemployed immigrants, youths who cannot find work—and all those who struggle to change this state of affairs.

—The exploitation of events, like those of Clairvaux. They conceal, behind these individual attempts, an entire series of struggles that the prisoners have collectively carried out against the administration:

Grenoble, August 1971: a hunger strike of 160 prisoners against the intolerable conditions of their incarceration. Strike victorious.

Melun, September 1971: a workers' strike against the guards.

Fleury-Mérogis, February 1971: a hunger strike against the inertia of preventive detention; September 1971: against the brutalities of the screws.

—Systematic misrepresentation of the revolts that have taken place abroad (Attica, Turin, Kingston): they speak only of indiscriminate slaughter; they don't speak of the specific strategies of the rebels, who demanded the abolition of political and racial repression in prison, work for all, freedom to unionize, etc.

The GIP continues the work of political prisoners against the penitentiary regime (hunger strike of January 1971). First victory: newspapers allowed in all prisons beginning on August 1, 1971.

The GIP brings together former prisoners, families of prisoners, lawyers, and all those who want to struggle against the prison regime.

It publishes information that comes from prisoners themselves; GIP members lead inquiries alongside the prisoners into the conditions of incarceration and into the kinds of violence that are perpetrated there.

It supports the collective struggles carried out by prisoners against the penitentiary administration and, on the whole, against the justice system.

For example, at Fleury-Mérogis, the GIP:

—exposed the beatings of September 24;
—helped families come together and initiate a collective action;
—provoked the intervention of lawyers;
—compelled the investigating officer to open an investigation.

On the basis of these experiences, the GIP now proposes the creation of groups of collective action, which will intervene with lawyers, tribunals, and the penitentiary administration, on behalf of the rights of prisoners and their families, who are faced with bourgeois justice.

On What Does the Penitentiary System Rely?

DANIEL DEFERT

The text of a speech by Daniel Defert, delivered during a meeting at La Mutualité on November 11, 1971.

On what does the penitentiary system rely?

Fundamentally, the prison regime rests on division between prisoners. Division along the lines of money, division along the lines of work (scarcity, unequal salaries, tasks of differing severity—as we see in the queues at Clairvaux).[1] Division along the lines of race, informant status, offense (whether theft or sexual abuse), and gang rivalry.

Everything on which the bourgeois regime is built can be found in prison. The foundation of the penitentiary regime is racism, division.

"It is impossible to live with no privacy, 23 out of 24 hours in a cell, without hating each other."

They tell us: At Clairvaux, it is a kingdom of gangsters *[caïds]*, prisoners are armed with knives. This is not the crisis of the penitentiary regime but its success, its truth. It is the anti-Attica, where white and black prisoners perish side by side under a barrage of police fire, never having touched their hostages.

What, then, is the spirit of the prison movement?

To recognize its true enemies: not such and such prisoner, but the screw, the snitch, the penitentiary administration, lawyers, judges, cops, the officers who take us there, the few big crooks used by the bourgeoisie to justify repression.

A prisoner from Turin writes: "We are involuntarily serving the repression of the proletariat."

Prisoners who agree to name their true enemies no longer name enemies inside the prison regime, but class enemies, rightly identified outside the prison. As the prison movement develops, it encounters an external buttress to prisons.

Let's return to the example of Attica.

Last July, prisoners ended several months of discussion and organization with a plan, composed of 28 points, addressed to Governor Rockefeller.

In September, prisoners declared themselves a people's council. Not a common tactic, apparently. In reality, if the administration refused their demands as incompatible with the law, it was because the administration recognized that the prisoners were not engaged in a struggle for amelioration but rather meant to be recognized as a force; it was a struggle for existence.

The proof is that they—whites and blacks together—accepted death in order to declare their demands.

The situation in France is not at that point of development. The prisons are not primed and the most politicized elements are carefully isolated (as a communist, in a *maison centrale* for eight years, wrote to us).

But the growing unemployment among young people and the appalling working conditions available to them ensure that prisons are progressively filled with youths, the most rebellious portion of the population since '68 (57 percent of prisoners are under 30 years old, 17 percent under 21). In those prisons with the highest number of young people, dissent grows. There is a large number of imprisoned draft dodgers or deserters who don't plan to remain idle in prison.

Established last February, the GIP assumed the task not of addressing the problems of the prison, but of giving the floor to prisoners by befriending their visitors outside prison doors. The first information-inquiries concerned the material conditions of detention.

But the material conditions of detention convey not a budget deficit, but a conscious will to degrade prisoners.

"We are men, we aren't dogs!" rang out from every prison in France.

To struggle against current material conditions is to support struggles for the dignity of those imprisoned.

The GIP has quickly been enlisted as a means of bringing together struggles inside and outside the prison. Isolated, local struggles, each of which gathered different people together. The GIP publicized:

—at Grenoble, the mass hunger strike of prisoners; in working-class districts, where the families of prisoners live, they gathered and, for the first time, were defined by their political struggle and not by (infamously) their relation to prison;

—at Lyon, prisoners and their families organized a support action with unjustly imprisoned workers;

—at Toulouse, families of immigrant prisoners formed a support group and initiated a public campaign against the insufficient care of Dr. . . . , a prison physician;

—at Melun, families enabled a workshop strike to be publicized for the first time.

And while it took two years to publicize the bloody repression of the hunger strike and the Algerian revolt at La Santé in July '67 (there were certainly deaths), it took two days last September to communicate to families and the press the beatings by which, on the 24th, the Fleury-Mérogis screws avenged Clairvaux on the young prisoners there. Those responsible have been identified and denounced: Mr. X . . . , Mr. Y . . .

Judges were forced to set up an inquiry and we are following the case.

Some families recently proposed to create their own committee.

These multiple forms of intervention encourage us today to call upon families of current prisoners, former prisoners, and all concerned to create prison-specific support groups and former-prisoner support groups for the employment of those with a criminal record.

These different local committees enable the formation of a real movement

—to defend the rights of prisoners,

—to respond immediately to and counter the beatings in police stations and prisons,

—to abolish criminal records, and

—to get prisoners either to join this association or to form their own interior organizations.

Starting this evening, all those who want to participate in the formation of groups can get in touch with us through the GIP booth, set up every Saturday afternoon, at 73 Rue Buffon. We ask from now on that all those who want to pose questions or bear testimony do so in writing if they wish to protect their anonymity. We are going to go through the audience to collect questions.

Note

1. [Eds.] Clairvaux prison had a large number of workshops. Prisoners rose early, assembled in the yard (ranked according to their workshop), and were escorted to their workshops in single file.

Pleven Eliminates the Detainees' Christmas Packages

GROUPE D'INFORMATION SUR LES PRISONS (GIP)

A GIP leaflet probably drafted on the occasion of the demonstration by families on December 4, 1971, at Place Vendôme, in front of the chancellery, protesting the elimination of Christmas packages. It was the first demonstration to mobilize the families of common-law prisoners seeking greater justice on an issue of daily life in prison. This demonstration followed in the footsteps of the meeting on November 11, 1971.

WHO ARE THE PRISONERS?

BIG REAL-ESTATE SPECULATORS? NO.

For every Rochenoir[1] in prison, there are hundreds of immigrant workers rotting away for months for having stolen food from a Prisunic.[2]

BIG DRUG DEALERS? NO.

For every ex-agent of the SDECE,[3] hundreds of youths, picked up for drug-related offenses, are incarcerated in preventive detention for months at Fleury-Mérogis.

WHAT IS LIFE IN PRISON LIKE?

THE DEPRIVATION OF FREEDOM? NO.

Degradation, humiliation, beatings, and the absence of work. Some occasional mind-numbing jobs: threading tags with string at La Santé, making Christmas wreaths at Fresnes, folding Dior stockings at La Petite Roquette, preparing Amora pickles at Dijon, weaving rush seat chairs at Caen.

FOR WHAT PAY?

One to three francs once the administrative deductions have been

220

made. The prisoner uses this money to purchase the nourishment that allows him to maintain his health. Once a year, prisoners had the right to receive a Christmas package, which improved upon the daily fare, and which for them represented the preservation of an affective tie to their families.

Pleven is eliminating the Christmas packages in order, he says, to assure the safety of the guards. THIS IS ABSURD.

It is a matter of ADDITIONAL HARASSMENT intended to remind the prisoners that in prison a custom is not a right, that a prisoner, even if only accused, has no rights, that everything is arbitrary. Everything granted to them is a favor. Which can be bought with snitching, complicity, and money. Order in prison does not lie in the hands of the guards. It rests in the division that the administration maintains between the prisoners.

THE FAMILIES OF PRISONERS REFUSE THIS ARBITRARY MEASURE AND ARE PROTESTING TODAY IN THE STREETS.

THE PRISONERS ARE PROTESTING WITH LABOR AND HUNGER STRIKES at La Centrale de Poissy, at La Santé, at L'Hôpital de Fresnes, at the St. Paul Prison of Lyon, etc.

JEAN LACOMBE, confined in isolation at Fresnes, has decided to STAGE A HUNGER STRIKE UNTIL DECEMBER 25. IN ORDER TO GET A CHRISTMAS PACKAGE? NO. In order to denounce the prison system, its arbitrary measures, its violence, the role that money plays in it, in order to remind us that in contemporary society it is impossible to rehabilitate anyone in prison.

LET US NO LONGER ACCEPT THE PRISON REGIME.

Special Printing House of the GIP, 73 Rue Buffon, Paris 5

Notes

1. [Eds.] Victor Rochenoir was indicted in August 1971 for his part in an investment scandal. He was tried in October 1973 and sentenced in March 1974 to imprisonment along with Robert Frenkel and André Rives-Henrÿs.

2. [Eds.] Prisunic was a popular supermarket chain, established in France in 1931 and bought out by Monoprix in 1997.

3. [Eds.] The Service de Documentation Extérieure et de Contre-Espionnage (SDECE) was a French intelligence agency active from November 6, 1944 to April 2, 1982.

Demands

Declaration to the Press and the Public Authorities Coming from the Prisoners at Melun

GROUPE D'INFORMATION SUR LES PRISONS (GIP.)

A text read during the press conference of January 17, 1972, organized by the GIP on the premises of the Chancellery and then at the offices of the Agence de presse Libération (APL). This document was republished in the APL Bulletin, *no. 16 (January 18, 1972), in* Cahiers de revendications sortis des prisons lors des récentes révoltes *in April 1972, and then in* Révolte à la prison Charles-III de Nancy *(GIP-Nancy, May 1972).*

We have two means of raising public awareness: the violent method, with which everyone is familiar, and the method we are employing today in drafting the present statement. We preferred the latter and sincerely hope this is sufficient to have our demands taken into consideration—demands that we lay down calmly and with confidence, conscious of our duties as prisoners, but also of our rights as men.

It may be that certain newspapers will be tempted to pass over this missive in silence. But let them above all not forget that their scorn risks driving us, against our better judgment, to violence, because that would then remain our sole means of making ourselves heard. Would they not speak of us then? So why not do so right now, without waiting for the sensational headline that the show of force we want to avoid would give them?

Following the publication of the report of the Schmelck Commission, the Minister of Justice hastened to reassure the public by maintaining that it was necessary to refrain from making a hasty generalization, since the system employed at Toul is far from being employed everywhere. Happily, this is true. At Melun, for example, abuses are nonexistent and the climate between the guards and the prisoners is fine enough, on the whole, even though it could be much better if a reactionary politician, having arrived from on high, didn't make the guards impose an often finicky, superfluous, and dated system of discipline. But we digress. That is not the real problem. No two institutions being designed in the same way, no two having the same internal logic, it is clear that each has its own dilemmas to resolve in relation to particular facts and circumstances. That is why our goal is to go beyond the framework proper to one prison or another. Finding oneself at Melun, at Toul, at Nîmes, or elsewhere simply amounts to carrying out one's punishment in different, more or less agreeable (or disagreeable), disciplinary and penitentiary conditions. But ultimately the vital question remains the same everywhere: when and how will our return to free life be secured?

Before succinctly stating the principal requests that matter most to us, we believe it necessary to explain the postulate that lies at the origin of the present communication: "The reintegration of prisoners into society can only be the work of prisoners themselves." This is a fundamental principle without whose acceptance nothing is possible. To reject it is to reject us, it is to doom the most generous prison reforms to failure.

In witness whereof, we maintain, before all else, the urgent need to institute in the prisons (at least in the *maisons centrales*) a committee of responsible prisoners, democratically elected by the entire penal population of each institution, under the jurisdiction (without any sort of pressure) of the Local Placement Commission, directed by the Executive Magistrate. These delegates will have the right to hold discussions with the directors, as well as the possibility of speaking and making demands on specific issues in the name of all the prisoners, without, for all that, finding themselves taken to be ringleaders. (And for that matter, ringleaders of what? The time has passed when mutinies were able to take on catastrophic proportions. Now, all it takes is the slightest alarm and the CRS is there.) No ringleaders, no sanctions, no shows of force, just dialogue. That is what we demand, first and foremost. It is in starting with this dialogue between the administration and the penal collectivity, through the intervention of prisoners who are responsible and conscious of their responsibility, and only in starting with this, that everything is possible, in particular the discussion of the following prison improvements, which we consider to be so many suggestions that the Minister of Justice would perhaps do well to take as his inspiration when developing the reform that he proposes to undertake:

(1) Application of the law (which exists: Article 723, Article D136 and following of the Criminal Procedure Code [CPP]) regarding day parole. It allows convicts whose remaining sentence amounts to less than a year to work on the outside.

(2) Application of the law (Article 729 of the CPP) concerning conditional release. Which is to say, the possibility of release halfway through the sentence for first-time offenders and two-thirds of the way through the sentence for recidivists. Something that never takes place in practice. Currently, in the Melun prison, even though it is a reform prison, at least 240 out of a prison population of around 480 prisoners legally qualify for conditional release. What are they doing in prison? Why are they not being given their chance? Why is the law not applied on those rare occasions when it is favorable to us?

(3) Commutation of life sentences at the end of a maximum trial period of seven years. (If this principle had existed, it is likely that the nurse and guard at Clairvaux would still be alive. For a man from whom all reason to hope has been taken, whether or not he be a criminal, often has no recourse other than to kill himself or to fight to the death.)

(4) Participation by the guards and the prisoners concerned (in ways still to be defined) in different Classification Commissions presided over by the Executive Magistrate.

(5) Abolition of criminal records, which are no guarantee for the employer and only a hindrance to the released prisoner. In reality, if a wrongdoer wants to get himself into a business, you can be sure that he will be quite capable of producing a fake record and counterfeit papers.

(6) Work certificate provided by the prison administration (under the heading of whatever public service) in such a manner that the prisoner seeking employment upon release can establish his professional qualifications and prove his experience. So that, to the famous question, "Who was your last employer?," one will finally be able to respond without having to explain with a lie or with a gap of several years in one's professional life.

(7) Elevation of convicts to the status of ordinary workers: social security, right to a pension, paid holidays, paid vacation (of which the payment of the holiday allowance would constitute a reserve for release), gradually increased salaries, such that they would reach the SMIG[1] after a reasonable period. (Is it really right to pay a man to whom one claims to have given back a taste for social life 1.50 francs a day? Is it acceptable that after years of work in prison, a releasable prisoner still finds himself in debt with legal fees that he cannot possibly have settled, having been insufficiently remunerated, and that would justify his being imprisoned for debt for up to two years, because the fees exceed 8,000 francs?) It goes without saying that, once remunerated decently, the prisoners would take charge of their [own] nourishment and take over the state's role in food subsidy payments. A subsidy that could even be doubled. Which would allow us to finally have proper meals every day, and no longer just twice or three times each week. This suggestion should, of course, be investigated further and the forms it might take should be defined by a joint committee: administration, educators, guards, and elected prisoners. We do not want to impose anything. We are therefore unable to study this idea without the agreement of the administration. But our opinion is that with lots of goodwill on both sides, a *maison centrale* could very well one day become a real factory, sufficient unto itself. The manpower isn't lacking. What is necessary is to want it, to finally admit the need for a dialogue, to finally admit that we are men, to no longer handle us and make use of us as numbers, to trust us and afford us our dignity. But will Mr. Pleven want that? That is the whole question.

(8) Right to work for every prisoner deemed fit for release, and for him to leave dressed decently and supplied with a sum of money

that will allow him to live and house himself for at least a month (thanks to the holiday allowances, for instance).

(9) Abrogation or revision of the laws prohibiting us from communicating with the outside. We wish to be able to make our grievances and our demands known to the outside without being obliged to revolt (the sticks of the CRS are hard and they are none too friendly when they are let loose on us) or to expose ourselves to grave disciplinary sanctions and penalties to do so. In any event, if our demands are unjustified, the public will see that this is the case. If they are reasonable, why hide them? Reform is not silence. At Melun, at the time when reform was really believed in, there was a newspaper written by the prisoners—*Le trait d'union.*[2] Why was it suppressed? What prevents it from being printed anew?

Mr. Minister of Justice, you have promised to look into the means of putting a stop to the ills that currently reign in the prisons. That's great and we thank you for it. But you are going to do it with the help of technicians and technocrats who often only know about the prison problem through what they have read and what they have learned through statistics and reports bereft of warmth and life. Our propositions are not technical, but they are human. They rest upon an experience lived on the inside. The only experience that matters, as you know.

We are not being remote-controlled from the outside. Our objectives are commendable and we are sincere. The best proof of which is the writing of this letter.

That is why we all express the hope of seeing you take the preceding suggestions into consideration and why we thought it necessary to express this without violence, in the manner of men who, even in punishment, want to be responsible for their destinies and futures. Taking measures, that's great. But to take them too hastily and without even listening to those primarily concerned, namely, the prisoners, is to risk deciding them badly and to risk merely deferring the problem and seeing the events of today break out again tomorrow and for similar reasons.

"The reintegration of prisoners into society can only be the work of prisoners themselves." We reaffirm it. It is therefore in the name of this fundamental principle that we request an interview with the authorities responsible at the highest level as soon as possible. The members of the Schmelck Commission, for example. They will necessarily select local officials, with whom it will be equally useful for everyone to work. Some of the authors of this declaration will then present themselves, as deputized prisoners, before this commission, to which they will put forward their points of view in person. Their only requirement: not to expose themselves to any punishment for the present initiative. They reject the idea of violence as long as it isn't necessary. They hope that the administration will have the heart to do likewise.

We hope that the public authorities will understand the necessity of taking the present request into consideration as soon as possible. We believe that it will be in the interest of all. We sincerely believe that.

Notes

1. [Eds.] The Salaire Minimum Interprofessionnel Garanti (SMIG), now the Salaire Minimum Interprofessionnel de Croissance (SMIC), is the French minimum wage for all adult wage earners.

2. [Eds.] This circular appears to have been issued in the 1950s. See an extract from the 1957 February issue, "Marginales," written by René-Charles and reprinted in *Prisons et Prisonniers* (120 Rue Cherche-Midi, Paris: 1958), 117–18: http://data.decalog.net/enap1/Liens/fonds/Prisons_Prisonniers_1958_1.pdf.

Toul Prison List of Demands

GROUPE D'INFORMATION SUR LES PRISONS (GIP)

This list of demands was developed by prisoners at Toul Prison and published in the GIP booklet Cahiers de revendications sortis des prisons lors des récentes révoltes *in April 1972.*

We have requested:

1. Improvement of the staple diet (nourishment);
2. Improvement of communal showers;
3. Better treatment vis-à-vis prisoners who have sustained abuse, both moral and physical;
4. Better work compensation;
5. Elimination of marks for good behavior so that everyone has access to exercise;
6. Elimination of isolation units;
7. Regulation of dental care;
8. Improvement of disciplinary units (heating);
9. That the authorization, given by competent personnel outside the prison, to correspond with registered family members, lovers, and children be respected;
10. Improvement of the canteen;
11. Elimination of the rationing of bread;
12. Improvement of heating in the cells.

Fresnes

GROUPE D'INFORMATION SUR LES PRISONS (GIP)

This list of demands was developed by prisoners at Fresnes Prison and published in the GIP booklet Cahiers de revendications sortis des prisons lors des récentes révoltes *in April 1972.*

—Right to a radio in each cell.

—Improvement of the staple diet.

—End of isolated exercise for prisoners in maximum security.

—Right to buy paperback books from the canteen.

—Right to obtain new releases for the prison, titles not yet in the library.

—Right to religious services for those isolated in maximum security.

—Expanded visiting hours.

—Cinema for everyone (only those authorized to work *[les classes]* have access to it).

—Elimination of the warden's right to oversee disciplinary matters within the prison.

—Plus all the demands from Melun.

Tract Made and Launched by Insurgent Prisoners at Nancy

GROUPE D'INFORMATION SUR LES PRISONS (GIP)

This list of demands was developed by prisoners at Nancy Prison and published in the GIP booklet Cahiers de revendications sortis des prisons lors des récentes révoltes *in April 1972.*

Penitentiary Region
Strasbourg
Nancy Prison
Nancy, January 15, 1972

Demands from the Penal Population at Nancy Prison

—We ask for a more equitable system of justice within the prison, on the part of the guards and supervisory staff.

—The prisoners demand an honorable justice, together with the elimination of administrative supervision *[tutelle]* and the travel ban.

—Every Monday, Tuesday, and Wednesday, prisoners passing before the correctional tribunal at Nancy experience much heavier punishments than their counterparts receive other days of the week. WHY?

—We demand the improvement of nourishment provided by the staple diet.

—That the canteen be improved.

—We demand that newspapers no longer be censored.

—We demand decent hygiene, and heating in all the sleeping quarters.

—We demand that prisoners no longer be beaten by the guards for slight infractions.

The Prisoners at Nancy Prison

The GIP Proposes a Commission of Inquiry

GROUPE D'INFORMATION SUR LES PRISONS (GIP)

*A GIP tract, circulated on December 11, 1971, calling for the creation
of an independent commission of investigation into the Toul revolt.
The demands of prisoners at Toul were also attached.*

The events at Toul, following those at Lyon, Poissy, Clairvaux, Gragu-
ignan, and Nîmes, have highlighted a number of facts:

(1) The French penitentiary administration does not perform its task:
"the reeducation of prisoners."
(2) It failed in its supposed mission: "the humanization of prisons."
(3) It blocked what the public could know about what happens inside prisons and what prisoners could make known on the outside
about their demands and the conditions of their existence.

In order to respond to this failure, the Prisons Information Group
calls for the formation of a commission of inquiry that would include
among its members journalists, legal experts, doctors, and the families of prisoners. Their task would be to answer a number of specific
questions. For example:

—Is harassment and abuse in fact practiced in all of the prisons for
which the GIP would be able to furnish a list? Have the complaints
that the prisoners have filed on this subject reached the Public Prosecutor's department?
—What kind of medical care is guaranteed in most French prisons?
—For prisoners who revolted at Toul, what fate is waiting for them
in the prisons to which they have been transferred?

Concerning Something New in the Prisons...

GROUPE D'INFORMATION SUR LES PRISONS (GIP)

A GIP tract distributed in December 1971 after the Toul revolt and during a street performance, by actors from Ariane Mnouchkine's Théâtre du Soleil, of a comedy sketch, "Whoever steals bread goes to prison, whoever steals millions goes to Palais-Bourbon."[1]

At this point, the scandal of prison conditions is flaring up in the eyes of the public.

The suppression of Christmas packages by Pleven, Minister of "Justice," made prisoners' anger—an anger already exacerbated by the scandalous and intolerable conditions of prisons—reach new heights. Strikes and hunger strikes have taken place in numerous prisons across France: Poissy, Lyon, La Santé, Grenoble, etc.

But families of prisoners have also mobilized to protest against the suppression of Christmas packages:

—in Paris, they marched a petition straight to the Minister of Justice;
—in Toulouse, they blockaded the prison doors with empty packages.

So, these are the erupting revolts: at Toul, where 80 percent of the prisoners are young people locked up for stealing cars and the conditions of detention are particularly atrocious: prisoners are chained to restraint beds for up to 8 consecutive days! Prisoners have revolted twice:

—the first revolt aimed to secure the dismissal of the warden;
—the second occurred because Pleven lied to them.

All of this has stirred up public opinion: the wall of silence surrounding prisoners' living conditions is now broken.

Some newspaper articles and radio shows are explaining the prisoners' revolt and talking about the conditions of their detention.

Today, actors are performing for us a skit with the following motif: "Whoever steals bread goes to prison, whoever steals millions goes to Palais-Bourbon."

They want to discuss prison conditions with us, but also certain forms of repression that follow prisoners after they get out: the criminal record, for example.

But the families suffer, too: *they suffer from the greed of lawyers, the arbitrary restrictions on visitation; they are forced to form a long line and wait outside in the cold.*

Right now:

We can pressure the penitentiary administration to get rid of the waiting line and get a waiting room!

Note

1. [Eds.] The Palais-Bourbon is the seat of the French National Assembly, the lower legislative chamber of the French government.

To Escape Their Prison

MICHEL FOUCAULT

The transcription of an unpublished manuscript that Michel Foucault prepared for a Comité Vérité Toul press conference on the Toul Prison Revolt in January 1972.

To escape their prison, prisoners at Toul used to use the same means as other prisoners across the world: breakout or suicide. But the other day, they did not jump the wall; they formed a barricade. They confined themselves within a prison of which they were now masters, and from which they chased the administration: no one could enter without their express permission. They occupied it like one occupies a factory, a place of struggle. They made it a fulcrum to demonstrate their demands and to assert their rights. They inverted the functions of the wall, the bars, and imprisonment itself. On that day, they did not want to get out of prison, but rather to be free of their status as humiliated prisoners.

Thus did a new type of struggle appear. New at least for French prisons and French prisoners. For, it is doubtless the same type of struggle we saw already in the United States and Italy; the same type of struggle undertaken by the fifty-seven Algerian prisoners in La Santé.[1]

The prisoners of Toul did not take hostages. Journalists raised this astonishing fact, while the administration tried to deny it—one can easily imagine why: the administration's power holds only if the prisoners opposite them are not in and of themselves, by their number and by their collective decision, a force. By not taking hostages and by guiding guards to the gate of the occupied prison, it was as if prisoners said: we do not need a ruse, blackmail, or possibilities of rebellion in order to be a force. We are a force by ourselves, because we have decided together to kick the administration out and not let it return until it has recognized us as a force with which one negotiates, to which one cedes, and in reference to which one is engaged.

It appears that, in order to make order reign throughout the prisons, the administration relies on relations of money,[2] prestige, and physical force that divide the prisoners. The other day at Toul, those forces were redistributed and, suddenly, the game[3] took on another meaning: prisoners, because they were detained, humiliated, used, and exploited, became a collective force in opposition to the administration. And it is in this way that they entered into a struggle.

Organization? It's still difficult to say. There were delegates—both leaders and spokespersons.

Objectives? Lists of demands were circulated. These began with the essential demands, those most difficult to obtain (transfer of the warden, chief of the guard, etc.), and they moved to the more detailed ones (shower temperature, meals, etc.); but these are not merely details, or rather, every detail is essential when one struggles to obtain, against a boundless arbitrariness, a minimum of juridical status, when one struggles to have the right to demand. It is important to have the right to wash, but it is essential when one obtains it in this way.

Tactics? To occupy strategically important places, like the roofs from which they can be seen and heard on the outside, from which they can demonstrate (beyond the cordoning off, the consignment, the silence, and the lies of the administration) that they exist, that they struggle, and why they struggle. To destroy or, on the other hand, to protect symbolically important places (to burn the library and with it all the hypocrisy of prison education, moral rectification, and professional formation; to protect the chapel, because the chaplains "treated us well"); not to negotiate directly, without witness, with an administration whose methods are known all too well, but by reliable intermediaries and guarantors (which is why prisoners asked that negotiations pass through the chaplains).

It appears that, after negotiations, the prisoners, or at least some among them, returned to their cells, following the settlement to the letter; they passed before the guards, hands behind their back, eyes fixed on the ground, and, lifting their hats, said, "Good evening, chief."

This was not an image of defeat but of action: they had negotiated force to force; the administration had ceded; and for their part, they kept their end of the bargain: they really and symbolically returned "to order."

Had they been shamelessly lied to? It is true. Had they let themselves be duped? Perhaps. I, however, think everything that has happened represents a double victory for the prisoners:

—with respect to these "common-law" prisoners, to whom the penitentiary administration claims to teach morality, justice, good and evil, that administration has been caught in the very act [en flagrant délit] of lying and abusing trust.

But above all:

—the prisoners of Toul exhibited a political struggle in prisons. For I think we can call "political" any struggle against established power, when it constitutes a collective force, with its own organization, objectives, and strategy.

Now, there is something terrifying about this, something they tried to mask. The newspapers worked one angle: the dilapidation of premises, the absence of funds, the inanity of regulations, the arbitrariness of wardens; as if these events at Toul were but the final result of long wear and tear or too much neglect, in any case the inevitable culmination of a process begun long ago. In fact, what happened at Toul is the beginning of a new process: the first time a political struggle was led against the entire penal system by the same social stratum that forms its primary victim.

Notes

1. [Eds.] In 1967, Algerian prisoners at La Santé launched a prison protest movement that, while violently repressed, nevertheless constituted an acknowledged precedent for the GIP prison resistance movement.

2. [Trans.] The phrase d'argent is not entirely clear in the original. The transcription places [?] here.

3. [Trans.] Foucault's scrawl is notoriously difficult to decipher. Although the transcription takes this word to be pas, we read it as jeu (also noting its graphological differences from other instances of pas in the piece).

Toul Hell

GROUPE D'INFORMATION SUR LES PRISONS (GIP)
AND COMITÉ VÉRITÉ TOUL (CVT)

*Testimonials received by the GIP and the Comité Vérité Toul (CVT)
from prisoners and guards, published first by the* Agence de
presse Libération *(January 9, 1972), then reprinted in* La Cause du
peuple—J'accuse, *and reprinted again in the CVT's* La Révolte de
la Centrale Ney *(Paris: Gallimard, 1972).*

Toul Hell (Testimonials)

Prétoire (from a Guard)

After a prisoner has "committed an infraction," he is led to the *prétoire* to face Warden Galiana. The warden is behind a large table. On
the floor is a mark (a circle): the prisoner stands there, arms at his
side, flanked and held by two guards, one on each side. There is an
additional guard at the door. There is always a guard waiting to take
the sanctioned prisoner away. It is very rare to see prisoners acquitted; when they are, it is because they are in collusion with the administration.

Isolation

Some prisoners stay in isolation seven to eight months. They get out
only for a half-hour walk each day. With promises of more. Under the
slightest pretext, they do another month or two. Most often when
they leave isolation, they have a nervous breakdown, they break completely. At that point, they are strapped to a restraint bed for eight
or ten days. They aren't even unstrapped when they need to relieve

237

themselves, they are just left in their excrement. They are fed with a small spoon. Sometimes one hand is freed, sometimes not.

It is the warden who gives the order to strap them down.

One prisoner said, "Once, a guy who had just been to the *prétoire* and got back to his cell began to break down. When the guards got there, they brought him back and the warden said: 'I've had enough, strap him down.' So they strapped him down."

Nurse and Doctor (from a Prisoner)

When the guy was strapped down, they didn't call the doctor. And when they called the nurse, the nurse didn't even come. She didn't give a damn. She laughed. I even saw her one day, when they said: "Oh! There's a new one strapped down!" And I saw her laugh as if it pleased her, as if she was happy. She couldn't care less about her responsibilities. She did her work as if she were caring for animals, if that. Me, I've seen animals cared for a lot better than this. These people are far more concerned about an animal with an abscess than a guy who cuts his wrists.

A guard: "I've witnessed 35 prisoners seen in 20 minutes. Can even the best of doctors see 35 prisoners in 20 minutes?"

A prisoner: "There was even a doctor who had the horrible habit of writing up all the prisoners who went to see him without proper cause. Me, I don't see what the point of that is on the inside. If we go to see a doctor, it's because we don't know what we have. We may very well have nothing. We may just be apprehensive and want to see a doctor. If the doctor writes us up, after he determines we are fine— that is not his role."

Beatings (from a Guard)

I saw a guy who had gone mad, a prisoner. He'd lost it; it took two guards to take him away. Naturally, that didn't just happen. We had to put him in chains, bound hand and foot. There were eight of us. We didn't hurt him, we tried to hold back. But, to amuse themselves, two young guards grabbed him when he was five meters from the wall and sent him flying headfirst into it with all their strength. And that happened when he had already been under control for five minutes. I looked at the nurse's file; the young man was the biological son of a black doctor. He was a pyromaniac. He had wanted to burn down his grandmother's house because he never met his father. He was in prison.

Searches (from a Prisoner)

The main thing is still the searches. The systematic searches. When we get back from yard, for example, they search us nude in the refectory of Building C. It's really demoralizing. It's a thing that has always irritated me. Still, I've never said anything. One goes through a search completely naked. There are guards who push you around. They make you turn around and bend over. There is no respect for anyone. Go ahead, look in my anus! Three-quarters of the time, it's done out of spite. Besides, there are some guards who never do it.

Some Guards Lurk Around (from a Prisoner)

There are some guards who hang around outside the door and like to slip their key into the lock, without anyone noticing. And when they enter, they're really pleased with themselves. Can you imagine being the prisoner who sees a guard enter his cell like that?

The Watchtowers

You are there sitting in a chair for eight hours a day and three months at a stretch. The work runs on trimesters. The first eight days are more or less fine. But afterwards, a guard can't fall asleep anymore, he loses sleep, and he becomes incapable of the least physical exertion.

A guard said: "If the general doesn't like the look of you, he'll try to trip you up. He can do it in different ways. He makes the rounds. You have to salute and say: 'nothing to report.' At night, it gets worse. You have the timekeeper, and you have to clock in every 45 minutes past the hour.

"The night vigils are split into segments. There are 15 segments. Each guard has five stations, and he has a 4-hour shift in the watchtower."

Another guard: "Sometimes, you're tired. You have the red light, the rounds, the clock-ins. By the end, you don't even know your own name. Then in the morning, some old guards are completely insane."

In general, the guards take the night shift once every 5 or 6 nights. So, they never sleep at regular hours, they never work at regular hours, their whole life cycle is thrown off.

A guard: "There's a chair there, you can take two or three steps, you can stand up, turn around, but ultimately you get claustrophobic. There is nothing to do, you are trapped, you feel confined, oppressed, almost as if you were imprisoned in a cell. Almost. . . ."

Harassing the Guards (from a Former Guard)

What makes life impossible at Ney is a general climate of suspicion that hounds everyone, prisoners and guards alike. The guard is afraid of his superior, afraid of being written up for a misapplication of the rules. If he is too easygoing with the prisoners, they think he's a "wimp" who doesn't know how to get respect. As a result, he finds himself consistently assigned to the watchtower.

A guard: "There are guards who have signed up for another three months in the watchtower. There are others who never stop, even at gate 2 (the gate of entry: the guard works between 4 gates, which he spends time opening and closing). A guy bangs out maybe 20 or 30 kilometers during one 8-hour shift."

The guard is in a difficult position. In his book, a former political prisoner at Toul wrote: "Poor guards. Always caught between a rock and a hard place." Another prisoner: "In the penitentiary world, the guard is not above the prisoners but opposite them." A guard: "You can't trust anyone, anyone at all. I was able, over the course of several years, to make just 4 or 5 friends I could trust, that's all. Prisoners know intimate details about the guards' private lives."

The "Stripes" System (from a Prisoner)

It's from the get-go. It starts like this: we earn the first stripe at the end of six months if we haven't "screwed up," if we've never been to the *prétoire*. You have to have never been reported. That gives you the right to a ration of additional cigarettes, every ten days. So, at the end of six months, if you haven't screwed up, you earn the right to two bonus packs and, I believe, 20 or 30 francs more per month.

If you live in a cell, it's practically impossible to spend all your time there without screwing up. In your cell all day long, something is bound to happen. Take the bedsheets, for example. Suppose that your bedsheets are poorly folded and that you bump into a guard who's a real animal and he strips your bed. You get back to your cell and it ticks you off to see your bed stripped. When you see that, you yell, you scream. It's normal. There are some guards who conduct a decent search, we don't even see the signs. But then there are some who, when they do a search, it's over, they have zero respect for your things, they toss the whole place. When you see that, if you don't hold yourself back, you can't help but scream.

The "Notebook" and Informants (from a Prisoner)

I have a flaw, I'm curious. I love sticking my nose into everything. Over there, there's a cell registry, in Building C. It has a list of guys who have been marked down as "homosexual." Whose attention do they want to draw to these guys? Me, I think we shouldn't see this notebook. This notebook, it was at someone's gate, on the table, open, and I stumbled on it, I learned that a guy was gay. That made for a fantastic story. I think it's true, but these things should remain confidential.

A guard: "It's a vicious circle, all of it, because the prisoner on janitorial service is charged by the chief to watch the guard *[le surveillant-chef de surveiller le surveillant]*" ... A guard: "You have to really get this. We, we watch. At the same time, a prisoner is charged by the chief guard to watch us *[le surveillant-chef de vous surveiller]*. Simultaneously, the prisoner wheels and deals with people at his level: 'During yard, you'll give my buddy some chocolate,' later, the exchange of letters, etc. ... Guards who refuse to participate are automatically viewed poorly by the chief because the prison rat goes and gives them up to the chief. You see, it's a vicious cycle. Clearly, the chief doesn't give a damn about this prisoner. He wants to be informed, that's all. These prison rats aren't there just for the guards, but for both the prisoners and the guards. There is no difference for the chief: for him, it's a piece of intelligence, it's always better to be a step ahead."

A guard: "It's a setting in which you can't even trust your own shadow. In each cell, they put a prisoner (generally for sex scandals) who informs the administration. In prison, there are only scuttlebutts, gossips. A trifle takes on enormous proportions."

Suicides (from a Guard)

During night shift, on our floor, we were on suicide watch over a guy, one guy and then another guy, whose names they'd given us.

Some Caseworkers (from a Prisoner)

More than anything else, caseworkers play the role of auxiliary guards. They have the chief within easy reach, and they have their favorites. I mean it; they go to see their favorites and they're always visiting them. There are 200 guys, two caseworkers, and maybe 20 guys get seen. They don't talk to the others, they don't even bother with them.

They go to see guys after they're completely broken, when they've cut their wrists. There's one of them whose mother was on her death-bed. He cut his wrists and the caseworker finally decided to go and see him.

When a guy cuts his wrists, they call the nurse, they bandage him up, and they strap him down.

Report by Doctor Rose, Psychiatrist at Toul Prison

ÉDITH ROSE

This report, drafted by Dr. Édith Rose, was sent to the penitentiary administration's Inspector General, to the President of the French Republic, to the Minister of Justice, and to the National French Order of Physicians the day after the Toul revolt. This report was read aloud by Michel Foucault during the Toul press conference on December 16 and published in La Cause du peuple—J'accuse, *no. 15 (December 18, 1971), then in* Le Monde, *where Foucault and other public figures, including Simone Signoret, had purchased a page, and finally in* Psychiatrie d'aujourd'hui, *no. 7 (January/ February 1972).*

This is the exact text of a statement I gave this afternoon in front of Mr. Bouyssic

To the Inspector General of the Penitentiary Administration, with copies being sent to the President of the French Republic, to the Minister of Justice, to Mr. Bouyssic (Inspector General of the Penitentiary Administration), to the President of the National French Order of Physicians, and one that I will also make public, because our society and those who lead it ought to be informed about how that public is protected. I have to pose a fundamental question to the public: are you interested in condoning prison regulations and correctional techniques that force prisoners into pipelines of murderous violence and that embitter them to such a degree that their only solution, upon release, is to "relapse"? Or should we, together with good-hearted people, develop techniques to neutralize their aggression, an aggression that we sense is growing and that scares us so much?

In this regard, I am going to give some concrete examples concerning Ney, the Toul Prison:

—Prisoners do not have the right to play sports here unless they have earned a "stripe" (one year of detention without sanction). *Honestly, is that much credibility really necessary to warrant giving them a ball and letting them spend their time playing soccer in the penitentiary's giant yard? Do you not think their demand is justified: "sports for all"?*
—Do you not find it inhumane that young men of 18 are confined all day long in a cell, 3 meters by 2 meters,[1] occupied with meaningless work?
—Prison regulations here forbid prisoners from having more than a certain number of photos: I had to care for a young man with "mental disorders" from whom they had confiscated a picture of his little brother, which his mother had sent him. I ask myself the question: *what harm is this photo?*

My medical authority was very limited.
My primary job, however, was to issue medical certificates permitting them to put two prisoners into one cell, who, after months or even a year of total isolation, presented with mental disorders, or, conversely, to put those who could no longer endure the constant overcrowding into a cell by themselves. Regulation would then no longer allow them their five or six cigarettes a day. Far be it from me to praise the benefits of tobacco, but, for those who have nothing, these cigarettes were important!

It shocked me to learn on Friday in Mr. Le Como's office that it was left to the discretion of each doctor, *though not mine (in any case).* The prisoners were, I believe, well cared for on strictly medical terms: we did not hesitate to conduct physical exams or the requisite paraclinical tests. They had the right to accept or reject treatment and came to get their medicine in the infirmary. Once, a very depressed man came to me. I ascertained that an aggressive treatment plan was necessary and proposed it to him. He replied: *"Ms. Rose, I would like to, but I have to work every day and you know these anti-depressants will not allow me to do my job."* The authorities with whom I checked said: *"They are here to work and, if we make exceptions, there will no longer be anyone in the workshops."*

A mentally ill prisoner, who had three or four suicide attempts under his belt (and numerous medical reports to support his illness) and whom I had transferred out to Château-Thierry,[2] had been placed in a corrective wing because he didn't "want" to work. I can confirm under oath that, because of his disorders and necessary medications, he could not work.

But the thing that most nauseated and pained me was seeing people strapped down for a week or more.

I can affirm under oath that they do not unstrap them to eat. I heard my office nurse call a guard to spoon-feed them. A guard told me himself how unpleasant that was for him, beyond the additional work it represented. Some witnesses even said that these prisoners were left strapped down in their own excrement. I did not see this.

I very often expressed to the nurse my horror at these techniques and my desire to see the people freed. And when I expressed this, I was invariably told that it was a matter of administrative regulation, applied to men who had attempted suicide or self-mutilation. (I note that prisoners made these attempts in an effort to get evacuated and transferred to regional hospitals, to escape Toul Prison.) I was invariably told that both general and personal safety had to be respected, for these men disrupted the established order. I hit a wall; I seemed to be living in a Kafkaesque world.

Overwhelmed by the principle of the administration's absolute power, I didn't dare continue my impassioned stand against these practices.

The mentally ill were sent to me either after they saw my medical colleague, the nurse, or when they asked to see me. They were brought to my office. No one ever showed me the people strapped down. I happened to catch a glimpse of them through a crack in the door, when they were in the first cell. But they were perhaps deeper in and clearly scattered throughout the building.

I can affirm under oath that I was never consulted on the necessity of a restraint bed, and I demand to take the witness stand. Do I not specialize in treating the "mad," the agitated, those who hit themselves? I never signed a script for a restraint bed, and you could confirm this because my medical prescriptions are written in black and white in the prison infirmary's file.

I affirm under oath that I was never called to treat one of these attacks of violent, destructive agitation that might explain the restraint bed, and yet I live in Toul, they have my number, and I have never failed to show up at the prison whenever they asked.

I was very surprised to learn from Mr. Le Como in his office last Friday that it was by medical orders these people were strapped down. Obviously, if I had known beforehand, I would have talked about this with my colleague.

For several years, I interned at psychiatric hospitals and of course I saw people in a state of extreme agitation; never did I see them strapped down for more than a few hours at a time to administer a sedative. I trust my teachers and colleagues at these hospitals will not dispute this. *In fact, they are bound to support my statements.*

One day, I went by myself—on my own authority and without being asked—to a cell where a man was strapped down. He had attempted suicide by hanging on February 22, 1971, because, for administrative reasons, he was not permitted to write to his partner, with whom he had lived for at least five years and had several children. I saw him the morning of February 26. He was strapped down and I can affirm under oath that he was not in a state of agitation or insanity warranting this restraint. I spoke with him in peace for about a half hour in front of the nurse and a guard.

I affirm having been struck, upon my arrival at Toul, by the extreme frequency of suicide attempts: hangings, severing the femoral artery, swallowing spoons, forks, fluorescent tube lights, etc. These prisoners were often transferred without seeing me. Having never spent much time in other prisons, I thought it was like this everywhere. And another thing: several times I received complaints from adult prisoners who were preparing for their exams (CEP, BEPC, even the baccalauréat).[3] They claimed to be absolutely unable to work on their courses at night, after returning from the workshop, because they lived in a cell of six and the others would turn the radio on, play cards, etc., . . . all on the one, lone table in the cell. I asked the relevant authorities if it was possible to set them up somewhere else—not only on Saturday afternoons, when they worked with the instructor, but also for some quiet hours during the workweek. I was told that this compromised security but that they would try to put prisoners who did the same sort of work together.

If I had my medical reports, I might be able to specify the precise number of these complaints.

Were prisoners really put together? It would take an investigation to track this down and interrogate the prisoners. I could still cite two dark informant stories recounted by prisoners, which I explained in detail to Mr. Bouyssic (I could give him even more specifics if I had my medical reports).

But I am going to move on to how I occupied my time on December 10, 1971.

Friday, the day of my appointments at the prison, I got there, as usual, to do my work. The nurse, Mrs. Rors, showed me the juvenile center and its wreckage; I then followed her to the premises of the administration. She first checked in with the secretary and *I swear under oath to having seen the list of prisoners who had been strapped down.* This sheet of paper was a little smaller than the one on which I now write and bore two vertical columns of names written top to bottom. I could read some of them, including the names of about five or six people that I knew. The nurse was then called into Mr. Le Como's office and I said I would follow her, although he had not called me. Except for a few details, I gave the statement above. Mr. Bouyssic, who also came, took notes on my statement, notes that I neither read nor signed.

On Saturday morning, December 11, 1971, I had naturally called Abbot Velten, as well as Pastor Amedro, to give them my testimony and communicate my sympathies. I knew neither of them.

On Monday morning, December 13, 1971, at 8:30, following the first revolt, which had supposedly involved no violence, I showed up at the prison to do some work I hadn't been able to finish on Friday. *The guards refused to let me in;* so I requested authorization from Mr. Divisia, who authorized me to go look in the detention center for my file of prescriptions and observations, but he refused to let me see any prisoners.

What horrified me, in entering the courtyard, was seeing through the windows several prisoners with bandaged heads and hearing them cry out: "We are hurt."

It was impossible for me to remain unaffected and since, as I'd read in the papers, they were allowed to see the chaplains, I thought they'd also be able to see me, so I shouted up to them: *"Act crazy!"* (I am a psychiatrist), and my emotions kept me from finding the right words... *"Try to have me called in...."* Believing, naive and guileless as I am, that if they wanted to see me I could go to them. I swear I was moved only by the desire to help and reassure them. If they were asked, they would say they yelled, "We're hurt . . . ." The nurse and the two guards accompanying me can attest to this. The nurse, to whom I said: *"But, Mrs. Rors, they are hurt,"* told me, *"This is nothing. They act like that a lot, doubtless to entertain themselves."* I was disgusted, and, as Mr. Bouyssic can attest, I cried in front of him when I told him about it, and I hadn't for a moment tried to keep my attempted intervention from him.

Not finding my clinical observations at the infirmary, I went to check in the legal affairs office; files of transferred prisoners were strewn about everywhere and I was surprised that medical records that usually take so long to send were pulled so quickly this time . . . . As for the files of current prisoners, we didn't have time for me to find them, so I was left empty-handed.

At 1:00 on Monday, a telephone call warned me that the prison riot had started again.

I quickly informed the chaplains and joined up with them. My medical aid to the prisoners was refused by Mr. Divisia, the penitentiary administration's regional warden, who called in Dr. Gérardin and two military doctors. He told us that it was nothing serious (4 prisoners were gravely wounded, according to the count issued over the radio by Nancy's CHR).[4]

Since apparently it was nothing serious, Abbot Velten, Pastor Amedro, and I asked to enter the detention center and have unrestricted access to the prisoners. After consulting with his superiors, Mr. Divisia denied this clear and simple request.

We didn't see what happened. . . .

Under these conditions, and seeing the underhanded and completely unjustified attacks to which the two chaplains were subjected (which is to say, these two kindhearted men were accused of organizing the rebellion to selfishly attract attention), *I decided to speak my mind,* already upbraiding myself for not flagging these unwarranted restraints to higher authorities and for not opening this dispute to public opinion, because people have the right to be informed. . . .

We do not have "hardened criminals" at Ney Prison.

Few of these guys are criminals (80 percent are here for car theft, driving without a license, etc.), especially among the youth. The problem with adults is a little different: I would say that there are very often people here who are truly mentally ill and who absolutely do not belong in prison (I am thinking of one extremely dangerous person in particular, who has been here for a number of years. I requested his transfer, but transfers are the exception).

Here, I am going to offer a quick police sketch of my clients for your consideration:

Coming from broken homes, child of an alcoholic father, rejected by a stepfather or stepmother, or carted around from l'Assistance Publique[5] to child care, from education centers to juvenile detention facilities. Some are on their own by the age of 12, and I could cite some harrowing and poignantly sad reports here. I am ready, if I find them, to add them to this record. Many start their stints in prison at age 14. As soon as they get out, with an average nest egg of 100 francs in their pocket, and every door closed in front of them, they have only one thing on their mind: to realize this beautiful dream they've been nursing all their years in detention—to tear down the road in a sweet ride. They steal a car and go back to prison: they then become "dangerous recidivists." *They can't, like middle-class kids (like me), just take their mom or dad's car!*

When we think about how people who embezzle hundreds of millions enjoy legal pardon and yet these guys are in here!...

So far, I have only talked about prisoners, but I also have to address the other victims: the guards.

One need not imagine that all of them are brutes. If a kind, intelligent man lets a prisoner without a stripe into the yard to play soccer with the others, he gets harshly reprimanded by his superior.

They have to abide by idiotic and arbitrary rules all the time; for example, don't talk in the ranks, eyes on the ground, waste time and dignity feeding a man strapped down.

Let's recall that these men, who live day in and day out with the prisoners, have no say in meetings where judgment is passed on the latter. They are present, but only in order to ensure the physical security of the officers (I also want to note that, as a medical psychiatrist, I am not invited).

They may also have some authority over the prisoners, when, as frequently happens, they are assigned to watch a work group of 100 guys. Is their security ensured given that some people with serious mental illnesses are thrown in with all the others? I am thinking in particular of a dangerous paranoiac, who has been here for several years and for whom I requested a transfer two months ago. He is still here.

These men work in materially and morally appalling conditions. What can they do given that they have no right to speak and no right to strike (they sign a document on their first day, putting themselves entirely in the service of the administration). I think that, at Toul, they are right to demand an increase in staff.

The doctors notice how mentally drained these men are and what regrettable repercussions that can have on their family life. They have no alternative but to come and ask us for a work-release note. The absenteeism at Toul this year was horrible. To console them, the administration made glasses of wine available for 30 centimes each and in unlimited supply. After I had remarked that this risked facilitating alcoholism, I was told: "No, just the opposite. It tells me who the drinkers are so I can keep an eye on them." And when Mr. Le Como objected that the injection of a temporary sedative leads to addiction . . . take from that what you will.

I would add that I have no particular political orientation, no religious affiliation, just goodwill.

I refuse to believe that a man is irrevocably damned at the age of 20, as so many people at Ney think. I challenge all who read me. I beg them not to remain indifferent and—like the Abbott, the Pastor, and me—to get involved!

I close by affirming that not once, over the course of the past year at Ney, has a prisoner acted aggressively toward me, nor shown me any disrespect.

I asked my five-year-old daughter, who was bugging me as I wrote this report, if she could lend her mama for one afternoon to these young men who have no one to love, care for, and soothe them; she answered yes and, seeing my own sadness, left in tears.

Notes

1. [Eds.] These measurements equal roughly a cell of 7 x 10 feet. A typical solitary confinement cell in the United States is 8 x 10.

2. [Eds.] Le Centre Pénitentiaire de Château-Thierry was known for

treating difficult prisoners, the majority of whom suffered from mental illness.

3. [Eds.] The baccalauréat is roughly equivalent to a college entrance exam.

4. [Eds.] CHR stands for Centre Hospitalier Régional. These are area hospitals that also offer highly specialized care and expertise. In France, most CHRs have joined forces with universities in order to become CHRUs, regional centers for medical research and care.

5. [Eds.] The Assistance Publique—Hôpitaux de Paris (AP–HP) is a public hospital system of Paris and its suburbs.

The Toul Speech

MICHEL FOUCAULT

*A statement by Michel Foucault during the Comité Vérité Toul press
conference on January 5, 1972. This intervention was published in*
Le Nouvel observateur, *no. 372, December 27, 1971–January 2, 1972,
and in the* APL Bulletin, *no. 12, on January 9, 1972.*

On Thursday of last week, the prison psychiatrist at Toul spoke. What
did she say? Many things we already vaguely knew and with which we
have now become quite familiar: for days, men are bound hands and
feet to a bed; there are suicide attempts nearly every night; a regular
alternation between punishments and sedatives, detention-injection,
dungeon-valium (oh tranquilizing morality!); and, at twenty years old,
car thieves are converted into delinquents for life.

   But listen for a moment to how she said it. She did not say: the restraint bed is an old practice utilized in both the prison and the asylum; penitentiary personnel have not known how to get rid of it. She
did not say: too little respect, therefore too little personnel, therefore
too little surveillance, therefore brutalities and injustices. She does
not lash out at the structures themselves, at their dilapidation. She
says: "Such and such day, in such and such place, I was there and I
saw: at such and such a moment, so and so told me . . . and I understood; I made such and such demand; here is the response I got from
the warden and I testify to it under oath." Listen to the trembling of
this voice that no longer hesitates: it is a singular voice and one we
have never heard on the outskirts of the prison.

   Our institutions feign to recoil when they are critiqued from
within; but they accommodate those critiques; they live through
them; it is the glamour of their style and the blush in their cheek. But

what they do not tolerate is when someone suddenly turns their back and begins shouting in the other direction: "This is what I just saw, here, now, this is what is happening. This is the event."

You remember the Algerian War. It was one thing to accuse the army of practicing torture (of course, it was forbidden to print such a thing, but people knew it and said as much). It was another thing to stand up, like some men did, to cry: "Captain X tortured Y; he left this many cadavers in such and such police precinct." Those who took this risk put their lives in jeopardy.

I doubt that Dr. Rose's life is in danger. But I can already see the campaign of denigration and malice. They say: (1) this is not important, these are just anecdotes, "mere details"; (2) this is slander, and as such it is immoral; (3) in any case, this is the work of journalists, it is not your work.

Well, pay a little attention to what Dr. Rose recounts.

In the mere details she exposes, what is hidden—or rather, what comes out? Someone's dishonesty? Someone else's mistakes? Hardly. Rather, it is the violence of power relations.

Society painstakingly requires everyone to avert their eyes from events that betray true power relations. The administration speaks only in tables, statistics, and bell curves; unionists speak in terms of working conditions, budgets, loans, and staff recruitment. Only rarely do people want to attack evil right "at the root," that is, where no one sees it or experiences it—far from the event, far from the forces that confront us and from the act of domination itself.

But this is exactly the place from which the Toul psychiatrist spoke. She shook things up and broke the big taboo. As someone within a system of power, instead of critiquing how it operates, she denounced what happened there, what had just happened, on a certain day, in a certain place, under certain circumstances.

More than outrage, the response was really a widespread stupor. Around her voice there collected a kind of silence. An uneasy hesitation. Everything needed to be put back in its place. Habitual news circuits needed to reassert their rightful role: those responsible for reporting the event needed to do so; those capable of conducting a critique needed to do so. Everything Dr. Rose said was therefore "redistributed" in the papers: in some articles, the facts were reported as if they were anonymous tips or the result of an investigation; in other articles, you would find, carefully placed within quotations marks, passages in which Dr. Rose alluded to faults of the institution, the psychosociology of prisoners, the situation of the guards, etc.

But what of this voice that said "I"? What of this woman who, after all and if only by virtue of her knowledge, was "of" power, "in" power, what of this woman who had the unique courage to say: "I just saw, I just heard"? What of this refrain throughout the text: "I swear it, I attest to it, I agree to a face-to-face confrontation"? All of this has been snuffed out. But it is this that I want us to read and recognize *[reconnaisse]*—or rather, notice *[connaisse]* for the first time. The "Toul Speech" may well be a critical event in the history of the penitentiary and psychiatric institution.

One further remark. The commissioners designated by Pleven heard Dr. Rose's testimony the other day. They pressed her very hard. As if the goal of these men was not to know the truth but to erase what had been said. They questioned her: "You swear that the prisoners in restraints were not freed for meals. Did you witness this yourself?" And Rev. P. Rousset insisted several times: "It is very serious, Ms. Rose, for a doctor to swear to something when she hasn't witnessed it herself."

Now, Dr. Rose had testified not that she had seen it but that she knew it. She knew because a guard had said: "In certain cases, we freed one hand." Another had clarified, regarding these spoon-fed meals: "We lost time doing this." And the nurse testified: "In any event, we did free them when they had to relieve themselves." But the reverend father decided he would have to see for himself; it couldn't be alleged just like that, out of thin air; he returned to this point several times, emphasizing it heavily, almost menacingly.

I begged Dr. Rose to ask the reverend father if he had seen, with his own eyes, the man nailed hands and feet between two thieves.

Concerning Psychiatrists in the Prisons

GILLES DELEUZE

A statement by Gilles Deleuze during the Comité Vérité Toul press conference on January 5, 1972. This address regarding the reception of Dr. Édith Rose's report among psychiatrists was published in the APL Bulletin, *no. 12, on January 9, 1972.*

Over the past ten days or so, psychiatrists and psychoanalysts have put forward testimonies of support for and solidarity with Dr. Rose. In this short period, close to 100 signatures have been received—whether in the form of group motions or individual letters to Dr. Rose—from the most diverse and most prestigious of psychiatric teams. We are right to think that this campaign is going to take on considerable proportions. There is one point of commonality among all the letters and motions: unequivocal support, the affirmation of solidarity. But the tone varies: some call for the development of a plan of action; others emphasize the analogy—notwithstanding indications to the contrary—between hospital psychiatry and prison psychiatry; still others underscore the importance of the fact that a psychiatrist had dared say what so many of them, each in his own sector, had wanted to say.

These demonstrations by psychiatrists and psychoanalysts take on all the more importance given that a movement is currently taking shape, led by certain ministry representatives and penitentiary association leaders, to eliminate psychologists and psychiatrists from the prisons, as so many potentially troublesome witnesses.

It is crucial, on the contrary, that troublesome witnesses be multiplied and that psychiatrists who, even outside the prison, so often find themselves confronted with the psychological consequences of incarceration, participate more and more in the denunciation of the penitentiary regime in France.

The Nancy Uprising

I Would Like, on Behalf of the GIP, to Dispel a Misunderstanding ...

GROUPE D'INFORMATION SUR LES PRISONS (GIP)

A GIP communiqué, unsigned but likely written by Michel Foucault in January 1972, refuting potential critiques of the GIP over the attitude of the prisoners at Nancy on January 15, 1972. Denis Périer-Daville, a journalist for Figaro, *had actually critiqued the revolt of Charles-III, Nancy, which occurred right as the Schmelck Report acknowledged certain dysfunctions of the Toul Prison.*

I would like, in the name of the GIP, to dispel a misunderstanding. Certain newspapers have thought and said that the GIP denounced the recent action on the part of prisoners at Nancy. This is a huge mistake. And for a simple reason: there is nothing for the GIP to denounce in the collective forms of action that prisoners have decided upon as means of supporting or expressing their demands. The GIP reckons that the prisoners are old enough. The GIP is not an intellectual tribunal, which would judge the legitimacy of these actions, nor is it, as the Minister would have it, a subversive group that inspires prisoners from the outside. Since its inception, the GIP has proposed not to speak for the prisoners or in their name, but to ensure that the prisoners and their families may finally be able to speak for themselves. It was initially said in the newspapers and on the radio that the action on the part of Nancy prisoners was a savage act, devoid of any demands; that is false, the prisoners had precise demands, which the administration tried to stifle. It was said on television that there had been a "massacre," the word *massacre* was used twice, while this same television station showed images in which the only ones massacred were the iron bed frames. It was said that the prisoners should have waited and been patient for the Schmelck Report and for the inquiry ordered by the Minister; but it is precisely this report that fails to take into account even the most moderate of the demands made by the prisoners themselves. The prisoners know that there would have been no Schmelck Report without the actions taken at Toul; they know that no real change will come about without an unrelenting continuation of their action. It is a great success, as much at Nancy as at Nîmes and at Melun, that they have been able to make their demands known by diverse means. And for its part, the GIP takes up these issues without reservation and reckons that a commission of inquiry could never be serious without the participation of the workers, on the one hand, and the prisoners themselves or ex-prisoners, on the other.

What the Prisoners Expect from Us . . .

GILLES DELEUZE

*An opinion piece by Gilles Deleuze, speaking for the GIP, published
in* Le Nouvel observateur, *January 31, 1972, 24. The text responds to
accusations that the GIP was a subversive group that orchestrated
the prison revolts from the outside. The English translation by
Michael Taormina was published as "What Our Prisoners Want
from Us . . .," in Gilles Deleuze,* Desert Islands and Other Texts,
1953–1974, *ed. David Lapoujade (New York: Semiotext(e), 2004),
204–5. The translation has been revised for this volume.*

Something new is happening in and around the prisons. Prisoners
are deciding what form they wish to give their collective action within
the context of each specific prison (for example, since Toul, the latest
cautionary missive from Melun, the labor strike at Nîmes, the material destruction and occupation of the roofs at Nancy). Across this
variety, however, a series of precise demands have surfaced that no
longer even address themselves to the penitentiary administration,
but rather address themselves directly to power and appeal to the
people. These common demands deal essentially with censorship;
with the "*prétoire*" and "solitary confinement" as forms of brutal repression without any possible defense from the prisoner; with the
exploitation of work in prison; with conditional release, the travel
ban, and criminal records; and with the call to establish monitoring
commissions independent of [penal] power and the administration.

The very fact of penalty and imprisonment, however, has not yet
been called into question; and yet, a front of political struggle is already forming in the prisons. That prison is a matter of class, that it
concerns above all the working class, and that it also has to do with

the labor market (repression will be all the more harsh, especially on the young, to the extent that unemployment is a threat and the markets have no use for them)—this awareness *[prise de conscience]* is becoming clearer and clearer in the prisons. The essential principle articulated by the prisoners at Melun is that *"the social reintegration of prisoners can only be the work of the prisoners themselves."*

An active grassroots base inside the prisons is not enough; an effective grassroots base on the outside that supports and propagates prisoners' demands is also necessary. The GIP is not, as both Minister Pleven and the *Minute* newspaper would have it, a subversive group inspiring the actions of prisoners from the outside. Nor is it a group of intellectual dreamers as Mr. Schmelck, president of the Toul Commission of Inquiry, would have it. Rather, the GIP proposes to organize effective external aid, which must be led first by former prisoners and prisoners' families, but which must recruit more and more workers and democrats to the cause.

In this regard also, something utterly new is happening. At Toul, Lille, and at Nancy, among others, a new type of gathering is developing that has nothing to do with the genre of "public confession," and which is not the classical type of meeting either: former prisoners, settled in the very city where they paid their debt, are coming forward to say what has been done to them, what they have seen, physical cruelty, reprisals, lack of medical care, etc. It is this *personalized critique,* for which the report of Doctor Rose provides the example, that is joining forces with the cause of current prisoners.[1]

This is what took place in Nancy, in an extraordinary gathering that brought together more than one thousand people, and yet about which all the press remained silent.

This is what took place at Toul when the guards, stationed in the back rows [of the meeting], were shouting, and were silenced only by former prisoners who did not hesitate to say why they had gone to prison, to recognize this or that guard, and to remind them of his brutality. The statement by which the guards sought to intimidate the prisoners: *"I recognize him,"* became the statement by which the prisoners silenced the guards.

The day is coming when not a single prison guard will be able to beat a prisoner without, the next day or a month later, being publicly denounced by the prisoner he beat or by a witness in the very city where it happened. Former prisoners, like current prisoners, have stopped being scared and ashamed.

Faced with such a movement, power has countered only with the announcement of increased repression (CRS is constantly ready to intervene in the prisons) and administrative reforms (where prisoners and former prisoners have no right to give their opinion). It is a question of restoring powers to the prefects:[2] which amounts once again to the Ministry of Justice passing the buck to the Ministry of the Interior. Between the Pleven reforms and the most moderate of the prisoners' demands there is an abyss that lays bare the relations of class, force, and power.

Notes

1. [Eds.] Both Dr. Rose's report and Michel Foucault's essay in response are collected in this volume.

2. [Eds.] Prefects, serving under the Minister of the Interior, are state representatives to local governments charged with overseeing issues of security, safety, documentation, immigration, and legality.

It Was about a Year Ago

MICHEL FOUCAULT

*Michel Foucault's statement on the Nancy Prison Revolt from the
GIP press conference of January 17, 1972. The meeting began at the
Ministry of Justice, Place Vendôme, with Foucault reading a public
statement from the prisoners at the Melun Prison. The protesters,
who included Jean-Paul Sartre, Gilles Deleuze, Jean-Pierre Faye,
Claude Mauriac, Jean Chesneaux, Marianne Merleau-Ponty, Alain
Jaubert, Daniel Defert, Jean-Luc Godard, and Michelle Vian, were
forcibly removed from the ministry portico and they reassembled
at the offices of the Agence de presse Libération (APL), where
Sartre spoke first, followed by Foucault. Foucault's statement was
published in the* APL Bulletin, *no. 16 (January 18, 1972).*[1]

It was about a year ago that a hunger strike among political prisoners unfolded. It was this hunger strike that, for the first time, posed
to public opinion the problem of detention, and not only of political
detention, but of detention as such. To tell the truth, these problems
were posed a long time ago, and they were posed to prisoners and for
prisoners. Long ago, the same people were sent to prison. Long ago,
youths from working-class districts were the police's favorite clien-
tele and consequently also the prison's. Long ago too, there were beatings in prison. But thanks to the political prisoners' hunger strike, the
problem of prisons has been posed and, by the struggle of prisoners
themselves, this problem has been taken up and now carried to the
point at which you know it today.

It is because prisoners took their own struggles in hand, it is because they knew how to give [themselves] to their struggle *[donner
à leur lutte]*, that we can gather together this evening, hold a press

261

conference before the doors of the Ministry of Justice, and repeat the message prisoners communicated to us. We can call that a victory. The victory lies not so much in the Schmelck Report;[2] the victory lies in the process of struggle that has been initiated and has developed to this day. This victory, well, it is the possibility for prisoners to organize their struggles collectively, the possibility they have had, they have been given, to formulate precise demands. It is the possibility they have been given—given by force and by violence—to appeal, to appeal directly to public opinion, on the roofs of their *maison centrale* and their *maison d'arrêt*. And their victory, well, it is the support they received from a number of external organizations and movements, the support they received from the public.

That said, I think there are a number of remaining threats and this press conference is actually tied to threats still weighing on the movement, threats to prisoners: on Thursday evening, as I will remind you in a moment, the prisoners of Melun were sent to solitary confinement after leaving their demands in the hands of the penitentiary administration. Even today, in the prison at Nancy, they are trying to make the distinction between leaders and led; evidently, it is the leaders who are being threatened. But the threat, really, falls through their leaders onto all the prisoners. There are also threats to external groups—see Pleven's declaration on subversive movements trying to profit from the movements of prisoners. The threat, finally, lies in the very way in which the newspapers recounted Monday's events at Nancy.

This evening, the GIP will hold a press conference where it will state a certain number of things. I will try to summarize for you, here, the principal, and most significant, elements. Clearly, they will give you more details, which they have amassed over the course of yesterday and today. Here I am giving you whatever was transmitted to me by yesterday evening, and which, on a number of points, really corrects the image of the movement the press has been giving.

Over the past few months, there have been an important number of hunger strikes in the Nancy Prison. They were linked to a number of demands: some dormitories are not heated; guards beat the prisoners; there is no medical care. The doctor of the *maison d'arrêt* brags he never spent more than ten minutes a week in the prison, and medical visits never last longer than a minute. This doctor is the city's former UDR[3] mayor.

A large proportion of the prisoners are young people: there seem to have been a dozen prisoners under 18 years of age. It is illegal to hold persons under 18 in a *maison d'arrêt*. One of the minors seems to have been wounded in a brawl.

An important point is that *last Thursday,* prisoners formulated demands and brought them to the administration. *Friday, the prisoners who brought these demands were thrown into solitary confinement.* The insurrection Saturday morning broke out following these retaliation measures taken by the administration.

Consequently, when the newspapers, the penitentiary administration, and the Ministry of Justice say that this mutiny broke out without any demands, they are telling a double lie: there were demands and those who bore them were punished. From the beginning, when the mutiny began at 8 o'clock, prisoners threw a leaflet from the roof. There were between 40 and 60 young people, some of whom appeared to be armed.

They had printed leaflets in which they formulated their clear, distinct, legible demands on Nancy Prison letterhead:

Demands of the penal population of Nancy Prison.

We ask for equitable justice, within the prison, on the part of guards and supervisory staff.

Prisoners demand honorable justice, including the suppression of criminal supervision and residency prohibition.

On Monday, Tuesday, and Wednesday, prisoners who went before the correctional court at Nancy received punishments much heavier than those dispensed on other days. Why?

We request the improvement of food standards and the canteen. We demand that newspapers no longer be censored. We demand decent hygiene and heated dormitories. We demand that prisoners no longer be beaten by the guards over slight infractions.

Interestingly, there is now a traditional body of prisoner demands concerning nourishment, beatings, etc. Moreover, they demand legal and juridical protection within prison. They also ask that conditions of release and the way they are monitored after release by the penitentiary administration be improved.

Finally, and this is very important, they are in a *maison d'arrêt,* and not in a *maison centrale,* and thus they have much more frequent contact with the legal system and the correctional court. It is the first time this has been evident in the demands of prisoners in revolt: they have posed the problem of justice and the way in which it is administered. To the extent that the revolts progress and develop, demands stack up, pile up, and take over new regions of the global repressive system. At the outset, these demands were concerned exclusively with the penitentiary system and now they put in question the distribution of the penitentiary administration and even the legal system.

It is up to us to follow these demands and lend them our support. The prisoners wrapped this leaflet around stones and threw them.[4] It was the police's job to collect all the leaflet-wrapped stones so that no one would know what the prisoners wanted. GIP militants got hold of one of these leaflets, immediately reproduced it, and distributed it in the street. Police descended on the leaflets to suppress them and threatened to arrest all those who gathered and distributed them. There was a dialogue between the prisoners on the roof and a group of former prisoners, prisoner families and sympathizers, youths, activists, and students. Prisoners even threw down provisions they had taken from the canteen: nougats to be precise,[5] so the crowd could bear with them and be able to eat! That is the truth beneath the assertion that the prisoners were drunk. Those who saw these roofs and the slope of their frame, those who saw the prisoners throw stones with great precision, could guarantee that the prisoners were clearly not in an inebriated state: there were some 300 bottles of beer for 400 detainees.

All of the above attempts to emphasize the systematic business of distorting truth that the radio, television, and newspapers have undertaken. GIP militants and a number of sympathizers spoke out with a megaphone. We sent a message saying they were not alone and we would make their demands known as widely as possible.

Among the prisoners on the roofs, several were very near release, and, if they participated, it was despite the risk and out of profound solidarity with the prisoners who would remain. There was a lively discussion within the crowd: they were not sympathetic at first but they became so after talking with the prisoners, observing the attitude of the cops, and witnessing certain fascists demand, for example, that "submachine guns be fired on the prisoners." The police intervened to hide the leaflets and to arrest leftists as well as a former convict. The prisoners then shouted: "Help us young folk!" and "They killed a 16-year-old minor!" It seems he was not killed, but perhaps he was the one transferred to a hospital. We know, through an intern at the Nancy hospital, that there was a prisoner with a significant head injury and it is possible he is the one: obviously, his presence there is illegal and it will be difficult to establish.

That is the gist of what the Nancy GIP is going to publicize this evening.

With regard to the text that we are going to read from the prisoners at Melun, it is interesting to know how it was written. Its composition followed a rather large collective discussion. Among the prisoners, there were two camps. Some thought that the Schmelck Report had something to it, that it should be taken into consideration, that they should wait to see what effects it would have. Others thought that the Schmelck Report was worthless, that it promised nothing: that it was one of Pleven's smokescreens, that they should continue the movement begun at Toul.

The second group prevailed.

They disseminated this text not in order to negotiate, but to address the public as a whole. Bypassing the penitentiary administration, bypassing even the Ministry, to whom they nevertheless insisted the text be sent, they wanted to inform the public that they had demands, before whatever was going to happen came to pass.

Notes

1. [Eds.] Alain Jaubert's eyewitness account of this event, along with photographs by Élie Kagan, are available in *Michel Foucault, une journée particulière* (Lyon: Ædelsa Éditions, 2004).

2. [Eds.] Given the more than one hundred prison revolts in France during 1971 and 1972, two of the country's most preeminent judges were selected to conduct inquiries: Judge Schmelck in 1971 and Judge Arpaillange in 1972 and 1973.

3. [Eds.] Union pour la Défense de la République (UDR), 1968–71, or Union des Démocrates pour la République (UDR), 1971–76, was a Gaullist political party in France.

4. [Eds.] Jacky Hoffman, one of the incarcerated leaders of the Nancy revolt, recalls stuffing the demands in nougat bars and throwing them from the roofs. See Nicolas Drolc's film *Sur les toits* (2014).

5. [Eds.] Nougats are French confections composed of sweetened egg white, mixed nuts, and sometimes pieces of fruit.

Aftermath

The Great Confinement

MICHEL FOUCAULT

This interview with Michel Foucault conducted by Niklaus Meienberg originally appeared under the title "Die grosse Einsperrung" in Tages Anzeiger Magazin, *no. 12 (March 25, 1972): 15, 17, 20, and 37.*

NIKLAUS MEIENBERG.: Does a relationship exist between your structuralist, philosophical works and your engagement in the GIP?

MICHEL FOUCAULT: First of all, I am not a structuralist, I never said I was a structuralist, in fact I have always insisted that I am not a structuralist, and I've revisited the issue several times. Nothing, absolutely nothing in what I have published, nothing in my methods or in my concepts, evokes, even from a distance, structuralism. You would have to be named Piaget to imagine I am a structuralist.

N. M.: Then where does it come from—this general conviction that you are a structuralist?

M. F.: I suppose it is a product of stupidity or naïveté.

N. M.: Was it Piaget who labeled you a structuralist philosopher?

M. F.: I hardly think so; he is not capable of it, poor fellow. He never came up with anything himself.

N. M.: So, let me say this: the relationship between your engagement in the GIP and, quite simply, your philosophical work. Or would you prefer to be characterized as a historian?

M. F.: Decide for yourself! I have claimed neither one characterization nor the other. I would like you clearly to emphasize what I said about structuralism: that is, I am not a structuralist, I have never been one, and only the foolish and naive—let's call them Piaget—can claim that I am. The foolish, the naive, and the ignorant. Usually, this label is utilized by those who lost their contemporary relevance, so they judge others. But these considerations are hardly of interest, let us speak rather of serious things.

N. M.: By all means.

M. F.: I would really like us to establish no relationship between my theoretical work and my work in the GIP. That is very important to me. But there probably is a relationship. What I studied in *History of Madness* had something to do with this singular phenomenon of Western society that, in the seventeenth century, they called "confinement." I think one of the most unsettling pieces ever painted in the West is Frans Hals's *The Regentesses*,[1] an extraordinary work of which Claudel said some very beautiful things.[2] It relates to a very original practice which was, in a certain sense, a brilliant invention of the classical era. End of the sixteenth, beginning of the seventeenth century. I believe we can identify different types of civilizations. There are civilizations that exile, namely, those that react to offenses or crimes, or even insufferable individuals, by chasing them from society, exiling them. Then there are societies that slaughter, societies that torture, that retaliate against these individuals by torture and the death penalty. And then there are societies that confine. I think not many societies of this type exist. You know, in the Middle Ages prisons were practically nonexistent; in that era, dungeons were preeminently a kind of court antechamber—they seized a person for collateral, in order thereafter to kill him, or punish him in some other manner, or to have him ultimately pay a ransom for his freedom. In that era, the dungeon was a passageway: passageway to death or to freedom, the latter being bought at a price. The idea that prison could be a punishment in itself was completely foreign to the Middle Ages, and practices of this kind did not exist in medieval society. It is only when capitalism, in its early stages, found itself confronted with new problems, above all those of the workforce and the unemployed, and when societies of the seventeenth century saw great, popular insurrections, in France, in Germany, etc., in England too—only at that moment did they resort to confinement. Why?

Because the old method of repressing insurrections no longer seemed appropriate. Up until that point, they would normally send a mercenary army simultaneously to slaughter people and destroy property, in a kind of parallel invasion that affected the wealthy and poor equally. This was an absolute massacre, the army stayed in the country for weeks or months, devouring everything, it made a clean sweep, the big landowners could no longer bring in property taxes, it was a general economic catastrophe. Thus, they invented the prison to ultimately obtain a differential result, namely, prisons permitted them to eliminate, as dangerous, a select portion of the population, yet without this elimination having catastrophic economic consequences, as in the case of invading insurgent regions. A prophylactic, of some kind.

N. M.: In the Middle Ages, dungeons and prisons already existed.

M. F.: But they confined people only until they were judged, until they paid ransom, or until they were executed. The cells contained very few prisoners awaiting their destiny. Confinement en masse did not yet exist—not like in seventeenth-century Paris, where more than 6,000 prisoners were permanently confined. This was an enormous number in those days, for Paris contained but 300,000 inhabitants. Which had its demographic and economic consequences—for who was it that was confined? The vagabonds, the people without work and without home. To escape confinement, one had to practice a trade, accept salaried work, however poorly paid. Consequently, the lowest salaries were stabilized by the threat of incarceration. Obviously, the political and social consequences were important; for they could eliminate all the so-called agitators in this way. Thus, it was an extraordinarily elegant solution, if one can still speak of elegance here, a miraculous remedy in the period of nascent capitalism.

N. M.: People were not taken to court; they were incarcerated directly.

M. F.: Directly. Thanks to the police, an institution that was perfected in this era and fulfilled a quasi-judicial function. Its power was nearly absolute; in Paris, the police lieutenant had the power to confine mendicants and vagabonds without further ado.

N. M.: Speaking of the historical background you described in *History of Madness,* did you hit upon the present function of prisons after that?

M. F.: I would have been much happier with some other research subject. After May '68, when the problem of repression and of legal proceedings became more and more acute, it's likely that it jolted me and rekindled a memory. For one had the impression, well before May '68, that we were returning to the very general sort of confinement that once existed in the seventeenth century: a police force with extensive discretionary powers. In that era, they confined, without any discrimination, the old, the infirm, people who couldn't work or wouldn't work, homosexuals, the mentally ill, spendthrift fathers, and prodigal sons; they confined everyone together in the same place. Then, at the end of the eighteenth and beginning of the nineteenth century, in the era of the French Revolution, they made distinctions: mentally ill in the asylum, young people in the reformatories, delinquents in prison, to which they added a whole arsenal of discriminatory measures, residency prohibition, etc. And today, for reasons I still do not understand very well, they are returning to a kind of general, undifferentiated confinement. The Nazi concentration camps introduced a bloody, violent, inhumane variant of this new confinement—Jews, homosexuals, communists, vagabonds, Gypsies, political agitators, workers, everyone in the same camp. And today, we see the same thing take shape in a more discrete, more shrouded form, in an apparently scientific manner. The famous psychiatric asylums of the Soviet Union are beginning to function in this way. All these institutions that, in France, appear so humanitarian, so medical, and so scientific—the prophylactic centers, youth centers, and schools—are overseen and directed by people who look like social workers, educators, and doctors, but who are, in the end, police: in this broad range of professions, so different in appearance, one notices a common function that links them together: the turnkey. All of these professions have as their common function surveillance, the maintenance under lock and key of marginal existences that are neither really criminal nor really pathological.

N. M.: At first glance, the range of discriminations at the beginning of the nineteenth century led to a humanization: the mentally ill and so-called problem kids were separated from delinquents proper. But, on the other hand, the schema of the prison was extended to schools, asylums, and barracks.

M. F.: Let's say that the technique of confinement has been generally applied. Equally across asylums, barracks, and schools ... For example, at the Collège de France, we presently offer a seminar on medicolegal affairs. In 1835, one can already see lawyers defending murderers who are obviously mentally ill. They tell the judges: "The main thing is to confine this sort of person. It matters little whether that be in the prison or in the asylum, as far as my client is personally concerned. If I ask you to give preference to the asylum, it is so that his family's honor would not be tarnished." One clearly sees that, in the eyes of a lawyer, in 1835, there is no difference between being imprisoned and being committed to an asylum.

N. M.: If I understand you correctly, another form of confinement was forcing vagabonds to work and putting them in factories. Others were sent to the barracks, with an eye to the conquest of new markets in these early stages of imperialism. Have you noticed a correlation between the development of productive forces, in Manchester capitalism, and different techniques of confinement?

M. F.: For me, that is one of the enigmas posed by penal proceedings in the West. The great confinement has generally been practiced in capitalist societies. It is something very archaic and unjustified, its consequences are demonstrably costly. Everyone knows that presently, in France, there are 30,000 prisoners, of which about 3,000 to 4,000 are criminals, properly so-called. The rest are petty thieves or people who wrote bad checks, small fry; for them, clearly one does not need to use the costly, archaic, and ungainly methods of confinement. You have, then, an enormous carceral organization of which you might ask whether it ultimately corresponds to an economic need because at the strictly penal level its existence is unjustified. If you consider that, besides the 30,000 permanent inhabitants of the prison, 100,000 per year pass through it and the same 100,000 regularly return, then you see that in France, *grosso modo,* 300,000 people pass in and out of prison.[3] That does not represent even 1 percent of the French population. From an economic perspective, then, you don't see what good it does to subtract 300,000 people from a population of 50 million. Compared, for example, to the number of car accident victims, prisoners hold no weight. And yet, society finds them vastly important. It has this costly apparatus of prisons and prison guards, and, when we want to critique it, when we want to show its absurdity, people in power react with incredible vigor! The entire society reacts, too, and this gives rise to press campaigns.

N. M.: Perhaps, within "innocent" people, there is a profound psychological need for scapegoats, ultimately to foreground their "innocence" against the backdrop of prisoners' culpability.

M. F.: I don't know. There is surely a reason. At present, within the confines of my university work, I am occupied with the penal system of the Middle Ages. And recently—perhaps I am a little naive for not having seen it earlier—I've found the snag: at issue is the confiscation of goods. The penal system of the Middle Ages contributed, almost more than the bank, to the circulation of goods. This was one of the determining factors in the establishment of royal power. Because royal power, to the degree that it was also judicial power, retained either the whole or a large portion of confiscated goods. And the extension of royal power, which is to say the establishment of absolute monarchy, the concentration or, at the very least, the control of a great part of national wealth by royal power, this entire process was accomplished via the penal system. That I can understand. But in our day, that is no longer really the case. The portion of goods confiscated by today's penal system is utterly negligible. I am looking for reasons, but still do not see them clearly. The role of the medieval penal system was nearly as important as the prohibition of incest in primitive societies. The prohibition of incest equally had as its goal the circulation of goods, notably the dowry and the paraphernalia.[4]

N. M.: Why do you say you would prefer to be occupied with historical work that would not lead you back into the vicinity of the modern execution of punishments?

M. F.: Guess!

N. M.: It is a mystery to me. A scientific work that organically leads to the praxis of the present is still more useful than producing essays for specialists and snobs.

M. F.: If I occupy myself with the GIP, it is only because I prefer effective work to university yakking and book scribbling. To write a sequel today to my *History of Madness,* one that would cover material up to the present era, is devoid of interest for me. On the other hand, a concrete political action in favor of prisoners appears to me charged with meaning. An aid in the struggle of prisoners and, ultimately, against the system that puts them in prison.

N. M.: It strikes me as interesting to compare what you say at this juncture with your former declarations. In an interview, in 1966, you said: "We experienced Sartre's generation as, of course, a courageous and generous generation, which had a passion for life, politics, and existence . . . But we discovered another thing, another passion: a passion for the concept and for what I will call the 'system.'"[5] At the time, that sounded like a profession of faith in favor of an apolitical, disengaged structuralism.

M. F.: Since then, many things have fundamentally changed. This is probably because my generation has moved closer to that of Sartre. Less than a week ago, Sartre and I joined a demonstration before the Ministry of Justice to read publicly a manifesto sent to us by prisoners.[6] Clearly, I have changed, but doubtless Sartre has also, because up until that point he had believed that what I had written was a refusal, a negation of history. Today, he no longer seems to believe that. Because I have changed? I don't know.

N. M.: They chased you from the Ministry of Justice. Would you like to speak to Pleven, the Minister of Justice?

M. F.: We don't speak to his kind. He deceived prisoners, he made promises he didn't keep, he lied. It is absolutely useless to speak to Pleven. The demonstration before the Ministry of Justice had a symbolic value. There were two or three journalists, radio reporters, etc. But, naturally, our statement was not aired on the radio. That is typical of the system.

N. M.: How can you struggle effectively against the present penal system if the information network suppresses your statements?

M. F.: It is hard work. They said to me a thousand times: "Write an article on your ideal prison." And a thousand times, I answered: "Shit, that doesn't interest me." On the contrary, if we pitch a text, drafted by prisoners, in which they say: "We want such and such," newspapers won't publish it. *La Cause du peuple* itself censored a prisoner's text. The piece didn't correspond to their ideas, they preferred revolts on roofs. When prisoners speak, it poses such a problem. The text I read with Sartre was not published by *La Cause du peuple*. Because, as soon as prisoners speak, we are at the heart of the debate. The first step to take, then, is to give the floor to prisoners.

N. M.: Currently, members of Secours Rouge are distributing GIP tracts in the marketplace. In doing so, they noticed that moderate people, who manifested sufficient comprehension of Secours Rouge's antiracist campaign, were no longer compelled by the campaign on prisons. They heard reactions like: "Do we have to build four-star hotels for these crooks?"

M. F.: It is utterly apparent that the proletariat is itself the victim of crime. Old folks obviously have no particular tenderness for the sort of young delinquent who steals their last bit of savings because he wants to buy a Solex. But who is responsible, in the first instance, for the fact that this young man doesn't have enough money to buy a Solex and, in the second, for the fact that he has such a strong desire to buy one? The nineteenth century practiced its specific type of proletariat repression. The proletariat was accorded diverse political rights, freedom of assembly and union rights, but, conversely, the bourgeoisie obtained the promise of good political behavior and the renunciation of open rebellion from the proletariat. The popular masses could exercise their meager rights only by complying with the rules of the game established by the ruling class. In this way, the proletariat interiorized a part of bourgeois ideology. The part concerning the use of violence, insurrection, delinquency, the subproletariat, and the margins of society. Today, we see the first reunion, the first reconciliation between a portion of the proletariat and the nonintegrated portion of the marginal population.

N. M.: On the contrary, if we consider the reactions of the Communist Party, we get the impression that the segment of the proletariat that has a political consciousness neatly distances itself from the subproletariat, the marginal population.

M. F.: That is correct in a certain sense. Ideology puts more and more pressure on the working class. This ideology of order and virtue, of the acceptance of laws, of what is decent and what is not. It's true that this ideology is more and more interiorized. And yet, surprisingly, the violent marginal strata of the plebeian population are regaining their political awareness. For example, there are these young gangs in the projects, in some districts of Paris, for whom their criminal status and their marginal existence take on a political significance.

N. M.: Does the fact that delinquents openly stand on the ground of their delinquency allow us to conclude they have a political consciousness?

M. F.: This consciousness exists. In Renault, for example, there are today perhaps more than a thousand young workers who have a criminal record. Up until recently, they hid it, they were ashamed of it, and no one knew anything about their past. Today, they are starting to talk about it. And they explain that, because of their criminal record, they have difficulty finding work, or they have difficulties after finding work, or they explain that those who have already been convicted are always the first to be laid off, or to be assigned the meanest work. It is an entirely new phenomenon, which is linked to the appearance of new plebeians. Or again, take the former prisoners who, in a public gathering at Nancy, took the floor *[pris la parole]* to speak about their detention. There were public meetings at Nancy, Toul, Lille, Poitiers, and prisoners often took the floor there. They mounted the platform to say: "I spent two years in this prison, or five years in that."

N. M.: Let's take, for example, the meeting last Wednesday at La Mutualité. The audience was composed of noisy sympathizers, a milieu heavily defined by young leftists.

M. F.: This meeting was at once interesting and deceptive. Because, for the first time in Paris, there were ten or twelve former prisoners, introduced by name, who spoke out in public to express what they thought of their detention. On this score, it was singularly interesting. It was also deceptive, because currently a kind of four-year-old tradition exists: We go to La Mutualité, or, as they say, to La Mutu, there is always the same leftist audience, which, moreover, behaved even more badly that evening than usual. Naturally, they were unimpressed. A quarter of them didn't stop chattering, coming and going, the normal mess at La Mutu. What happened before their eyes was all the same to them, the main thing was to be at La Mutu. The gathering had not been organized by the GIP. When we organized something in November, the audience was a little different.[7] The local discussions in youth centers and clubs, villages, small circles, the marketplaces seem more interesting to us. They are more fruitful. The leftist ritual is sterile. These kinds of mass gatherings are no more the barometer of revolutionary mobilization than 11 o'clock village Mass is a barometer for the intensity of faith.

N. M.: You also said, in an interview in 1966: ". . . we are returning to the seventeenth-century perspective, but with this difference: putting in God's place not man, but an anonymous thought, knowledge without a subject, and the theoretical without identity."[8] If we start from this theory, can we still be active in the political realm, given that the subject is abolished? It seems to me that the logical consequence of such a position would be a feeling of lethargy and impotence, of standing by knowledge and renouncing action, in brief: structuralist contemplation.

M. F.: On the contrary, it only signifies the renunciation of personalization; it does not signify immobility. To the GIP, that means: no organization and no leader, they really do everything for it to remain an anonymous movement that exists only by the three letters of its name. Everyone can speak. Whoever the one speaking might be, he does not speak because he has a title or a name, but because he has something to say. The GIP's only watchword is: "Speech to the prisoners!"

N. M.: You said in 1966: "The task of current philosophy . . . is to bring to light this thought before thought, this system before any system."[9]

M. F.: OK, don't constantly go back to things I said before! When I say things, they are already forgotten. I think in order to forget. Everything I said in the past is absolutely without importance. One writes something when one has already worn it out in one's head; one writes the bloodless thought, voilà. What I wrote does not interest me. What interests me is what I could write and what I could do.

N. M.: But you cannot stop your readers from reflecting on your previous ideas, or reflecting on their coherence. At what point in their development should we consider your ideas uninteresting and without importance for the Foucault who has continued to develop?

M. F.: I really don't care. What disturbs me, and the reason why your question makes me a little peeved, is that you could say: "You

already said that," or, "What you said there is the natural development of this other thought." It bothers me when you suggest there
is no relationship between *History of Madness* and my work in
GIP. You could also list all the possible and imaginable sentences
I might have written or said that would contradict what I do today,
and I would respond to you simply: first, I don't give a damn, and,
second, it gives me pleasure. What I mean by that is I don't feel
either attacked or critiqued or embarrassed by the fact that I no
longer say the same things as before. And that gives me pleasure,
for that proves that I don't have a narcissistic relationship to my
discourse.

N. M.: The issue is not to trap you in contradictions; in fact, what interests me is the idea that today you do the work of a philosopher.

M. F.: You want to know my idea of a philosopher's work? Philosophers don't work! What characterizes the philosopher is that he
distances himself from reality. He can't come near it.

N. M.: It would be a great time to abolish philosophy, and perhaps
also philosophers!

M. F.: Philosophy is already abolished. It is no more than a vague little
university discipline in which people talk about an entity's totality,
"writing," the "materiality of the signifier," and other such things.

N. M.: A couple of serious philosophers, who "totalize" as Sartre would
say, still exist outside the university.

M. F.: Yes. *(Long silence.)* Wherever Sartre totalizes, he distances himself from reality. And each time he grasps a determinate problem,
has a determinate strategy, or struggles, he approaches reality.

N. M.: The GIP's fight, which you lead with Sartre and other activists,
aims not at the center of society, the relations of production and
appropriation, but at its periphery. Can the situation of prisoners
change if, in France, the same class remains in power?

M. F.: No. Why should they want to change detention conditions
when they are in power? During the revolt staged at Toul Prison,
we received messages of support from foreign countries. The most
vigorous encouragement came from Uppsala Prison in Sweden.
That means that the prison revolts put into question not details,
like whether or not to have television or permission to play soccer, but, on the contrary, the status of the marginal plebeian in

capitalist society. The status of the derelict. In our day, there are a large number of young people who want to be engaged in the GIP and with other problems of the marginal population. But what they lack are analyses. For, the Communist Party, or the French Marxist tradition in general, has hardly improved what services we extend toward marginal people, what we understand as their problems, and what we present as their demands. Leftists them-selves have the greatest repugnance for doing this work. In the end, we need analyses of power in order to give meaning to this political struggle that is now beginning.

N. M.: Do you know of a model prison?

M. F.: No. But there *do exist* better prisons than those in France. In Sweden, fifteen years ago, on the road from Uppsala to Stock-holm, I saw an establishment that resembled a very comfortable French school building. The problem is not a model prison or the abolition of prisons. Currently, in our system, marginalization is effected by prisons. This marginalization will not automatically disappear by abolishing the prison. Society would quite simply institute another means. The problem is the following: to offer a critique of the system that explains the process by which con-temporary society pushes a portion of the population to the mar-gins. Voilà.

Notes

1. [Eds.] Frans Hals, *Les Régentes* (1664).

2. [Eds.] See Paul Claudel's "Introduction à la peinture hollandaise," in *L'œil écoute* (Paris: Gallimard, 1967), 9–68.

3. [Eds.] Foucault's calculation here appears to be incorrect.

4. [Eds.] It is worth recalling that the term "paraphernalia," commonly applied to various specialized accoutrements, originally referred to prop-erty owned by a married woman (from the Greek *para* [apart from] and *pherna* [dowry]).

5. [Eds.] "Entretien avec Madeleine Chapsal," *La Quinzaine littéraire*, no. 5 (May 16, 1966): 14–15, reprinted in DE I, no. 37, 513–18 (where the pas-sage quoted appears on 514) and DEQ I, no. 37, 541–46 (passage appears on 542).

6. [Eds.] See "It Was about a Year Ago" (this volume) for Foucault's statement from the press conference held after this protest.

7. [Eds.] See "A Movement of Struggle Is Developing Today . . ." (this volume) for the flyer announcing this event and "On What Does the Penitentiary System Rely?" (this volume) for Daniel Defert's speech from this meeting.

8. [Eds.] See "Entretien avec Madeleine Chapsal."

9. [Eds.] Ibid.

Intellectuals and Power

MICHEL FOUCAULT AND GILLES DELEUZE

A discussion between Michel Foucault and Gilles Deleuze recorded on March 4, 1972. It was published in L'Arc, no. 49 (1972): 3–10.

MICHEL FOUCAULT: A Maoist once said to me: "I can easily understand Sartre's purpose in siding with us; I can understand his goals and his involvement in politics; I can partially understand your position, since you've always been concerned with the problem of confinement. But Deleuze is an enigma." I was shocked by this statement because your position has always seemed particularly clear to me.

GILLES DELEUZE: Possibly we're in the process of experiencing a new relationship between theory and practice. At one time, practice was considered an application of theory, a consequence; at other times, it had the opposite sense and was thought to inspire theory, to be indispensable for the creation of future theoretical forms. In any event, their relationship was understood in terms of a process of totalization. For us, however, the question is seen in a different light. The relationships between theory and practice are far more partial and fragmentary. On one side, a theory is always local and related to a limited field, and it is applied in another sphere, more or less distant from it. The relationship that holds in the application of a theory is never one of resemblance. Moreover, from the moment a theory moves into its proper domain, it begins to encounter obstacles, walls, and blockages that require its relay by another type of discourse (it is through this other discourse that it eventually passes to a different domain). Practice is a set of relays from one theoretical point to another, and theory is a relay from one practice to another. No theory can develop without eventually encountering a wall, and practice is necessary for piercing this wall. For example, your work began in the theoretical analysis of the context of confinement, specifically with respect to the psychiatric asylum within a capitalist society in the nineteenth century. Then you became aware of the necessity for confined individuals to speak for themselves, to create a relay (it's possible, on the contrary, that your function was already that of a relay in relation to them); and this group is found in prisons—these individuals are imprisoned. It was on this basis that you organized the Prisons Information Group (GIP),[1] the object being to create conditions that permit the prisoners themselves to speak. It would be absolutely false to say, as the Maoist implied, that in moving to this practice you were applying your theories. This was not an application; nor was it a project for initiating reforms or an inquiry in the traditional sense. The emphasis was altogether different: a system of relays within a larger sphere, within a multiplicity of parts that are both theoretical and practical. A theorizing intellectual, for us, is no longer a subject, a representing or representative consciousness. Those who act and struggle are no longer represented, either by a group or by a union that appropriates the right to stand as their conscience. Who speaks and acts? It is always a multiplicity, even within the person who speaks and acts. All of us are *"groupuscules."*[2] Representation no longer exists; there's only action-theoretical action and practical action that serve as relays and form networks.

M. F.: It seems to me that the political involvement of the intellectual was traditionally the product of two different aspects of his activity: his position as an intellectual in bourgeois society, in the system of capitalist production and within the ideology it produces or imposes (his exploitation, poverty, rejection, persecution, the accusations of subversive activity, immorality, etc.); and his proper discourse to the extent that it revealed a particular truth, that it disclosed political relationships where they were unsuspected. These two forms of politicization did not exclude each other, but, being of a different order, neither did they coincide. Some were classed as "outcasts" and others as "socialists." During moments of violent reaction on the part of the authorities, these two positions were readily fused: after 1848, after the Commune, and after 1940. The intellectual was rejected and persecuted at the precise moment when the facts became incontrovertible, when it was forbidden to say that the emperor had no clothes. The intellectual spoke the truth to those who had yet to see it, in the name of those who were forbidden to speak the truth: he was conscience, consciousness, and eloquence.

In the most recent upheaval,[3] the intellectual discovered that the masses no longer need him to gain knowledge: they *know* perfectly well, without illusion; they know far better than he and they are certainly capable of expressing themselves. But there exists a system of power that blocks, prohibits, and invalidates this discourse and this knowledge, a power not only found in the manifest authority of censorship, but one that profoundly and subtly penetrates an entire societal network. Intellectuals are themselves agents of this system of power—the idea of their responsibility for "consciousness" and discourse forms part of the system. The intellectual's role is no longer to place himself "somewhat ahead and to the side" in order to express the stifled truth of the collectivity; rather, it is to struggle against the forms of power that transform him into its object and instrument in the sphere of "knowledge," "truth," "consciousness," and "discourse."[4]

In this sense, theory does not express, translate, or serve to apply practice: it is practice. But it is local and regional, as you said, and not totalizing. This is a struggle against power, a struggle aimed at revealing and undermining power where it is most invisible and insidious. It is not to "awaken consciousness" that we struggle (the masses have been aware for some time that consciousness is a form of knowledge; and consciousness as the basis of subjectivity is a prerogative of the bourgeoisie), but to sap power, to take power; it is an activity conducted alongside those who struggle for power, and not their illumination from a safe distance. A "theory" is the regional system of this struggle.

G. D: Precisely. A theory is exactly like a box of tools. It has nothing to do with the signifier. It must be useful. It must function. And not for itself. If no one uses it, beginning with the theoretician himself (who then ceases to be a theoretician), then the theory is worthless or the moment is inappropriate. We don't revise a theory; we make new ones, we have no choice but to make new ones. It is strange that it was Proust, an author thought to be a pure intellectual, who said it so clearly: treat my book as a pair of glasses directed to the outside; if they don't suit you, find another pair; I leave it to you to find your own instrument, which is necessarily an instrument for combat. A theory does not totalize; it is an instrument for multiplication and it also multiplies itself. It is in the nature of power to totalize and it is your position, and one I fully agree with, that theory is by nature opposed to power. As soon as a theory is enmeshed in a particular point, we realize that it will never possess the slightest practical importance unless it can erupt in a totally different area. This is why the notion of reform is so stupid and hypocritical. Either reforms are designed by people who claim to be representative, who make a profession of speaking for others, and they lead to a division of power, to a distribution of this new power that is consequently increased by a double repression; or they arise from the complaints and demands of those concerned. This latter instance is no longer a reform but revolutionary action that questions (expressing the full force of its partiality) the totality of power and the hierarchy that maintains it. This is surely evident in prisons: the smallest and most insignificant of the prisoners' demands can puncture Pleven's pseudo-reform. If the protests of children were heard in kindergarten, if their questions were attended to, it would be enough to explode the entire educational system. In truth, this system in which we live *can't stand anything*: hence, its radical fragility at every point and at the same time its global force of repression. In my opinion, you were the first—in your books and in the practical sphere—to teach us something absolutely fundamental: the indignity of speaking for others. We ridiculed representation and said it was finished, but we failed to draw the consequences of this "theoretical" conversion—to appreciate the theoretical fact that only those directly concerned can speak in a practical way on their own behalf.

M. F.: And when the prisoners began to speak, they possessed an individual theory of prisons, the penal system, and justice. It is this form of discourse that ultimately matters, a discourse against power, the counterdiscourse of prisoners and those we call delinquents and not a theory *about* delinquency. The problem of prisons is local and marginal: not more than 100,000 people pass through prisons in a year. In France at present, between 300,000 and 400,000 have been to prison. Yet this marginal problem seems to disturb everyone. I was surprised that so many who had not been to prison could become interested in its problems, surprised that all those who had never heard the discourse of prisoners could so easily understand them. How do we explain this? Isn't it because, in a general way, the penal system is the form in which power is most obviously seen as power? To place someone in prison, to confine him there, to deprive him of food and heat, to prevent him from leaving, from making love, etc.—this is certainly the most over-the-top manifestation of power imaginable. The other day I was speaking to a woman who had been in prison and she was saying: "Imagine, that at the age of forty, I was punished one day with a meal of dry bread." What is striking about this story is not the childishness of the exercise of power but the cynicism with which power is exercised as power, in the most archaic, puerile, infantile manner. As children we learn what it means to be reduced to bread and water. Prison is the only place where power is manifested in its naked state, in its most excessive form, and where it is justified as moral force. "I am within my rights to punish you because you know that it is criminal to rob and kill. . . ." What is fascinating about prisons is that, for once, power doesn't hide or mask itself; it reveals itself as tyranny thrust into the tiniest details; it is cynical and at the same time pure and entirely "justified," because its practice can be totally formulated within the framework of morality. Its brutal tyranny consequently appears as the serene domination of Good over Evil, of order over disorder.

G. D.: Yes, and the reverse is equally true. Not only are prisoners treated like children, but children are treated like prisoners. Children are submitted to an infantilization that is alien to them. On this basis, it is undeniable that schools resemble prisons and that factories are its closest approximation. Look at the entrance to a Renault plant, or anywhere else for that matter: three tickets to get into the washroom during the day. You found an eighteenth-century text by Jeremy Bentham proposing prison reforms; in the name of this exalted reform, he establishes a circular system where the renovated prison serves as a model and where the individual passes imperceptibly from school to factory, from factory to prison, and vice versa. This is the essence of the reforming impulse, of reformed representation. On the contrary, when people begin to speak and act on their own behalf, they do not oppose their representation (even as its reversal) to another; they do not oppose a new representativity to the false representativity of power. For example, I remember your saying that there is no popular justice against justice; the reckoning takes place at another level.

M. F.: I think that it is not simply the idea of better and more equitable forms of justice that underlies the people's hatred of the judicial system, of judges, courts, and prisons, but—aside from this and before anything else—the singular perception that power is always exercised at the expense of the people. The antijudicial struggle is a struggle against power and I don't think that it is a struggle against injustice, against the injustice of the judicial system, or a struggle for improving the efficiency of its institutions. It is particularly striking that in outbreaks of rioting and revolt or in seditious movements the judicial system has been as compelling a target as the financial structure, the army, and other forms of power. My hypothesis—but it is merely a hypothesis—is that popular courts, such as those found in the Revolution, were a means for the lower middle class, who were allied with the masses, to salvage and recapture the initiative in the struggle against the judicial system. To achieve this, they proposed a court system based on the possibility of equitable justice, where a judge might render a just verdict. The identifiable form of the court of law belongs to the bourgeois ideology of justice.

G. D.: On the basis of our actual situation, power emphatically develops a total or global vision. That is, all the current forms of repression (the racist repression of immigrant workers, repression in the factories, in the educational system, and the general repression of youth) are easily totalized from the point of view of power. We should not only seek the unity of these forms in the reaction to May '68, but more appropriately, in the concerted preparation and organization of the near future. French capitalism now relies on a "margin" of unemployment and has abandoned the liberal and paternal mask that promised full employment. In this perspective, we begin to see the unity of the forms of repression: restrictions on immigration, once it is acknowledged that the most difficult and thankless jobs go to immigrant workers; repression in the factories, because the French must reacquire the "taste" for increasingly harder work; the struggle against youth and the repression of the educational system, because police repression is more active when there is less need for young people in the workforce. A wide range of professionals (teachers, psychiatrists, educators of all kinds, etc.) will be called upon to exercise functions that have traditionally belonged to the police. This is something you predicted long ago, and it was thought impossible at the time: the reinforcement of all the structures of confinement. Against this global policy of power, we initiate localized counterresponses, skirmishes, active and occasionally preventive defenses. We have no need to totalize that which is invariably totalized on the side of power; if we were to move in this direction, it would mean restoring the representative forms of centralism and a hierarchical structure. We must set up lateral affiliations and an entire system of networks and popular bases; and this is especially difficult. In any case, we no longer define reality as a continuation of politics in the traditional sense of competition and the distribution of power, through the so-called representatives in the Communist Party or the General Confederation of Labor (CGT). Reality is what effectively happens today in a factory, in a school, in a barracks, in a prison, in a police station. And this action carries a type of information that is altogether different from that found in newspapers (this explains the kind of information carried by the *Agence de presse Libération*).

M. F.: Isn't this difficulty of finding adequate forms of struggle a result of the fact that we continue to ignore the problem of power? After all, we had to wait until the nineteenth century before we began to understand the nature of exploitation, and to this day, we have yet to fully comprehend the nature of power. It may be that Marx and Freud cannot satisfy our desire for understanding this enigmatic thing that we call power, which is at once visible and invisible, present and hidden, ubiquitous. Theories of government and the traditional analyses of their mechanisms certainly don't exhaust the field where power is exercised and where it functions. The question of power remains a total enigma. Who exercises power? And in what sphere? We now know with reasonable certainty who exploits others, who receives the profits, which people are involved, and we know how these funds are reinvested. But as for power . . . We know that it is not in the hands of those who govern. But, of course, the idea of the "ruling class" has never received an adequate formulation, and neither have other terms, such as "to dominate," "to rule," "to govern," "group in power," "state apparatus," etc. This whole set of notions needs to be analyzed. We should also investigate the limits imposed on the exercise of power—the relays through which it operates and the extent of its influence on the often insignificant aspects of the hierarchy and the forms of control, surveillance, prohibition, and constraint. Everywhere that power exists, it is being exercised. No one, strictly speaking, has an official right to power; and yet it is always exerted in a particular direction, with some people on one side and some on the other. It is often difficult to say who holds power in a precise sense, but it is easy to see who lacks power. If the reading of your books (from *Nietzsche*[5] to what I anticipate in *Capitalism and Schizophrenia*)[6] has been essential for me, it is because they seem to go very far in exploring this problem: under the ancient theme of sense, of the signifier and the signified, etc., you have developed the question of power, of the inequality of powers and their struggles. Each struggle develops around a particular source of power (any of the countless, tiny sources—a small-time boss, the manager of "HLM," a prison warden, a judge, a union representative, the editor in chief of a newspaper). And if pointing out these sources—denouncing and speaking out—is to be a part of the struggle, it is not because they were previously unknown. Rather, it is because to speak on this subject, to force the institutionalized networks of information to listen, to produce names, to point the finger of accusation, to find targets, is the first step in the reversal of power and the initiation of new struggles against existing forms of power. If the discourse of prisoners or prison doctors constitutes a form of struggle, it is because they confiscate, at least temporarily, the power to speak on prison conditions—at present, the exclusive property of prison administrators and their cronies in reform groups.[7] The discourse of struggle is not opposed to the unconscious, but to the secretive. It may not seem like much; but what if it turned out to be more than we expected? A whole series of misunderstandings relates to things that are "hidden," "repressed," and "unsaid"; and they permit the cheap "psychoanalysis" of the proper objects of struggle. It is perhaps more difficult to unearth a secret than the unconscious. The two themes frequently encountered in the recent past, that "writing is repressed" and that "writing is automatically subversive," seem to betray a number of operations that deserve to be severely denounced.

G. D.: With respect to the problem you posed: it is clear who exploits, who profits, and who governs, but power nevertheless remains something more diffuse. I would venture the following hypothesis: the thrust of Marxism was to define the problem essentially in terms of interests (power is held by a ruling class defined by its interests). The question immediately arises: how is it that people whose interests are not being served can strictly support the existing power structure by demanding a piece of the action? Perhaps, this is because in terms of *investments,* whether economic or unconscious, interest is not the final answer; there are investments of desire that function in a more profound and diffuse manner than our interests dictate. But, of course, we never desire against our interests, because interest always follows and finds itself where desire has placed it. We cannot shut out Reich's cry: the masses were not deceived; at a particular time, they actually wanted a fascist regime! There are investments of desire that mold and distribute power, that make it the property of the policeman as much as of the prime minister; in this context, there is no qualitative difference between the power wielded by the policeman and the prime minister. The nature of these investments of desire in a social group explains why political parties or unions, which might have or should have revolutionary investments in the name of class interests, are so often reform oriented or absolutely reactionary on the level of desire.

M. F.: As you say, the relationships between desire, power, and interest are . . . more complex than we ordinarily think, and it is not necessarily those who exercise power who have an interest in its execution; nor is it always possible for those with vested interests to exercise power. Moreover, the desire for power establishes a singular relationship between power and interest. It may happen that the masses, during fascist periods, desire that certain people assume power, people with whom they are unable to identify since these individuals exert power against the masses and at their expense, to the extreme of their death, their sacrifice, their massacre. Nevertheless, they desire this particular power; they want it to be exercised. This play of desire, power, and interest has received very little attention. It was a long time before we began to understand exploitation; and desire has had and continues to have a long history. It is possible that the struggles now taking place and the local, regional, and discontinuous theories that derive from these struggles and that are indissociable from them stand at the threshold of our discovery of the manner in which power is exercised.

G. D.: In this context, I must return to the question: the present revolutionary movement has created multiple centers, and not as the result of weakness or insufficiency, since a certain kind of totalization pertains to power and the forces of reaction. (Vietnam, for instance, is an impressive example of localized countertactics). But how are we to define the networks, the transversal links between these active and discontinuous points, from one country to another or within a single country?

M. F.: The question of geographic discontinuity that you raise might mean the following: as soon as we struggle against exploitation, the proletariat not only leads the struggle but also defines its targets, its methods, and the places and instruments for confrontation; and to ally oneself with the proletariat is to accept its positions, its ideology, and its motives for combat. This means total identification. But if the fight is directed against power, then all those on whom power is exercised to their detriment, all who find it intolerable, can begin the struggle on their own terrain and on the basis of their proper activity (or passivity). In engaging in a struggle that concerns their own interests, whose objectives they clearly understand and whose methods only they can determine, they enter into a revolutionary process. They naturally enter as allies of the proletariat, because power is exercised the way it is in order to maintain capitalist exploitation. They genuinely serve the cause of the proletariat by fighting in those places where they find themselves oppressed. Women, prisoners, conscripted soldiers, hospital patients, and homosexuals have now begun a specific struggle against the particularized form of power, the constraints and controls that are exerted over them. Such struggles are actually involved in the revolutionary movement to the degree that they are radical, uncompromising, and nonreformist, and refuse any attempt at arriving at a new disposition of the same power with, at best, a change of masters. And these movements are linked to the revolutionary movement of the proletariat to the extent that they fight against the controls and constraints that serve the same system of power.

In this sense, the overall picture presented by the struggle is certainly not that of the totalization you mentioned earlier, this theoretical totalization under the guise of "truth." The generality of the struggle specifically derives from the system of power itself, from all the forms in which power is exercised and applied.

G. D.: And which we are unable to approach in any of its applications without revealing its diffuse character, so that we are necessarily led—on the basis of the most insignificant demand—to the desire to blow it up completely. Every revolutionary attack or defense, however partial, is linked in this way to the workers' struggle.

Notes

1. [Orig. Eng. Ed.] Foucault's books *I, Pierre Riviere*, trans. Frank Jellinek (Lincoln: University of Nebraska Press, 1982), and *Discipline and Punish* (New York: Vintage Books, 1977) both result from this group.

2. [Orig. Eng. Ed.] Cf. Michel Foucault, "Theatrum Philosophicum," in *Foucault Live: Collected Interviews, 1961–1984*, ed. Sylvère Lotringer (New York: Semiotext(e), 1996), 185.

3. [Orig. Eng. Ed.] May 1968.

4. [Orig. Eng. Ed.] See Michel Foucault, "Discourse on Language," in *The Archeology of Knowledge* (New York: Random House, 1972), 215–37.

5. [Eds.] *Nietzsche et la philosophie* (Paris: P.U.F., 1962), in English translation as *Nietzsche and Philosophy* (New York: Columbia University Press, 1983).

6. [Eds.] *Capitalisme et schizophrénie*, vol. 1, *L'Anti-Œdipe*, in collab-

oration with Félix Guattari (Paris: Éditions de Minuit, 1972), in English translation as *Anti-Oedipus: Capitalism and Schizophrenia* (Minneapolis: University of Minnesota Press, 1983).

7. [Eds.] Foucault appears to be referring here to Doctor Édith Rose, the psychiatrist at the Ney Prison in Toul, whose report, written in the aftermath of the Toul Revolt, documented many of the daily atrocities at the prison. See the "Report by Doctor Rose" and Foucault's own analysis of the report, "The Toul Speech" (this volume).

On Attica

MICHEL FOUCAULT

An interview with Michel Foucault conducted in Buffalo, New York, on April 21, 1972, by John Simon after their tour of the Attica Correctional Facility, the site of a major revolt in September 1971. It was translated by John Simon and appeared in Telos *19 (1974): 154–61. The translation has been revised for this volume.*

JOHN SIMON: We just recently visited the prison at Attica and I know that in addition to your studies about exclusion—exclusion of the sick, exclusion of all sorts—you have been interested for a year or a year and a half in prison reform in France. I would like to know your reactions to this visit. It's the first time, I believe, that you set foot in a prison.

MICHEL FOUCAULT: Well, yes, since in France one does not have the right to visit prisons. You can enter a prison only if you are yourself a prisoner, a guard, or a lawyer, and I have not, practically speaking, belonged to any of these three categories. I have never been detained by the police for more than twelve hours, and consequently I have not really been able to get to know prisons in France. It is thus thanks to you that I was able, for the first time in my life, to enter a prison, and obviously, for a Frenchman, the sight of Attica is completely overwhelming. Even though I have never entered French prisons, I have heard a lot about them from people who have spent time there, and I know that they are decrepit and dilapidated places, with the prisoners often crammed on top of one another in cells that are repellent with filth. Attica is obviously not that at all. At Attica, what struck me perhaps first of all was the entrance, that kind of phony fortress à la

291

Disneyland, those observation posts disguised as medieval towers with their *machicoulis*.[1] And behind this rather ridiculous scenery, which dwarfs everything else, you discover it's an immense machine. And it's this notion of machinery that struck me most strongly—those very long, clean, heated corridors that prescribe, for those who pass through them, specific trajectories that are evidently calculated to be the most efficient possible and at the same time the easiest to oversee, and the most direct. Yes, and all of this ends in those huge workshops, like the metallurgical one, that are clean and appear to be close to perfection. A former Attica prisoner whom I saw the day before yesterday told me that, in reality, those famous workshops that they display so willingly are very dangerous, that a lot of people are hurt in them. But actually, at first sight you have the impression you are visiting more than just a factory, that you are visiting a machine, the inside of a machine.

So, the question one obviously asks is what does the machine produce, what is that gigantic installation used for, and what comes out of it? At the time of the creation of Auburn and the Philadelphia prison, which served as models (with very few modifications even to the present day) for the great machines of incarceration, it was believed that something indeed was produced: "virtuous" men. Now we know, and the administration is perfectly aware, that no such thing is produced. That nothing at all is produced. That it is a question simply of an extraordinary sleight of hand, a curious mechanism of circular elimination: society eliminates by sending to prison people whom prison breaks down, crushes, physically eliminates; and then once they have been broken down, the prison eliminates them by "freeing" them and sending them back to society; and there, their life in prison, the way in which they were treated, the state in which they come out ensures that society will eliminate them once again, sending them back to prison, which in turn ... Attica is a machine for elimination, a kind of prodigious stomach, a kidney that consumes, destroys, breaks down, and then rejects, and that consumes in order to eliminate what it has already eliminated. You remember that when we visited Attica they spoke to us about the four wings of the building, the four corridors, the four large corridors A, B, C, and D. Well, I learned, again through the same former prisoner, that there is a fifth corridor, which they didn't talk to us about—it's corridor E. And you know which one that is?

J. S.: No.

M. F.: Ah, well, it is quite simply the machine of the machine, or rather the elimination of the elimination, elimination in the second degree: it is the psychiatric wing. That is where they send the ones who cannot even be integrated into the machine and whom the machinery cannot succeed in assimilating according to its norms, that it cannot crush in accordance with its own mechanical process. Thus, they need an additional mechanism.

J. S.: You have studied the process of exclusion as a sort of abstract concept, and I know that you are acquainted with the inside of hospitals and other institutions. To have visited a place like this—I mean physically visited—did that effect any emotional change in your attitude toward the process of exclusion? Or has the visit simply reinforced your ideas about exclusion?

M. F.: No, they have rather been undermined; in any case a problem has arisen for me that is rather different from ones that I had previously been puzzling over; the change was perhaps not absolutely determined by the visit to Attica, but the visit surely precipitated it. Until then I envisioned exclusion from society as a sort of general function, a bit abstract, and I tried to plot that function as in some way constitutive of society, each society being able to function only on condition that a certain number of people are excluded from it. Traditional sociology, sociology of the Durkheim type, presented the problem in the following way: How can society hold individuals together? What is the form of relationship, of symbolic or affective communication that is established among individuals? What is the organizational system that permits society to constitute a totality? In a way, I was interested in the opposite problem, or, if you will, in the opposite response to this problem, which is: through what system of exclusion, by eliminating whom, by creating what division, through what game of negation and rejection can society begin to function?

Well, the question that I ask myself now is the reverse: prison is an organization that is too complex to be reduced to purely negative functions of exclusion; its cost, its importance, the care that one takes in administering it, the justifications that one tries to give for it seem to indicate that it possesses positive functions. The problem is, then, to find out what role capitalist society has its penal system play, what is the aim that is sought, and what effects are produced by all these procedures for punishment and exclusion? What is their place in the economic process, what is their importance in the exercise and the maintenance of power? What is their role in the class struggle?

J. S.: I wondered precisely to what degree you remained conscious of the political context while walking through the corridors of Attica. I myself was so terrified by the purely human side, by the sense of latent suffering and repression, that there were moments, paradoxically perhaps, when I completely forgot the political context.

M. F.: It is very difficult for me to reply on the matter of the human and sheer physical horror of what goes on at Attica. I believe that I had the same impression as you; but possibly I am less sensitive than you and perhaps a bit thick-skinned. When you go through those long corridors, which are—let me repeat—clean, a Frenchman has the impression of being in a somewhat austere private or parochial school; after all, nineteenth-century *lycées* and *collèges* were not that much more pleasant. But finally, after thinking it over, what appeared most terrifying to me at Attica was the strange relationship between the periphery and the inner part. I mean the double game of bars: those that separate the prison from the outside and those that, inside the prison, set apart each of the individual cells. The former, the bars on the gates—I am well aware how prison theoreticians justify them: society must be protected. (Of course, one might say that the greatest dangers for society are not produced by car thieves, but by wars, famines, exploitation, and all those who permit and provoke them, but let that pass . . .) Once the first bars have been passed through, you might expect to find a place where the prisoners are "readapted" to community life, to a respect for law, to a practice of justice, etc. Well, you perceive instead that the place where prisoners spend 10 to 12 hours a day, the place where they consider themselves "at home," is a terrifying animal cage: about two yards by one and one-half yards, entirely grated on one side. The place where they are alone, where they sleep and where they read, where they dress and take care of their needs, is a cage for wild animals. And there lies the entire hypocrisy of the prison. One suspects that the representative of the administration who conducts the visit must really be chuckling inside. You have the impression that he must be saying to himself and also to us something like: "You have handed over to us robbers and murderers because you thought of them as wild beasts; you asked us to make domesticated sheep of them on the other side of the bars that protect you; but there is no reason why we, the guards, the representatives of 'law and order,' we, the instruments of your morality and your prejudices, would not think of them as wild animals, just the same as you. We are identical with you; we are you; and, consequently, in this cage where you have put us with them, we build cages that reestablish between them and us the relationship of exclusion and power that the large prison establishes between them and you. You signaled to us that they are wild beasts; we signal in turn to them. And when they have learned it well behind their bars, we will send them back to you." The only way for prisoners to escape from this system of training is by collective action, political organization, rebellion. It appears that the American prison, much more easily than European prisons, can be a place for political action. American prisons in fact play two roles: a role as a place of punishment, as there has existed now for centuries, and a role of "concentration camp," as there existed in Europe during the war and in Africa during the European colonization (in Algeria, for example, during the period when the French were there). One must not forget that there are more than one million prisoners in the United States out of 220 million inhabitants, compared with 30,000 in France for 50 million inhabitants. The proportion is not at all the same. Then, in the United States, there must be one out of 30 or 40 Black men in prison: it is here that one can see the function of massive elimination in the American prison. The penal system, the entire pattern of even minor prohibitions (too much drinking, speeding, smoking hashish) serves as an instrument and as a pretext for this practice of radical concentration. It is hardly surprising that the political struggle for penal justice has progressed further in the United States than in France.

J. S.: One of the things that occurred to me was the question of whether such a prison, in the context of American society, might be considered a symbol, simply a microcosm of society in general, or—you said a moment ago that the prison resembled schools as they were formerly . . .

M. F.: In Europe, in Europe . . .

J. S.: Yes, in Europe, but in America, now you have become acquainted with many no-man's-lands, areas on the outskirts of cities, suburbs; you have spoken to me in rather precise terms of drugstores in airports, places that seem to be nowhere. And, of course, there are bars everywhere in our society like those in prison. Is it such a big jump from the center of a city—from a ghetto, for example—to the situation of a prison that the latter cannot be naturally encompassed as a normal part of American society or, on the contrary, isn't the prison simply an extension of this society, an extremity of it, as it were?

M. F.: I think that your question is very much to the point because, indeed, Attica does resemble America in a profound way—in any event, America as it is viewed by a European who is a little bit lost and not very resourceful like me; that is to say, gigantic, technological, a little terrifying, that Piranesi aspect that permeates the view of many Europeans about New York.[2] It is true that what we have seen resembles American society, but you cannot, I think, simply be satisfied to say, "Oh, yes, American prisons are the image of American society, just as European prisons are the image of Europe"; for, if you say that too much, you are ultimately saying this, that in the final analysis we are all in prison, that, after all, in the street, in a factory, in a dormitory, one is similarly in prison. It is true that we are caught in a system of continuous surveillance and punishment. But prison is not only punitive; it is also part of an eliminative process. Prison is the physical elimination of people who come out of it, who die of it sometimes directly, and almost always indirectly insofar as they can no longer find a trade, don't have anything to live on, cannot reconstitute a family anymore, etc., and, finally, passing from one prison to another or from one crime to another, end up by actually being physically eliminated.

J. S.: Well, then, where does one begin to reform prisons, because just as with the Vietnam War, those who seek to reform prisons may be deluding themselves in feeling that they are cleaning up the source of evil simply by making the most visible symptom of it disappear? Is it not, then, an illusion to hope for reform inside prisons? Are not the prisons so much a part of the fabric of society that nothing can be achieved by beginning there?

M. F.: The group that we have formed in France is not first and principally concerned with the reform of prisons. Our project is, I really think, quite radically different. In France (I know that in America the situation is a little bit different because of the army) the penal system and imprisonment weigh in a privileged and most insistent manner upon a certain fringe of the population that is really not integrated into the working class, controlled to a certain extent by the large unions. We have often been told, on behalf of certain political organizations, that the problem of prisons is not part of the proletarian conflict. There are several reasons for that. The first one is that the fringe of the lower class that is constantly in contact with the police and law is to a large extent made up of people who are outside the factory. Whether their unemployment is voluntary or involuntary, their form of opposition to bourgeois society does not express itself in demonstrations, politically organized struggles, and professional or economic pressures such as strikes. The second reason is that the bourgeoisie often uses this fringe of the population against the working people: it may be made into a temporary workforce or even recruited by the police. The third reason is that the proletariat has been fully imbued with the bourgeois ideology concerning morality and legality, concerning theft and crime.

So we are currently at a state where different strata of the people seek to overcome conflicts and oppositions that had been established and maintained between them by the capitalist system; where struggles in the factories are linked more than they used to be with struggles outside the factories (concerning housing, the question of the "quality of life," etc.); where it is recognized that the general ideological struggle is an integral part of the political struggle. For all these reasons, the isolation of that fringe of the lower class, at the outset under the domination of police pressure, is in the process of slowly disappearing. Its reintegration into political struggles is the prime objective of our group.

J. S.: In this regard, the story that you told us about Genet and the

distinction that was made between certain types of prisoners—
has that sort of thing become better recognized by the proletariat
in France as well as in America?

M. F.: You are evidently referring to what Genet told me one day about
prisons. During the war he was in prison at La Santé and he had
to be transferred to the Palais de Justice in order to be sentenced;
at that time the custom was to handcuff the prisoners two-by-
two to lead them to the Palais de Justice; just as Genet was about
to be handcuffed to another prisoner, the latter asked the guard,
"Who is this guy you're handcuffing me to?" and the guard replied:
"It's a thief." The other prisoner stiffened at that point and said,
"No, I'm a political prisoner, I'm a Communist, I won't be handcuffed with a thief." And Genet said to me that from that day on,
with regard to all forms of political movement and action we have
known in France, he has had not merely a distrust, but a certain
contempt...

J. S.: I wonder to what extent, since that time, those who are involved
in politics have become aware of the lack of distinction among different forms of prisoners, of the possibility that these other prisoners, victims of social problems that are at the source of their own
political struggle, are not political prisoners in the proper sense of
the word, but are still more profoundly prisoners, politically, than
they themselves?

M. F.: I believe that there has been a historical mutation, if you will,
in the course of the nineteenth century. It is almost certain that
labor movements and their leaders, in Europe and particularly in
France, in order to escape from police repression in its more violent and savage form, were obliged to distinguish themselves from
the entire criminal population. Efforts were made to present these
labor movements as organizations of murderers, as hired killers,
thieves, alcoholics, etc. There was thus the necessity to avoid falling victim to these accusations and to the consequent punishments; thus, also the obligation they felt to take up, as if it were
their own, the responsibility for a whole system of morality that
came from the ruling class, and finally to accept the bourgeois
division between virtue and vice, respect for the property of others, and so on. They were obliged to re-create for themselves a
sort of moral puritanism that was for them a necessary condition

for survival and a useful instrument in the struggle as well. That kind of moral rigorism finally remained with them as a part of the proletariat's daily ideology, and still now, until recent times, the proletariat and its union or political leaders had certainly continued to grant that separation between the common-law offenders and political prisoners. And, after all, you must keep in mind all the struggles, all the efforts that were necessary in the nineteenth century so that the leaders of the workers were not treated and punished like crooks.

The change occurred a short while ago in France at the time of the imprisonment of certain Maoists. When Maoists were put in prison, they began, it must be said, by reacting a little like the traditional political groups, that is to say: "We do not want to be assimilated with the common-law criminals, we do not want our image to be mixed with theirs in the opinion of people, and we ask to be treated like political prisoners with the rights of political prisoners." This was, I think, a sort of political mistake that was rather quickly felt; there were discussions on this subject, and it was at this time that we founded our group; the Maoists quickly understood that ultimately the prison's elimination of common-law prisoners was part of the system of political elimination of which they were themselves the victims. If one makes the distinction, if one accepts the difference between political law and common law, that means that fundamentally one recognizes bourgeois morality and law as far as respect for the property of others, respect for traditional moral values, etc., are concerned. The cultural revolution in its widest sense implies that, at least in a society like ours, you no longer make the division between common-law criminals and political criminals. Common law is politics; it is, after all, the bourgeois class that, for political reasons and on the basis of its political power, defined what is called common law.

J. S.: Then, what the Maoists understood was not simply a political mistake that they had committed—I mean, in the eyes of the public, the idea that they were excluding themselves, that they intended to remain an elite in prison—but this was something they learned as well in connection with politics in a much deeper sense.

M. F.: That's right, I believe that it was for them an important deepening of their understanding, the discovery that ultimately both the penal system in its entirety and the entire moral system were the result of a power relationship established by the bourgeoisie and constituted an instrument for exercising and maintaining that power.

J. S.: In listening to you, I am reminded of a scene in the film *The Battle of Algiers*. This is simply one example among others, but there is a certain asceticism on the part of revolutionaries that results in their refusing to indulge in drugs and looking with disgust upon prostitution. I am reminded of that film where the heroes were sketched as being very pure, and one of them refused to go off with a prostitute. This attitude seems still to prevail in Algeria, as a matter of fact. To what extent does that asceticism on the part of certain revolutionaries who want to remain pure (and which is very likely the product of a bourgeois education) become a quality that prevents the true revolutionary from eventually succeeding in being accepted within a popular movement?

M. F.: One can say in reply to your first question that the rigorism of the revolutionary certainly reveals his bourgeois origins, or, in any case, a cultural and ideological affinity with the bourgeoisie. Nevertheless, I think that we must link that to a historical process; it seems to me that until the beginning of the nineteenth century, and even during the French Revolution, popular uprisings were led at one and the same time by peasants, small craftsmen, by the first laborers, and then by that category of restless elements poorly integrated into society that might be highway robbers, smugglers, and so on—at any rate, all who had been rejected by the reigning system of legality, the law of the state. And in the nineteenth century, in the course of political struggles that permitted the proletariat to have itself recognized as a power with compelling demands, that permitted the proletariat to escape, all the same, from violent elimination and constraint, in the course of these political struggles the proletariat was obliged in some way to establish a separation between it and that other "agitated" population. When labor unionization was founded, in order to have itself recognized, it needed to dissociate itself from all the seditious groups and from all those who refused the legal system: We are not the murderers, we are not attacking either people or goods; if we stop production, it is not in an outburst of absolute destruction, but in conjunction with very precise demands. Family morality, which had absolutely no currency in popular circles at the end of the eighteenth century, had become by the beginning of the nineteenth century one of the means by which the proletariat was able in some way to establish its respectability. Popular virtue, the "good" worker, good father, good husband, respectful of the legal system—that is the image that since the eighteenth century the bourgeoisie proposed and imposed on the proletariat in order to turn it away from any form of violent agitation, insurrection, any attempt to usurp power and its rules. That image the proletariat took up and used, as a matter of fact, in an often very efficient way to support its struggles. That "morality" was, up to a certain point, the marriage contract between the proletariat and the petty bourgeoisie during the entire second half of the nineteenth century, from 1848 to Zola and Jaurès.[3]

Now, your second question: Isn't this puritanism an obstacle for the revolutionary leader? I would say, currently, yes. There exists indeed—at least that is the opinion of our group, in any event—there exists today in our societies truly revolutionary forces made up of just those strata who are poorly integrated into society, those strata who are perpetually rejected, and who, in their turn, reject the bourgeois moral system. How can you work with them in the political battle if you do not get rid of those moral prejudices that are ours? After all, if one takes into account the habitually unemployed who say, "Me, I prefer not working to working"; if one takes into account women, prostitutes, homosexuals, drug addicts, etc., there is a force for questioning society that one has no right, I think, to neglect in the political struggle.

J. S.: If one followed your line of thought logically, one would say almost that those who are involved with the rehabilitation of prisoners are perhaps the most virulent enemies of the revolution. And then, that fellow who guided us through Attica, if I may come back to my first question, and who gave us the impression of being a very well-intentioned guy—"decent," as you would say, but totally devoid of imagination—he would be the most dangerous enemy.

M. F.: Yes, I think what you say is profoundly true. Look, I do not want to go further, because you have presented the problem very well, but this man who is responsible for the cultural programs at Attica and who took care of our visit, I think that one can say also that he is dangerous in an immediate sense. One of the former prisoners of Attica whom I saw after our visit said to me: "He is one of the most vicious among the guards."

But afterwards we met some psychologists who were clearly very nice people, very liberal, who saw things with a good deal of accuracy. For them, stealing the property of someone else, pulling off a holdup in a bank, committing prostitution, sleeping with a man if one is male, etc.—if those acts are psychological problems that they must help the individual to resolve, are they not also fundamentally accomplices of the system? Aren't they masking the fact that ultimately committing a misdemeanor, committing a crime, questions the way society functions in a most fundamental way? So fundamental that we forget that it is social, that we have the impression that it is moral, that it involves people's rights . . .

And you see in what way one can present the problem. So that I subscribe completely to what you say, doesn't everything that concerns reintegration, everything that is a psychological or in-dividual solution for the problem, mask the profoundly politi-cal character both of society's elimination of these people and of those people's attack on society? All of that profound struggle is, I believe, political. Crime is "a coup d'état from below." That phrase is from *Les Misérables*.[4]

Notes

1. [Eds.] *Machicoulis* are box-shaped openings in defensive battle-ments through which stones, boiling water, or water might be thrown down on attackers.

2. [Eds.] Giovanni Battista (or Giambattista) Piranesi (1720–78) was an Italian Classical archaeologist, architect, and artist famous for his etch-ings of Rome and of fictitious and atmospheric "prisons" *(Le Carceri d'In-venzione, 1750–1761).*

3. [Eds.] In 1898, novelist Émile Zola was sentenced to prison for hav-ing publicly accused the President of France of anti-Semitism in the case of military officer Alfred Dreyfus. Jean Jaurès, future leader of the French Socialist Party, spoke and wrote on Zola's behalf.

4. [Eds.] Cf. Victor Hugo, *Les Misérables,* vol. 1 (Paris: Gallimard, 2009): "le vol, le meurtre, tous les crimes n'étaient que des formes de la rébellion" (426); cf. *Les Misérables* (New York: Simon and Schuster, 2005): "all crimes were only forms of rebellion" (55).

Pompidou's Two Deaths

MICHEL FOUCAULT

This piece, written by Michel Foucault, addresses Pompidou's execution by guillotine, in December 1972, of Claude Buffet and Roger Bontems, the prisoners at Clairvaux who took hostages during an escape attempt. It originally appeared in Le Nouvel observateur *421 (1972): 56–57. It was translated by Robert Hurley in* Power, *ed. James Faubion (New York: New Press, 2000), 418–22.*

There is a man living in Auteuil who, during the night of last Monday to Tuesday, earned 1,200,000 francs. Mr. Obrecht pulled on the cord twice: 600,000 old francs for a head falling in a basket.

That still exists, forms part of our institutions, convokes around its ceremony the magistracy, the Church, the armed police, and, in the shadows, the president of the republic—in short, all the powers that be. There is something about it that is physically and politically intolerable.

But the guillotine is really just the visible and triumphant apex, the red-and-black tip, of a tall pyramid. The whole penal system is essentially pointed toward and governed by death. A verdict of conviction does not lead, as people think, to a sentence of prison or death; if it prescribes prison, this is always with a possible added bonus: death. An eighteen-year-old boy gets six months for one or two stolen cars. He's sent to Fleury-Mérogis, with isolation, idleness, a megaphone as his only interlocutor. It suffices for him to receive no visits or for his fiancée to stop writing to him; then his only recourse will be to beat his head against the walls or twist his shirt into a rope and try to hang himself.

So begins, already, the risk, the possibility, worse, the temptation, the desire for death, the fascination with death. When a prisoner is released, there will be the police record, unemployment, the relapse, the indefinite repetition until the end, until death. Let us say, in any case, until the twenty-year sentence or confinement in perpetuity—"for life," as they say. "For life," or "for death," the two expressions mean the same thing. When a person is sure that he will never get out, what is there left to do? What else but to risk death to save one's life, to risk one's very life at the possible cost of death? That is what Buffet and Bontems did.

Prison is not the alternative to death: it carries death along with it. The same red thread runs through the whole length of that penal institution that is supposed to apply the law but that, in reality, suspends it: once through the prison gates, one is in the realm of the arbitrary, of threats, of blackmail, of blows. Against the violence of the penitentiary personnel, the convicts no longer have anything but their bodies as a means for defending themselves and nothing but their bodies to defend. It is life or death, not "correction," that prisons are about.

Let us give this some thought: one is punished in prison when one has tried to kill himself; and when the prison is tired of punishing you, it kills you.

Prison is a death machine that has produced, with the Clairvaux affair, two deaths times two. And one must bear in mind that, in the past, Buffet had gone through the Foreign Legion, that other machine in which one also learns the dreadful equivalence of life and death.

People told themselves: Pompidou is going to kill Buffet—harsh profile—and he will pardon Bontems—gentle profile. But he had both men executed, and why was that?

An electoral scaffold? No doubt. But maybe not because 63 percent of French people, according to the IFOP,[1] are in favor of keeping the death penalty and the right of pardon. It's probably more serious than that; if the numbers were reversed, I think he would have done the same thing. He wanted to show that he was a tough, uncompromising man, that, if necessary, he would resort to extreme measures—that, if the circumstances required, he was prepared to rely on the most violent and reactionary elements. The sign of a possible orientation, the sign of a course of action already decided upon rather than a faithfulness to the nation's majority impulse. "I will go that far when I need to."

To that first calculation another was added. Here it is, summed up in three propositions:

1. If Buffet alone had been executed, he would have appeared to be the last person guillotined. With him, after him, no one else. From that point on, the machine would have been blocked. And by the same token, Pompidou would have been the last to operate it. Bontems enables it to go on indefinitely; his execution generalizes the guillotine all over again.

2. Bontems was not convicted for murder but for complicity. His execution is actually addressed to all prisoners: "If you undertake, together with an accomplice, any action whatsoever against the penitentiary administration, you will be held responsible for anything that may happen, even if you didn't do it." A collective responsibility. Here the refusal of mercy is in the spirit of the antiwreckers law.

3. It is undeniable that Buffet helped a good deal to get Bontems convicted. So, it may look as if he shared the responsibility for his execution—at least that's the official calculation. "You shouldn't get worked up about this Buffet; he lured his accomplice into death; the nasty world of crooks, with its hatreds and its betrayals, is manifested again in this double execution." Pompidou is not alone in having killed Bontems.

Such was the calculation, no doubt. Let us hope that it will be foiled and that it will have to be paid for.

But I'm speaking as if the two condemned men and the president were the only ones onstage, as if it were only a question of the legal machinery. Actually, there is a third element to consider, the penitentiary system and the battle that is now under way in the prisons.

We know about the pressures that were applied by the unions of prison guards in order to obtain this double execution. An official of the CGT spoke of a plan that was ready in case their desire for revenge was not satisfied. One has to know what the atmosphere was at La Santé last Monday: Pompidou had just come back from Africa. Now, executions traditionally take place on Tuesday, a day when there are no visits. So, everyone knew it would be that night. A young guard said before witnesses: "Tomorrow we'll have a head with vinaigrette sauce for dinner." But well before them, Bonaldi (FO)[2] and Pastre (CGT) had made imperative and inflammatory statements without being called to order.

Once again, the penitentiary administration overstepped the legal system. Before the trial and before the appeal for mercy, it demanded, and imposed, its own brand of "justice." It loudly claimed and was granted the right to punish, this administration which should only have the obligation to calmly apply penalties whose principle, measure, and control belong to others. It established itself as a power, and the head of state has just given his assent.

Is he unaware that this power he has just sanctioned is being combated today, everywhere, by prisoners struggling to gain respect for the rights they still have; by magistrates who insist on controlling the application of penalties they have prescribed; by all those who no longer accept either the machinations or the abuse of the repressive system?

It's true there is nothing in common between Buffet and Bontems and a mother who lets a bill go unpaid.[3] And yet, "our" repressive system imposed a common "measure" on them: prison.

And so, once again, death came for some men and for a child.

We accuse the prisons of murder.

Notes

1. [Eds.] The Institut Français d'Opinion Publique (IFOP) is an international polling and market research firm.

2. [Eds.] The Force Ouvrière (FO) is a major labor union in France founded in 1948.

3. [Orig. Eng. Ed.] Yvonne Huriez, mother of eight children, sentenced to four months in prison with no possibility of remission for having failed to respond to a court that ordered her to pay a bill of 75 francs for the rental of a television set. Her fourteen-year-old son, Thierry, who couldn't stand hearing his mother called a thief by his school buddies, committed suicide.

Prisons and Revolts in Prisons

MICHEL FOUCAULT

*This interview with Michel Foucault conducted by Bodo
Morawe originally appeared under the title "Gefangnisse und
Gefangnisrevolten" in* Dokumente: Zeitschrift für übernationale
Zusammenarbeit, *no. 2 (June 1973): 133–37.*

BODO MORAWE: There are, first of all, prison revolts in numerous
French penitentiaries, at Aix, Clairvaux, Baumettes, Poissy, Lyon,
and Toul, that have drawn the public's attention to what happens
behind bars and concrete walls. These revolts, which have been
making headlines in France since 1971, have taken different forms:
riots, acts of desperation, collective resistance, and protest movements with concrete demands. In your opinion, where does the
significance of this revolution reside? Is it effectively a new phenomenon?

MICHEL FOUCAULT: First, we need to recall here that in all the political revolutions of the nineteenth century—1830, 1848, 1870—
there was a tradition: either there were revolts inside prisons and
prisoners stood in solidarity with the revolutionary movement
unfolding outside, or revolutionaries went to prisons to force
open the doors and free prisoners. This was a permanent feature
of the nineteenth century. Conversely, in the twentieth century,
owing to a series of social processes—for instance, the rupture
between the politically and union organized proletariat and the
lumpenproletariat—political movements have no longer been associated with movements in prisons. Even if newspapers practically never spoke of prison revolts, thus giving the impression that
calm reigned for seventy-one years, that in no way corresponded to

reality. There were prison revolts in this period; there were protest movements within the penitentiary system, often suppressed in a violent and bloody fashion, as in 1967 at La Santé. But this remains unknown. A question, then, poses itself: how has this liaison between a political movement outside prisons and the politicization of a movement within prisons reappeared? Several factors were in play: first and foremost, the presence of a large number of Algerian prisoners, during the Algerian War. There were thousands of them and they fought to make their political status known; by means of passive resistance and the refusal of obedience, they succeeded in demonstrating that it was possible to force prison management to back down. That was already something very important. Then, there were political prisoners after May 1968, mainly Maoists. Finally, there was a third important factor: after the foundation of the Prisons Information Group, prisoners knew there was an outside movement interested in them, a movement that was not simply one of Christian or lay philanthropy, but a movement devoted to the political contestation of prison. This series of phenomena—the politicization inside prisons, thanks to Maoists and before that to Algerians, and the politicization outside prisons of the problem of the penitentiary—crystallized a certain situation. Following a campaign led by the GIP, the government accorded to prisoners, for the first time in history, the right to read daily newspapers, papers that until July 1971 were not allowed to penetrate prison walls. So, in July 1971, they allowed prisoners to read newspapers. In September 1971, the prisoners heard about the Attica revolt; they realized that its problems were their own and that these problems were political in nature—that, for this reason, they had support on the outside, for these problems existed all over the world. The tremor was strong and the realization of the size and political significance of the problem was acute at that particular moment. Now, over the course of the next two weeks, two prisoners from Clairvaux, one of the harshest French prisons, attempted a break out by taking two hostages: a prison guard and a nurse. During this attempt, they killed their hostages. In fact, we know today that, if this hostage taking was not overtly organized by the administration, the latter facilitated it, and let's say in any case that the administration tolerated it, being aware that a plan was being hatched, even if they didn't know what it was. So, to squash this growing movement of agitation, which was already political, the administration let the two young fellows go through with it. That finally ended the drama. Immediately afterward, the penitentiary authorities, the government, and several newspapers initiated a campaign saying: "You see what prisoners are." At this precise moment, a very important change occurred in French prisons: prisoners became aware that individual or semi-individual struggles—a breakout by two, three, or more—was not the right method and that if the prisoner movement wanted to reach a political dimension, it had, first of all, to be a really collective movement that included the entire prison and, second, it had to appeal to the public that, as prisoners knew, was starting to get interested in the problem. That led to a totally different form of revolt. In December 1971, two months after Clairvaux, two and a half months after Attica, four months after the authorization of newspapers, one year after the foundation of the GIP, a revolt exploded at Toul as hadn't been seen since the nineteenth century: an entire prison in revolt, prisoners up on the roofs, throwing leaflets, unfurling banners, making appeals on the megaphone, and explaining what they wanted.

B. M.: What demands did the prisoners express? And can we really say that their revolt was the result of political awareness? I ask the question because you speak explicitly about "political movement."

M. F.: First of all, we have to distinguish between the political and the nonpolitical form of an action. I would say that a breakout by two, after taking hostages, even if it is a matter of political prisoners, or those who have political awareness, is a form of action that is not political. On the other hand, it is a political form of action when, for example, the following demands are posed: better diet, heating, not being condemned to absurd punishments for piddling infractions—demands, then, that exist in the domain of their immediate interest and that are posed in a collective fashion, by drawing on public opinion, by addressing not their superiors, the prison wardens, but power itself, the government, the party in power. From this moment, their action has a political form. Perhaps you will say that there is still no political content. But isn't that precisely what characterizes current political movements:

the discovery that the most quotidian things—the way one eats or is nourished, the relationship between employee and employer, the way one loves, the way in which sexuality is repressed, familial constraints, prohibition of abortion—are political? In any case, politics today consists in being the subject of a political action. Consequently, the political or nonpolitical character of an action is no longer determined by the sole end of this action, but by the form, the manner in which objects, problems, disturbances, and sufferings, that the European political tradition of the nineteenth century banished as unworthy of political action, are politicized. They don't dare speak of sexuality. Since the nineteenth century, they have barely spoken of the diet of prisoners as a serious political problem.

B. M.: In the inquiries made by the Prisons Information Group, you occupy yourself concretely with the conditions of detention and the system of enforcing punishments in France. What facts have you come up against? What was the group's proposed goal for these inquiries?

M. F.: Certainly most of these facts were already known: absolutely deplorable material conditions; penitentiary work at the level of the most shameless exploitation, of slavery; nonexistent medical care; assaults and violence on the part of the guards; the existence of an arbitrary tribunal whose only judge is the warden and which inflicts supplementary punishments on prisoners. These facts, after all, were known and we could have linked them to reports gleaned from the right and the left, with the help of some "traitors" from the penitentiary administration. But, for us, the main thing was that this information should be communicated to the public by prisoners themselves. Thus, we haven't gone to the penitentiary authorities, we haven't asked them questions, not even the doctors or social workers who work there. We illegally passed questionnaires into the prisons, and prisoners returned them to us in the same way, so that in our booklets prisoners themselves have taken the floor and revealed the facts. Because these facts were known only within circumscribed milieus, it was important that the public hear the voice of prisoners, and that prisoners know they were the ones speaking. And this produced something extraordinary, at least according to some: the Ministry of Justice has not been able to refute a single one of these facts. Thus, prisoners told the truth, absolutely and entirely.

B. M.: The facts published in the GIP's booklets—decayed premises, sadistic abuse, repeated disregard for medical prescriptions, illicit punishments followed by the administration of tranquilizers, etc.—are in shocking opposition to the stated intentions of the French legislature, which, starting in 1945,[1] in the reform of the penal law, put it thus: "Punishment by the privation of liberty has as its primary end the betterment of the condemned and their reintegration into society." Do you agree with this conception? And why, in your opinion, has it not yet been actualized?

M. F.: This sentence, which French magistrates currently cite with so much deference, was formulated in the same terms more than 150 years ago. When prisons were first put in place, it was as instruments of reform. That failed. It was imagined that confinement, the break from society, solitude, reflection, obligatory work, continual supervision, and moral and religious exhortations would lead the condemned to self-reformation. One hundred and fifty years of failure has not put the penitentiary system in the position to ask for our continued confidence. This sentence has been repeated so often that now we can hardly give it any credit.

B. M.: That's your answer?

M. F.: Yes, absolutely.

B. M.: Well, let me clarify my question: is it desirable to reform the present penitentiary system in order to alleviate the conditions of detention? Or is it necessary to break with all the traditional ideas about penal law, the application of punishments, etc.?

M. F.: The penitentiary system, which is to say the system that consists in confining people, under special supervision, in closed establishments, until they are reformed—or so we suppose—has completely failed. This system forms part of a larger, more complex system that we might call the punitive system: children are punished, students are punished, workers are punished, and soldiers are punished. Ultimately, we are punished our whole life long. And we are punished for a number of things, though no longer the same as those in the nineteenth century. We live in a punitive system. That is what we must put in question. Prison, in itself, is only part of the penal system and the penal system is only part of the punitive system. It will do no good to reform the penitentiary system without reforming the penal system and penal legislation. But legislation has to have pretty much its current form if it is true that the stability of a capitalist society depends on this entire network of punitive pressure exerted on individuals.

B. M.: So, we have to change the whole system?

M. F.: We have the penal system we deserve. There is an analysis, supposedly Marxist, rather simple, that consists of attributing all of that to superstructures. At that level, one can always imagine adjustments and modifications. But, in fact, I don't think that the penal system forms part of the superstructures. In reality, it is a system of power that penetrates deeply into the lives of individuals and bears on their relation to the production apparatus. Viewed in this way, it is not at all a matter of superstructure. In order for individuals to be a workforce available for the production apparatus, a system of constraints, coercion, and punishment is necessary, a penal system and a penitentiary system. These are just expressions.

B. M.: Can we prove that historically?

M. F.: There has been, since the beginning of the nineteenth century, a whole series of institutions that have functioned on the same model, that obey the same rules, and whose almost unbelievable first representation can be found in Bentham's famous *Panopticon*:[2] institutions of surveillance *[surveillance]* where individuals were hooked up to a production apparatus, to a machine, a trade, a workshop, a factory, or to a scholarly apparatus, or to a punitive, corrective, or sanitary apparatus. They were hooked up to this apparatus, constrained to obey a certain number of rules of existence, encompassing their whole lives—and they were placed under the supervision *[surveillance]* of a certain number of people, of managers (foremen, nurses, guards), who had at their disposal the means of punishment, which consisted in fines in the factories, physical or moral corrections in the schools and asylums, and a certain number of violent and essentially physical punishments in the prisons. Hospitals, asylums, orphanages, colleges, reformatories, factories, workshops with their discipline, and, finally, prisons, all formed part of a kind of great social form of power, which was put in place at the beginning of the nineteenth century and has doubtless been one of the conditions for the functioning of industrial—of, if you prefer, capitalist—society. In order for man to transform his body, his existence, and his time into labor power *[force de travail],* and put it at the disposal of the production apparatus that capitalism aims to mobilize, a whole apparatus of constraints is necessary;[3] and it seems to me that all these constraints that take man from the nursery and school and to the old folks home, by way of the barracks, all the while threatening him with prison or the psychiatric hospital—"Either you are going to the factory, or you will end up in prison, or in the lunatic asylum!"—these constraints point to the same system of power. In most other domains, these institutions have relaxed, but their function remains the same. People today are no longer surrounded by misery, but by consumption. As they were in the nineteenth century, even if in another mode, they are relentlessly drawn into a credit system that obliges them (if they bought a house, furnishings . . .) to work all day long, to take on additional hours, to stay connected. Television offers its images as objects of consumption and prevents people from doing what they already feared so much in the nineteenth century: going to cafés and bars where political meetings were held, where the local and regional gatherings of the working class risked producing a political movement, perhaps even the possibility of overturning the whole system.

B. M.: You said that other institutions have relaxed. And prisons?

M. F.: Prisons are anachronistic and yet profoundly bound to the system. In France, at least, they have not relaxed; this is different from Sweden or the Netherlands, where the functions of prison are absolutely consistent with the functions no longer provided by the old colleges or by psychiatric hospitals as they once were, but by relatively relaxed institutions, what in France we call "sector psychiatry," outpatient psychiatry, medical control, psychological and psychiatric supervision *[surveillance]* to which the population is exposed in a diffuse manner. The same function is always at stake. The prison is consistent with the system, except that the penal system has not yet discovered these insidious and relaxed forms already found by pedagogy, psychiatry, and general societal discipline.

B. M.: One last question to conclude: is a society without prisons imaginable?

M. F.: The answer is easy: there have indeed been societies without prisons; it was not so long ago. As a punishment, prison was invented at the beginning of the nineteenth century. If you look at the texts of the first criminal lawyers of the nineteenth century, you will notice that they always begin their chapter on prisons by saying, "The prison is a new punishment that was still unknown a century ago." And the president of one of the first international penitentiary congresses, a congress that, if memory serves, took place in Brussels in 1847, said: "I am quite old and I still remember the time when we did not punish people with prison, when Europe was covered in gibbets, shackles, and various scaffolds, when we saw mutilated people who had lost an ear, two thumbs, or an eye. Such were the condemned."[4] He evoked this landscape, at once stark and colorful with punishment, and he said: "Now, all of that is confined behind the monotonous walls of the prison." People of this era were perfectly aware that a positively new punishment had been born. You want me to describe a utopian society where there would be no prison. The problem is to know if we can imagine a society in which the application of rules would be controlled by the groups themselves. It is the whole question of political power, the problem of hierarchy, of authority, of the state and state apparatuses. It is only when we have cleared away the underbrush from this immense problem that we will finally be able to say: yes, we should be able to punish this way, or, it is completely useless to punish, or again, society should respond in such and such a manner to this irregular conduct.

Notes

1. [Eds.] See Jean-Michel Le Boulaire and Claude Faugeron, "La création du service social des prisons et l'évolution de la réforme pénitentiaire en France de 1945 à 1958," *Déviance et société* 4 (1988): 317–35.

2. [Eds.] See Jeremy Bentham, *Panopticon or, The Inspection-House* (1791) in his *The Panopticon Writings,* ed. Miran Bozovic (New York: Verso Books, 2011).

3. [Eds.] Foucault makes this claim about the relationship between the body and disciplinary practices and institutions beginning with his 1972–73

316 | PRISON REVOLTS (1971-1972)

lecture course at the Collège de France; see *The Punitive Society,* trans. Graham Burchell (London: Palgrave, 2015), 232–33. He returns to the thesis in the 1974–75 course (*Abnormal,* trans. Graham Burchell [New York: Picador, 2003], 87–88) and, finally, once again, albeit only in passing, in *Discipline and Punish: The Birth of the Prison,* trans. Alan Sheridan (New York: Vintage Books, 1977), 25–26.

    4. [DE Eds.] These are the opening remarks of Mr. Van Meenen, President of La Cour de Cassation de Bruxelles, at the Second Congrès Pénitentiaire International, September 20–23, 1847, in Brussels. A transcription is published in *Débats du Congrès Pénitentiaire de Bruxelles* (Brussels: Deltombe, 1847), 20.

Prisoners gesture from windows during revolt at Ney Prison in Toul, France, in December 1971. Photograph by Gérard Drolc.

Part IV
Transition (1972–1973)

The GIP ceased its primary operations in December 1972, although evidence of some minimal activity appears as late as May 1973. This section documents some of the final discussions, both internal to the group and in the public domain, that took place as the organization sought to take stock of its shared work and to identify the potential axes on which the struggle against the intolerable might continue, transition, and develop.

Prison Suicides (1972), the final report in the *Intolerable* series, which was published in February 1973, was cosigned by two newly formed organizations: the Comité d'Action des Prisonniers (CAP) and the Association pour la Défense des Droits des Détenus (ADDD). These groups, which were both founded in November 1972, were inspired by the GIP and took its unique structure and militancy as their model. The booklet thus signaled the GIP's official dissolution and the transferal of its struggles to these new groups.

The organizers of the CAP were former prisoners (among them Serge Livrozet, Michel Boraley, and Claude Vaudez), all of whom had been involved in the Melun prison revolt. The group was the first organized instance of common-law prisoners raising their collective voice both to denounce the prison and to assess it politically. The CAP was decidedly reformist and even abolitionist in its approach to incarceration and it was pivotal in securing the abolition of the death penalty in France in 1981. Its main organ of communication was a widely distributed newspaper, *Le CAP, journal des prisonniers* (1972–81), created for and by prisoners, whether formerly or currently incarcerated. In its January 1973 issue, the CAP announced its eleven basic concerns: (1) the abolition of criminal records; (2) travel bans; (3) imprisonment for debt and court fees; (4) the death penalty; (5) life sentences; (6) preventive detention and parole supervision; (7) the reorganization of prison labor; (8) the right to free speech; (9) medical care; (10) legal appeal and defense; and (11) freedom of association. In its September 1973 issue, it added a twelfth: (12) the elimination of prisons. Michel Foucault's name actually appeared as a coeditor of the first issue, which addressed the relationship between the GIP and the CAP, and he was listed as a member of the editorial team for two further issues.

The ADDD was founded by nonprisoners—the writer and illustrator Vercors (the pseudonym of Jean Bruller, who also cofounded Les Éditions de Minuit) served as its president—and functioned as a legally registered support organization. Its basic work was to foster the formation of a lawyers' association that provided legal counsel to prisoners and their families. It organized several public events with the GIP that assisted prisoners and their families in initiating legal action, fighting, in particular, for the right to organize and join unions and, taking up an initiative central to the work of the GIP, having criminal records expunged so that former prisoners could pursue gainful employment. It also pursued greater means for the public to exercise direct control over penal institutions.

The GIP's innovative methods and principles served as models for the creation of several other groups during this period as well: (1) the Groupe d'Information sur la Santé, which was devoted to public-health issues such as lead poisoning, the role of profit in the pharmaceutical industry, securing the legality of abortion, and the oppressive use of forms of knowledge by medical professionals; (2) the Groupe d'Information sur les Asiles, which was established to work on issues related to psychiatric hospitals; and (3) the Groupe d'Information et de Soutien aux Travailleurs Immigrés, devoted to migrant workers' issues.

Flowing from the alliances formed during the GIP, Foucault wrote a supportive preface for the CAP leader Serge Livrozet's memoir and manifesto, *De la prison à la révolte* (1973), and for the 1975 French translation of Bruce Jackson's collection of interviews with prisoners in Texas, *In the Life: Versions of the Criminal Experience* (1972).

Forms of Mobilization and Axes of Struggle

GROUPE D'INFORMATION SUR LES PRISONS (GIP)

An unsigned, internal GIP document that dates from April 1972 and analyzes its existing forms of mobilization and the axes of struggles to come. At this time, there seem to be two opposing currents at the heart of the group: a more moderate one, which favored focusing the struggle on prisons and prisoners alone, and a more critical one, which favored an expansion of the struggles.

(1) Monitor the prisons by multiplying the groups concerned with prisons. This year, starting with the presence of militants in the waiting lines and visiting rooms, these places of almost total censorship became places in which one speaks of prison (inquiries of the GIP).

(2) Inquiries-counterattacks, of the sort carried out with the families at Fleury-Mérogis following the beatings of September 24. The secret of solitary confinement cells was revealed in leaflets: lawyers and judges were forced to do their jobs.

(3) Unite the prisons with one another: before the admittance of newspapers and since, leaflets have been read regularly in various prisons. Two-sided "newspapers," in name and in fact. Ex.: Toul front and back, a newspaper made by prisoners' families about that prison.

(4) Organization of families: mutual assistance, child care for pregnant women (Toulouse), support for an imprisoned worker (Lyon).

(5) The arbitrariness internal to prisons extends to families: one judge grants and another denies visitation: collective struggle for rights to be respected, denunciation of the judges.

(6) Support the struggles: know them and their objectives, amplify them. The warden of the prison at Toulouse complains in a report to Paris of a "siege."

(7) Ask, as a citizen, to go inside a prison and see so as to put an end to the arbitrariness in all of its manifestations.

(8) Help the families of the rebels at Toul who have been transferred to other prisons to exchange news, to bring the truth about Toul to light, to bring civil actions. Some of them have banded together. Those who wish to contact this initial group, write to *Esprit,* 19 Rue Jacob, Paris, 6e.

(9) The prisoners at Loos have asked that the GIP be their intermediary. Starting with the multiplication of "prison groups," an association (law 1901)[1] composed of families and all citizens could be created and the right for prisoners to be members of it could be imposed.

Gatherings

Popular forums (neighborhoods, train stations, factory gates) have indicated a way of resolving a contradiction within the people as regards prisoners:

(1) Concretely see who is going to prison by relying on the case of a former prisoner who relates the succession of repeat offenses beginning with his first "offense." It is a matter of freeing the speech *[parole]* of the "freed."

(2) Bring together a group of leftist youths from a particular neighborhood. For example, in a neighborhood following a display of hostility toward the young, discussions revolved around the ways in which they were rejected: scarcity of housing, absence of law (... ?), unemployment, wages ..., all the way up to the proposal of an investigation for five imprisoned youths. One sees (sketched) the possibility of social struggles against the oppression of everyday life, and so of forging common cause.

(3) In addition to protesting at the prison gates, many intellectuals (actors, psychiatrists, teachers) can participate in forums and make connections between (prison) groups and neighborhood groups.

(4) Neighborhood groups can be strengthened as a result of this ideological mobilization. In the experience of the GIP, these groups are able to respond to the needs of youths who are constantly subjected to judicial repression. Conducting popular counterinvestigations, getting plaintiffs to withdraw their complaint, these are actions that the youths require.

Creating popular neighborhood tribunals would allow us to see better what this justice is:

— who really steals the work from others in the neighborhood?
— who ruins the health and lives of human beings?

(5) Struggle for the employment of people who have a criminal record or to get them HLM housing (which is refused to those who have a record).

Note

1. [Eds.] Association Loi de 1901 permits and governs the creation of nonprofit organizations.

The Second Front (The Neighborhoods)

GROUPE D'INFORMATION SUR LES PRISONS (GIP)

An unsigned, internal GIP document that dates from the spring of 1972 and analyzes the possibility of making neighborhoods the second front of the struggle, following the work done by Lotta Continua in Italy.

Over the course of shared experiences and discussions, a certain number of formulations have come up frequently:

—"Achieve Justice through the intermediary of the neighborhoods"
—"The neighborhood as the unit where the control of the justice system is exercised"
—"The neighborhood as an attack unit of the judicial apparatus"

It struck us that, while the SR [Secours Rouge] struggles primarily against the municipal apparatus, the GIP must lead a defense, by each neighborhood, of victims of the judicial system, it must advance the idea of a popular justice at the level of neighborhoods.

From this perspective, the neighborhood represents two distinct populations:

—the families (of youths, of former prisoners)
—the youths

The problem is establishing a connection between these two groups.

Social workers, various aids, and agents of the judicial system collect around groups of youths. They are not all scoundrels bankrolled by those in power. Hence the need to intensify the ideological struggle with them.

The neighborhood is a site of:

—police control
—seizure of delinquents
—the judicial apparatus's differential treatment based on social differences.

In view of our present strengths, the opening of a second front would consist in:

Giving ourselves the means of contacting folks and collecting information (direct contact with groups of youths, with MJC,[1] social workers, families, connections with lawyers, etc.), in order to stimulate the creation of local popular committees for checking the judicial system and for defending its victims, whether current or intended.

Note

1. [Eds.] Created in 1948, Maison de Jeunes et de la Culture (MJC) is an organization that aims to acculturate youths through popular education.

To Have Done with Prisons

JEAN-MARIE DOMENACH

This article by Jean-Marie Domenach was published in Esprit, *no. 415 (July–August 1972), and represents the most radical statement of his position.*

In ten years, the horror of the French penitentiary system will be as obvious to the public as the torture in Algeria is today, and Minister René Pleven will appear just as Minister Guy Mollet[1] did for having tried to conceal the intolerable. In the meantime, we are, with respect to this scandal, in the same exact position as we were concerning torture in 1960: the public pays no heed, those in charge sidestep it[2] or appoint yet another commission of inquiry.

The conviction of six young people at Nancy, accused of having organized the mutiny at the Charles-III Prison, confirms the Schmelck Report: the minister makes use of a respectable man in order to transform something that is not the general rule, but certainly has its place in the majority of French penitentiary establishments, into an exception. It had been officially recognized that the regulations had been violated at Toul and that the penitentiary reform undertaken in 1945 had been betrayed.[3] It was recognized because the mutinies at Toul and at Nancy wouldn't permit silence. But while they were acquitted at Toul (what else could be done, since without the rebels there wouldn't have been a "Schmelck Report"?), they were charged and convicted at Nancy. The rebels at Toul are therefore justified: their revolt, which was harsher and more costly than that at Nancy, led to an official report and to promises of reform. But to acquit the rebels from Nancy would have been to admit that Toul was not an exception, that the same shame existed at Nancy and elsewhere. And it was the same investigating officer who refrained from pursuing the rebels at Toul and who charged six young men[4]—six of the 250 who shouted their misery from the rooftops, six young men denounced by a provocateur and sent to trial to serve as an example.[5] So it goes with our justice system. So it goes with the prison administration: at Toul, the Catholic and Protestant chaplains were fired, along with Dr. Édith Rose, while the prison warden received a promotion, the mafia that directs the prison administration remains ever in place, and, in Nancy, they convict the "ringleaders" of the revolt at the Charles-III prison . . .

Here, in the first place, are Casamayor's reflections, written on the eve of the trial.[6]

> In Nancy, six young people are judged by the criminal court. It is an interesting trial because the agenda, to a large extent, exceeds the framework of the *prétoire*. Everything that the trial hides needs to be known. It is true that at issue is a prison revolt, but it is not true that it is the only thing at issue. Let us begin with the revolt. In practice, it led to violence, each side can fault the other, and if justice were the same for everyone, members of both camps, prisoners and guards, would be convicted.
>
> But it is a long way from theory to practice. Practice consists in holding a trial instead of implementing reforms, and if we are to consider this practice, we must break through the walls of the courtroom.
>
> Everyone knows that the prisoners didn't want to harm this or that guard, but were expressing their will to achieve a change in the system. If blows were dealt, it is well beyond the bodies that were affected by the blows that the intended goal is to be found. Men of justice, who are blessed no less than others with a certain faculty of vision, know this, but blind themselves to it willingly. One frequently condemns an individual in order not to condemn an institution, and it is in that domain that jurisprudence continues its little existence, surviving, but only as a fossil.
>
> Listen, let there be no mistake. The institution is not everything and the individual man is not nothing as regards his own conduct. But the degree to which he is directly responsible is variable. To quite a great degree in the case of a corrupt businessman—though it can't be total, given that he benefits from possibilities that are offered to

him by a capitalist society—and to a very small degree in the case of a violent alcoholic—though it can't be entirely absent, given that he is neither constantly drunk, nor constantly violent.

At Nancy, there is no doubt that the prison is to blame. This is not a reason to destroy everything the good apostles say, forgetting that violence is in the service of all causes, the good as well as the bad, and that even the best have not triumphed without violence. But as soon as it is a question of violence, one needs to know who started it. And in order to respond to this crucial question, one must grant the same credence to every testimony. The moment you refuse the testimonies of one group, in order to take into account only the testimonies of another, the moment you believe the civil servants (the Minister of the Interior or the Minister of Justice) and not the prisoners, it becomes impossible to know. No truth can result from such debates. Thus, failing to begin with the source of the ill, the tribunals intervene at the level of secondary manifestations and place their seal[7] on an inequality whose injustice is known.

At Nancy, those in power had ulterior motives. Just as the goal of the rebels was well beyond the individual guards, the goal of the government went beyond the rebels. It was not a matter of texts published regarding acts of violence, blows, or wounds, but rather of the famous antiwreckers law. We recall that this law, presented as being inspired by the honorable idea that the instigators are more guilty than the perpetrators, actually didn't spare the latter precisely so as to strike at the former. It strikes at everyone, enlarges the domain of repression, and pushes citizens back into a state of fear-induced prudence. Thus, in offering, little by little, more guilty parties to public opinion, it is gradually brought farther and farther away from the source of the ill, which is our deplorable penitentiary system. Those in power want to turn our attention away from it. Should one go as far back as Peking, as the Minister of Agriculture told the farmers, one would still find it necessary to focus all the hostility of a scandalized nation toward those who protest, so that the real scandal is forgotten. Justice is an excellent alibi: a fine-tuned machine, in which oral discussion is free and public, cannot but lend confidence to public opinion. It will judge the judgment, it will find it to be good or bad, and the trick will already have been played, for no one will see that the trial that unfolds before them is not the real trial.

Things are arranged in such a way that the necessarily partial and ineffective decision is presented as just and useful. Ultimately, judges, guards, and prisoners—in decreasing order of good fortune—are all in the same bag, which those in power have carefully cinched, so that nothing good may come of it. Good things are whatever has not been locked away, whatever has remained outside. What are we talking about? Precisely the debates, the depositions, everything that has been able to make its way out to public opinion. Contrary to what we believe, the more something falls outside of the trial, the more it is at the center of the drama, the more it is true.

Casamayor

Since the hypocrisy of the responsible parties has been established, the moment has come for us to take our denunciation up once more and refine it. For six months, documents and testimonies have abounded in the press and in publishing.[8] And what has been published is only a small fraction of a wealth of information, which is difficult to utilize because it most often comes from prisoners who would suffer consequences were it to be published. We will, however, cite several pages from the hundreds we have read. One day, these witnesses will speak publicly; they are already beginning to do so, and their courage should urge onward all those judicial, social, medical, and religious personnel who often do good in a shortsighted manner, and who, though they are in less danger, have still not dared to say openly what they know.

A Universe without Law

We received an accurate testimony from a group of prisoners in the Mende Prison, which is so accurate that it cannot be published and could only be of service in the lawsuit that one day will have to be brought against those in charge (including the sinister Galiana, who went on to distinguish himself as the warden of Toul Prison). Several of the guards appear in a terrible light:

And let's not forget B. d. B.! He deserves his recognition: a fascist, a self-righteous ass. In 1953, at Clairvaux, he broke the forearm of D.—a psychiatric patient—with a billy club, and then plunged it several times into boiling water, aided by S., the guard.

Some prisoners advised D. to file a complaint. The latter responded

(X., a prisoner, was present): "Don't worry about me. B. d. B. and S. came to see me in the infirmary and instructed me to say that I broke my arm in a fall and said that if I happened to open my yap, they would hang me; they had brought ropes with them." D., in tears, begged the other prisoners not to do anything.

The affair came to light and the prosecutor of Troyes twice went to see D., who kept his mouth shut. The warden of Clairvaux protected the two guards and promised D. a pardon in return for silence.

In 1963, some prisoners went back to see D. in the Poissy infirmary, his arm atrophied. These prisoners, C., D., and R., advised D. to consult the League of the Rights of Man. He refused. C., D., and R. were relegated to isolation cells as punishment—the reason: "bad advice."

B. d. B. was there again during the attempt to drown six prisoners who tried to escape from Clairvaux, and during the ferocious beating that incited the indignation of prisoners as well as certain officers—including the Executive Magistrate (JAP) of Justice—and that paved the way, through the climate itself, for the deaths of the nurse and the guard.

It would be interesting and revealing if a commission of the International Red Cross would seriously visit Mende . . . As for the Declaration of the Rights of Man . . . France hasn't ratified it . . .

Mende, a place of terror, where the most ferocious guards are sent.

In the face of such instances of inhumanity, can one speak—without cynicism, without shame, without deception—of Justice?

As regards the attempted escape from Clairvaux that was just mentioned, here is a straightforward account, coming from a prisoner, that includes all the documentation needed to authenticate it. The situation at Clairvaux was lamentable: cold, humidity, bullying, and provocations. The following scene took place alongside a hunger strike at the beginning of 1970:

They were killing us with hunger. The butchery in our section continued, certain guards deliberately provoked the prisoners in the workshops just so they would have cause to report them, and—so, so many other little details that break the camel's back . . .

Also, in March or April (I don't know exactly anymore) prisoners decided on an indefinite hunger strike for several reasons:

(1) elimination of work on Saturday afternoons;

(2) improved nourishment;

(3) money order increase;

(4) authorization to receive packages of linens (undergarments);

(5) authorization to receive books for study;

(6) granting doctors complete liberty to do their job.

A general hunger strike is always feared: you never know when and how it will end. Also, during the days of the strike, the guards won't get too close to you and won't try to do anything abusive. On the contrary, they allow you an almost complete freedom of movement. Some of them will even go so far as to say that they understand, etc. (sure!).

After three days, the warden passes through the workshops without saying a word. Everything he observes is expected and doesn't please him one bit, yet he can't do anything about it and doesn't ask any questions. When he passes through, we are all at our stations, there isn't a sound, everyone follows him with their eyes, but no one works. This isn't a refusal to work; rather, work became an impossibility.

What bothers them the most is that everything is so calm: no one among us argues, no one fights. For once, I see harmony. We do our own policing. A single case could have ended very badly, but we intervene and they literally "hand over" the prisoner to us. Prisoners, we cannot let ourselves lose our shit. This one guy had just written to his mother for her birthday and had drawn a rose in the corner of the letter as a token of his love from far away. The letter was returned to him with the drawing crossed out in red pen and the note: "this is forbidden." Seized by rage, he treated the guard to every name imaginable (and in prison there are some really awful ones!). The guard was none too pleased and kept repeating: "But I couldn't do anything about it . . ."

Finally, we brought him to the back of the refectory. To let off steam, he grabbed a storage rack and smashed it against the wall. We let him do this; it did him good.

The next day, our demands were met and the regional warden[9] (in the Marti era, since deceased) gave his word that this would be respected.

But the improvement was only temporary and the situation began to deteriorate once again:

I should recount an event that took place during the night of May 15–16.

Some prisoners attempted to escape through the sewers. They came so very close, but didn't make it. A shame. But here's what happened next:

These sewers are quite large; you can walk in them standing up straight. Sluice gates close off the mouth of a little, underground canal that terminates in these sewers, which makes it possible for someone to flood the whole thing in a matter of minutes. When the guards notice that people are missing from their cells, they sound the escape alarm: one time only, lasting three minutes. Then they institute lockdown. In more than four watchtowers, where the guards are armed day and night, two guards armed with rifles get into position on each side of the prison, in the corner towers (there are four), while two groups of two armed guards each make the rounds: one in one direction, the other in another. It is impossible to get past them. What's more, at night the rampart walk is more illuminated than a boulevard: every six meters, a fluorescent light!

On the inside, all the night personnel begin the search with several successive roll calls in all the cells. Those at home taking a day off need to come in immediately as backup.

This is what happens. After an hour and fifteen minutes of searching, a guard hears a recurring, muffled sound. That's when they got it and remembered the sewers. The escapees were using a crowbar to try to work loose a protective grate that was placed there precisely to stop someone from getting out that way. They only had a little more work to do. Just a couple minutes (maybe three) and they would be free and clear.

But, up above, someone heard them in there. Then their strange reaction (for they don't go down there, even though they're all armed, they have stage fright! The prisoners later hear about this from several who were present), which was to open the sluice gates and force the escapees to come out. If not, they would simply drown them "like rats." (This expression was used by several guards!) And the six escapees owe their lives to Mr. Valvet, the civil electrician charged with the prison's entire electrical system, who, having heard what was going on, immediately closed the sluice gates himself. (Later we learned that the water stopped rising 30 centimeters from the ceiling of the vault.)

So, the six were done for. A manhole cover in a certain location was opened in order for them to exit; all around it, the "butchers" waited. No one wanted to go down to look for them. Then a brave guard went in (all throughout the butchery, he would interpose himself between the prisoners being beaten and the guards). The guys came out, one by one. As soon as they were back on the surface, blows began to fall from every direction: rifle butts, batons, kicks . . . From there, they were led through a shower of blows all the way to the control room. They were clearly soaked. Their clothes were torn off, after which a veritable horde of human beings fell upon them. They had no more than their underwear clothing them.

We, in detention, watched them pass by the windows of our cells, we witnessed the butchery! Everyone shouted insults and threats at the brutalizers! The doors were kicked and beaten with benches. It made an appalling din. It was 2 in the morning and it came within a hair of being a revolt. If a single door had opened, it would have been over, all the others would have opened, too.

On top of the six naked men there were more than thirty guards armed with rifles, billy clubs, and batons. And officers. And the assistant warden, who didn't strike, but let it happen. And the warden, who took part in the brawl to such a degree that, afterward, he had to wash his blood-soaked hands in one of the control room sinks (this, too, we learned later on).

The rest is known and it is atrocious. The Executive Magistrate, A. Petit, who had attempted to curtail the injustice and who had denounced the situation in a report to his superior, was stripped of his duties following a maneuver by the warden of the penitentiary administration, Mr. Le Corno.[10] The situation deteriorated still further. Several prisoners attempted suicide. One burned himself alive. Finally, two prisoners sentenced for violent crimes took a guard and a nurse hostage, whom they killed when their demand for freedom was refused.

The repercussions are also well known: in retaliation, guards lynched prisoners at Fleury-Mérogis, the Minister banned Christmas packages, there were revolts at Toul and Nancy, the strike at Melun, the protest and lynching at Fresnes, the Schmelck Report, and the trial at Nancy.

A Universe without Progress

> Laughter is an amusement and an external manifestation of the heart's joy; neither can be permitted in a prison, where everything is serious, strict, penal, and where the improvement of the guilty is expected, through atonement for the crime committed and repentance, all of which is only pain.

This lovely text is an excerpt from the "Rapport à M. le comte de Montalivet, pair de France, ministre de l'Intérieur, sur les prisons de l'Angleterre, de l'Écosse, de la Hollande, de la Belgique et de la Suisse," by Louis-Mathurin Moreau-Christophe, Inspector General of France's prisons (Paris, Imprimerie nationale, 1839). Reading it, I was remarking to myself that we have made progress over the past 130 years. And then I met up with a lawyer whose client, a prisoner, had been thrown into solitary confinement for having laughed. And I received the testimony of a prisoner recounting how one of his companions was just punished with several days in solitary ("the hole") for having yawned . . .

Certain practices have disappeared, of course, at least in certain prisons. A minority of prisoners now benefit from new legal benefits like day parole. But the carceral universe essentially remains the same and produces the same effects, as the texts published later in this issue demonstrate: a system of humiliation, of mutual fear, implicating both prisoners and guards, a system of the destruction of personhood, a degrading hierarchy in which the brutality of the strong and the cunning of the weak triumph.

A Universe without Hope

Contrary to the legislature's stated intention, the most certain effect of prison is to sap the prisoner of all hope and to drive him to recidivism. Work, expected to be an instrument of reeducation, often consists of absurd and demeaning tasks and only fetches the prisoner 1 to 5 francs a day (except in some rare exceptions).[11] Nothing is done to prepare for the "reintegration" about which people talk so much. But the criminal record and the travel ban are there to prolong the punishment. From a prisoner in Lyon:

How am I to have confidence and courage when, upon my release, I will no longer have a roof to shelter me, a bed to sleep upon, silverware to eat with, work to live on, or money to let me survive?

How am I to have confidence when, instead of understanding the reasons behind my delinquency and remedying them, they have instilled me with hatred, resentment, and the spirit of revolt and vengeance?

For a year, my imprisonment consisted only in waiting. But waiting for what? My release, of course, but what else? Upon my release, I would not have the right, for three years, to go to what remained of my family, nor the right to visit my friends, since, my fifteen long months in prison not being enough to satisfy them, the court gave me a three-year travel ban. Exile, as it were, and that on the brink of the twenty-first century!

Where am I going to go? What am I going to do? How will I live? What kind of existence am I going to have when I have to leave for a "wide-open" world without money, without family, without guaranteed work?

The rate of recidivism is overwhelming—47 percent for all detainees and 53 percent for those sentenced—and they are much higher when the punishment is mild and the prisoner is young. What would people say of a hospital where folks entered with bronchitis only to leave, a year later, with tuberculosis?

The Product of a Class Justice

—Four-fifths of all prisoners are juvenile delinquents.

—93.8 percent have not received their *certificat d'études* (CEP) or are illiterate.

—About half are younger than 25 years old.

These three facts suffice to characterize the bulk of the prison population (which amounts to 30,000 prisoners). They allow us to conclude, with Henri Varennes, that "prisoners are members of the poorest and most deprived part of the proletariat, and are, for the most part, young proletarians."[12] The same author, who, by "proletarian," means salaried agricultural workers, laborers, and skilled and specialized workers, notes that of this group, which represents around 35 percent of the male population over the age of 18, 62 percent are convicted of assault and battery or of public lewdness or indecent exposure, 58 percent have committed a theft, and 50 percent abandoned their families.

This hyperdelinquency of the proletariat is, in the first place, the consequence of judicial discrimination. An unpublished inquiry conducted by the GIP into a month of charges in Paris provides surprising results:

—48 percent of charges affect members of the working class (additionally, 8 percent concern domestic workers);

—80 percent of the accused belonging to the bourgeois class are granted interim release, as opposed to 32 percent of those belonging to the working class;

—90 percent of those convicted belonging to the bourgeois class receive a suspended sentence, as opposed to 33 percent of those belonging to the working class.

The fact remains that certain offenses are committed more frequently by youths, by the illiterate, and by proletarians than by the bourgeoisie: theft, especially car theft, assault and battery, insulting an officer, etc. These are not the high-profile cases of fraud that are discussed in the newspapers and that require an advanced education (especially in law) and a developed network of relatives, friends, and acquaintances: it is petty delinquency, whose form is clearly linked to a social model that is controlled by money and publicity, to a type of stifling urbanization, and to a generalized normalization of life, which drives youths, for whom every fantasy and every celebration are forbidden, to seek transgression in crime.

Nevertheless, rehabilitation—true rehabilitation—is on its way. After Toul, Nancy, and Melun, a growing number of prisoners are becoming aware of their trampled dignity and getting back on the right track by demanding their rights. An association was recently founded to help them do so.[13] The best testimony to this growing awareness is the texts written by the prisoners themselves. Here we have one that circulated at the beginning of the year in the Ensisheim prison:

It is inadmissible, intolerable that we should forever be the scapegoats, the whores, the beasts of burden, the shiteaters. Let's stir up this pile of manure, this trash heap that is our society. We are what it made us. Let's make ourselves Men! From now on, wherever we might be, it will be necessary to make society, our society, the way we want it to be from the bottoms of our hearts.

We are treated as subhumans and at every moment it is thrown in our faces—brutally or hypocritically, it all amounts to the same. Every day we need to do a little to show that we are Men in our own right. We must make them admit it.

Let's not obey slavishly, automatically, no matter who wants what! Why that? What is the point of it? Who will profit from it? We must ask ourselves questions, we must not allow the smallest details of our lives to be determined for us—submission is often only the abdication of human dignity—and we must know and act accordingly, for our true interests, not for whatever dangling carrot. Let's organize elected committees for effective representation. In the USA, they have unions in their prisons. Let's demand the abolition of criminal records. Let's obtain real "conditionals."[14] Let's request normal salaries, vocational training that lives up to our hopes, the right to vote (Denmark has this, with visits from journalists and politicians), vacation time like in Sweden, Germany, Denmark, etc. Even more, the abolition of prisons (like in Tanzania)!

We are considered livestock, but even the littlest calf kicks. We are considered dogs, but even the most crossbred pup bites when you attack it. Are we less than that?

Yes, it's true, we're guilty of not sufficiently opposing bureaucracy, that sort of society that oppresses us, that crushes us, that wants us to be responsible for its own putrefaction. If it isn't the Jews, the Arabs, it's the convicts! It's for the tranquillity of their consciences, their positions, their careers, or their honors that they make us rot.

Delinquents, criminals, who are we? Why do they dog us like destitution does the gaunt Indian? Why is fate so against us? Could it be because we are against the established order, which is so favorable to certain people and so terrible for others, for the majority?

Are tuberculars punished? If we are sick, are we responsible for our sickness? If our unstable, broken, or negligent families raised us poorly, so to speak, educated us badly, is that our fault?

The familial setting in which we developed was noxious, if only it had been that of the privileged—is it our fault it wasn't? Does that make us guilty? But of course we're guilty and responsible! Otherwise, society would be revolting, rotten, and criminal; otherwise, our relatives—bless their hearts!—would be oblivious, exploited, and alienated; otherwise, the proper course, the right track, and the good path would be synonyms for slavery, submission, and collaboration with exploiters. Who profits from crime? Look at the bank accounts!

So, in order to allow our families to be brave and the brave to be honest and intelligent "good citizens," who have had mishaps with "their progeny"—in order to allow society and its privileged members to congratulate one another, to mutually honor one another in good conscience, to stuff their pockets and enjoy themselves in peace and quiet, we have to be guilty.

In this farce, in this comedy, "they" play the leading role. We are made to measure! We are the foils of those gentlemen. No, that's enough, comrades! Let's become conscious of our Human state, today we must open our eyes, understand, and rise up! Righteous anger! Are we not weak for having waited so long?

If we were sick, we should have been cared for. If our relatives were incapable, they should have been taught. If society is rotten—and each day the stench grows stronger—it has to be toppled and returned to dust. It isn't a matter of climbing onto the rooftops—which does nothing!—of demolishing, of settling our personal scores. It isn't a matter of cutting throats; they'd simply say we were insane.

But we have to show, to demonstrate in a thousand and one ways, with acts, speeches, writings, oppositions of all kinds, that we aren't responsible for all the ills on Earth. It is the current political system of our country that must be called into question, it and its values, its profiteers, who are direct causes of our misery and our errancy. The cops, the judges, the prison guards, they are its pillars, its supports. We have only duties, we need to have rights, too! The basic right to speak, to write, to contest the system in which we live, which wants us to be submissive bums, zombies, wrecks, which humiliates us in order to kill us off better, in order to subdue us, to teach us to live . . . according to "our best interests."

And above all, comrades, no illusions! Even if we are promised a 4 star,[15] we would only be its bellboys and flunkies. Let's look beyond the primary objectives, the dangling carrots. Our crimes, our offenses are only clumsy and reckless protests against the hand we've been dealt. Our society has made us into criminals and wants us to remain so! But we, the aware, anticapitalist criminals, we are becoming revolutionaries! Enough sales pitches, enough false promises: enough hypocrisy and lies, enough humiliations. Let them release us from these absurd, idiotic places; let them pay us, let them teach us a trade; let them abolish criminal records, let them allow us a normal, human life if they want to be taken seriously, if they want to show us that this society is something other than complete shit: "Steal a crown, you'll be hanged, steal a kingdom, you'll have a crown."—We're worse than hung!

Let's not forget, comrades, that the Union is our only strength, that we must move forward side by side and remain unwavering in the face of the demagoguery, the carrots—and beware those acting in both "good and bad faith!"

In order to cease being subhuman, let us unite and fight for another life, as Men!

Let's constantly exert our pressure on the enemy and let's not forget that we must count only on our own strengths; let's think about the fact that the ocean is made up of drops of water, that the relentless waves erode even the hardest stones.

Let's be convinced of the justice of our cause and no longer convicted by the injustice of the privileged and their lackeys.

With all the rebels in prisons—Toul, Nancy, and others—in factories, in the odious life to which we are subjected—with them we are united!

—*Le Comité de Défense d'Ensisheim*

The tone of this text—which is one among many—should suffice to make clear what is going on. I say it again because it is on this point that the keen intellects criticize us. We do not oppose the category of prisoners to that of "honest folk," and it is not because a man has been convicted in court that we take him to be a rebel or a savior. But we also know, in our hearts and from experience, that a convicted man in court is not necessarily condemned to infamy; we know that, under certain circumstances, he is capable of conducting himself more honestly and courageously than many of the people who despise and condemn him. Sometimes this can be seen during national catastrophes. We must dare to name what public decency has always concealed: among the early maquis,[16] there were a number of "repeat offenders." Perhaps their past predisposed them to adventure. But they could have chosen the black market or collaboration [with the Nazis], and they chose the Resistance. At that time, nearly all the French officers waited in their homes for the Liberation and judges from the free zone sent the Resistance fighters to Vichy prisons.

Breaking Down the Walls

The time has come to put an end to the scandal of the prisons. No one can claim to be ignorant of it anymore, and the only question is knowing if we will still have to wait ten years for new revolts, new lynchings, new repressions—and new commissions of inquiry. Attorney General Schmelck, who has begun uncovering the shame of Toul, President Rolland,[17] who had the courage, during the colloquium held at the beginning of June in the Palais de Justice in Paris, to say concerning torture in Algeria: "We should have spoken up," the moment has come to speak up. What do you think of the sentencings at Nancy? Ask for an audience with the President of the Republic. Take hold of public opinion. Later on, you might blame yourself for having waited too long to intervene.

All the reforms are worthwhile, but they don't get at what is essential. It is really a question of breaking down prison walls, of destroying the carceral universe, which doesn't mean, as they feign to believe, entering into a universe without sanctions overnight. To apply the law according to both its letter and its spirit, that, already, would empty our prisons by three-quarters: of the majority of those awaiting trial, of the bulk of juvenile delinquents, and of the percentage of the mentally ill that they house. As for the tiny minority of dangerous criminals, it is easy, in their cases, to institute measures of social protection that would put an end to the obsession with escape and security that weighs on the entire penitentiary administration and on the bulk of prisoners.

Breaking down prison walls, it is a risk to be taken with eyes wide open—a risk that will be less costly, in any case, than that of carceral degradation. It will be necessary to invent institutions and forms of conduct that, rather than responding to delinquency with repression, will treat its causes and will thereby compel the transformation of a society that is encouraging crime more and more. Penitentiary sadism is the extreme point of a contempt for humanity and of a violence that imprisons our social life. It has nothing to do with justice. It is the very opposite of justice, as vengeance is the opposite of sanction. Is it really extraordinary to imagine a society without prisons? After all, since we are just a few days short of July 14, it is appropriate to remember that France's national holiday is nothing other than the commemoration of the end of a prison.[18]

Notes

1. [Eds.] Guy Mollet (1905–75) served as Prime Minister of France from 1956 until 1957. Presiding over the Algerian War, especially the Battle of Algiers and its corollary torture campaign, Mollet is famous for having been pelted with tomatoes ("la journée des tomates") at a demonstration for Algeria in 1956.

2. Not only those in power but also those belonging to the opposition. One finds no mention of prisons in the copious government program *[programme de gouvernement]* devised by the Communist Party and only one, very vague line in that of the Socialist Party.

3. [AL Eds.] Jean-Marie Domenach, "Les détenus hors la loi," *Esprit* 411.2 (1972): 163–70.

4. [Eds.] The "Nancy Six," as they were called, are as follows: Jean-Claude Depoux (butcher, 26 years old), Charles (Jacky) Hoffman (waiter, 20 years old), Daniel Jacques (boilermaker, 24 years old), Gérard Lapointe (painter, 25 years old), Michel Magnier (mechanic, 21 years old), Gilbert Villière (welder, 25 years old).

5. [AL Eds.] For a narrative of the Nancy trial, see Philippe Meyer's "La Justice est Passée," in the section "Journal à plusieurs voix," in this same issue, *Esprit* 415.7/8 (1972): 101–2.

6. [Eds.] Casamayor (pseudonym of Serge Fuster, 1911–88) was a judge, GIP collaborator, and frequent critic of the French police. A prominent Catholic, he was well known for his denunciations of French torture during the Algerian War and in the Ben Barka Affair. Michel Foucault initially invited him to lead the GIP with him, but Casamayor, as a sitting judge, declined. He suggested that Foucault contact Jean-Marie Domenach, the author of the present essay, editor of *Esprit,* and a major representative of left-wing Social Catholicism for the position. Domenach accepted, along with Pierre Vidal-Naquet, a historian of ancient Greece and an important critic in his own right of French torture during the Algerian War. Casamayor wrote several books, including *Si j'étais juge* (Paris: Arthaud, 1970),

Les Juges (Paris: Seuil, 1973), *La Police* (Paris: Gallimard, 1973), and *Questions à la justice* (Paris: Stock, 1974). And, in 1979, Casamayor joined Foucault in a lengthy interview regarding "Le nouveau contrôle social" (http://www.archives-video.univ-paris8.fr/video.php?recordID=111).

7. [Eds.] Casamayor appears to be capitalizing on two senses of *seal*. There is the general sense of "seal of approval" and the legal sense of René Pleven's authorization, as Minister of Justice, Keeper of the Seals.

8. In particular, Marc Kunstlé and Claude Vincent have just published *Le Crépuscule des prisons* (Paris: Julliard, 1972). It is a very well-documented study that does not hesitate to implicate those in charge of the penitentiary administration, calling them out by name. We await the reaction of the interested parties with great curiosity. In addition, the GIP just published a new booklet, *Cahier des revendications sorties des prisons lors des récentes révoltes.*

9. [AL Eds.] The regional warden of the penitentiary administration.

10. The latter held him responsible for the failure of a prisoner, who had received special permission to attend his wife's funeral service, to return to prison.

11. On this subject, read the remarkably well documented book by Christine Martineau and Jean-Pierre Carasso, *Le Travail dans les prisons* (Paris: Champ libre, 1972).

12. Henri Varennes, "Des prisons, pour quoi faire?," a well-documented article in the issue on prisons published by *Politique aujourd'hui* (April–May 1972): 15-40.

13. An association for the rights of the imprisoned was recently created under the presidency of Vercors. It includes, most notably, Claude Bourder, Père Boyer, Gilles Deleuze, Jean-Marie Domenach, Dominique Éluard, Mrs. de Felice, Jacques Madaule, Mrs. Matarasso, Claude Mauriac, and Mrs. Thévenin. The work of the prisoners in the prisons, of the GIP on the outside, and the growing awareness of the public are at the origin of this association. It will work to make known and respect the rights of prisoners and it will intervene to denounce all abuses taking place in the prisons. The association is open to the families of prisoners, to those close with prisoners, to ex-prisoners, to prisoners themselves when it is possible for them to join, and to anyone interested in whatever way and wishing for an effective, democratic control over the prisons. Postal address: Association pour la Défense des Détenus (ADDD), 18 Rue du Douanier, Paris, 14e.

14. [Trans.] This term refers to conditional release [i.e., parole].

15. Allusion to a kind of demagoguery that refers to prisons as four-star hotels.

16. [Eds.] The Maquis *(maquisards)* were a group of French Resistance fighters during World War II.

17. [Eds.] Maurice Rolland (1904–88) served as Président de la Chambre Correctionnelle de la Cour de Cassation from 1964 to 1974.

18. [Eds.] Bastille Day commemorates July 14, 1789, a day during the French Revolution when the resistance stormed (and eventually demolished) the Bastille and freed its prisoners. Built as a medieval fortress in the late fourteenth century, the Bastille was converted into a prison in the mid-seventeenth century.

Preface to Serge Livrozet's *De la prison à la révolte*

MICHEL FOUCAULT

A preface, penned by Michel Foucault, to Serge Livrozet's De la prison à la révolte *(Paris: Mercure de France, 1973), 7–14.*

Lacenaire,[1] Romands,[2] that was already more than 130 years ago . . . The condemned have no grounds for complaint: from the moment they could speak, they have had the chance to say what they needed to say. The attention we lend them honors them—and flatters us: we are not dupes of the system that condemned them, after all; their very books prove it, since we make sure to shelve them with the others, even if we leave their authors on the inside.

We have only one condition for such authors: that they recount their lives. *They must* recount their lives. Beneath the facade of tolerance, this is a strict rule. What does it impose? In the first place, that the criminal conviction and the time in prison appear to be singular adventures. Only fate or something completely outrageous could have brought them about. Whoever finds himself caught up in such things has no doubt summoned them through some sort of weakness or obscure genius: this could only happen to him. The encounter, the opportunity, the act, the flight, the capture, the evidence, the conviction, the escape—a sum of improbabilities and lucky breaks that come together only once, and bear only one name.

At the heart of our relationship with justice we place, and want to see nothing but, chance. After all, it takes a lot of chance to make a criminal; a lot of chance to commit a crime; a lot of chance for him to be discovered. It is essential that we believe that the penal machine functions only every now and then, triggered each time by an incredible combination of circumstances. In order to convince ourselves of this, we have two opposed kinds of stories: the detective novel (a maximum of improbabilities, indecipherable traces, a chance discovery that sets the most meticulous calculations in motion) and the tale of criminal adventures (which should be something like the inverse of the detective novel: luck, hard luck, worse luck, fate, foiled plans, miraculous providence, the unexpected flap of a butterfly's wings). In response to the unimaginable adventure that happens only once, there is the unerring detection that discovers the improbable each time. Thus are our minds put to rest.

Thus we find conjured away everything quotidian, familiar, extremely likely, and ultimately central to our relationship with the police and the justice system.

Thus we find it established that the condemned cannot have thoughts because he must only have memories. His memories alone are permitted, not his ideas. Behind his act, there is nothing more than a mad desire that set it all in motion, or inevitable circumstances that plotted the course: but always exceptional, and without it being possible for there to be a communicable meaning in it, or a truth that could be the truth of several. The offense is not committed so as to be thought; it must only be *lived,* then recalled. We don't tolerate the system, but only the simple memory of the crime.

Thus we also find it established that the condemned will always be a man alone. He can have accomplices or cellmates, but that is only because he crossed paths with them. He will have made contact with them in a chance convergence or a shared fate, but they will each have been alone together anyway. Their memories can certainly cross paths or overlap, but they will always remain the memories of one or the other of them. There is no question, then, of their being able to hold together a unified narrative that would be theirs collectively, and in which they would be able to state, by common consensus, not what they once lived through, but what they think today.

"You will therefore recount your memories to yourself, you will say what you did, why you were caught, how you spent your time in prison, how you managed to escape. Be as extreme and as unique as possible. Recall your impressions, revive your feelings. Say what you have lived. The community, the group, that through which we communicate? Don't worry about that: this isn't a question of thought or reflection, it's just writing. It's through the work, the beauty, the measured originality of your writing that you will be recognized. Remember, writing is our sacred place and our universal element. Stop, at all costs, wanting to say what you think. Write. And write it the right way, which is to say, the way we want you to. You don't know how? You use profanities, you repeat yourself, you lapse into idle speculations when you're asked for the *writing* of your own lived experience? No matter. We'll get a tape recorder, you're going to recount your life. We, we are going to write it. We'll split the profits."

And yet, are we not in a good position to see that the infraction, the court, the punishment are not—in any case, are not only—matters of individual adventure? For a long time now—more or less since we read Lacenaire's *Mémoires* and acquired the habit of listening to the memories of the condemned—we have had a sociology and a psychology of delinquency. We know, then, that there is a steady stream of infractions in our society and that the suppression of crimes is one of our society's central functions; that, beyond the events of singular adventures, delinquency exists as a general phenomenon; that the criminal is not simply a player or a plaything, but one who carries a certain number of characteristics, symptoms, physical traits; that this is a case—a normally abnormal case.

But here precisely is what is significant: in order for the condemned to cease to be the simple subject of his adventures, an expert gaze must be trained on him; a discourse, armed with concepts, must speak of him; an institution—"sociology," "psychiatry," "psychology," "criminology," the name doesn't matter—must take him as its object; he must not speak and be listened to, but rather must answer questions that are posed to him so that what he says may then be examined. The condemned exist in the plural only as the effect of and by the grace of a "scientific" discourse managed by an official. They form a group because they have been gathered together under general categories; if they must have words and ideas in common, it is the words by which they are designated and the notions that are applied to them. Analysis and reflection come from the outside: one doesn't ask them for their analyses and reflections, analysis and reflection are practiced on them as precisely as possible. The truth illuminates them from above.

That way we can be sure that they will never form anything but a collection; never a collective movement bearing its own reflections.

We must not be mistaken: the tale of unique adventures lived by the condemned forms a part of a certain distribution of roles, in which criminology and the detective novel also figure. Memory, writing, chance, certainty, truth, all of that has a thoroughly determined place within this distribution. Here's the scene: you, you are the individual, the adventure, the memory; you will speak in the first person, but only under the conditions of a kind of writing whose laws we alone possess; for this price, you will be heard and pardoned. We, we will listen to the fictive stories (disturbing-reassuring) in which your irregular adventure will be continued, reconstructed, captured, mastered by a certain rational calculus that will triumph over your ruses and solve the riddle with an ingenious discovery. And while we delight ourselves with these fictions, you others, you experts, you will be the only ones capable of transforming the singular adventure that recounts an individual memory into a general phenomenon, which, in the name of science, you designate and disarm using the term "delinquency."

A moment ago I said that criminology appeared in the same era as when Lacenaire's *Mémoires* (written in prison, just before his execution) was enthusiastically welcomed by the public. Yet it is necessary to recall that these *Mémoires* appeared only in censored form. There is no way for us to reconstruct what has been suppressed, of course. We can, however, surmise what was there, since the editor replaced the expurgated passages with ellipses. Nothing was excluded that could have been considered a memory or an adventure: the thefts are recounted, the murders and the attempted murders, the way he got caught, the good and bad luck, the number of blows he was dealt. All the censored sentences clearly deal with the relations between crime, the state, politics, religion, and the economy. It is not the practice but the theory of crime that is blotted out. The regime of Louis-Philippe[3] could certainly handle a murderer looking back on a murder; but not a criminal reflecting on crime, on the political question of crime, or making an analysis that others (whether criminals or not) could take up and work on as a common oeuvre.

And it is precisely in the blank space of this explicitly forbidden (and not "repressed") discourse that criminology and the sociology and psychology of crime found their place: in their turn, they took charge of making criminality exist as a general phenomenon, and in such a way that it would express itself only as an object of knowledge, as a field of analyses, as a theme for reflections, conducted by others and for others. Don't be surprised, then, if such "sciences" decompose criminality into a sum of little individual adventures, as products of good and bad luck, like the mother's possessiveness, the father's absence, the destructuring of the family, or the immaturation of the superego: sociopsychological rotten luck.

A skilled and docile partner, criminology responds ably to the tale of adventures. It sings the same tune, but in a different octave and with different words. And, on the other hand, it echoes the detective novel: just as the latter unravels the incredible mystery using the certainty of calculation, criminology reduces all the irregularities of the individual adventure to a general profile, bearing the name of "deviance."

Don't tell me I'm exaggerating. An American psychoanalyst had listened to criminal clients with such attention he was able to understand how and why any given crime was committed. So the police consulted him: and faced with a dead body, he reconstructed the psychological portrait for his client (this time the police) so well that he succeeded in unmasking the guilty party. His name: Brussels.[4] The scene of which I am speaking is that of the Lacenaire-Gaboriau-Lombroso trio.[5]

Serge Livrozet's book upsets this distribution. He picks up the thread of a discourse that Lacenaire's censors would have wanted to interrupt. He undertakes to see—from the point of view of the perpetrator—the political meaning of the infraction. These are not the *Mémoires* of a prisoner. I don't mean to say that it would be useless to provide testimonies, in the form of memories, that could be valuable as critiques and denunciations. What I mean to say is that it is time to listen to something else, which is both new and very old.

New, because those who have the courage to publish such things are rare. New, because we aren't used to these texts, in which memories that have only just begun are interrupted; they are there for an instant just to give one the right to say, without "scientific qualifications:" "Since it is a question of crime, of law, of infraction, of delinquency, here is what I think; here is what I thought or wanted when I broke the law and committed a crime." The first person who speaks throughout the book is less the first person of memory than the first person of theory. Or rather, a first person who, in recalling his crimes, affirms the right for a "delinquent" to speak of the law; a first person who refuses to be stripped of this right by the permission granted him to recount his memories. Of my life, Serge Livrozet says, you know only the minimum necessary for you to be able to establish the following fact: whether by transgressing the law in the past, or by leading a life that is not at odds with it today, I have never stopped attacking it with armed discourse. What's more, this is a right that my crimes gave me then and that I hold on to now far more tightly than to the memories that they have left me.

In this way, Serge Livrozet's book belongs to an ancient tradition that has been systematically brushed aside and misunderstood. For there has long been a *thought* of the infraction intrinsic to the infraction itself; a certain reflection on the law tied to the active refusal of the law; a certain analysis of power and law that was conducted by the very ones who were engaged in a daily struggle against law and power. Strangely, this thought seems to have caused more fear than illegality itself, for it has been more severely censored than the deeds that accompanied it, or of which it was the occasion. From time to time, we have seen it appear with a bang in some anarchist movement, for instance, but usually only in secret. It is passed on, nevertheless, and it is developed.

Here it is, bursting forth today in this book. And it is bursting forth because, in the prisons, among those getting out as much as those on their way in, it has acquired, through revolt and struggles, the strength to express itself. Serge Livrozet's book forms a part of this movement, which, for years, has been disrupting our prisons. I don't want to say that it "represents" what all or surely even a majority of prisoners think. I am saying that it is an element in this struggle; that it is born of this struggle and will play a role in it. It is an individual and a strong expression of a certain collective *[populaires]* experience and thought of the law and of illegality. A philosophy of the people.

Serge Livrozet was one of the organizers of the movement of struggle that developed at the Melun Prison during the winter of 1971–72.

After his release, he was one of the founders of the Comité d'Action des Prisonniers.

Notes

1. [Eds.] Pierre François Lacenaire (1803–36), incarcerated for murder, is author of *Mémoires, révélations et poésies* (Paris: Marchands de Nouveautés, 1836). Foucault also discusses Lacenaire in *Discipline and Punish: The Birth of the Prison,* trans. Alan Sheridan (New York: Vintage Books, 1977), 283–85.

2. [Eds.] We have been unable to establish the referent of this term.

3. [Eds.] Louis-Philippe I (1773–1850) was the king of France from 1830 until 1848.

4. [Eds.] James A. Brussel (1905–82) was a psychologist, criminologist, and New York State's assistant commissioner of mental hygiene. An early developer of psychological profiling, Brussel assisted in the arrest of George Metesky, the "mad bomber," and Albert DeSalvo, the "Boston strangler." Dubbed "Sherlock Holmes on the Couch," Brussel published his book *Casebook of a Crime Psychiatrist* (New York: Grove Press) in 1968.

5. [Eds.] Foucault here refers to Pierre François Lacenaire (1803–36), Émile Gaboriau (1832–73), and Cesare Lombroso (1805–1909): the criminal (the first romantic figure of his kind), the novelist (a pioneer of the detective novel), and the criminologist (referred to as the father of criminology).

Preface to Bruce Jackson's *In the Life: Versions of the Criminal Experience*

MICHEL FOUCAULT

Michel Foucault's preface to Bruce Jackson, Leurs prisons: Autobiographies de prisonniers américains *(Paris: Plon, 1975), i–vi. Originally published in English as Bruce Jackson,* In the Life: Versions of the Criminal Experience *(New York: Holt, Rinehart, and Winston, 1972).*

The book before you is composed of interviews with prisoners, recorded by Bruce Jackson in several Texas prisons. Or rather, it is composed of long monologues rekindled from time to time by barely perceptible questions. This great outpouring of stories, memories, fables, of tiny details and great flourishes, of defiance, rage, and bursts of laughter has plenty to astonish us—we who are accustomed to hearing about crimes only when they are draped in the modesty of difficult admissions, and about prison only when it is shrouded by a prohibition against seeing and hearing. This is doubtless true of America, sure, but Texas?

We others, we Europeans, live in the continuum of our history. America, however, perpetually lives the birth and death of the law. Our categories are victory and defeat. Theirs are violence and legality. Our mascot is the commander in chief or the soldier. Theirs is the sheriff.

But, whereas in the land of the Western we see moral law and order, pure and simple, reconstructed at the hands of the "lawman" on the foundation of violence and savage land-grabbing, in Bonnie and Clyde's country, between Dallas and Houston, the law becomes corrupt, dissolves, decays, and dies; and from its sunbaked corpse a swarm of crimes is born, some large, some small, but all eager to talk.

Maybe we are more Texan than we think. Claude Mauriac once said that, "Over there, politics, the police, and the whole environment are one and the same." But there is clearly a restrained irony in his use of "over there."

In the Life does a good job of showing that prison walls owe their formidable force less to their material impermeability than to the innumerable threads, the thousands of channels, and the countless, crisscrossing lines that traverse them. The strength of a prison is the incessant capillarity that feeds it and empties it; it functions thanks to a whole system of large and small valves that open and close, suck in and spit out, discharge and refill, devour and expel. It is situated in a mess of junctions, loops, return routes, and pathways leading in and out. We mustn't see it as a lofty fortress enclosing the lords of revolt or the damned of humanity, but as a halfway house, a brothel, the inevitable roadside motel. Across the continent, from Texas to California or Chicago, these people meet up and are reunited with folks they knew in Chicago, California, and Texas time and time again. They meet them, or traces of them, their memories, their friends, or their enemies. One thinks of those photos taken at night, in which the headlights flying by, one after the other, leave behind a network of white, immobile lines. This spider's web extends across the entire United States. Four large highways lead to prison: drugs, prostitution, gambling, and forgery *[les chèques]*. Delinquency out of the blue? Not at all. Rather, a more or less quick graduation first from the tolerated, to the semilegal, and to the partially illicit; then branching out to a kind of criminal activity that is accepted, protected, even integrated into all "honest" work, and of which prisoners are at once the feverish workforce, the slick and yet indiscriminate subcontractors, and the easiest victims. We say with such ease—whether to psychiatrize or to lionize them—that they are "marginal." But the margins in which they move are not branded as the frontiers of exclusion; they are the discreet and worn-down spaces that allow the most honorable story to be told, and the most austere law to be put into practice. What a certain lyricism calls the "margins" of society, what one imagines to be a sort of "outside," are the internal gaps, the little, interstitial distances that allow society to function. Jackson's interlocutors' thousand stories are eloquent on this very point, even when it is a question of robbery, that is, of a criminal practice that marks a degree of rupture much greater than that of the daily grind of prostitution, swindling, or gambling. Read the story of the gangster who went to rob a supermarket early in the morning when it was still nearly empty: the first customers take him for the cashier, he gives them their change and draws up a receipt for the gagged manager. Or the cashier who, when robbed of cash but not his checks, thanked the thieves and told them he hoped they'd be the ones to come next time, too.

Bosses, cashiers, insurance agents, cops, robbers—each plays his own role and follows his own path down an already well-worn track. And—this is the important thing—that is perfectly tolerated, not by "the people" or "the public" (in whom, to the contrary, they try to instill fear), but by those who possess both the money and the power.

Law and order—whether American or European—have their fringes, which are not fractious or poorly controlled regions they seek to wrest from their adversaries; rather, such fringes are the very conditions of the exercise of law and order. To render the law (as a relation to power) collectively acceptable, the illegalism of delinquency must be cultivated with care and constructed as a permanent danger. Love of the law, or at least general docility, is bought at the price of these complicities, which, in the end, are hardly costly. The police-delinquency theater, which occupies such a prominent place in everything we've read and seen since the nineteenth century, is one of the complements and indispensable counterweights of universal suffrage. For the law to be able to have clear value in its secret violence, for order to be able to impose its constraints, these zones of "danger"—which are silently tolerated, and then suddenly glorified in the press, in crime fiction, in film—must exist, and not at the outer limits, but in the very center of the system, like some kind of playground for its machinery. And, in the end, it hardly matters whether the criminal is presented as a hero of pure rebellion or as a human monster barely emerged from the forest, provided he creates fear.

Yet that is where the formidable irony, the red and black[1] enthusiasm of the stories gathered by Bruce Jackson take on their meaning.

In the nineteenth century, a tradition took shape, the traces of which have yet to be effaced across Europe. It organized the discourse of delinquency into two registers. On the one hand, we other delinquents, we are the products of society: products, since in its cruelty it has exploited us, rejected us, excluded us, driven us to violence despite ourselves, and pushed us to war; products, also, since we resemble it: our violence is its violence, and if there is some malice and madness in us, it put them there with its own hands. We are descendants who resemble society too much for it not to hate us. On the other hand, if the delinquent is a "product," delinquency itself, as a gesture, is represented as a revolt: the true social war. It is the theft that opposes itself to that other theft: property. It is the murder that answers the sometimes slow, sometimes swift death of wartime massacres, or that responds to this whole factory of exploitations society imposes on individuals. In sum, two registers: the delinquent-victim and delinquency-rupture.

In the present book, however, this discourse is completely reversed. What Bruce Jackson's prisoners repeatedly say is that delinquency itself, in its circuits and its procedures, in its swindles, its thefts, and its murders, functions in toto to give the system its greatest profit and highest yield; that all the robberies are tolerated, that prostitution and gambling are set up, that there are opportunities for drugs and fraud everywhere, that everything is possible and even outlined in advance; that the police are always a part of it. But what ultimately makes the delinquent (the obstinate, recidivist delinquent, whom Jackson is addressing) is less the pathos of a situation lived in common with so many others than a sort of singular strength in the midst of this irony. It's because he lays it on thick, he keeps doing it, he can't stop himself—player rather than plaything. If there's a subversion in all that, it is not in the form of delinquency as revolt, but in the intensity of determination, in a series of repetitions, in a frenetic course that ends by blowing open the widest doors and the broadest channels. And suddenly the scandalous thing appears, the intolerable truth that must be covered up by making the guilty party disappear definitively: that from the top of the system to the bottom, everything has been arranged so that the illegalisms would function and the most profitable delinquencies would multiply. It is not by turning against established law, but by endlessly converging on pre-arranged illegalisms that the Texan prisoners interviewed by Jackson

cause a scandal, politically. And the political effect cannot be dissoci-
ated from the tremendous laughter that traverses all their stories. No
admission, never a cry of innocence, nor the least justification. But
the accumulation, the feast, the orgy of offenses, the excess, the fiction, of course, the overdose of deeds and of "action" that those Pan-
tagruels[2] of criminality tirelessly recount. It is a raging delinquency,
Margot la Folle,[3] laughing hysterically and going on and on about her
transvestite's garb, her gear for armed robberies, her gangster's machine gun, the sheriffs, the police, the lieutenants, the mayors, and
the senators—the entire idiotic staff of law and order.[4] Count how
many holdups Bob and Ray were able to pull off, how many times Big
Sal was locked up, how many ploys Webster devised, how many times
Bebop used up his stash of heroin, how many suckers Slim fleeced
with his dice, how many times Maxwell got fucked.

In France, and undoubtedly in all of Europe, the traditional form of
the scandal was the condemned innocent and the entire machinery
of justice working to impose and maintain that condemnation. In
the United States, it is the exaggeration of the guilt of the guilty, that
astonishing accumulation of all that he was able to perpetrate, the
wide avenues that were open before him, the moments of tolerance
he benefited from, and finally the complicity of the entire machinery, not in his condemnation, but in his criminality itself. On the one
hand, Jean Valjean or Monte-Cristo. On the other, Al Capone, Bonnie and Clyde, or the Mafia. The "European" kind of scandal—let us
say, rather, the old kind of scandal, the nineteenth-century sort—was
the Dreyfus Affair, in which the entire state machinery, all the way
up to the highest level, is compromised in the persecution of someone who isn't guilty. The "American" kind of scandal is Watergate,
where from a minor infraction we climb little by little up the network
of continuous illegalisms, in accordance with which the machinery
of power functions. In this case, the scandal was not that those in
power had wanted to cover up a crime that was useful to them; it
wasn't even that the most powerful person in the world had been a
rather crude common-law delinquent, but that his power was exercised and could only have been exercised daily through the most ordinary delinquency. Finished is that individual and total criminality of
the Shakespearean kings, which surrounded them with a monstrous

aura and, in a certain manner, sanctified them. We have long been in the age where the functioning of power and the administration of illegalisms go hand in hand.

Listen to those shrill, voluble, ferocious, ironic voices that Bruce Jackson has recorded. They don't sing the hymn of the accursed in revolt. They make law and order—and the power that functions through them—"sing," in the name of all the tricks that they have played on one another.

Notes

1. [Eds.] The red and black is one version of the communist flag; the red stands for socialism and the black stands for anarchism.

2. [Eds.] Foucault is referring here to a collection of five novels, *La vie de Gargantua et de Pantagruel,* which were published in the sixteenth century (1534–62) by the writer François Rabelais. The stories tell of the adventures of two giants, Gargantua and his son Pantagruel, and Pantagruel's friends. They are filled with satire, humor, and violence. Interestingly, Foucault discusses the use of the "proximity of extremes" by one of Pantagruel's attendants, Eusthenes, in his book *The Order of Things: An Archeology of the Human Sciences* (New York: Pantheon Books, 1970), xvi.

3. [Eds.] A reference to Willy Vandersteen, *Bob et Bobette: Margot La Folle,* v. 78 (Belgium: Éditions Erasme, 1967), whose protagonist, Margot, is described here.

4. [Trans.] In English in the original.

A crowd amasses as revolt breaks out in Charles-III Prison in Nancy, France, on January 15, 1972. Photograph by Gérard Drolc.

Part V
Reflections (1979–1980 and After)

The GIP was an experiment in forging a new kind of critical movement. And, as such, it was fraught with tensions throughout its short history, tensions over tactics and principles, even over strategies and goals, but, in the end, the GIP consistently struggled to draw public attention to the problems raised by incarceration as a technique of punishment, to make the public aware that there was something there in the penal system that, as Michel Foucault put it reflecting back on this experience in 1979, "people didn't tolerate and is not tolerable."

This final section collects assessments of the GIP by some of its most prominent members: Foucault and Gilles Deleuze, each made from the vantage of some seven years after its dissolution, as well as Hélène Cixous, looking back on the GIP today. The appraisals are honest, critical, nuanced, and insightful about the group's limitations and its innovations.

The first two selections derive from a 1979 roundtable organized by the journal *Esprit* to reflect on the GIP's work nine years after its birth ("Struggles around the Prisons"). It featured three participants. Two had been active in various ways in the GIP: Antoine Lazarus, a former doctor who had worked at the prison at Fleury-Mérogis, and Louis Appert (a pseudonym that Foucault assumed for this publication), an intellectual who presents an insider's view of the history and evolution of the group. The third participant, François Colcombet, a former member of the judicial system, served as a kind of interviewer.

The publication of the roundtable was preceded by an introduction, authored by Paul Thibaud, who had recently taken over the editorship of the journal from Jean-Marie Domenach. The piece claimed that groups such as the GIP were largely ineffectual because they failed to produce concrete proposals for reforming the prison system and that this was due to their reliance on intellectuals as the primary leaders. Foucault, stepping out from behind his pseudonym, and Jean-Marie Domenach engaged Thibaud in a follow-up exchange ("Still Prisons") that was published in a subsequent issue.

The penultimate selection ("Foucault and Prisons") is an interview with Deleuze from May 1985, published in *History of the Present.* It represents Deleuze's reflections on Foucault's militancy and their distinctive approaches to the question of social order as he prepared the two lecture courses he was to deliver in October 1985 through May 1986 that laid the foundations for his own study *Foucault* (1988).

Finally, the collection closes with a new interview with Hélène Cixous, conducted expressly for the present publication. In it, she contextualizes her work with the GIP within the tangled arc of her political activism and her calling as a writer.

Throughout these reflections, former GIP members grapple with what counts as success and failure not only in the broad realm of political activism but in the specific acts of resistance to the prison, itself an eerie exemplar of a failing instance of justice and yet a resounding success as a judicial institution.

Struggles around the Prisons

FRANÇOIS COLCOMBET, ANTOINE LAZARUS, AND LOUIS APPERT

*A roundtable discussion in 1979 on the work of the GIP with
François Colcombet (a former member of the court system),
Antoine Lazarus (a former prison doctor), and Louis Appert (a
pseudonym for Michel Foucault). The discussion was published in*
Esprit, *no. 11: "Toujours les prisons" (November 1979): 102–11.*

LOUIS APPERT: It has been a completely normal, ordinary, and long-
standing activity of the bourgeois intellectual to occupy himself
with prisons, really since the beginning of the nineteenth century.
What changed, in 1971, was the manner in which he occupied himself with them.

It seemed interesting to grapple with the general question of
penalty—because that was already in question—starting with the
prison, this region with which so many people had been occupied
for so long, but that had never been taken as the angle through
which to interrogate the penal system. We were occupied with the
prison, but as the penal system's underground chamber *[sous-sol]*,
its storeroom *[chambre de débarras]*.[1] The idea was to start inter-
rogating the penal system through its storeroom.

Then, there was a fuss or uneasiness among certain political
groups. They worried: what is the significance of posing political
questions that don't stem from the perspective of class struggle,
the proletariat against the bourgeoisie?

ANTOINE LAZARUS: Though at the beginning some people tried to
show that the prison was a privileged place of class struggle, where
they confined only the proletarians and subproletarians, and that

the prisoners' words, driving passions, and revolts constituted political discourse.

L. A.: Yes, but within the GIP we were fortunate to get neither support nor OPA[2] from any political group.

A number of months after the GIP was formed, we held a large meeting in a public place, to which many people, families of prisoners, prison visitors, etc., came. A very clumsy political intervention was made by two young lads who were doubtless well-meaning but believed it was absolutely necessary to politicize everything. That scared off a lot of people and it was really difficult to regroup. This was right at the beginning, in 1971.

One of the PC-CGT's newspapers asked: why don't they stop these people? *Temps modernes*[3] offered no help at all, just a few small venomous slanders. As for the Socialist Party, forget about it, and the same for the Trotskyists. The Maoists offered only some support, and one Maoist who wanted to "put down roots" in the GIP, poor fellow, was thrown into ridicule . . . All the political groups either voluntarily turned away from the movement or bashed their heads against it.

FRANÇOIS COLCOMBET: What portion of public opinion appreciated the GIP's discourse? Who bought its booklets?

L. A.: People who "weathered" May '68 and who either didn't want to or couldn't be integrated into groups. For example, folks from VLR,[4] '68 folks who remained individualists.

Very early on, there was a great response from certain prison personnel: not from judges or penitentiary personnel properly so-called, but from educators and visitors. Some doctors, too. And above all, the families of prisoners. For, contrary to what has been said, the GIP always included prisoners—that was its basic principle.

F. C.: Political prisoners or common-law prisoners?

L. A.: There were some political prisoners from the beginning. But they were few in number and we immediately saw that this was not the best way in. The best way was the visiting rooms, the families who formed the queue: there, we immediately got a sizable response.

The GIP was created at the beginning of 1971. The events marking its creation were the political prisoners' hunger strike and the hunger strike on the outside led in solidarity with those who demanded political status—that is to say, by Geismar's Gauche Prolétarienne.[5] At the time, they embraced the ideology of the "new resistance." In the Resistance, it had been very important to emphasize that resisters were not common-law prisoners, despite the assimilation that Germans and the Vichy government wanted to enforce. The struggle to have a political status was absolutely essential for the Resistance. (Genet recounts that, one day in 1942, in order to take him to the courthouse, or La Santé, they wanted to cuff him to a communist, but the latter refused, saying: "Not with a thief!") But in 1971, the demand for political status immediately raised questions, not only critiques aimed at Maoists but debates among Maoists. In discussing the above, they said: we must pose the problem not of the political regime in prisons, but of the prison regime itself.

From that moment on, reference to the problem of psychiatry came into full play. In the sixties, antipsychiatry had given up on the question: what is madness? Is it of social origin or not? Is it social alienation or mental alienation? Reification, objectification, bad conscience, false consciousness . . . Antipsychiatry said instead: it doesn't matter what the mad are. What do we do with them? What is it to be confined? And what is this psychiatric practice?

To approach the problem of penalty not by asking, "Is society responsible for delinquents?" but rather by posing the smaller question, which has the effect of deflating these grand considerations: What do they make of the situation? With the GIP, people came (the families of prisoners came), prisoners sent us documents, and the question was never asked: what did you do? And the interesting thing is, they didn't ask that question themselves. Together, and very quickly, we sensed from within and without that the problem was this: what is prison?

A. L.: In my memory, the GIP is obviously different. I was already a doctor at Fleury-Mérogis. It was a very difficult period: we were on call 48 hours straight and paid 700 francs a month. For us, the GIP was directly inscribed in a continuum of struggles, whether carried out among students or elsewhere. Whatever political analyses enabled us to act on the student world or within the political

context were the same tools available for an analysis of prison—
the prison that, while a kind of caricature or distillation of the exterior world, was easier to get hold of and move through protest.

The GIP people I came across were looking for information,
working to draft a booklet on Fleury published toward the end of
1971. I had a very curious thought: what do people on the outside
have to say about all this? Some intellectuals were in the mood for
practical, activist work . . . On the other hand, I sensed a profound
relief that there was a relay station in place.

The hunger strike, led by detained militants from the Gauche
Prolétarienne, posed a fundamental problem with the demand
for political status. If they were given the status of political prisoners, they became elite and recuperated privileges. Even in this
struggle to publicize the prison and defend other people, they had
to situate themselves on the side of those who had the privilege
of being known and distinctly recognized by the administration:
how could we say: "Let's all be common-law prisoners" and demand political status? We could certainly say: "All common-law
prisoners are political," but that no longer worked because there
was a tremendous divide between a political activist who finds
himself in prison, who has reached a new level of personal evolution, a maturity (or who manages his neurosis, we might say),
but who is, nevertheless, capable of being invested in a problem
outside himself—a terrible divide between him and the young
common-law prisoner, who lives so badly in his environment that
he constitutes a kind of egoistic delinquency (his sole manner of
survival) and who is absolutely incapable, barring a long evolution, of being invested in a problem outside himself.

Did the GIP have an organic constitution?

L. A.: No, not at all. It was a meeting ground. The group was not constituted. To every person who wanted to do something, we said:
Go do it. Sure, we discussed what was most effective, but we did
not give orders. Outside of Paris, groups were formed and wrote to
us; we exchanged information. For it was very important to really
demonstrate that we knew what was happening in prisons. We
had to show the penitentiary administration and journalists that
we knew what had happened in prison the night before. This was
a tool to agitate within prisons and to call prison into question,

but it was also a means of making the penitentiary administration and journalists uneasy: prison is not a static place where nothing happens and all we know of it is that some unfortunate wrecks get out; it is a place in which events happen every day: hunger strikes, refusals of nourishment, suicide attempts, revolts, fights . . . We tried to publicize on a day-to-day basis this whole seething life of the prison, which literally didn't "exist," even for those who wrote great pieces on prisons. And to that, the press generally reacted quite well.

We had to put prison in the news, not under the sign of a moral problem, or a problem of general management, but as a place where history, the everyday, and life itself happened, where events took place of the same order as a workshop strike, a neighborhood movement, a low-income housing [H.L.M.] protest . . .

It was understood that three people, with some notoriety,[6] would be put in the spotlight—people who had to employ a certain etiquette and hide how things happened, hiding above all the fact that there was nothing to hide, that there was no organization. It was crucial that the penitentiary administration not even know whether there was organization or not.

It was also understood that, whenever a core of former prisoners was sufficiently numerous and willing to take over the whole movement, they would do so. And, that is indeed what happened after three years, when people from the CAP, with whom we had worked for a long time, left and established their own movement. At the time, we thought it might be good, in addition to the CAP—in which former prisoners would actually, and in an overt fashion this time, be the leaders—to have a movement in which, to the contrary, the apparent leaders were nonprisoners (the Association for the Defense of Detainees Rights, ADDD). Then it turned out things worked well enough for that not to be necessary . . .

A. L.: So, very quickly, even in the GIP, we made use of the know-how of intellectuals, their speaking ability, and their knowledge of how to be heard in order to get information out, but they were only the amplifiers of a sincerity and of a conviction provided by the presence of prisoners.

L. A.: I would be hard-pressed to identify the part each played. For example, in these booklets we made, in a sense there wasn't a single line not written in the hand of a former prisoner. We added nothing, fabricated nothing. Things were said to us and written to us. True, we had a basic format *[grille]*, some questions we posed, and information we wanted to obtain. But there was never a conflict between former prisoners, prisoners, and us in the drafting process. They always saw eye to eye; we didn't know where things came from, or who actually did what. We had practically no lies; there were some errors, but a very limited number of them, and one that appeared once in *Le Monde* was a very small error in data that we had no means of verifying. That proves that those who informed us (prisoners and former prisoners) were not trying to lie, nor were they drunk. In and around prisons, there was a real effort to make things known.

A. L.: Had there already been this alliance between the discourse of common-law prisoners and that of intellectuals?

L. A.: The first texts to come from prisons were published around 1825 by a philanthropist[7] who traveled from prison to prison and had prisoners, serious criminals, recount their previous lives: these people were adventurers who had seen the Revolution, the imperial armies, who led wild lives across Europe, failed to be reintegrated in Restoration France, and spent years in the prisons of Charles X.

Perhaps, during the campaigns against penal colonies, before the First World War, and between the two wars, there was a real collaboration between journalists and convicts. But still, that was always to publish individual testimonies; there wasn't this kind of collective and anonymous work.

A. L.: Some of those testimonies may also have been from intellectuals or notable persons who found themselves in prison for political reasons.

F. C.: And the outcome of all this?

A. L.: I am not sure what to say. I might be too optimistic, but I think those who collaborated in the GIP experience perceived this kind of work positively. The mode of operation strikes me as quite important. This opportunity for tying practical and theoretical work together was completely different from what you get in a political group where doctrine binds and practice restrains. Here, knowledges, analyses, sociological practices, a bit of historical knowledge, a dash of philosophy, some anarchist ideas, and readings, all of that was in play; it circulated, forming a kind of enveloping placenta.

F. C.: The paradox is that it operated apropos of the prison.

A. L.: The means of expression included articles, press conferences, and films.

L. A.: Yes, René Lefort made a film: *Les Prisons aussi.* Its production was an important element in the group. Material difficulties, lack of money, and slow development meant it was barely finished when the GIP was handing things over to the CAP in 1974. I am not convinced the film had a very large impact. But the fact that we knew we made a film, the fact that we interviewed former prisoners, was very important.

Very quickly, we got some journalists to integrate these prison events into the general news: Périer-Daville in *Figaro,* for example.

At some point, the papers regained control; notably in *Figaro,* they took swipes at some of the GIP's apparent leaders. But journalists continued to publish news about prisons and to take an interest in them. Newspapers, all the while demarcating themselves from us, kept talking about prisons.

F. C.: Do you sense that what the GIP conveyed had an impact on the so-called contemporary "reformer"?

L. A.: I don't know.

F. C.: The Arpaillange reports, for example.

L. A.: Before talking about the Arpaillange Report, we would have to talk about the Schmelck Report on revolts, which was the first official administrative response to the prison revolt movement. Everyone in the GIP saw it as a scandal. And we knew that the claim "Schmelck was a good soul and an honest man" was false. The way he tried to split the difference in the Toul affair, to admit certain facts while concealing those responsible, to give an absurd promotion to Toul's warden, all of that proved to everyone that this man was dishonest.

F. C.: Among those holding magisterial office or within a certain sector of public opinion, the Schmelck Report was not seen that way; for them, he at least deserved credit for breaking the silence.

L. A.: What we in the GIP did not see was that, in relation to what could be said in an official report on prisons, the Schmelck Report already introduced a considerable modification.

F. C.: That demonstrates, moreover, the difficulty of finding common cause with reformers, who have a tough time getting engaged with movements like the GIP.

A. L.: One question posed to me after Toul was: should we stay in the administration? I had the impression that the answer, stated in a vague way, but reflecting the sentiments of those from the GIP, was that we had to desert this institution and that all struggle should be led from outside.

L. A.: Not necessarily. I'm not sure I can accurately transcribe everyone's opinions, but it seems to me that, for us, the problem was not to say: such and such a thing is wrong and thus here are some conditions that might be right; it was simply to say: there is a problem here, there is something here people didn't tolerate and isn't tolerable. The idea that a critical movement, which is at the same time very strongly tied to practice, shouldn't be obliged to be a reform movement or to authorize a reform proposal is something we have always maintained. I know that for some people, especially those working in prisons, there was a problem and they said to us: what do you propose? I trust we had no impression of being evasive when we said: we have nothing to propose, in the sense that it's not up to us to propose anything; I trust this was not illogical, that it was not too self-limiting for, after all, we didn't create the prisons, nor did we work there. We said that the existence of prisons posed problems, just as much as what happened there. In this group, we wanted no prescription, no recipe, and no prophecy.

A. L.: Critiques of this type reflect the impossibility of conceiving all social intervention as substituting one power for another. We inform people about something and then, to change things, we send people back to their responsibilities, whatever they make of them.

L. A.: We can respond to the information on prison with revolt, with reform, or with the destruction of prisons.

F. C.: Do you think that the GIP's initiative has had repercussions on what the prison is today?

L. A.: I think that the GIP's initiative has been as much a symptom as a cause. How could something percolate in the thought or sensibility of some former '68 folk and intellectuals that was also percolating in the prisons? The Toul Revolt posed a problem for us: many people asked if the GIP had organized it and we ourselves said: perhaps it was a tract ... How far does that go? If ten guys are shot at, shot down ... We weren't always at ease ... But that wasn't what we did, it is what happened. And indeed, something happened, passing from prisons to the outside and from the outside into prisons, that was quite specific to this period. Similar things happened in American, English, Italian, and Spanish prisons: this wasn't the GIP ... The GIP was rather a microsymptom, in the middle of this whole ensemble, testifying to the impossibility of societies like ours justifying the fact of punishment.

F. C.: Don't you think that this kind of discourse has been better understood by intellectuals, including those from the right? Giscard d'Estaing[8] moving to shake hands with a prisoner, for example, didn't that strike you as a result of the GIP's initiative?

L. A.: Well, there was the secretary of state for prison conditions.[9] If the GIP is a leftist movement, it is the only one that can take credit for a state secretary! Here it is absolutely necessary to make a distinction. It is true that the prison, as a traditional place of philanthropic benevolence, was an ideal place for a government, wanting to be slightly liberal and modernist, to make some promises. But that produced exactly nothing, it seems to me. The complex of problems and the movement itself, now taken over by the CAP, have remained what they were.

A. L.: It produced some improvements that the era in any case required: new age groups are coming to prison with a different culture and different levels of intolerance—for parental restrictions, for example, or educational or professional ones; this is why a certain kind of carceral restriction can no longer last. Lecanuet and Mrs. Dorlhac's circulars, in response to the 1974 revolts, were superficial, reinforcing the humanization of prisons: to have a little more warmth, guards a little less heavy-handed, a little more warmhearted.[10] But, in relation to its announced objectives: the prison ought only to deprive prisoners of their liberty, or again: the prison ought to help people get out, to be reintegrated into society (hence Giscard's initiative to create the GENEPI,[11] an organization that sends students from the *grandes écoles* into prisons to supply a bit of outside culture)—in relation to those objectives, the outcome is nothing. They removed the irritating thorns that were liable to trigger an explosion.

What is surprising, when we see, after the fact, the content of recorded demands, is that they ask for basic comfort: nourishment, bedclothes . . . Prisoners display, sometimes at the risk of their own lives, an enormous need to change things, to be heard, and simultaneously they demand all the little things.

L. A.: There is a very interesting point here. What struck us in our investigative work was the importance of these problems of heating, chocolate bars, physical problems. From the beginning, we were a little surprised, but this was very important. It proved that among prisoners there was absolutely no shame in emphasizing and putting to work the problem of being hot or cold, the problem of chocolate or grub, even if it killed someone. This represented, it seems to me, a deculpabilization.

F. C.: Why a deculpabilization?

L. A.: At the end of the nineteenth century, people reproached prisons because the criminal left still a little more criminal than before, but I doubt they would have come up with criticisms like: we are really too cold. That whole literature was steeped in: surely, what I did is dreadful, I must atone for it, I am here to pay my debt to society.

A. L.: When I arrived at Fleury, in 1970, a fifty- or sixty-year-old prisoner, whose offense, moreover, was not very significant, said to me: "I don't understand, here I am treated well, it is warm, we are well nourished, you are a doctor, you take care of me: this is not hard enough, I am not paying enough." That was the old way . . . It has completely disappeared.

L. A.: I wonder if it changed around '68. Now people say: "Yes, I killed someone, but this is no reason for me to be cold."

F. C.: In the nineteenth century, they had no possibility of expression. One of the new changes is to have given possibilities of expression to people who didn't have the ability to speak about prison.

L. A.: Certainly, but it is important to point out that the people with whom we corresponded and who gave us information composed a tiny fringe of the prison population. What is interesting is that their comrades don't seem to have disowned them and that, to the contrary, those comrades accepted their role as spokespersons quite well.

A. L.: I wonder if, in a number of cases, the discourse of demands was not retained by the gangsters, by those who already held power in prison and who enhanced their gang power by the protest action; in a circle of the oppressed, the gangster serves as intermediary between other oppressed people and the penal authority; he enjoys certain privileges and the respect of both sides.

L. A.: Yes, but I would say, rather than a sublimated form, a parallel form of gang power. Those who wrote to us were, more than anything, the little people, those who suffered under the gangsters, or who would have loved to be gangsters. At one time, the movement became strong enough—thanks to the CAP rather than the GIP—for a gangster like Mesrine[12] to use and multiply his effects of prestige through this spokesperson function.

A. L.: I wonder if the key isn't really the fact that you touched families. We got information from prisoners, or from doctors, educators, and chaplains . . . The families, even if someone dear to them is in prison, had a discourse beyond prison. The society outside gained awareness that the prison was a wound even for those who weren't inside. That facilitated the effects of projection.

F. C.: You mentioned, a moment ago, that what was interesting about this manner of approaching prisons was that it allowed an approach to the problems of justice and of repression more generally . . .

L. A.: The traditional critique of prison was very localized and even marginalized in relation to the general problems of justice. At the time of the GIP, we realized that the prison, and also the police, must be considered as an essential piece of penality. Magistrates, moreover, increasingly realized that their moment to intervene in the penal circuit was extraordinarily short and they had little control; everything upstream was ensured by the police, everything downstream by the prison, its administration, and the "games" they permit, with conditional releases, etc.

F. C.: Do you think that augmenting the zone in which judges can act would be a positive thing?

L. A.: The Syndicat de la Magistrature itself critiques the restrictions of the judicial sphere, the limitations we impose on it, or the smallness of its role, but, while it does lay claim to a little more power for the judiciary, it doesn't do so without a little fear of its extension.

F. C.: This is a relatively recent attitude. There was a time when judges didn't disapprove of reducing the judiciary.

L. A.: Yes, and then there was a time when they said: "Return to the judiciary, return to the law," and it seems to me that for some months now they've been hesitating again.

In relation to all other forms of disputes and damages, the little illegality has a sad fate, since it is first dealt with by the police who make their own law, who choose what should and should not be judged, and then it is consigned to a judicial status of the worst sort: the *flagrant délit*. Compared to the cushy way we arbitrate a fiscal fraud, it is terrible. Is an administration like that of the police and the legal system the best format for mopping up these little infractions? We go so easy in other domains.

A. L.: It is a matter of arbitration, on one hand, and, on the other, of naming something that is nonarbitrable a posteriori, when the offense has already been committed and is violent.

L. A.: The distinction of penal and civil, of arbitrable and nonarbitrable, is recent.

A. L.: I wonder if we aren't headed toward a civilization where physical restriction will seem less crushing than the constraint of university knowledges, to which people are subjected without the means of counterargument.

In fact, over the last ten years, in our consciousness and the collective unconscious, the place of prison has been slightly modified. It lost its reference to an ideology of good and evil, and it is now looking for support in pedagogy and education.

L. A.: Rather, I would say it lost its evidence, the chain of evidence that causes us to admit that those who have committed a crime should be punished and that the most satisfactory form of punishment is confinement. These two things are, in a certain sector of the public, being put into question.

One of the effects of this critique of prison is to say: "In fact, prison can't be good and it can't but have bad effects." This is to say that, for anyone who runs the risk of being released from prison, it would have been better not to put him there, but, on the other hand, for anyone whose release risks being dangerous to society, we just have to leave him there; and that if prison is not good, it's good that it's not good. One of the current trends is the idea of a prison dump, an absolute dump—from which one doesn't get out, coupled with a host of alternative penalties: fines, work, and social activities.

From there we might reach two conclusions: (1) a whole series of alternative penalties for people who, their misdemeanor not being too serious, would one day be reintegrated into society, who we then wouldn't want to put through prison; (2) but for the other people, conversely, "if they went to prison, they are not getting out;" this would be the prison-cul-de-sac, then, which makes sense only if it is for life.

A. L.: This is the idea of the penal colony. For the young guys interviewed at Fleury, the penal colony meant living together, being mates.

L. A.: That has been the scourge of the penal colony in France: guys wanted the penal colony so much that they committed crimes, exaggerating the number of stabs as needed in order to be sure of going to the penal colony. Certain murders were committed during robberies that were hardly essential to the robbery, but were indispensable for securing a place in the penal colony.

A. L.: The youths I saw at Fleury wanted to live together, but not in Paris; there was an ecological nuance to it: a society of men, with shared values and a commitment to aiding one another.

On the other hand, people who called in to *Les Dossiers de l'écran*[13] in 1975 said: "They should be put on highway crews to crush stones." For these people, prison was not a place of camaraderie, but a place of forced labor.

Notes

1. [Trans.] There is a certain irony in this phrase. The term "*débarras*" most basically refers to an area in which otherwise encumbering (or barring) objects have been stored (hence, a storeroom, closet, junkyard, etc.). The phrase "*bon débarras*," meaning "good riddance," captures the relief of unencumbering oneself by confining things elsewhere. In this case,

society debars its life by consigning prisoners to the barred realm of the *débarras*.

2. [Eds.] Offre Publique d'Achat (OPA) is the acronym for a takeover bid.

3. [Eds.] *Les Temps modernes*, published from 1945 to 2019, was a French literary journal founded by Simone de Beauvoir and Jean-Paul Sartre.

4. [Eds.] Vive la Révolution (VLR) was a Maoist group, smaller than the Gauche Prolétarienne.

5. [Eds.] Alain Geismar was one of the most prominent figures in the events of May 1968 and a leader, with Benny Lévy, in the early seventies of the Gauche Prolétarienne.

6. [Eds.] Jean-Marie Domenach, Michel Foucault, and Pierre Vidal-Naquet.

7. [Eds.] Benjamin Appert (1797–1847) was a French pedagogue and philanthropist who introduced a system of mutual instruction into the regimental schools and eventually published a *Manual* setting forth his system. He subsequently taught prisoners at Montaigu and was accused and convicted of assisting two of his pupils in escaping. He was himself imprisoned and, upon his release, devoted the rest of his life to bettering the condition of prisoners. He carried out a large-scale study of prison discipline throughout Europe and wrote several books on the subject.

8. [Eds.] Valéry Giscard d'Estaing, center-right politician, served as President of France from 1974 until 1981.

9. [Eds.] In June 1974, the position of Secrétaire d'État à la Condition Pénitentiare (secretary of state for prison conditions) was formed, in response to the turmoil (see Stanislaw Plawski, *Droit pénitentiare* [Paris: Publications Universitaire du Septentrion, 1976], 91). The position was filled by Hélène Dorlhac, one of four women in significant governmental positions at the time. (See Claire Laubler, *The Condition of Women in France: 1945 to the Present—A Documentary Anthology* [New York: Routledge, 1990], 90.) Dorlhac went on to write *Changer la prison* (Paris: Plon, 1984).

10. [Eds.] Jean Lecanuet served as the Minister of Justice (Keeper of the Seals), 1974–76. Hélène Dorlhac (Borne) was the State Secretary to the Minister of Justice during this same period.

11. [Eds.] The Groupement Étudiant National d'Enseignement aux Personnes Incarcerées (GENEPI) was established in 1976.

12. [Eds.] Jacques Mesrine was the most notorious criminal in modern French history. He was declared "public enemy number one" in the early

1970s and was ultimately arrested and sentenced to twenty years in prison in September 1973. He famously escaped from La Santé on May 8, 1978.

13. [Eds.] *Les Dossiers de l'écran* was a television broadcast, addressing grand social issues, that ran from 1967 until 1991. Each installment began with a short film and was followed by debate.

Still Prisons

JEAN-MARIE DOMENACH, MICHEL FOUCAULT, AND PAUL THIBAUD

A series of letters exchanged between Michel Foucault, Jean-Marie Domenach, and Paul Thibaud prompted by a critique that Thibaud, who had recently taken over the editorship of Esprit, had included in the introduction to the November issue of the journal, "Toujours les prisons," arguing that the GIP, among other groups, had ultimately proved ineffective in fostering social reform because it failed to articulate a program and that this was due to the specious leadership of intellectuals, particularly Foucault. It originally appeared in the correspondence section of Esprit 37 (January 1980): 184–86.

Your article, published as an introduction to your November issue on prisons, calls for a certain number of clarifications. For it concerns a work done collectively.

(1) A group like the GIP once was—diverse, predominantly spontaneous, without either hierarchy or fixed organization—relies on an elementary moral code: if, the work having been accomplished, one wants to reflect on, critique, put into question the role or the influence of so-and-so, fine and good; but only if one does so together with those who did the work and especially those one wants to critique. Perhaps the genre of pointing fingers has its charm, but there is also something about it that is too easy, puerile, minimally correct, and not very elegant.

(2) In the GIP, we came from different backgrounds. We didn't get together because, with divergent perspectives, we shared the same indignation. But instead because, by having discussions and fumbling around, we together defined a mode of action, objectives, means, and a specific significance for this action. Each being free

to speak, to write, to stay or to go, the two or three from *Esprit* who traveled with us, and whose aid was priceless, never contested their fundamental agreement.

(3) One of our principles was in some way to make it so that prisoners and, around them, an entire fringe of the population, could express themselves. The GIP texts were not the elaborations of a noxious intellectual, but the result of this attempt. That is why the GIP never considered itself charged with proposing reforms. That is also why the GIP (as anticipated from the beginning) was dissolved once former prisoners were able to organize their own movement. All of that was the result of our cause and not the effect of contradictions.

(4) Am I one of those intellectual "theoreticians," with whom "activists" who are too docile and "social workers" who are too naive are quite wrongly fascinated—and apparently also one that weekend magazines these days denounce? Perhaps. But you see, after the GIP experience, I undertook and finished my book on prisons.[1] And what bothers me isn't that you have the bizarre idea of deducing from my book, which I fear you didn't understand very well, my poisonous influence on the GIP, but that you don't get the really simple idea that this book owes much to the GIP and that, if it contains two or three good ideas, it gleaned them from there.

You see, all you needed to do, if you wanted to discuss all of that, was to let me know,[2] to make me part of your critiques, to tell me some false impressions you might have, after the fact, of an action in which you didn't have the chance to participate; all you needed to do was to ask me to speak with you, like people from *Esprit* once spoke with us. Maybe we could have arrived at results a little more interesting than the "It's so-and-so's fault"—always a little nasty. Come, come, *Esprit* didn't sup with the devil, so this heartburn, seven years later, is too much.

Michel Foucault

It is true, as Paul Thibaud notes in his editorial for the issue "Toujours les prisons," that my perspectives in this matter were not identical with those of Michel Foucault. This, however, is not why the GIP "avoided all proposals." From the beginning, Michel Foucault and I, along with all the initiators of the GIP, agreed not to propose a reform plan and not to substitute our discourse for that of the prisoners. We

380 | REFLECTIONS (1979–1980 AND AFTER)

kept this commitment, and, for me, this was the most encouraging experience since the Resistance—this spontaneous action, without permanence, without "organization," and nevertheless perfectly articulated in its aim, which was not the success of one ideology against another, but the dignity and the free expression of a minority treated in an inhumane fashion.

Jean-Marie Domenach

Jean-Marie Domenach forwarded your letter to me concerning my introduction to *Esprit*'s prison issue.

On one point at least I have to admit you are right. It would have been better if I had raised these objections with you before.

As for the rest, I believe you are mistaken if you think I see you as the devil and blame you for a certain failure of this prison reform movement, to which you dedicated so much time and energy. That is not the problem; rather, the problem is the dramatic clog that we currently see in reformist energies. Why did the great critiques of post-'68 (those of Illich or your own) wash over us in all their force and truth, without provoking an equivalent wave of creativity? To me, this fact obliges us to ask ourselves together certain questions about the way in which culture and politics function in our country. The landscape that we have in front of us—far less reactionary than it is discouraged and self-abased—obliges us, whether we want to or not, to ask some painful questions.

So much for the background of the reflections that I put in extremis at the beginning of this issue, inspired in fact by a certain anger that was not aimed at you specifically but at us. And also at you, the GIP "reformists," who, technically, succeeded no better than others in finding a way out of the present impasses.

I appreciate the note in which you said you were ready to get to the heart of the matter. I would like that too. The question for me is that of post-'68, of the oblivion into which critiques and utopias of the time seem to fall, and the field left open to the peacefully reactionary and cynically degrading discourses of "our" ministers.

Paul Thibaud

Thank you for your letter. I am all the more appreciative since it constitutes, I think, a giant step forward.

You write in your article: the prison reform movement "comes up against a radical critique. The dominant influence among activists and certain social workers was *in fact* that of M.F." You now tell me that you "are not blaming me for a certain failure of the prison reform movement." Let's leave it to inflexible minds to say there is something of a contradiction here. I believe in evolutions and I see here a completely positive progress.

You also write: "My anger was not aimed at *you* specifically, but at *us*." This "us," certainly, gave me pleasure; failing to have been considered as a possible dialogue partner, I felt satisfied to be reintegrated as a partial object of your anger. The impression that you were vigorously beating another man's breast dissipated immediately. It is doubtless that you struck your neighbor's chest quite accidentally: which is hardly important now that we know you want to correct your own fault.

You also say, and it is the most precious part of your letter, that you want "to ask ourselves *together* certain questions" and that you want to "get to the *heart* of the matter." If we are to believe your article, the heart of the matter is the disastrous "fascination" exercised by "intellectuals" and above all intellectual theoreticians. Some might say that, if that is the real heart of the matter, it is a rather insipid one. But I am not of that opinion: it seems to me that if your explication lacks interest, it is very interesting that you give it. It is an already old theme, which assumes a greater and greater place in the current media and that you utilize in fact "*together*" with people like Mr. G. Suffert.[3]

J.-M. Domenach told you, I think, that we strongly desire our two texts concerning your November "editorial" to appear as soon as possible. Their very moderate tone avoids (and will avoid, I hope) the indefinite play of polemical responses and counterresponses. By adding thereto your very clear letter and the one I am presently writing, readers of *Esprit* can see how to continue the work of serene discussion, after reading the articles. And for the most general debate that you generously offer, I can suggest a little text: "On the Denunciation of Intellectual Theoreticians: Study of a Genre."

Michel Foucault

The aim of the introduction to which Michel Foucault refers was not demagogically to critique all theory, but to note the fact that, in France, a productive equilibrium has not been found, with respect to prisons as in other domains, between principled critique and reformist activism. That is due to the concealment of the question of law and right, as I said in this text where Michel Foucault sees only a personal quarrel.

Paul Thibaud

Notes

1. [Eds.] *Discipline and Punish: The Birth of the Prison,* trans. Alan Sheridan (New York: Vintage Books, 1977), originally published as *Surveiller et punir: Naissance de la prison* (Paris: Gallimard, 1975).

2. It is true that, through third parties, you asked me to recount the GIP experience. That has nothing to do with a discussion of your critiques and objections, for which I was and am always ready.

3. [Eds.] Georges Suffert, a prominent writer and editor, published a critique of the role of intellectuals in public life, *Les intellectuels en chaise longue* (Paris: Plon, 1974).

Foucault and Prisons

GILLES DELEUZE

*This interview with Gilles Deleuze, conducted by Paul Rabinow
and Keith Gandal on May 25, 1985, was originally published in
translation by Paul Rabinow as "The Intellectual and Politics:
Foucault and the Prison" in* History of the Present *2 (1986): 1–2,
20–21. A French version, based on a transcription of the original
recording, was published in* Deux régimes des fous, *ed. David
Lapoujade (Paris: Minuit, 2003), and this version (which differs
in some respects from the first English version) was included, in a
translation by Ames Hodges and Mike Taormina, in* Two Regimes
of Madness, *revised edition, ed. David Lapoujade (New York:
Semiotext(e), 2007), 277–86. The translation has been revised for
this volume.*

HISTORY OF THE PRESENT: Before moving to more general questions
   on intellectuals and the political arena, could you explain your relationship to Foucault and the GIP?
GILLES DELEUZE: So, you want to begin with the GIP. You will have
   to double-check what I tell you. I have no memory; it is like trying
   to describe a dream, it's rather vague. After '68, there were many
   groups, very different groups, but necessarily compact ones. It was
   post-'68. They survived, they all had a past. Foucault insisted on
   the fact that '68 had no importance for him. He already had a history as an important philosopher, but he was not burdened with a
   history from '68. That is probably what allowed him to form such
   a new type of group. And this group gave him a kind of equality
   with other groups. He would never have let himself be taken in.
   The GIP allowed him to maintain his independence from other

groups like the Gauche Prolétarienne. There were constant meetings, exchanges, but he always preserved the complete independence of the GIP. In my opinion, Foucault was not the only one to outlive a past, but he was the only one to invent something new, at every level. It was very precise, like Foucault himself. The GIP was a reflection of Foucault, a Foucault–Defert invention. It was one case where their collaboration was close and fantastic. In France, it was the first time this type of group had been formed, one that had nothing to do with a party (there were some scary parties, like the Gauche Prolétarienne) nor with an enterprise (like the attempts to revamp psychiatry).

The idea was to make a "Prisons Information Group." It was obviously more than just information. It was a kind of thought experiment. There is a part of Foucault that always considered the process of thinking to be an experiment. It's his Nietzschean heritage. The idea was not to experiment on prisons but to take prison as a place where prisoners have a certain experience and that intellectuals, as Foucault saw them, should also think about. The GIP almost had the beauty of one of Foucault's books. I joined wholeheartedly because I was fascinated. When the two of them started, it was like stepping out into the darkness. They had seen something, but what you see is always in darkness. What do you do? I think that is how it started: Defert began distributing tracts among the families waiting in lines during visiting hours. Several people would go, and Foucault was sometimes with them. They were quickly singled out as "agitators." What they wanted was not at all to agitate, but to establish a questionnaire that families and prisoners could complete. I remember that in the first questionnaires, there were questions about food and medical care. Foucault must have been very reassured, very motivated, and very shocked by the results. We found something much worse, notably the constant humiliation. Foucault the observer then passed the mantle to Foucault the thinker.

The GIP was, I think, a forum for experimentation leading up to *Discipline and Punish*. He was immediately sensitive to the great difference between the theoretical and the legal status of prisons, between prison as a loss of freedom and the social uses of prison, which is something else altogether, since not only do they deprive an individual of his or her freedom, which is already huge, but there is systemic humiliation—the system is used to break people, and that is separate from taking away one's freedom. We discovered, as everyone knew, that there was a form of justice with no supervision that had taken shape in prison ever since the creation of a prison within the prison, a prison behind the prison, known as the "*mitard*" [solitary confinement]. The QHS[1] did not yet exist. Prisoners could be sentenced to solitary without any possibility of defending themselves. We learned a great deal. The GIP worked alongside the prisoners' families and former prisoners. Like everything special, there were some very funny moments, like the time we first met with former prisoners and each one wanted to be more of a prisoner than the others. Each one had always experienced something worse than the others.

H. P.: What was the group's relationship to politics?

G. D.: Foucault had a keen political intuition, which was something very important for me. Political intuition, for me, is the feeling that something is going to happen and happen *here,* not somewhere else. A political intuition is a very rare occurrence. Foucault sensed that there were little movements, small disturbances in the prisons. He was not trying to take advantage of them or cause them. He *saw* something. For him, thinking was always an experimental process up until death. In a way, he was a kind of *seer.* And what he saw was actually intolerable. He was a fantastic seer. It was the way he saw people, the way he saw everything, in its comedy and misery. His power of sight was equivalent to his power to write. When you see something and see it very profoundly, what you see is intolerable.

These are not the words he used in conversation, but it is in his thinking. For Foucault, to think was to react to the intolerable, the intolerable things one experienced. It was never something visible. That was also part of his genius. The two parts complement each other: thinking as experimentation and thinking as vision, as capturing the intolerable.

H. P.: A kind of ethics?

G. D.: I think it served as an ethics for him. The intolerable was not part of his ethics. His ethics was to see or grasp something as intolerable. He did not do it in the name of morality. It was his way of thinking. If thinking did not reach the intolerable, there was no need for thinking. Thinking was always thinking at something's limit.

H. P.: People say it is intolerable because it is unjust.

G. D.: Foucault did not say that. It was intolerable, not because it was unjust, but because no one saw it, because it was imperceptible. But everyone knew it. It was not a secret. Everyone knew about this prison in the prison, but no one saw it. Foucault *saw* it. That never stopped him from turning the intolerable into humor. Once again, we laughed a lot. It was not indignation. We were not indignant. It was two things: seeing something unseen and thinking something that was almost at a limit.

H. P.: How did you become a part of the GIP?

G. D.: I was completely convinced from the start that he was right and that he had found the only new type of group. It was new because it was so specific. And like everything Foucault did, the more specific it was, the more influence it had. It was like an opportunity that he knew not to miss. There were completely unexpected people involved who had nothing to do with prisons. I am thinking, for example, of Paul Éluard's[2] widow, who helped us a great deal at one point for no special reason. There were very consistent people like Claude Mauriac, who was very close to Foucault. When we made connections at the time of the Jackson affair and problems in American prisons, Genet stepped forward. He was great. It was very lively. A movement inside the prisons was formed. Revolts took shape. Outside, things were going in every direction, with prison psychiatrists, prison doctors, the families of prisoners. We had to make booklets. Foucault and Defert took on endless tasks. They were the ones with the ideas. We followed them. We followed them with a passion. I remember a crazy day, typical for the GIP, where the good and tragic moments came one after the other. We had gone to Nancy, I think. We were busy from morning to night. The morning started with a delegation to the prefecture, then we had to go to the prison, then we had to hold a press conference. Some things took place at the prison, and then we ended the day with a protest. At the start of the day, I told myself I would never make it. I never had Foucault's energy or his strength. Foucault had an enormous life force.

H. P.: How did the GIP disband?

G. D.: Foucault did what everyone else was contemplating: after a while, he disbanded the GIP. I remember Foucault was seeing the Livrozets frequently. Livrozet was a former prisoner. He wrote a book for which Foucault did a beautiful preface. Mrs. Livrozet was also very active. When the GIP disbanded, they continued its work with the CAP, the Prisoners Action Committee that was going to be run by former prisoners. I think Foucault only remembered the fact that he had lost; he did not see in what way he had won. He was always very modest from a certain point of view. He thought he had lost because everything closed down again. He had the impression that it had been useless. Foucault said it was not repression but worse: someone speaks but it is as if nothing was said. Three or four years later, things returned to exactly the way they were.

At the same time, he must have known what an impact he had made. The GIP accomplished many things; the prisoners' movements were formed. Foucault had the right to think that something had changed, even if it was not fundamental. It's an oversimplification, but the goal of the GIP was for the prisoners themselves and their families to be able to speak, to speak for themselves. That was not the case before. Whenever there was a show on prisons, you had representatives of all those who dealt closely with prisons: judges, lawyers, prison guards, volunteers, philanthropists, anyone except prisoners themselves or even former prisoners. Like when you do a conference on elementary school and everyone is there except the children, even though they have something to say. The goal of the GIP was less to make them talk than to design a place where people would be forced to listen to them, a place that was not reduced to a revolt on the prison roof, but would ensure that what they had to say came through. What needed to be said is exactly what Foucault brought out, namely: we are deprived of freedom, which is one thing, but the things happening to us are something else altogether. They own us. Everyone knows it, but everyone lets it happen.

H. P.: Wasn't one of the functions of the intellectual for Foucault to open a space where others could speak?

G. D.: In France, it was something very new. That was the main

388 | REFLECTIONS (1979–1980 AND AFTER)

difference between Sartre and Foucault. Foucault had a notion,
a way of living the political position of the intellectual that was
very different from Sartre's, one that was not theoretical. Sartre,
no matter what his force and brilliance, had a classical conception
of the intellectual. He took action in the name of superior values:
the Good, the Just, and the True. I see a common thread that runs
from Voltaire to Zola to Sartre. It ended with Sartre. The intellectual taking action in the name of the values of truth and justice.
Foucault was much more functional; he always was a function-
alist. But he invented his own functionalism. His functionalism
was seeing and speaking. What is there to see here? What is there
to say or think? It was not the intellectual as a guarantor of certain values. I know that he later discussed his conception of truth,
but that was different. "Information" was not the right word ultimately. It was not about finding the truth about prison, but producing statements about prison, once it was said that neither the
prisoners nor the people outside prison had been able to produce
any themselves. They knew how to make speeches about prison,
etc., but not how to produce them. Here as well, if there was any relationship between his actions and his philosophical work, it was
that he lived like that. What was so exceptional about Foucault's
sentences when he spoke? There is only one man in the world I
have ever heard speak like that. Everything he said was *decisive,*
but not in the authoritarian sense. When he entered a room, it
was already decisive; it changed the atmosphere. When he spoke,
his words were decisive. Foucault considered a statement to be
something very particular.

Not just any discourse or sentence makes a statement. Two
dimensions are necessary: seeing and speaking. It is more or less
words and things. Words are the production of statements; things
are the seeing, the visible formations. The idea is to *see* something
imperceptible in the visible.

H. P.: Does producing statements mean letting someone speak?

G. D.: In part, but that is not all. Like others, we said (it was our
theme): others must be allowed to speak, but that was not the
question. Here is a political example. For me, one of the most fundamentally important things about Lenin was that he produced
new statements before and after the Russian Revolution. They
were like signed statements, they were Leninist statements. Can

we talk about a new type of statement or one that emerges in a certain space or under certain circumstances that are Leninist statements? It was a new type of statement. The question is not to seek the truth like Sartre, but to produce *new* conditions for statements. 1968 produced new statements. They were a type of statement that no one had used before. New statements can be diabolical and very annoying and everyone is drawn to fight them. Hitler was a great producer of new statements.

H. P.: Did you find that politically sufficient at the time?

G. D.: Was it enough to keep us occupied? Certainly. Our days were completely full. Foucault brought with him a type of practice that had two fundamentally new aspects. How could that not have been sufficient? Your question is too harsh in a way. Foucault would have said that it was not sufficient because in one sense, it failed. It did not change the status of the prisons. I would say the opposite. It was doubly sufficient. It had a lot of resonance. The main echoes were the movement in the prisons. The movement in the prisons was not inspired by either Foucault or Defert. The GIP amplified the movement because we also wrote articles and spent our time hassling the people in the Ministry of Justice and the Ministry of the Interior. Now there is a type of utterance on prisons that is regularly made by prisoners and nonprisoners that would not have been imaginable before. It was successful in this way.

H. P.: You have a much more fluid view of the social world than Foucault. I am thinking of *A Thousand Plateaus*. Foucault uses more architectural metaphors. Do you agree with this description?

G. D.: Completely. Unfortunately, in the final years of his life, I did not see him much, and of course I now regret it deeply, because he was one of the men I liked and admired the most. I remember we talked about it when he published *The Will to Knowledge*. We did not have the same conception of society. For me, a society is something that is constantly escaping in every direction. When you say I am more fluid, you are completely right. It flows monetarily; it flows ideologically. It is really made up of lines of flight. So much so that the problem for a society is how to stop it from flowing. For me, the powers come later. What surprised Foucault was that faced with all of these powers, all of their deviousness and hypocrisy, we can still resist. My surprise is the opposite. It is flowing everywhere and governments are able to block it. We approached the problem from opposite directions. You are right to say that society is a fluid, or even worse, a gas. For Foucault, it is an architecture.

H. P.: You spoke with him about this?

G. D.: I remember that at the time of *The Will to Knowledge,* which was, I think, the start of a kind of intellectual crisis, he was asking himself many questions. He was in a kind of melancholy and at the time, we spoke a great while about his way of viewing society.

H. P.: What were your conclusions? Did you grow apart . . .

G. D.: I always had enormous admiration and affection for Foucault. Not only did I admire him, but he made me laugh. He was very funny. I only resemble him in one way: either I am working, or I am saying insignificant things. There are very few people in the world with whom one can say insignificant things. Spending two hours with someone without saying a thing is the height of friendship. You can only speak of trifles with very good friends. With Foucault, it was more like a sentence here or there. One day during a conversation, he said: I really like Péguy[3] because he is a madman. I asked: Why do you think he is a madman? He replied: Just look at the way he writes. That was also very interesting about Foucault. It meant that someone who could invent a new style, produce new statements, was a madman. We worked separately, on our own. I am sure he read what I wrote. I read what he wrote with a passion. But we did not talk very often. I had the feeling, with no sadness, that in the end I needed him and he did not need me. Foucault was a very, very mysterious man.

Notes

1. [Eds.] Quartier de Haute Sécurité (QHS) refers to supermax incarceration, where discipline is stringent, isolation is commonplace, and prisoners are presumed unusually dangerous and likely to attempt escape. See Roger Knobelspiess, *Quartier de haute sécurité* (Paris: Masson, 1980), with a foreword by Michel Foucault.

2. [Eds.] Paul Éluard (1895–1952), a French poet, was one of the founders of the Surrealist movement.

3. [Eds.] Charles Péguy (1873–1914), a controversial French poet and essayist.

Hope Is the Blood of It
On the GIP, Paris 8, and the Urgency of Writing
An Interview with Hélène Cixous

PERRY ZURN

This conversation took place in Hélène Cixous's apartment in Paris on March 14, 2019. The interview was conducted in English and subsequently revised for publication.

PERRY ZURN: I met your writing first through feminism, then again through Jacques Derrida, and yet again through the work of Michel Foucault and the GIP. It seems that you are there at every turn—that you follow me, or I carry you. By way of beginning, then, I want to express how grateful I am for the words that you have created already and those that you will share today.

    You have led a life of activism and letters. Besides being the author of innumerable works, you were involved, among other things, in May '68, the GIP, establishing the University of Paris 8, and founding the first Center of Feminist Studies in Europe. What do you see as the relationship between writing and activism, between a life of letters and a life of politics?

HÉLÈNE CIXOUS: In how many words?

P. Z.: However many you like.

H. C.: I'll try to be short, then: it's the same drive. Writing for me, first of all, is the most decisive, and necessary, and vital action and urgency in my life. The other actions are corollaries of writing, because I've experienced the necessity of writing as a reaction and an answer to everything that was threatening and painful in my childhood. That was a mixture of personal mourning, personal losses of beloved beings, the experiences I had with the different racisms, anti-Semitism, etc. Because I was born inside the Second World War, in a colonial country, and all this I vividly understood. When I was just three, I was politically aware—really, and not superficially.

I wonder how kids feel the world around them now. I'm very glad, for instance, that they are afraid of the possibility of an end of the planet, because I thought about that when I was three. Except that then, it wasn't for climate reasons, but because of evil, the different types of evil that I was a witness to. So, I thought there's no issue, except climbing a tree and escaping somehow, and that's how I started thinking in terms of books, of nests, of surviving: my answer was really a response with words. My father disappeared in a week, when I was ten, and the whole planet seemed to me a complete abyss, and I wondered how you cross it. So, I had to make a bridge with words.

Then later, it was a succession of horrors, which I could analyze politically, from one war to the other, from Nazism, to which my German family was subjected, to colonialism, since when we left the Second World War, it was to open onto decolonization. When I was nineteen or twenty, I discovered the predicament of women, because, at first, it wasn't my main urgency at all. It was only upon arriving in France that I realized that everything was rotten with misogyny. Of course, it was the same thing in Algeria, but it wasn't visible because there was torture, exclusion, deportation, etc. So, things weren't so different, as I have always been active regarding the rights of every category of persecuted people.

And also, that's French history. I lived all my life under right-wing governments, until 1958. Then comes de Gaulle, I thought we were going back to monarchy, and I was desperate about that. I was about to have my first child, my daughter, and I thought, "I'm going to call her Republic," but this didn't work. With de Gaulle, actually, in 1958, the decade that led to '68 began. And I started seeing that things were moving a little, that it was also a matter of generations, and that there were some people around with whom I could speak. That was a major improvement. For instance, I met Derrida in 1963. I didn't guess anything about what was going to happen later, but there was somebody who spoke and thought in a direction that I could recognize.

And very quickly, in a couple of years, I was in touch with others, Foucault, Lacan, the intellectually alive, and the great writers who were all in exile in Paris, the Latin Americans who were in Paris. I was close friends with Carlos Fuentes, with Julio Cortázar, etc. So, it made for a little air to breathe in. When '68 came, I personally was ready for it. I even had weapons: I had friends. So '68 of course was a moment of total happiness for everyone. For ten years people were happy. The young were happy. The elders were happy. It was a moment of major change, and yet I was prudent. My past was there, very readable, and I thought, '68, it's paradise: it won't last. So, we have to save something out of it. And that was Vincennes, Paris 8 University.[1]

When the rebellion died down, all of the urgent causes followed. I had been a friend of Foucault since 1968, and he immediately got committed to the GIP. For me, it was obvious. Of course, I always excluded joining a political party, because I knew it means giving up your freedom. You have to obey. So, this was excluded, but doing things in a concrete way—that fit.

P. Z.: So, you got involved in the GIP simply through your friendship with Foucault?

H. C.: Yes. It was very banal. We were doing things together. We were friends. He improvised the GIP. There were few people involved. I joined immediately. It was earnest, but it was fun. Excuse me. *[phone call]* That was my daughter, who was a militant in the GIP when she was a baby. And my son, too.

P. Z.: How old were they?

H. C.: During the GIP period, they were very tiny, but they were with me in '68. They knew all those people. For them it was a golden childhood. It was the contrary of mine, because at least there were answers everywhere. So, they would demonstrate with me. For the GIP, for instance, when we had publications to distribute, they would come along. My daughter was born in '58, which was the time I thought I would call her Republic, and my son three years later. They're both university people. My son is a mathematician, and my daughter is the head of all the research centers that deal with gender in Paris. They know more about those times than I do, because for them, since it was their childhood, it's very vivid. Sometimes when I forget a detail, it's easier to ask them.

P. Z.: Some of the GIP meetings happened here, yes? What were they like?

H. C.: Yes. Here, right here. It was very familiar. It was not exactly the same layout. Here *[gestures across the living room],* there were three rooms. So, we would actually meet there *[gestures to the far end].* There was a wall here. Maybe Foucault was sitting here, where you are. We had discussions, perhaps twenty of us sitting on the floor. We were close friends; the group was also rather mobile, limber, it wasn't like an army. Another friend of mine who was involved was Gilles Deleuze. We would discuss the next actions. There were a number of possibilities all the time. We would decide which prison we would try to besiege.

It's how I met Ariane Mnouchkine, because in 1972, I first saw *1789*,[2] one of her major plays. I didn't know her at all, but she was performing close to Paris 8 University. We were in the same forest. I attended a performance, and I thought, "Phew, we can do something with this woman." I told Foucault, "You should come with me and meet Ariane Mnouchkine, we're going to describe what we do with the GIP, and they may help us." So that's what we did. We explained to Ariane how we were actively doing all kinds of things that had to do with prisons, and she joined with a couple of actors. I always say it's very funny that the first play we did, Ariane and I, was four minutes long. It was a kind of nursery rhyme which ran: *Qui vole un pain va en prison, qui vole des millions va au Palais-Bourbon.*[3] Palais-Bourbon is where the parliament takes place.

Ariane with a couple of actors would meet in front of a prison. They would hurriedly build a little stage. Then the actors would try to perform. Except that I never saw the end of the play because the police were on us immediately.

P. Z.: I know that you and Ariane organized a number of short plays performed during GIP protests, outside prison or factory doors. Following the Nancy Prison Revolt in January 1972, you also converted the court transcript of the trial of the six ringleaders into a short play.[4] This piece, in which Ariane Mnouchkine played the role of the prisoners' lawyer, Henri Leclerc, was then performed by the Théâtre du Soleil after its regularly scheduled performances of *1789* at the Cartoucherie.[5] I am wondering quite simply about theater. What do you see as the political power of theater? And why was it a particularly appropriate or powerful vehicle for the GIP's actions?

H. C.: Because it's the most obvious opportunity to sum up a dramatic situation in a very short time in a way that is deep, short and deep.

P. Z.: As part of your work with the GIP, you also coedited, with Jean Gattegno, *Cahiers de revendications* (or *Lists of Demands*).⁶ This booklet captures the newly collective, political voices of prisoners. What led you to take on this project? And what was the process for assembling it?

H. C.: It wasn't difficult, because Foucault and others would visit prisons, as I did, later. This happened very often, we would meet with prisoners and hear their complaints. Things that, at that time, were seldom done. There was a huge amount of material. Then, we were joined by former prisoners, and some of them were quite clever. So, we published this material, which was a description of the conditions in prisons, and the prisoners' demands, because, given the situation in France, it was totally ignored, of course, publicly. I must have a copy somewhere. There are some at the National Library [Bibliothèque Nationale de France].

You have surely met Daniel Defert?

P. Z.: Yes! He's lovely. I asked to interview him as well, but he told me he has already said all he has to say about the GIP.⁷

Some of the prisoners' demands are simple, and some are grand. They demand the improvement of diet, the elimination of isolation units, the extension of visiting hours, but also something far bigger: an equitable, honorable system of justice. Is something about this breadth necessary to communicate the intolerable? Why this span from the quotidian to the abstract?

H. C.: It's the same thing, of course. I don't believe in abstract things. They are all inscribed in reality and in the flesh, so it would amount to nothing if it were only principles. You have to approach the real and inescapable pain of people. Which is why what Foucault was doing was important, and I appreciated the fact that it was totally concrete. Actually, one of the good memories I have is once when we were here, actually—because sometimes we would meet further up the street where there was a Protestant meeting place— for one of the last sessions. They were always improvised. And Foucault said, "Well, today I think we have to analyze the reasons why we've been involved in this action." I thought, "What? We're only doing the theory of it now?" To me this was most important because I realized that it was the other way 'round compared to what I thought it would be originally. That is, I had assumed it was first a theory devised by Foucault and then the practice. No, it was practice, then theory. So, the people who were there tried to ask themselves why they had taken part. For me, it was obvious because my main subject was the prison, ever since I was a kid. I didn't know what the others felt.

P. Z.: At the same time, you were part of the Mouvement de Libération des Femmes [Women's Liberation Movement].

H. C.: No, it wasn't at the same time. I got involved with women later.

P. Z.: What was the status of women in the GIP? I am thinking about women prisoners (e.g., at La Roquette), women prison personnel (e.g., Édith Rose), and women activists (e.g., you, Christine Martineau, Danièle Rancière, etc.). The GIP focused more on men's prison issues than women's, did it not?

H. C.: It was men. Not because it was men and not women, but because the group had contacts, and, as they were men, that gave them access to men's prisons. But, of course, there must have been women's prisons, too, but they are a minority compared to men's.

P. Z.: Was there any feminist sensibility in the GIP?

H. C.: No, not at all. I don't think anyone there thought about it. For myself, maybe my further commitment was partly triggered by the GIP, but it was only a little part, because women as a subject didn't ever exist. No one thought that leaders might be women, that leading discourse might have been created by a woman. No. I thought that this was a weakness. But, of course, for me it didn't mean criticizing the action, because it was defined very clearly. And it wasn't general. No, it was focused precisely on that subject: prison.

But, of course, what it led to was a friendship and more and more action with Ariane. Outside the GIP, except that we remained eternally friends with Foucault, etc. Then, later, actually three years later, I got carried away by the women's movement. I was late with the militancy of women, because I was first preoccupied with the founding of Paris 8, the experimental university. I wanted to change things in research, in the university. Paris

8 gave me an enormous freedom, personally, as a woman inside the university.

Still, I thought, "It's impossible to remain in universities as a woman. It's impossible to make room for women in academia. I have to do something." Then, in '74 there was an unhoped-for opportunity. Suddenly the government changed all the rules of research, and, in particular, of doctorates, etc. Everything had to be refounded. So, I immediately jumped on the occasion of founding a doctorate in "études féminines," women's studies. I met with difficulties, but since I had a little power inside my university, nobody opposed my desire.

That was in '74. There was a kind of feminist fortress inside Paris 8, which I founded, for sexual difference, etc., inside the university. And it was because of that, and because I started being active with sexual difference, or opposition, etc., inside intellectual research, that women militants outside came to me and asked me to join the women's movement.

P. Z.: On January 15, 1972, the first day of the Nancy Prison Revolt, you signed a statement insisting that "A GIP commission be given the means of (1) entering into Nancy Prison, (2) assessing the wounded and the care they received, (3) learning the fate of transferred prisoners, and (4) making sure that the prisoners' demands are taken seriously."[8] Then, on February 26, 1972, you participated in a day of protest outside Nancy Prison. You were among those "unexpectedly charged" by the police.[9] You yourself were "clubbed to the ground and left unconscious."[10] How did you make sense of this violence? Of losing consciousness? Of losing touch with your own body? Just as you were fighting to protect prisoners' own rights to bodily integrity?

H. C.: Yes, I was there. Deleuze was there, too. It was banal, you know. At the time, the police were much more violent than now. It was incredibly violent and terrifying. We were frightened all the time. We fled when we could.

P. Z.: But it didn't dissuade you from participating?

H. C.: No, of course not. Otherwise, I wouldn't have joined. I was used to that. For years and years there had been demonstrations against the Algerian War, in which, of course, I took part, etc.

P. Z.: That same day ended with a statement by former prisoners of the Algerian War, who stated their solidarity with the current prisoners at Nancy. What do you see as the correlation between the Algerian War and the crisis in French prisons with which the GIP was concerned? Do you see a connection?

H. C.: For me, there was one, because I was involved very closely with the Algerian War. It's rather obvious, but it wasn't the main subject. That was a French matter. The French government and institutions had to answer for the state of French prisons.

P. Z.: In your 1992 Oxford Amnesty lecture, you recall realizing retroactively a link between your commitment to the GIP and the themes of your first novel, *Dedans*.[11] You explain, "One day, in front of the Prison de la Santé, where I was demonstrating with Foucault's GIP, someone pointed out to me that my first book was the book of a prisoner. . . ."[12]

H. C.: It was at that meeting here, it wasn't in front of La Santé. It was that time when Foucault said, "Now, let's do the theory of it." So, we were all trying to explore our commitment to the GIP. For me, it was beyond explaining, I would have had to explain such a long history, which was my personal one, and which also had to do with colonialism, with anti-Semitism, with Nazism. My friends didn't have the same type of structure I had, and when I was musing, wondering what I was going to say, a guy who was there, and who I think wanted to be a writer, said to me, "But it's obvious, you've always written about prisons." I said, "No," because, in fact, for me in my texts it was a metaphor. But for him, it was obvious. He said, "Your first book starts with the first sentence which says that . . ."[13] And I realized it's true.

P. Z.: When you're recalling this moment in that lecture, you say that, "When prisons are constructed or deconstructed in my texts, I fail to see it. The prison precedes me. When I have escaped them, I have discovered them. When they have cracked and split open beneath my feet."[14] Does one always write, in some way, out from under prison? In search of freedom? As a means of escape?

H. C.: I do. But I can't say that for others. I did my thesis on Joyce. This choice was almost intuitive. I had wanted to write on Shakespeare. I was dissuaded, and even forbidden, because they told me, "There are so many theses on Shakespeare. Give it up." So, I turned my choice to Joyce, who seemed to me the most important. Then, same answer for other reasons: "No one has ever worked on Joyce." That was true, at that time. "Give it up." So, I said, "No. This time I'm going to stick to it."

For me, Joyce was the greatest writer in the twentieth century. He opened all the ways forward. And his main theme was exile. He had fled, as he says, out of the reach of threatening powers: the church, nationalism. Later, exactly as with Foucault, I found myself repeatedly in the same scene. I'm always in the same scene without realizing it: escaping by the same means.

P. Z.: The word. Words.

H. C.: Yes. Creation.

That was when I was twenty-two. So, it's like that. It's fatal.

P. Z.: When you look back at the GIP, do you see it as a success, or a failure?

H. C.: No, it wasn't a success, but it wasn't meant to be a success. It was meant to be a testimony. I personally thought Foucault very wisely ended it. Not that it was a main interest in my life; there were many others. But I didn't know where we would go, because we were repeating, after all. Were we going to change things? I was skeptical, but then, at one point, he said, "No. We've done our work, and we have to hand it over to those who are the main actors: the prisoners," which he did. So those prisoners who had joined us became the successors of their own cause.

P. Z.: Serge Livrozet, for instance.[15]

H. C.: Livrozet, yes. He became a writer.

P. Z.: When you judge the success of a political work or a piece of writing, is the standard the same: that it be a testimony?

H. C.: No. That was a testimony. It was political. Writing is exploring an idea that is totally unknown. It's always impossible. You don't know what you do, except that you have to overcome the feeling of impossibility.

P. Z.: In *Rootprints,* you define curiosity as "this urgency, this need to decipher what cannot be said, what is expressed otherwise than in verbal speech which nonetheless arouses the desire for words."[16] Then, in *Insister of Jacques Derrida,* you write that you and Derrida share "a curiosity for the signifier, a greediness for tastetexts," a "curiosity for sighs and hesitations," and a "curiosity for the abundantly stocked idiomatic storehouse of French of which, in any and every context, we exchange a few specimens that the worms had not gotten into."[17] I wonder if you also share a certain curiosity with the GIP, although perhaps of a different sort. "This urgency," as you say, "to decipher what cannot be said" but calls to be said about the prison itself, the experience of imprisonment, or simply the absence of freedom. Might the intolerable be "expressed otherwise than in verbal speech, but nevertheless arouse the desire for words"? And, therefore, might the GIP be understood as an organ of curiosity, in your sense?

H. C.: I don't think that the GIP aimed at that. It was humble. It wasn't a piece of writing. No, it was an activist type of thing, which I think is necessary. There are plenty of actions all the time, going on and being invented. The root of the movement, or the drive for individuals to get committed, to give time and empathy, is individual, except that people don't really know what they are doing when they join. Today, there is no idealist party in France, none, but when I was a young woman there was. Communists had a dream, etc.

Now, there are no dreams. But when there is a political dream, you wonder why. Of course, if you're an African American, it's obvious what you want—at least mainly. Of course, there are many personal secrets. Recently, I reread Richard Wright. I wonder even whether he's readable now, because he is so intrepidly truthful. The way he analyzes the damage done to people of color, as he as a kid had to discover it, is extraordinary. What is important in his work is, of course, that it is absolutely singular. Only one person can express the horror and the pain of the situation. You can describe it, but you cannot share it. The other person will have experienced something totally different, which he or she can show in turn.

I make a total, complete distinction between political, transitional movements, and art or writing. Indeed, I can't imagine being identified with a political cause forever. Particularly because critically, you can identify with a cause for a time—which is, of course, undefinable—but it can't last. It's impossible. At one moment, it will change, deviate, etc.

P. Z.: In contrast to political action, then, writing is driven by a certain curiosity.

H. C.: Except that it's not a simple curiosity. It's a deep curiosity of the creature. It's the origin of mankind and of science. It's Adam and Eve, discovery of everything, sin, loss, everything, and science, as you experiment all the time.

P. Z.: Whereas, political activity, you say, is driven by a dream . . .

H. C.: For me. Today, it doesn't have any meaning, except what happens now with climate change and the students, and young people waking up. It's a dream for them, and of course, it's necessary. It works, for a while.

P. Z.: But that seems to be the only dream?

H. C.: Right now, I don't see anything else.

Of course, there are fighters. There are fighters for women's rights everywhere, and it's most important.

P. Z.: What about hope? Is there a hope involved in writing, and a hope involved in political activism?

H. C.: Hope is the blood of it. Without hope there's nothing. It's a sign of hope, except that if you say it, there's no hope anymore. So, it's just a light, a little heat.

P. Z.: Is there anything else you recall about those few years of activism with the GIP that you'd like to share?

H. C.: I don't know, except that I speak now from a distance. But, of course, I personally haven't changed. I said it's transitory. You belong to a cause, completely. But you cannot belong, except for a short while. So, Foucault, as well, at one point probably thought, "Now, I think I'm getting bored. We have to change places, etc., stop."

P. Z.: When he came out with *Surveiller et punir (Discipline and Punish)*, did you see its connection to the GIP? It's a very different book than the GIP materials.

H. C.: It was the same movement for me. He was very coherent. That is, I think he was on the same path, all the time, with changing objects, of course. And also, discovering, because he himself didn't know himself completely. So, every time he would probably discover another aspect of his quest. In the end, with his last books, he gave them to me and said, "Don't read them, because I'm dissatisfied. I don't like them." I thought that was honorable. I thought it was fair to say that, because he was going further, which is normal.

Of course, he wasn't much interested in literature.

P. Z.: No?

H. C.: Philosophy, yes, but not literature. For instance, when I told him about the Théâtre du Soleil, he didn't go and attend the performance. It wasn't interesting for him.

P. Z.: How did you bring the two together then, if he didn't go?

H. C.: I didn't think it was compulsory for him to attend.

P. Z.: But you are drawn to theater.

H. C.: I? Yes, of course.

P. Z.: What is it that draws you there?

H. C.: I don't think I would have stayed if Ariane hadn't existed with the Théâtre du Soleil, because I have nothing to say against this. It's not corrupt. It's idealistic, all the time, which is extraordinary. It's inventive, all the time. I don't think I would have gone on with the theater otherwise, since I don't like the conditions of production, for instance. Except for the Théâtre du Soleil, because it's a real dream company. Moreover, I don't belong completely to the Théâtre du Soleil. I'm their writer. I'm their house playwright, but I do other things.

P. Z.: You say that you have remained the same. And yet, the breadth of your work is extraordinary. You find that it all comes from the same place, a place that has never changed?

H. C.: Yes.

And you, Perry?

P. Z.: And me? About my place, the place from which I write?

H. C.: Yes.

P. Z.: I am drawn to the GIP's work because I belong to, and live among, a number of excluded groups. So, I understand what it is not to have a voice, to fight for a voice, or to get into the academy and to try to claim a space for voice that isn't already there. I'm compelled by that. And what draws me to your writing, again and again, is my frustration with most academic writing. There seems to be something lost in the way we write. There is rarely anything literary in its nature.

H. C.: Which university are you from?

P. Z.: American University in Washington, D.C.

H. C.: I see. And where were you born?

P. Z.: Pennsylvania. I grew up in the foothills of the Allegheny Mountains.

But this is precisely what is missing. Room to breathe, to soar, to reimagine yourself. Not in service to the professionalized, bureaucratic machine, but because you listen to things themselves and the words between them. You respond to the real presence of an other, whether inside yourself or beyond. A space to slow down. A place to honor the power and the beauty of words, not crunch them like numbers (an idiom itself unjust to the elegance of mathematics). But I think about the pace and face of professionalized academic writing. There's so much that's lost . . .

H. C.: It has always been like that. It's not new. That's why I said that if I hadn't founded Paris 8, I would have left the university.

P. Z.: Tell me more about Paris 8.

H. C.: It was a dream come true, but it was thanks to all kinds of pieces of luck. It's incredible, actually. I, myself, can't believe it. During the movement in '68, to which I belonged, I realized (I was older: I was thirty; the students were twenty) they were going to fight like lions for three months, and then, out goes the fire. I thought, "We have to save something," and then, suddenly there was an opportunity because the dean of the Sorbonne, who was a friend of mine, who had really decided he would make a move with me, as a woman, as a young person, quite by chance offered me keys to this creation.

One day, he came out of the Ministry, telling me, "They are going to give me provisional buildings inside the forest . . . what do I do with that?" So, I said, "You make an experimental university." He said, "I can't do it. I don't know how to do it." He was old. He was sixty-five. I said, "You give it to me. I'll do it." So, that's it. That's how I did it. I had complete power for six months. So, I came out, called my friends, my first friend, Derrida. I told him, "I can do anything. I can do an experimental university, but I have to do it against the clock, in a short time. The government is going to change its mind when they realize it's going to be done."

So, very quickly I contacted the best in France. Derrida helped me. For instance, I needed Foucault's address. He was in Tunisia. He was going to leave France completely, definitively. So, on the way, I called him, explained to him what was going to happen, that I would make a completely free, open, modern, and intelligent university, which had never existed, where everybody would work with their peers, with their others. Deleuze was isolated in one university, Foucault in another one, and everybody was desperate, and caught in snares. Even though it was unbelievable, they believed me.

We did that—I did that with a number of friends—very quickly, and it happened. It happened. I kept thinking, "If I hadn't had that, I wouldn't have stayed." My first position was in Bordeaux, when I was twenty-five, and I resigned. After two years, I thought, "It's impossible. It's too stupid, too regressive, too ignorant." So, I resigned. Actually, it was my great friends and protectors in Paris, my research director, who was an extraordinary man, also sixty-five, and the future dean of the Sorbonne, who bet on me. I don't know why, but they credited me with everything. So, I built my own little tower, which was where I could stay.

P. Z.: And have you felt that you needed to create and protect that space for yourself, until now?

H. C.: For myself, then, I built a large world with my own creation. But teaching, I wouldn't have done elsewhere, because there I'm free. I do what I want. I say what I want. But I know it's a piece of luck, and it doesn't happen twice. I don't like the academy. I don't like those who belong to it. But in Vincennes, it's still free largely.

P. Z.: What is it about the academy that's so frustrating?

H. C.: I think that people get old when they are thirty or thirty-five. They forget that they were once young. Of course, there are always exceptions, which help you survive, which happened to me, too. If there hadn't been Mayoux, my director, and Las Vergnas, who was the head of the Sorbonne. But it was two out of five hundred. And this I've always known. It's always like that. So, you have to find out, or be found out by those two.

P. Z.: I'll keep looking for them.

H. C.: They exist. There's always one or two people. You have to find them out, but of course only if you're on the lookout, which I was. When I was nineteen or twenty, I thought, "It's not here. If it's not here, it's in the other city." It was not in Bordeaux, it must be in Paris. Arriving in Paris, I said, "But no, it's not there either." It went on like that. But I was lucky because when I thought there was no one to communicate with, I met Derrida. Because of that, because I was looking for another. He was too, actually.

But that is a kind of miracle. And you help. You have to imagine miracles exist, which I don't believe in, but they happen.

P. Z.: And you can't just wait for them.

H. C.: No, you can't.

P. Z.: But you can't force them either.

H. C.: No. No. So, it's very difficult, of course.

Notes

1. In 1968, Cixous was appointed by the French Ministry of Education to establish the academic structure of a new "experimental" university and to recruit the initial heads of department. Now known as University of Paris 8, the campus was located in the Bois de Vincennes on the outskirts of Paris until the early 1980s.

2. Ariane Mnouchkine, who founded the Théâtre du Soleil in 1964, wrote and directed *1789* to much acclaim. The play first opened in 1970 at La Cartoucherie, a former munitions factory in the Bois de Vincennes on the outskirts of Paris. See *1789,* a documentary film directed by Ariane Mnouchkine (Les Films Ariane, 1974).

3. "Whoever steals a loaf of bread goes to prison; whoever steals millions goes to the Palais-Bourbon."

4. Théâtre du Soleil/GIP, "Le Procès des Mutins de Nancy" (1972), in *Le Groupe d'information sur les prisons: Archives d'une lutte,* ed. Philippe Artières (Caen: IMEC, 2003), 239–57.

5. David Macey, *The Lives of Michel Foucault* (New York: Vintage, 1993), 284.

6. For a reproduction of the booklet's contents, see *Intolérable: Groupe d'information sur les prisons,* ed. Philippe Artières (Paris: Verticale, 2013), 221–66.

7. See Daniel Defert, "L'émergence d'un nouveau front," in Philippe Artières, *Le Groupe d'information sur les prisons,* 315–26; Daniel Defert, "Le moment GIP," in *Une vie politique* (Paris: Seuil, 2014), 55–76; Nicolas Drolc's film *Sur les toits* (Les Films Furax, 2014).

8. Artières, *Le Groupe d'information sur les prisons,* 192.

9. Ibid., 218.

10. Macey, *The Lives of Michel Foucault,* 283; cf. Didier Eribon, *Michel Foucault* (Cambridge: Harvard University Press, 1991), 233.

11. Hélène Cixous, *Dedans* (Paris: Grasset, 1969); published in English as *Inside,* trans. Carol Barko (New York: Schocken Books, 1986).

12. Hélène Cixous, "We Who Are Free, Are We Free?" *Critical Inquiry*

19.2 (1993): 203; cf. Hélène Cixous, "Biographie de l'écriture," entretien avec Alain Poirson, *Révolution*, no. 74 (July 31, 1981) : 18–20.

13. In the opening lines of *Dedans,* Cixous writes: "Ma maison est encerclée, Elle est entourée par le grillage. Dedans, nous vivons. [My house is surrounded. It is encircled by the iron grating. Inside, we live.]"

14. Cixous, "We Who Are Free, Are We Free?" 203.

15. Serge Livrozet, *De la prison à la révolte* (Paris: Esprit Frappeur, 1973); cf. Nicolas Drolc's film on Serge Livrozet, *La Mort se mérite* (Les Films Furax, 2017).

16. Hélène Cixous, *Rootprints: Memory and Life Writing* (New York: Routledge, 1997), 55.

17. Hélène Cixous, *Insister of Jacques Derrida,* trans. Peggy Kamuf (Stanford, Calif.: Stanford University Press, 2007), 137.

Chronology, 1970–1974

1970

March–April

In response to the wave of radicalism that arose after the student uprisings of May '68, the antiwreckers law is enacted. The law holds that anyone linked to a demonstration or protest where harm to persons or damage to property occurs could be charged as legally culpable for the destruction.

The Gauche Prolétarienne (GP), a Maoist group originally formed in October 1968 whose leaders had primarily been students of the philosopher Louis Althusser, had become the most prominent among the radical groups during the "extreme-left" period. It was particularly well known for its advocacy of the constructive role of violence in class struggle.

Entire print runs of the GP's paper, *La Cause du peuple,* were arbitrarily confiscated and its editor, Jean-Pierre Le Dantec, was arrested (on March 22) and charged with attacking state security. He was being held at La Santé awaiting trial.

The paper's interim editor, Michel Le Bris, was arrested on April 30 and was also charged with attacking state security. He too awaited trial at La Santé.

MAY 27

The trial of the editors of *La Cause du peuple* begins amid violent protests in the Latin Quarter (four hundred arrests).

The GP is officially banned by the state. The decree was issued by Raymond Marcellin, the infamous Minister of the Interior, who believed that all revolutionary groups were a threat to the French state and were directed and funded by foreign forces.

MAY 28

Le Dantec is sentenced to one year in prison, while Le Bris receives eight months.

JUNE

At the behest of his friend, Jacques Rancière, Daniel Defert joins the Organisation des Prisonniers Politiques (OPP), a cell of the banned, though still operating, GP that sought to provide support and advocate for the imprisoned GP leaders ("Report on the Prisons").

JUNE 25

Alain Geismar, director of the GP, is arrested on charges of leading a banned organization.

SEPTEMBER 1-15

The OPP organizes its first hunger strike, carried out by roughly thirty Maoist prisoners along with OPP members on the outside. They seek political status *(régime spécial),* rather than common-law status, for the GP leaders ("Declaration of Political Prisoners on Hunger Strike").

OCTOBER 20-22

Geismar is sentenced to eighteen months in prison.

NOVEMBER 24

In a second trial, this one before the State Security Court, Geismar is sentenced to two years in prison for reconstitution of the GP, an officially dissolved organization.

DECEMBER

In early December, the OPP began planning a second hunger strike to take place in mid-January. During these sessions, Defert proposes the formation of a commission of public inquiry to study the general conditions of the prisons and suggests that his partner, Michel Foucault, be its director.

At the end of December, a group gathers at the apartment that Defert and Foucault share to discuss the proposed study. Foucault begins the meeting by rejecting the model of a public tribunal for the group, arguing instead that they should seek to collect and make public information about prison conditions that would otherwise remain hidden.

Those assembled agree and Foucault signals the new direction of the group by proposing a distinctive name: the Prisons Information Group (Groupe d'Information sur les Prisons, the GIP).

DECEMBER 23

Le Dantec, editor of *La Cause du peuple,* is released from prison.

1971

JANUARY 14

Maoist prisoners begin a second hunger strike to claim political prisoner status ("Letter Addressed to the Families of Common-Law Prisoners").

JANUARY 22

In solidarity with the GP prisoners, militants from Secours Rouge (SR)—a group founded in June 1970 to serve as a support network for leftist organizations as they suffer massive government repression—begin a hunger strike at the Chapelle Saint-Bernard in Paris. The next day, a demonstration takes place in front of the doors of La Santé.

FEBRUARY 8

The SR ends its hunger strike with the announcement of several minor concessions granted by René Pleven, the Minister of Justice.

At the same event, Foucault announces the creation of the Prisons Information Group with a statement cosigned by Jean-Marie Domenach, the editor of *Esprit* and a former member of the Resistance, and Pierre Vidal-Naquet, distinguished classical historian and antiwar campaigner ("GIP Manifesto").

FEBRUARY 9

The Ministry of Justice announces the creation of the Pleven Commission, whose charge is to determine the criteria that prisoners must meet in order to gain political prisoner status *(régime spécial).*

MARCH 15

An interview with Foucault and Vidal-Naquet appears in *Politique Hebdo* ("Inquiry on Prisons: Let Us Break Down the Bars of Silence") in which they discuss the GIP's first proposed intolerance-investigation. The interview is accompanied by extracts of letters from several different prisoners.

On the same day, Foucault also publishes a statement in *J'accuse* discussing the first intolerance-investigation ("On Prisons").

MARCH 18

Police halt the distribution of the GIP questionnaire outside La Petite Roquette, a women's prison.

APRIL 24

The first public meeting of the GIP takes place on Buffon Street at a location that Félix Guattari made available to several groups.

MAY 1

The GIP distributes, as the first results of its intolerance-investigation, a manifesto in support of the abolition of criminal records, which is at the forefront of the demands made by prisoners and their families. "With the judicial process, there is no real liberation, only reprieve." Foucault, Domenach, and other members of the GIP are arrested at the gates of Fresnes and La Santé prisons while distributing this manifesto along with a sprig of lily of the valley. Foucault files a complaint ("Right to Information on the Prisons").

On the same day, Fleury-Mérogis prisoners demonstrate and confront their guards and the French National Police.

MAY 3

Publication in *Le Nouvel observateur* of an internal document obtained by the GIP and Michèle Manceaux titled "L'École des 'matons'" (The School of "Screws"), which details some of the training undergone by prison guards.

MAY 5

Eight young prisoners at Fleury-Mérogis revolt. A statement by Foucault about the arrests of GIP members that took place on May 1 appears in the journal *Combat* ("The Prison Is Everywhere").

MAY 24

The first combined issue of *J'accuse-La Cause du peuple* appears in which the GIP publishes several articles including the manifesto by Daniel Defert, "La Prison, enjeu d'un combat" (When Information Is a Struggle).

MAY 28

Publication of the first *Intolerable* booklet, *Investigation into Twenty Prisons,* by Champ Libre. The study is based on prisoner responses to the GIP questionnaire collected during the winter of 1970–71. The questionnaire was developed in large part by former prisoners, in collaboration with Danièle Rancière and Christine Martineau. Three thousand copies are printed in late May, the first edition quickly sells out, and a reprint is ordered in early June.

JUNE

Publication of the second *Intolerable* booklet, *The GIP Investigates A Model Prison: Fleury-Mérogis,* by Champ Libre.

JUNE 8

Le Monde reports on the first *Intolerable* booklet in an interview with Jean-Marie Domenach.

JUNE 9

The GIP organizes a meeting with families of prisoners at the Paris headquarters of the League of Human Rights.

JUNE 24

Police expel certain youths from Épinettes, a juvenile halfway house in Paris. Joined by some of their teachers, these youths make contact with the GIP, determining that educational and correctional centers are subject to the same critiques.

JUNE 25

An official circular authorizes prisoners to read a daily "nonspecialized general information or sports French news service" beginning July 12, "provided that it has not been seized in the past three months." This is considered the first victory of the publication of the intolerance-investigation.

AUGUST 10–14

Prisoners at the Saint-Joseph Prison in Grenoble begin a hunger strike to protest their conditions of detention, especially in terms of health. The GIP and the SR make this grievance known, for the seventh time in this facility in the past few years.

AUGUST 21

George Jackson, the author of the international bestseller *Soledad Brother: The Prison Letters of George Jackson,* an autobiography and manifesto of Black struggle and liberation, was serving a sentence for an armed robbery committed in 1961. During his incarceration, he cofounded the Maoist–Marxist Black Guerrilla Family, a group affiliated with the Black Panther Party.

In 1970, he had been charged, along with two others, with the murder of a prison guard in the aftermath of a fight. On August 21, after meeting with his attorney regarding a civil lawsuit Jackson had filed against the California Department of Corrections, he was escorted back to his cell when he allegedly tries to escape and is shot dead from a guard tower.

AUGUST 24

Josette d'Escrivan, a social worker at Fresnes Prison in Nancy, protests the egregious treatment of suicidal prisoners. D'Escrivan is blamed for the situation and fired. The GIP later publishes her full report of these events and depicts her as being summoned to testify in its theatrical representation of the Nancy trial.

SEPTEMBER 10-14

Provoked by, among other things, the killing of George Jackson, prisoners at Attica Penitentiary in New York State revolt. Forty-six guards are taken hostage. An assault was ordered by Governor Rockefeller to take back the facility and the uprising ended with the deaths of thirty-two prisoners and eleven guards. Images of the assault and the dead prisoners quickly circulate around the world.

SEPTEMBER 21-22

An escape attempt by two prisoners, Claude Buffet and Roger Bontems, at the Clairvaux Prison, led to the murder of two hostages (a nurse and a supervisor) by Buffet. Several officials questioned the harshness of the carceral system at Clairvaux and the institution's psychiatrist complained publicly about not being called in to mediate the situation. The case led to a government campaign of strong hostility toward prisoners based on their dangerousness.

SEPTEMBER 26

Four members of the GIP are fined for distributing leaflets at the gates of Fresnes Prison.

OCTOBER 16

Publication of a special issue of the daily newsletter *Agence de presse Libération* (APL) that contained a report prepared by the GIP regarding the violence perpetrated by guards at Fleury-Mérogis on young prisoners in September ("Violence at Fleury-Mérogis").

NOVEMBER 10

Publication of the third *Intolerable* booklet, *The Assassination of George Jackson,* by Gallimard.

NOVEMBER 11

The GIP organized a meeting at La Mutualité in Paris on the situation in French and American prisons. Before more than six thousand people, two films were shown detailing the prison conditions at Soledad and San Quentin in the United States; then former prisoners and families of prisoners testified publicly for the first time about the conditions in French prisons ("A Movement of Struggle Is Developing Today . . ."; for Defert's speech at this event, see "On What Does the Penitentiary System Rely?").

NOVEMBER 12

An official circular from the Minister of Justice, René Pleven, announces the cancellation of the delivery of Christmas parcels to the prisoners. The guards' unions welcomed the measure, which deprived the prisoners of a special food package in retaliation for the unrest that had gripped the prisons over the past year.

NOVEMBER

From November 14 through early December, prisoners—beginning at Draguignan and Poissy, but eventually including Lyon, Nîmes, Grenoble, Fresnes, and La Santé—went on hunger strikes and engaged in work stoppages to protest the rescinding of Christmas parcels.

DECEMBER 4

The GIP led a demonstration (known as the "piss packages *[colis de colère]*" protest) at the Place Vendôme in front of the chancellery and delivered a petition with 540 signatures protesting Pleven's action ("Pleven Eliminates the Detainees' Christmas Packages").

A delegation of around fifty family members of prisoners along with members of the GIP (including Claude Mauriac, Pierre Vidal-Naquet, and Jean-Jacques de Félice) held a meeting with Dominique Le Vert, the technical adviser to the minister. That same day in Toulouse, families blocked the doors of the prison at Saint-Michel with empty Christmas parcels.

DECEMBER 5-13

A revolt broke out at the Ney Prison in Toul against the brutal regime imposed by the warden, Georges Galiana, who had previously served as the director of an Algerian prison during the War of Independence. On December 5, a revolt first broke out at 5 p.m. in the young prisoners' cellblocks; the minister, Father Velten, played an important mediating role. On December 7, a work strike began. On December 9, there was a second revolt, with ransacking of the premises. On December 12, religious services were suspended and the prison administration forbade the chaplains and the psychiatrist access to the facility. On December 13, the announcement that the warden would be retained led to a third uprising that was then harshly repressed.

DECEMBER 6

Publication in *Le Nouvel observateur* of an open letter by Charles Dayant, former head physician of La Santé, detailing the daily suicide attempts in prison.

DECEMBER 7

Pleven declares on television that he now authorizes Christmas parcels for prisoners and those detained under the age of eighteen.

DECEMBER 11

The GIP proposes independent commissions of investigation into the prisons ("The GIP Proposes a Commission of Inquiry"), whereas the Toul city council supports the prison administration, as do the various associated unions a few days later.

DECEMBER 14

Robert Linhart, militants, and students form the Toul Truth Committee (Vérité Toul Committee, the CVT), which is charged with investigating the revolt and supporting this new "revolutionary front." An Inspector General of the Prison Service arrived on scene to conduct an administrative investigation while the GIP proposes an independent commission to report on charges of bullying prisoners and the fate of the leaders of the uprising.

DECEMBER 15

The Minister of Justice announces the creation of a commission to be chaired by the Attorney General, Robert Schmelck, to investigate the causes of the events at Toul.

DECEMBER 16

During a joint GIP–CVT press conference in Toul, in front of two hundred people, Foucault reads an official report by Dr. Édith Rose, the staff psychiatrist at the Ney Prison, denouncing the egregious treatment of prisoners, especially those with mental illness ("Report by Doctor Rose, Psychiatrist at Toul Prison"). On December 20, the guards' unions denounced the attitude of the doctor and the chaplains at their own press conference.

DECEMBER 18

A special supplement of *La Cause du peuple—J'accuse* is published bearing the title "Toul, the voice of the insurgents will be heard throughout France." Foucault and Simone Signoret take out a full-page advertisement in *Le Monde* to publish Dr. Rose's report as an open letter to the President of the Republic.

DECEMBER 23

In Toulouse, during a demonstration by the local GIP against the suppression of the Christmas parcels, violent skirmishes break out with the police; a protesting nun is wounded.

DECEMBER 24

On Christmas Eve, members of the GIP, including Claude Mauriac, Jean Chesneaux, Henri Leclerc, Jérôme Peignot, Alain Jaubert, and Michèle Manceaux, demonstrate with flares and firecrackers in front of La Santé. A message is sent to the prisoners at the cell windows: "We are all concerned because we are all potential prisoners; the prisoners will never be alone again; we are with you."

DECEMBER 27

Foucault publishes a piece in *Le Nouvel observateur* about the Toul Prison psychiatrist Dr. Rose and her report ("The Toul Speech").

DECEMBER 31

Borrowing a slogan from the workers' movement, the SR together with the GIP distributes a leaflet, "Whoever steals a loaf goes to prison. Whoever steals millions goes to Palais-Bourbon!" to denounce the condition of the prisoners. During the distribution, the Théâtre du Soleil, a prominent avant-garde theatrical troupe in which Hélène Cixous was involved, performs a skit under the same name.

DECEMBER 31–JANUARY 1

The GIP organizes New Year's Eve fireworks in front of the prisons at Fresnes, Toul, Besançon, Toulouse, and La Santé.

1972

JANUARY 5

At a CVT–GIP press conference on the revolt at Toul, an essay by Foucault is read ("To Escape Their Prison").

JANUARY 8

The Schmelck Report is published. Following the comments of Dr. Rose and Father Velten, the authors acknowledge a number of dysfunctions in the administration at the Toul Prison and officially acknowledge that there is a problem with the French prison system.

JANUARY 10

A revolt breaks out at the Loos-lès-Lille Prison. Fifty prisoners demand a dialogue with the public prosecutor in the presence of people whom they trust and along with representatives from the GIP. Two other revolts also take place that same day: one in Amiens, the other in Luxembourg.

JANUARY 14

In Fleury-Mérogis, about sixty prisoners demonstrate seeking an additional two hours of walking time. In the east, eight prisoners demonstrate against exercise schedules. The same day, the GIP organizes a demonstration in support of the prisoners in Paris.

JANUARY 15

A revolt breaks out at Charles III Prison in Nancy. By the end of the day, GIP members, including Hélène Cixous, Deleuze, Foucault, Michèle Manceaux, Marianne Merleau-Ponty, and Sartre, issue a statement titled "The Penitentiary Is Disqualified."

JANUARY 17

Foucault, Sartre, Deleuze, Jean Chesneaux, Michelle Vian, Claude Mauriac, and others, all in the name of the GIP, occupy the Ministry of Justice to denounce the detention conditions of prisoners, following the revolts at Toul and Nancy. A press conference follows at which both Foucault ("It

Was about a Year Ago") and Sartre speak. Deleuze attempts to speak but loses his breath, having had one lung removed.

Christine Martineau and Jean-Pierre Carasso publish *Le Travail dans les prisons* with Champ Libre. Documenting the injustices of prison labor, the book is the result of "six months of investigation undertaken conjointly with the GIP."

JANUARY 21

The GIP and the SR organize a demonstration in Paris that brings together eight hundred people. Several incendiary devices are launched against the Office of Penal Labor. The prison reform commissions that were created are immediately denounced by the Judicial Union as partisan.

JANUARY 26

The GIP and the SR organize a meeting at La Mutualité to discuss prisons and housing.

FEBRUARY 26

The GIP participated in a day of investigation and information outside Nancy Prison. The accompanying street protest, led by former prisoners (including some incarcerated during the Algerian War), was unexpectedly charged by the police; Hélène Cixous was clubbed to the ground and left unconscious.

MARCH 27

Saïd Belaïd, an Algerian minor incarcerated in Fleury-Mérogis, hanged himself after being threatened with deportation. His entire family lived in France. *Le Monde* reports his death.

APRIL 2

Publication by the GIP of *Lists of Demands from the Prisons during the Recent Revolts,* a booklet compiling lists of demands from the ten recent revolts.

APRIL 8

A circular from the Director of the Penitentiary Administration authorizes beauty products in women's prisons starting May 1.

APRIL 21

On a trip to the United States, Foucault visits Attica and meets the Committee for the Defense of Prisoners formed there in the wake of the revolt that had been violently repressed in September 1971 ("On Attica").

MAY 26

René Pleven, the Minister of Justice, declares at the Congress of the Federal Union of Magistrates that a plan for "the reform of the penitentiary system will be submitted to Parliament before the end of the session."

JUNE 5-8

In Nancy, on the eve of the trial of the prisoners accused of leading the revolt, many demonstrations take place. At the end of May, a black book on the revolt was published by the GIP–Nancy and a support committee was created for the accused in Nancy led by Dr. Jean-Pierre Gilles. Its manifesto is signed by 135 people, including Foucault and other GIP members. The next day, a public meeting of the GIP takes place under the direction of Jean-Marie Domenach regarding the prison conditions at Charles III (Nancy).

JUNE 21

Pleven presents the outline of his prison reform plan, which will be examined by the Parliament in autumn, to the Council of Ministers. Philippe Boucher, a journalist close to the GIP, wrote in *Le Monde*: "the revolt of the prisoners is no longer feared."

JUNE 29

The two escapees from Clairvaux, Buffet and Bontems, are sentenced to death.

JUNE 30

Two parliamentary information committees are constituted by the Commission on Law of the National Assembly: the first focuses on problems in the prisons, the second on the resources at the disposal of the judicial and penitentiary services.

JULY 2

At the Cartoucherie de Vincennes, the Théâtre du Soleil performs its director's (Ariane Mnouchkine's) play *1789*. Afterward, the group presents a new work developed in collaboration with the GIP, *The Trial of the Nancy Revolt*. Developed from notes of the proceedings taken by Michèle Manceaux and Ariane Mnouchkine, the play portrays the trial of the instigators of the Nancy Prison Revolt. Foucault, Deleuze, and Defert all participate in the performance.

JULY 14

Presidential pardon of several hundred convicted prisoners.

SEPTEMBER 25

Gérard Grandmontagne, incarcerated in Fresnes Prison and suffering from mental instability and suicidality, hangs himself after being sentenced to eight days in solitary for homosexuality. *Le Monde* reports on his death. The GIP later publishes a collection of his letters under the pseudonym H. M. ("Letters from H. M."). His is one of thirty-two GIP-recorded suicides in French prisons in 1972, a quarter of which were immigrants.

NOVEMBER

A public meeting of the Mouvement d'Action Judiciare is organized to address the crisis of prison suicides. Magistrates, lawyers, and former prisoners are in attendance, alongside members of the GIP and the FHAR (Front Homosexuel d'Action Révolutionnaire), for whom Grandmontagne had become something of a martyr.

NOVEMBER 7

Pleven restores the delivery of Christmas parcels to all prisoners.

NOVEMBER 28

Claude Buffet and Roger Bontems are executed by guillotine at La Santé at 5 a.m. Foucault publishes a piece in *Le Nouvel observateur* titled "Pompidou's Two Deaths."

DECEMBER 1

The first issue of the CAP (Prisoners' Action Committee) newspaper, *Le Journal du CAP*, appears, one year to the day after the revolt at Toul.

1973

FEBRUARY

At the beginning of the month, the GIP publishes its fourth and final *Intolerable* booklet, *Prison Suicides* (1972).

MARCH 8

Foucault and Claude Mauriac participate in an event in Paris in support of the CAP.

APRIL

Serge Livrozet, the cofounder of the CAP, publishes *De la prison à la révolte* with Mercure de France. Foucault contributes a preface ("Preface to Serge Livrozet's *De la prison à la révolte*").

MAY 1

During the May Day parade, a flyer of support for the prisoners signed jointly by the CAP, the GIP, and the ADDD is distributed.

There are a series of suicides across prisons in France, including Loos-lès-Lille, Strasbourg, Fleury-Mérogis, Château-Thierry, and Brest.

MAY 16

A delegation of the ADDD is received by the chief of staff of the Minister of Justice.

1974

JULY 19–AUGUST 5

Violent revolts break out in more than 120 prisons throughout France.

Guide to Key Terms, People, and Organizations

1945 French Penitentiary Reform: A commission convened by the Ministry of Justice drafted a plan, composed of fourteen principles, based on the concept that prisons are correctional institutions and that the rebuilding of lives and the ultimate social rehabilitation of prisoners is their primary objective.

Agence de presse Libération (APL, Liberation Press Agency): A popular leftist journal, modeled after underground circulars in France and abroad, founded on June 18, 1971, under the direction of Jean-Paul Sartre, Serge July, and Claude Mauriac, among others. After several rebirths, it continues to be published simply as *Libération.*

Jacques-Alain Miller: A French Lacanian psychoanalyst and author. He was coeditor with François Regnault of *Intolerable 2: Investigation into a Model Prison: Fleury-Mérogis* (1971).

Angela Davis: Distinguished Professor Emerita of History of Consciousness at University of California, Santa Cruz. She is author of numerous books, among them *Are Prisons Obsolete?* (2003). She was a longtime member of the Communist Party in the United States, ideologically affiliated with its leftist wing, formerly led by Charlene Mitchell. She is also the cofounder of the Critical Resistance movement, which works to abolish the prison–industrial complex.

Antiwreckers law: As part of its crackdown following May '68, the French government passed, in June 1970, the antiwreckers' law *[loi anti-casseurs].* This law found the organizers of demonstrations responsible for any disturbance or destruction; as such it permitted the easy imprisonment of a number of protesters under the auspices of "vandalism."

Pierre Arpaillange (1924–2017): A French judge and politician. He served in the Ministry of Justice from 1965 to 1974 and as Minister of Justice from 1988 to 1990. He is the author of *La simple justice* (1980).

Arpaillange Report: Working in the Ministry of Justice's Directorate of Criminal Affairs and Pardons in 1972, Pierre Arpaillange generated a report proposing significant reforms to the police and the penitentiary. The report, which unnerved Minister of Justice René Pleven and was suppressed by President Georges Pompidou, was later published as *La simple justice* (1980).

Association de Défense des Droits des Détenus (ADDD, Association for the Defense of Detainee Rights): A legal team dedicated to meeting prisoners' juridical needs, as well as recording and fighting prisoners' rights abuses. The team's work was made possible by the GIP's bridge building between current and former prisoners, their families, activists, lawyers, intellectuals, and media personnel.

Attica Prison and Revolt: Constructed in 1931, Attica Prison is a maximum/supermax security prison in New York. It was the site of the most famous prison revolt in U.S. history. Spanning September 9 through 13, 1971, the revolt, which occurred in protest of egregious prison conditions, mobilized approximately one thousand prisoners and resulted in a total of forty-three deaths (including both prisoners and correctional officers). The revolt was inspired, in part, by the death of George Jackson at San Quentin Prison on August 21, 1971.

Simone de Beauvoir (1908–1986): An existentialist and feminist French philosopher, author most notably of *The Ethics of Ambiguity* (1947) and *The Second Sex* (1949). After the incarceration of GP leaders, including the editors of *La Cause du peuple,* she and Jean-Paul Sartre organized the Association des Amis de *La Cause du peuple.* She was also instrumental in the founding of the Secours Rouge and was active in the Groupe d'Information Santé (GIS), which circulated information on women's reproductive health and rights.

Brevet d'Études du Premier Cycle (BEPC): A national set of examinations taken by French students at age fifteen and awarded a corollary diploma. It provides a Certificate of Secondary Education.

Claude Buffet and Roger Bontems: On September 21, 1971, prisoners Claude Buffet and Roger Bontems took Nicole Comte, a nurse, and Guy Girardot, a guard, hostage. Both Comte and Girardot were found dead the next morning. On September 24, a day set aside for remembrance, officers at Fleury-Mérogis beat prisoners sympathetic to the resistance. Buffet and Bontems were executed by guillotine at La Santé on November 28, 1972. Their defense lawyer, Robert Badinter, was a long-time champion of the abolition of the death penalty and wrote, most notably, *L'exécution* (1973), *L'abolition* (2000), and *Contre la peine de mort* (2006).

La Cause du peuple: Conceived as the militant, antiauthoritarian mouthpiece of the Gauche Prolétarienne (GP), the journal was founded in Paris on May 1, 1968. It published regular issues from 1968 to 1973 and then again from 1974 to 1978. Following the arrests of its first two editors, Jean-Pierre Le Dantec and Michel Le Bris in May 1970, Jean-Paul Sartre assumed the editorship until its first suspension in September 1973. *La Cause du peuple* was one of several important media venues for GIP activists.

Certificat d'Études Primaires (CEP): A diploma (granted from 1866 to 1989) certifying that students (by age thirteen) had acquired basic skills in reading, writing, math, science, and social studies.

Hélène Cixous: A prolific author and early voice in the French feminist movement, she was also a GIP activist, as were her two young children at the time. Besides hosting many GIP meetings in her apartment, Cixous edited one of the five GIP booklets: *Lists of Demands* (1972). She was particularly active in the aftermath of the Nancy Prison Revolt, attending an all-day investigation into the events on February 26, 1972, during which she was beaten and left unconscious by the police. She also codirected with Ariane Mnouchkine, through Théâtre du Soleil, the GIP play and several skits. In retrospect, Cixous understands her own beautiful and haunting novel *Dedans* (1969), translated as *Inside,* to prefigure this period of prison activism in her life and her long-standing interest in interiors and exclusions.

Clairvaux Prison and Revolt: Located in the former Clairvaux Abbey, Clairvaux Prison is a maximum-security prison best known for a high-profile revolt in 1971, featuring Roger Bontems, Claude Buffet, and others. In 2006, prisoners signed a manifesto asserting that, while the death penalty may have been abolished de jure in France, it remained de facto in effect in the form of life sentences without parole.

Comité d'Action des Prisonniers (CAP, Prisoners Action Committee): The successor to the GIP, which was led entirely by former prisoners, especially Serge Livrozet. The CAP worked for the immediate reform and ultimate abolition of both incarceration and the death penalty in France. It also published *Le Journal du CAP* from 1972 to 1980. For a history of the CAP, see Christophe Soulié, *Liberté sur paroles: Contribution à l'histoire du Comité d'action des prisonniers* (Bordeaux: Analis, 1995).

Compagnies Républicaines de Sécurité (CRS): The general reserve of the French National Police, primarily known for their work in riot control.

Confédération Générale du Travail (CGT, General Confederation of Labor): The French national trade-union center.

Confédération Nationale des Travailleurs en Éducation (CNTE): National Center for Distance Education.

Death penalty: The death penalty was abolished in France in 1981.

Josette d'Escrivan: A social worker at Fresnes Prison. She wrote a letter, addressed to the National Social Workers Association, regarding the unfair termination of her employment by the Red Cross, following her repeated objections to the abusive conditions under which suicidal prisoner Mr. Cicurel, whom she refers to simply as "C . . . ," was held. Her letter was later published as "Licenciement d'une assistante sociale" in the GIP booklet *Lists of Demands* (1972) and as "Peut-on ne pas dénoncer l'inacceptable?" in *Esprit* 413.4/5 (April–May 1972): 593–97.

Daniel Defert: A sociologist and political activist. A long-term partner of Michel Foucault, he suggested that Foucault assume a leadership role in the OPP, eventually leading to the formation of the GIP. Defert became deeply involved in the GIP, attending meetings and protests, launching investigations, giving press conferences, and publishing reports and opinion pieces. He was coeditor, with Christine Martineau and Danièle Rancière, of *Intolerable 1: Investigation into Twenty Prisons* (1971) and, with Gilles Deleuze, of *Intolerable 4: Prison Suicides* (1972). After Foucault's death from AIDS-related illnesses, Defert launched AIDeS, France's first AIDS awareness and advocacy group. He served as its president from 1984 to 1991. For his role in the GP, the OPP, the GIP, and AIDeS, see Daniel Defert, *Une vie politique* (Paris: Éditions du Seuil, 2014).

Gilles Deleuze (1925–1995): A French philosopher. Through his friendship with Foucault, Deleuze became heavily involved in GIP protests and occupations, prisoners' legal depositions, the antipsychiatry movement, and media statements and interviews. His fervor for protests and speeches was hampered only by his limited lung capacity, having had a tubercular lung removed in 1969. He spearheaded the ADDD and coedited, with Daniel Defert, *Intolerable 4: Prison Suicides* (1972). He is author, most notably, of *Capitalism and Schizophrenia: Anti-Oedipus* (1972) and *A Thousand Plateaus* (1980).

Jean-Marie Domenach (1922–1997): A Catholic leftist and a vocal opponent of French torture during the Algerian War. He worked as editor of *Esprit* (1957–76) and was succeeded by Paul Thibaud (1977–89).

Alongside Michel Foucault and Pierre Vidal-Naquet, he signed the GIP manifesto on February 8, 1971, and served in an unofficial leadership capacity.

Esprit: A French magazine established in 1932 under the auspices of Personalism and Nonconformism. To this day, *Esprit* maintains a radical mission: not to merely reform social structures but to deeply reimagine the social order.

Executive Magistrate (JAP, juge d'application des peines): A district court judge charged with the responsibility of overseeing convicted prisoners through their sentence and their reentry into the community. Created in 1958, the position aimed to adapt the terms and conditions of release to the individual needs of the prisoner. See Martine Herzog-Evans and Nicola Padfield, "The JAP: Lessons for England and Wales?" *Policy Brief, Criminal Justice Alliance* (2015).

L'Express: A weekly French leftist magazine founded in 1953, modeled after U.S. *Time* and German *Der Spiegel*. After its strong political stance against the Algerian War, especially the use of torture, *L'Express* was momentarily suspended by the French government. In 1964, several radical leftist journalists left to form *Le Nouvel observateur*.

Flagrant délit: The French legal system has three sorts of offenses: *délits* tried in the correctional courts, *contraventions* tried in the police courts, and *crimes* tried by the courts of assize. A *flagrant délit* is "an offense of the grade of '*délit*' which has just been committed or which is about to be committed." See Damon C. Woods, "The French Correctional Courts," *Journal of Criminal Law and Criminology* 23.1 [1932]: 20–27.

Michel Foucault (1926–1984): A French philosopher who played a key role in the genesis, naming, and development of the GIP. While he shared unofficial leadership of the group with Jean-Marie Domenach and Pierre Vidal-Naquet, most GIP meetings were held in Foucault's home and he is said to have done the majority of the organizing work. His involvement informed two lecture courses: *Penal Theories and Institutions, 1971–1972* (2018) and *The Punitive Society, 1972–1973* (2015), and two books, *I, Pierre Rivière* (1973) and *Discipline and Punish: The Birth of the Prison* (1975). Foucault insisted that if *Discipline and Punish* had two or three good ideas, they were directly attributable to the GIP.

Front Homosexuel d'Action Révolutionnaire (FHAR, Homosexual Revolutionary Action Front): Organization established in March 1971 by Guy Hocquenghem, author of *Homosexual Desire* (1972) and *The Screwball Asses* (1973). Beginning as a politically charged movement, FHAR became a primarily social organization focused on gay male sexual encounters. In 1976, it was replaced by the Groupe de Libération Homosexuelle (GLH).

Jean Gattégno (1935–1994): A French intellectual, with special expertise in Lewis Carroll and Oscar Wilde, who taught at the Université de Paris VIII and Nanterre. He was coeditor, with Hélène Cixous, of the GIP publication *Lists of Demands* (1972).

Gauche Prolétarienne (GP, Proletarian Left): A Maoist, non-Leninist organization founded at the end of 1968 when the libertarian militants of the March 22 Movement and the Union des Jeunesses Communistes Marxistes Léninistes (UJCML) joined forces.

Jean Genet (1910–1986): Writer and political activist whose youth was spent in and out of prisons for vagabondage, petty thievery, and sex work. A longtime supporter of the Black Panther Party, particularly in the cases of Angela Davis and George Jackson, he also worked with the GIP. He wrote the preface for *Intolerable 3: The Assassination of George Jackson* (1971). See Jean Genet, *L'ennemi déclaré: Textes et entretiens choisis, 1970–1983* (Paris: Gallimard, 2010).

Groupe d'Information sur les Prisons (GIP, The Prisons Information Group): A French prison activist organization, active from 1970 to 1973, focused on collecting and publicizing information about prison conditions and prisoner resistance efforts across France.

Groupe Information Asiles (GIA, Asylums Information Group): Established in 1972 by the Anarcho-Maoist contingent of the GP and the first awareness and advocacy group created for psychiatric patients in France. Originally concerned primarily with involuntary commitment and arbitrary institutionalization, its present concerns extend to all psychiatric abuses.

Groupe d'Information et de Soutien des Travailleurs Immigrés (GISTI, Immigrant Workers Information and Support Group): Established in 1972 by social workers and activists. The GISTI was named to expressly echo the GIP. It has fought and continues to fight racism and protect immigrant rights, including the right to a family, right to asylum, right to vote, right to social protection, and so on.

Habitation à Loyer Modéré (HLM, Rent-Controlled Housing): Refers to public, low-income, rent-controlled housing units.

H. M. (1940–1972): A pseudonym used in the reproduction of Gérard Grandmontagne's letters in *Intolerable 4: Prison Suicides* (1972). Born in 1940, Grandmontagne spent years in and out of detention, incarceration, and solitary confinement for petty crimes. Confined to solitary for homosexuality in 1972, Grandmontagne hanged himself from electrical wires he had torn from the ceiling.

J'accuse: Populist, revolutionary publication launched on January 15, 1971, aiming to reveal the truth of proletarian life silenced by the established media. *J'accuse* fused with *La Cause du peuple* from May 1971 to September 1973.

George Jackson (1941–1971): An African American prisoner, founder of the Black Guerrilla Family, a member of the Black Panther Party, and author, who, on August 21, 1971, was killed in an alleged escape attempt at San Quentin Prison. An investigation of this incident and of Jackson's thought was the subject of *Intolerable 3: The Assassination of George Jackson* (1971). He is author of *Soledad Brother* (1970) and *Blood in My Eye* (1971).

Serge Livrozet: A former prisoner, activist, and author of many books, including *De la prison à la révolte* (1972). With the support of Foucault, Livrozet established the CAP, in favor of which the GIP dissolved. For more on his life and work, see the film *La Mort se mérite* (Death Must Be Earned), directed by Nicolas Drolc (2017).

Maison de la Mutualité (aka La Mutu): A large Paris conference center, located at 24 Rue Saint-Victor.

Maisons centrales, maisons d'arrêt/maisons de détention: A *maison centrale* is a prison for convicted prisoners serving long sentences. A *maison d'arrêt* is a prison reserved for detainees awaiting trial, detainees awaiting transfer, or detainees whose remaining sentence is less than one year.

Christine Martineau: A prison scholar and GIP activist who helped draft the GIP questionnaire circulated to prisoners and their families. She then coedited, with Daniel Defert and Danièle Rancière, *Intolerable 1: Investigation into Twenty Prisons* (1971). The following year, she published, with Jean-Pierre Carasso, a study of prison labor, *Le Travail dans les prisons* (1972).

Claude Mauriac (1914–1996): A well-known French writer and journalist. He was a close friend of Michel Foucault and a GIP activist; his reflections on the GIP can be found scattered across his autobiographical writings. See, for example, Claude Mauriac, *Mauriac et fils* (Paris: Grasset, 1986).

May '68: A series of events that took place in France during May 1968 and beyond that indelibly marked French politics and culture. These events included demonstrations of unrest, demands, and protests across

France, from university students to blue-collar workers, producing not only high-profile clashes between the public and the police, but ultimately a nationwide labor strike. See Kristin Ross, *May '68 and Its Afterlives* (Chicago: University of Chicago Press, 2004).

Fleury-Mérogis Prison: Built in the 1960s in the southern suburbs of Paris, this is currently the largest prison in Europe. At the time of the GIP, it was supposed to be the most modern, least barbaric detention center, given its use of technology and solitary confinement. Its violations of human rights and dignity became the subject of *Intolerable 2: Investigation into a Model Prison: Fleury-Mérogis* (1971).

Minister of Justice: The director of the Ministry of Justice, the French government agency that oversees the juridical and penal systems. The Minister of Justice holds two positions (Ministre de la Justice and Le Garde des Sceaux) but is colloquially referred to simply as the "Minister of Justice."

Mouvement de Libération des Femmes (MLF, Women's Liberation Movement): An organization, founded in 1970 in the wake of May '68, that aimed to subvert the patriarchy and secure women's liberation (including sexual freedom, abortion rights, anticolonialism, and class equality). Like other groups of the period, the MLF operated through general assemblies, decentralized groups, and collective actions. In April 1971, the MLF's "Manifeste des 343," drafted by Simone de Beauvoir and published in *Le Nouvel observateur,* demanded greater information about and rights to women's reproductive health.

Nancy Prison and Revolt: The Charles-III Prison in Nancy was constructed in 1716 and demolished in 2009, replaced by the Centre Pénitentiaire de Nancy-Maxville. It is remembered best, perhaps, for the GIP-supported Nancy Revolt of January 15, 1972, in which prisoners clambered onto the roofs to throw lists of demands to witnesses below. See the film *Sur les toits* (On the Roofs), directed by Nicolas Drolc (2014).

Le Nouvel observateur (L'Obs): A weekly French magazine established in 1964 by journalists who had left *L'Express.*

Organisation Armée Secrète (OAS, Secret Army Organization): A terrorist movement opposed to Algerian independence.

Organisation des Prisonniers Politiques (OPP, Organization of Political Prisoners): An organization, formed in June 1970, in the wake of the incarceration of GP leaders during the events of May '68 and after, dedicated to defending arrested militants chiefly by advocating for their "political" status.

Parti Communiste Français (PCF, French Communist Party): The official communist party in France, founded in 1920.

Postes, Télégraphes et Téléphones (P&T): The French administrative apparatus overseeing postal and telecommunication services. Established in 1921, it was divided into La Poste and France Télécom in 1991.

René Pleven (1901–1993): A French politician who served as Minister of Justice from 1969 to 1973.

Pleven Reforms: René Pleven issued a government commission's report (the "Pleven Report") in January 1972 that investigated the conditions that led to the prison uprisings that had occurred in France in 1971–72. Based on its findings, the report recommended a number of reforms: (1) a statement of prisoners' rights and obligations, as well as a revision of disciplinary procedures; (2) development of job training and opportunities for paid work; (3) institution of a legal obligation for all prisons to establish "teams" around the warden consisting of guards, doctors, educators, social workers, and chaplains; (4) improvement in the system of inspection boards, which are provided by law for each prison but were found in many cases to be either nonexistent or superficial in their overseeing of prison conditions; (5) increases in the number and quality of special magistrates assigned to follow each prisoner and to recommend changes in their status; and finally, (6) simplification of the procedures by which prisoners may be put on probation or be allowed to work outside the prison. The proposals were adopted by the Pompidou cabinet on January 19, 1972.

Georges Pompidou (1911–1974): A moderate conservative who served as Prime Minister of France (1962–68) and President of the French Republic (1969–74).

Prétoire: A disciplinary court or disciplinary board, staffed by prison personnel, that adjudicates reports of prisoners' infractions committed while in prison and issues decisions on both punishment and clemency.

Danièle Rancière: A GP militant who employed Maoist methods to investigate violations of workers' rights in factories. When the GIP formed, she quickly joined. As perhaps her chief contribution, she helped develop the GIP questionnaire for prisoners regarding prison conditions. With Daniel Defert and Christine Martineau, she coedited *Intolerable 1: Investigation into Twenty Prisons* (1971).

François Regnault: A French philosopher and playwright. He was coeditor, with Jacques-Alain Miller, of *Intolerable 2: Investigation into a Model Prison: Fleury-Mérogis* (1971).

Restraint beds (contention): Across accounts of the Toul Revolt, there is disagreement over precisely what forms of restraint were used. Some report restraint beds (see, for example, Daniel Defert's *Une vie politique* [73]), while others report the use of restraint belts (see, for example, former prisoners interviewed in Nicolas Drolc's film *Sur les toits* [2014]).

La Roquette: A women's prison in Paris, opened in 1830, that was demolished in 1974.

Édith Rose: A psychiatrist at Toul Prison who was ultimately fired for her courageous description of intolerable prison conditions, especially for prisoners with mental illness.

La Santé: An infamous Paris prison founded in 1867. Conceived as the "house of health," La Santé is known for its high security and high-profile prisoners, including Jean Genet and Jacques Mesrine.

Jean-Paul Sartre (1905–1980): A French philosopher, playwright, and activist. He founded Secours Rouge in 1970 and cofounded, with Simone de Beauvoir, the Association des Amis de *La Cause du peuple,* later assuming the editorship of both *La Cause* and *Agence de presse Libération.*

Robert Schmelck (1915–1990): Author of *Pénalogie et Droit Pénitentiaire* (1967). He served as the director of the Penitentiary Administration (1961–64) and Attorney General to the Supreme Court of Appeal from 1964 to 1974. In 1972, he authored the Schmelck Report.

Schmelck Report: A report, published on January 8, 1972, under the direction of Robert Schmelck, that granted some legitimation to the widespread claims that prison conditions were unacceptable and that prison administrative personnel largely acted with impunity.

Secours Rouge Paris (SR, Red Aid): A group founded by Jean-Paul Sartre on June 11, 1970. Its aim was to ensure the political and legal defense of victims of repression and to provide them and their families with material and moral support. For more information on the Secours Rouge, see Julian Bourg, *From Revolution to Ethics: May 1968 and Contemporary French Thought* (Montreal: McGill-Queen's University Press, 2017).

Special status (régime special): The status of political prisoners who are exempted from the full extent of the criminal disciplinary regime.

State Security Court (Cour de Sûreté de l'État): Court established on January 15, 1963, specifically to judge acts of terrorism. It was abolished on August 4, 1981, when ordinary courts were given jurisdiction over these acts. In the interim, during the 1970s, the court was focused less on fighting terrorism and more on policing leftist political actors. See Jeremy Shapiro, "France and the GIA," in *Democracy and*

Counterterrorism: Lessons from the Past, ed. Robert Art and Louise Richardson (Washington, D.C.: United States Institute of Peace Press, 2007), 135–36.

Surveiller/Surveillance: A term notoriously difficult to translate into English in that it bears connotations both visual (surveillance and inspection) and managerial (supervision and oversight). This tension is drawn out in Foucault's book *Surveiller et punir: Naissance de la prison* (Paris: Gallimard, 1975), translated as *Discipline and Punish: The Birth of the Prison* (New York: Pantheon Books, 1977).

Syndicat de la Magistrature: A left-leaning judges' labor union founded on June 8, 1968, second in size only to the more conservative Union Syndicale des Magistrats.

Théâtre du Soleil: A Parisian avant-garde theater ensemble founded in 1964 by Ariane Mnouchkine and Philippe Léotard, rooted in physical theater and improvisation. Under the direction of Mnouchkine and Hélène Cixous, the Théâtre du Soleil collaborated with the GIP in a number of performances and a full play *(Le Procès de la mutinerie de Nancy)* to raise awareness of prison as a social problem.

Toul Prison and Revolt: The Ney Prison at Toul was founded in 1949. It is perhaps best known for the revolt that occurred on December 5–9, 1971, and set off a cascade of prison revolts across the country. Prisoners protested inhumane treatment and a commission of inquiry was instituted on December 15, 1971.

Travel ban: An order *[interdiction de séjour]* denying a former prisoner access to specific places.

Pierre Vidal-Naquet (1930–2006): A French historian, professor at the École des Hautes Études en Sciences Sociales, and political activist. Specializing in ancient Greece, his scholarly writing expanded to include denunciations of Holocaust denials as well as the French use of torture in the Algerian War. With Jean-Marie Domenach and Michel Foucault, he signed the GIP manifesto on February 8, 1971, and served as an unofficial leader of the group.

Further Reading

Historical Context

Philippe Artières. *68, une histoire collective, 1962–1981,* with Michelle Zancarini-Fournel. Paris: La Découverte, 2008.

———. *La Révolte de la prison de Nancy, 15 Janvier 1972.* Paris: Le Point du Jour, 2013.

Julian Bourg. *From Revolution to Ethics: May 1968 and Contemporary French Thought.* Montreal: McGill-Queen's University Press, 2007, Part 1.

Fabienne Brion and Bernard E. Harcourt. "Situation du cours." In Michel Foucault, *Mal faire, dire vrai. Fonction de l'aveu en justice.* Louvain: Presses universitaires de Louvain, 2012, 267–76.

———. English Translation: Fabienne Brion and Bernard E. Harcourt, "The Louvain Lectures in Context." In Michel Foucault, *Wrong-Doing, Truth-Telling: The Function of Avowal in Justice.* Chicago: University of Chicago Press, 2014, 271–322.

Comité Vérité Toul. *La Révolte de la centrale Ney.* Paris: Gallimard, 1972.

Loïc Delbaere. "Le système pénitentiaire à travers les luttes des dètenus de 1970 à 1987." Maîtrise d'histoire, UFR de sciences sociales, Université de Haute-Bretagne, Rennes II, 2002.

François Dosse. *Gilles Deleuze and Félix Guattari: Intersecting Lives.* New York: Columbia University Press, 2010, esp. "Deleuze and Foucault: A Philosophical Friendship," 306–30.

Stuart Elden. *Foucault: The Birth of Power.* Malden, Mass.: Polity, 2017, esp. chap. 5.

Didier Eribon. *Michel Foucault.* Cambridge: Harvard University Press, 1992 (1989), esp. chap. 16.

Alex Farquharson, ed. *The Impossible Prison.* Nottingham: Nottingham Contemporary, 2008.

Bernard Gendron. "Foucault's 1968." In *The Long 1968: Revisions and New Perspectives,* ed. Daniel J. Silverman, Ruud van Dijk, Jasmine Alinder, and A. Aneesh. Bloomington: Indiana University Press, 2013, 21–48.

Anne Guérin. *Prisonniers en révolte: Quotidien carcéral, mutineries et politique pénitentiaire en France (1970–1980).* Paris: Agone, 2013.

Bernard E. Harcourt. "Situation du cours." In Michel Foucault, *La Société punitive.* Paris: Gallimard/Le Seuil, 2013, 271–315.

Joy James, ed. *Warfare in the American Homeland: Policing and Prison in a Penal Democracy.* Durham, N.C.: Duke University Press, 2007, esp. chap. 7.

Alain Jaubert, Philippe Artières, and Elie Kagan, eds. *Michel Foucault, une journée particulière.* Lyon: Ædelsa Éditions, 2004.

Audrey Kiéfer. "Michel Foucault: Le G.I.P., l'histoire et l'action." Doctoral dissertation, Université de Picardie Jules Verne d'Amiens, 2003, esp. chap. 2. http://detentions.files.wordpress.com/2009/03/audrey-kiefer-foucault-le-gip-lhistoire-et-laction1.pdf (accessed January 12, 2012).

Roger Knobelspiess. *QHS: Quartier de haute sécurité.* Paris: Le Rocher, 1980.

Leonard Lawlor. "Prisons Information Group (GIP)." In *The Cambridge Foucault Lexicon,* ed. Leonard Lawlor and John Nale. Cambridge: Cambridge University Press, 2014, 394–98.

David Macey. *The Lives of Michel Foucault: A Biography.* New York: Pantheon, 1993, esp. chap. 11.

James Miller. *The Passion of Michel Foucault.* New York: Simon & Schuster, 1993, esp. chap. 6.

Dylan Rodriguez. *Forced Passages: Imprisoned Radical Intellectuals and the U.S. Prison Regime.* Minneapolis: University of Minnesota Press, 2006.

Christophe Soulié. *Liberté sur paroles: Contributions à l'histoire du Comité d'Action des Prisonniers.* Paris: Éditions Analis, 1995.

Edmund White. *Genet: A Bibliography.* New York: Alfred Knopf, 1993, esp. chap. 18.

Richard Wolin. "Foucault and the Maoists: Biopolitics and Engagement." In *The Wind from the East: French Intellectuals, the Cultural Revolution, and the Legacy of the 1960s.* Princeton, N.J.: Princeton University Press, 2012, 288–349.

Texts by GIP Activists

Louis Casamayor. *La Police.* Paris: Gallimard, 1973.

Hélène Cixous. "Biographie de l'écriture," Entretien avec Alain Poirson. *Révolution,* no. 74 (July 31, 1981): 18–20.

———. "We Who Are Free." *Critical Inquiry* 19.2 (1993): 201–19.

Daniel Defert. "L'émergence d'un nouveau front: Les prisons." Postface to *Le Groupe d'information sur les prisons: Archives d'une lutte 1970–1972*. Paris: IMEC, 2003, 315–26.

———. "Le moment GIP." In *Une vie politique: Entretien avec Philippe Artières et Éric Favereau*. Paris: Seuil, 2014.

Daniel Defert and Jacques Donz. "La charnière des prisons." *Magazine littéraire* (May 1976): 15–17.

Jean-Marie Domenach, Michel Foucault, and Pierre Vidal-Naquet. "Création d'un Groupe d'information sur les prisons." *Esprit* 401.3 (1971): 531–32.

Michel Foucault. *Discipline and Punish: The Birth of the Prison*. New York: Vintage Books, 1977.

———. *Dits et écrits*. Paris: Gallimard, 2001.

———. *Lectures on the Will to Know: Lectures at the Collège de France, 1970–1971*. New York: Palgrave, 2013.

———. *On the Punitive Society: Lectures at the Collège de France, 1972–1973*. New York: Palgrave, 2015.

———. *Penal Theories and Institutions: Lectures at the Collège de France, 1971–1972*. New York: Palgrave, 2018.

Serge Livrozet. *De la prison à la révolte*. Paris: Esprit Frappeur, 1999 (1973).

Christine Martineau and Jean-Pierre Carasso. *Le Travail dans les prisons*. Paris: Éditions Champ Libre, 1972.

Philippe Meyer. "La justice telle qu'on la rend." *Esprit,* nouvelle série, no. 417 (1972): 524–55.

Danièle Rancière. "Brève histoire du Groupe d'Information sur les Prisons (GIP), 1971–1972." *MANA, revue de sociologie et d'anthropologie* 5 (1998): 221–26.

Studies

Abu-Ali Abdur'Rahman. "Intolerable 1." In *Active Intolerance: Michel Foucault, the Prisons Information Group, and the Future of Abolition*, ed. Perry Zurn and Andrew Dilts. New York: Palgrave, 2016, 92.

Linda Martin Alcoff. "Does the Public Intellectual Have Public Integrity?" In *Queer Philosophy: Presentations of the Society for Lesbian and Gay Philosophy 1998–2008*, ed. Raja Halwani, Carol Quinn, and Andy Wible. Amsterdam: Rodopi, 2012, 69–82.

Kalinka Alvarez. "The Prisons Information Group (1970–1972): The Voice of the Voiceless." Doctoral dissertation, Columbia University, 2019.

Antipode Foundation. "Symposium on *Sur les toits*," with Anastasia

Chamberlen, Oliver Davis, Stuart Elden, Sophie Fuggle, Marijn Nieu-wenhuis, and Dominique Moran. June 23, 2016: https://antipodefoundation.org/2016/06/23/sur-les-toits-symposium/.

Philippe Artières. "Introduction: Foucault and Audiography." In *Speech Begins after Death*. Minneapolis: University of Minnesota Press, 2013, 1–22.

———. "La prison en procès: Les mutins de Nancy (1972)." *Vingtième Siècle, Révue d'histoire* 70 (2001): 57–70.

———. "Les écrits de la révolte: La prise de parole des détenus (1970-72)." *Drôle d'époque* 8 (2001): 37–47.

———. "Les mutins, la psychiatre et l'aumônier: Archéologie d'un silence foucaldien (Toul, décembre 1971)." *Le Portique* 13–14 (2004): 2–7.

———. "Parler" and "Mémoire." In Philippe Artières and Mathieu Potte-Bonneville, *D'aprés Foucault: Gestes, luttes, programmes*. Paris: Points, 2012, 79–92 and 261–80.

Jean Bérard. "Les révoltes des prisonniers et les critiques de l'enferme-ment." In *La Justice en procès*. Paris: Presses de Sciences Po, 2013, 63–97.

Jean Bérard and Gilles Chantraine. "Mai 68 et le prisons." *Vacarme* 44 (2008): 74–78.

Thomas Biebricher. "The Practices of Theorists: Habermas and Foucault as Public Intellectuals." *Philosophy Social Criticism* 37.6 (2011): 709–34.

François Boullant. *Michel Foucault et les prisons*. Paris: Presses Universitaires de France, 2003, 11–18.

Cecile Brich. "Foucault, Criminal Subjectivity, and the Groupe d'information sur les prisons." Doctoral dissertation, University of Leeds, 2006.

———. "The Groupe d'information sur les prisons: The voice of prisoners? Or Foucault's?" *Foucault Studies* 5 (January 2008): 26–47.

Alan Casamian. "Michel Foucault: Pouvoir et prison: Histoire d'un engagement." Doctoral dissertation, Université des sciences sociales de Toulouse, 1984–85, esp. chap 1.

Andres Fabian Henao Castro. "Can the Subaltern Smile? *Oedipus* without Oedipus." *Contemporary Political Theory* 14.4 (2015): 315–34.

Howard Caygill. "Philosophy and the Black Panthers." *Radical Philosophy* 179 (2013): 7–13.

Steve Champion. "Breaking the Conditioning: The Relevance of the Prisons Information Group." In *Active Intolerance: Michel Foucault, the Prisons Information Group, and the Future of Abolition,* ed. Perry Zurn and Andrew Dilts. New York: Palgrave, 2016, 95–104.

Natalie Cisneros. "Foucault's Punitive Society and Our Own: Sequestration, Elimination, and the Carceral System." *Carceral Notebooks* 12 (2017): 83–96.

———. "Resisting 'Massive Elimination': Foucault, Immigration, and the

GIP." In *Active Intolerance: Michel Foucault, the Prisons Information Group, and the Future of Abolition,* ed. Perry Zurn and Andrew Dilts. New York: Palgrave, 2016, 241–258.

Sylvain Dambrine. "Passages du mur: Des subjectivations de prisonniers." *Vacarme* 29 (2004): 146–49.

Oliver Davis. "Rancière and Queer Theory." *Borderlands* 8.2 (2009): esp. 3–7.

Jason Demers. "Prison Liberation by Association: Michel Foucault and the George Jackson Atlantic." *Atlantic Studies* 13.1 (2016): 165–86.

Stephen Dillon. "'Can They Ever Escape?' Foucault, Black Feminism, and the Intimacy of Abolition." In *Active Intolerance: Michel Foucault, the Prisons Information Group, and the Future of Abolition,* ed. Perry Zurn and Andrew Dilts. New York: Palgrave, 2016, 259–76.

Nicolas Drolc. "Prisoners Inside/Intellectuals Outside: The GIP and the French Prison Revolts, 1971–1972." *Carceral Notebooks* 12 (2017): 31–35.

Didier Eribon. "Resistance and Counterdiscourse." In *Insult and the Making of the Gay Self,* trans. Michael Lucey. Durham, N.C.: Duke University Press, 2004, esp. chap. 10.

Rolf S. de Folter. "On the Methodological Foundation of the Abolitionist Approach to the Criminal Justice System. A Comparison of the Ideas of Hulsman, Mathiesen, and Foucault." *Contemporary Crises* 10 (1986): 39–62.

Keith Gandal. "Michel Foucault: Intellectual Work and Politics." *Telos* 67 (1986): 121–34.

Michael Hames-García. "Are Prisons Tolerable?" *Carceral Notebooks* 12 (2017): 151–86.

Lisa Guenther. "Beyond Guilt and Innocence: The Creaturely Politics of Prisoner Resistance Movements." In *Active Intolerance: Michel Foucault, the Prisons Information Group, and the Future of Abolition,* ed. Perry Zurn and Andrew Dilts. New York: Palgrave, 2016, 225–40.

———. "The Creaturely Politics of Prisoner Resistance Movements." *Carceral Notebooks* 12 (2017): 47–56.

Bernard Harcourt. "A Dialectic of Theory and Practice." *Carceral Notebooks* 12 (2017): 19–29.

———. "The GIP as a Cynical Practice." *Carceral Notebooks* 12 (2017): 65–82.

Bernard Harcourt and Andrew Dilts. eds. *Discipline, Security, and Beyond: Rethinking Michel Foucault's 1978 & 1979 Collège de France Lectures. Carceral Notebooks* 4 (2008), esp. Guy Casadamont, "Masques de Foucault," 45–53.

Brady Heiner. "Foucault and the Black Panthers." *City: Analysis of Urban Trends, Culture, Theory, Policy, Action* 11.3 (2007): 313–56.

Marcelo Hoffman. "Foucault and the 'Lesson' of the Prisoner Support Movement." *New Political Science* 34 (2012): 21–36.

———. "Foucault, the Prisoner Support Movement, and Disciplinary Power." In *Foucault and Power: The Influences of Political Engagement on Theories of Power.* London: Bloomsbury, 2013, 15–46.

———. "Investigations from Marx to Foucault." In *Active Intolerance: Michel Foucault, the Prisons Information Group, and the Future of Abolition,* ed. Perry Zurn and Andrew Dilts. New York: Palgrave, 2016, 169–86.

———. *Militant Acts: The Role of Investigations in Radical Political Struggles.* Albany: SUNY Press, 2019, chap. 2.

Lynne Huffer. "The Untimely Speech of the GIP Counter-Archive." In *Active Intolerance: Michel Foucault, the Prisons Information Group, and the Future of Abolition,* ed. Perry Zurn and Andrew Dilts. New York: Palgrave, 2016, 41–58.

Antoine Janvier. "Le Groupe d'information sur les prisons: La philosophie politique à l'épreuve de l'évènement," présentée à l'ULg, à la journée d'études du Groupe belge d'études sartriennes du 23 février 2007 intitulée Qu'est-ce qu'un groupe?, organisée par Florence Caeymaex (FRS-FNRS/ULg) et Guillaume Sibertin-Blanc (Université de Lille III).

Jonathan Kahana. "Documentary Counterpublics: Filming Prison." In *Intelligence Work: The Politics of American Documentaries.* New York: Columbia University Press, 2008, 205–66.

Mads Peter Karlsen and Kasper Villadsen. "Foucault, Maoism, Genealogy: The Influence of Political Militancy in Michel Foucault's Thought." *New Political Science* 37.1 (2015): 91–117.

Michelle Koerner. "Line of Escape: Gilles Deleuze's Encounter with George Jackson." *Genre* 44.2 (2011): 157–80.

Colin Koopman. "Conduct and Power: Foucault's Methodological Expansions in 1971." In *Active Intolerance: Michel Foucault, the Prisons Information Group, and the Future of Abolition,* ed. Perry Zurn and Andrew Dilts. New York: Palgrave, 2016, 59–74.

Leopold Lambert. *The Funambulist Pamphlets,* vol. 2 (2013), esp. #18, "Prison Information Group: Michel Foucault, Jean-Marie Domenach, and Pierre Vidal-Naquet," 98–100.

Leonard Lawlor and Andrea Janae Sholtz. "Speaking Out for Others: Philosophical Activity in Deleuze and Foucault (and Heidegger)." In *Between Deleuze and Foucault,* ed. Daniel Smith, Thomas Nail, and Nicolae Morar. Edinburgh: Edinburgh University Press, 2016, 139–59.

Nancy Luxon, "The Disordering of Discourse: Voice and Ambiguity in the GIP." In *Active Intolerance: Michel Foucault, the Prisons Information*

Group, and the Future of Abolition, ed. Perry Zurn and Andrew Dilts. New York: Palgrave, 2016, 203–21.

Gérard Mauger. "Un nouveau militantisme." *Sociétés et Représentations* 3 (1996): 51–77.

Ladelle McWhorter. "The Abolition of Philosophy." In *Active Intolerance: Michel Foucault, the Prisons Information Group, and the Future of Abolition,* ed. Perry Zurn and Andrew Dilts. New York: Palgrave, 2016, 23–41.

Donald Middlebrooks. "Intolerable 3." In *Active Intolerance: Michel Foucault, the Prisons Information Group, and the Future of Abolition,* ed. Perry Zurn and Andrew Dilts. New York: Palgrave, 2016, 222.

Michelle Perrot. *Les Ombres de l'histoire.* Paris: Flammarion, 2001, esp. 27–38.

Derrick Quintero. "Intolerable 2." In *Active Intolerance: Michel Foucault, the Prisons Information Group, and the Future of Abolition,* ed. Perry Zurn and Andrew Dilts. New York: Palgrave, 2016, 141.

Jacques Rancière. "L'héritage difficile de Michel Foucault." In *Chroniques des temps consensuels.* Paris: Seuil, 2005, 183–87.

Michael Rembis. "Gender, Madness, and the Legacies of the Prisons Information Group." In *Containing Madness,* ed. Jennifer Kilty and Erin Dej. New York: Palgrave, 2018, 67–89.

Brigitte Robert. "Le GIP et la suite. . . ." *Classes dangereuses: Revue critique d'histoire et de politique* (Automone 1984): 33–40.

———. "Les Luttes autour des prisons 1971–1972: Le Groupe d'informaton sur les prisons à la naissance du C.A.P." Doctoral dissertation, Institut d'Études Politiques de Paris, 1981.

Dylan Rodríguez. "Disrupted Foucault: Los Angeles' Coalition against Police Violence (CAPA) and the Obsolescence of White Academic Raciality." In *Active Intolerance: Michel Foucault, the Prisons Information Group, and the Future of Abolition,* ed. Perry Zurn and Andrew Dilts. New York: Palgrave, 2016, 145–68.

Grégory Salle. "Le Groupe d'information sur les prisons (G.I.P.), ou le refus de l'"intolérable."" Doctoral dissertation, Institut d'Études Politiques de Paris, 1999–2000.

———. "Mettre la prison à l'épreuve. Le GIP en guerre contre l'"Intolérable."" *Cultures & Conflits* 55 (2004): 71–96.

———. "Statactivism against the Penal Machinery in the Aftermath of 1968: The Case of the French Groupe d'Information sur les Prisons." *PArtecipazione e COnflitto* 7 (2014): 221–36.

Falguni A. Sheth. "Unruliness without Rioting: Hunger Strikes in Contemporary Politics." In *Active Intolerance: Michel Foucault, the Prisons Information Group, and the Future of Abolition,* ed. Perry Zurn and Andrew Dilts. New York: Palgrave, 2016, 123–40.

Mischa Suter. "A Thorn in the Side of Social History: Jacques Rancière and *Les Révoltes logiques." International Review of Social History* 57 (2012): 61–85.

Dianna Taylor. "Between Discipline and Caregiving: Changing Prison Population Demographics and Possibilities for Self-Transformation." In *Active Intolerance: Michel Foucault, the Prisons Information Group, and the Future of Abolition,* ed. Perry Zurn and Andrew Dilts. New York: Palgrave, 2016, 105–22.

Anna Terwiel. "Foucault and the Lateral Body Politics of Hunger Strikes." Doctoral dissertation, Northwestern University, 2016.

———. "What Is the Problem with High Prison Temperatures? From Threat to Health to the Right to Comfort." *New Political Science* 40.1 (2018): 70–83.

Kevin Thompson. "Problematization and the Production of New Statements: Foucault and Deleuze on Le Groupe d'information sur les prisons." *Carceral Notebooks* 12 (2017): 187–252.

———. "To Judge the Intolerable." *Philosophy Today* 54 (2010): 169–76.

Janos Toevs. "Giving the Floor to Whom?" *Carceral Notebooks* 12 (2017): 131–49.

Michael Welch. "Counterveillance: How Foucault and the Groupe d'Information sur les Prisons Reversed the Optics." *Theoretical Criminology* 15 (2011): 301–13.

———. "Pastoral Power as Penal Resistance: Foucault and the Groupe d'Information sur les Prisons." *Punishment & Society* 12 (2010): 47–63.

Shannon Winnubst. "The GIP as a Neoliberal Intervention: Trafficking in Illegible Concepts." In *Active Intolerance: Michel Foucault, the Prisons Information Group, and the Future of Abolition,* ed. Perry Zurn and Andrew Dilts. New York: Palgrave, 2016, 187–202.

Benedikte Zitouni. "Michel Foucault et le Groupe d'Information sur les Prisons: Comment faire exister et circuler le savoir des prisonniers." *Les Temps modernes* 645–46 (2007): 268–307.

Perry Zurn. "Curiosities at War: The Police and Prison Resistance after May '68." *Modern and Contemporary France* 26.2 (2018): 179–91.

———. "The GIP and the Question of Failure." *Carceral Notebooks* 12 (2017): 37–46.

———. "Toward an Account of Intolerance: Between Prison Resistance and Engaged Scholarship." *Carceral Notebooks* 12 (2017): 97–128.

———. "Work and Failure: Assessing the Prisons Information Group." In *Active Intolerance: Michel Foucault, the Prisons Information Group, and the Future of Abolition,* ed. Perry Zurn and Andrew Dilts. New York: Palgrave, 2016, 75–91.

———. "The Politics of Anonymity: Foucault, Feminism, and Gender Non-Conforming Prisoners." *philoSOPHIA* 6.1 (2016): 27–42.

———. "Publicity and Politics: Foucault, the Prisons Information Group, and the Press." *Radical Philosophy Review* 17.2 (2014): 403–20.

Perry Zurn and Andrew Dilts, eds. "Affects, Active Intolerance, and Abolition." In *Theory and Event* 24.1 (2021).

———"Challenging the Punitive Society." *Carceral Notebooks* 12 (2017): 1–7.

———. *Active Intolerance: Michel Foucault, the Prisons Information Group, and the Future of Abolition.* New York: Palgrave, 2016.

———"Active Intolerance: An Introduction." In *Active Intolerance: Michel Foucault, the Prisons Information Group, and the Future of Abolition,* ed. Perry Zurn and Andrew Dilts. New York: Palgrave, 2016, 1–22.

Films

Nicolas Drolc. *La Mort se mérite.* Les Films Furax, 2016.

———. *Sur les toits. Hiver 1972: mutineries dans les prisons françaises.* Lew Films Furax, 2013.

Hélène Châtelain and René Lefort. *Les prisons aussi.* 1973; Paris: La parole errante, 2012.

Contributors

Louis Appert is a pseudonym for **Michel Foucault.**

Association pour la Défense des Droits des Détenus (ADDD, Association for the Defense of Detainee Rights) was a legal team dedicated to meeting French prisoners' juridical needs as well as recording and fighting prisoners' rights abuses.

Erik Beranek is a PhD candidate in philosophy at DePaul University. His translations include Jacques Rancière's *Béla Tarr, the Time After* (Minnesota, 2013), Étienne Souriau's *The Different Modes of Existence* (Minnesota, 2015), and David Lapoujade's *The Lesser Existences* (Minnesota, 2021).

Hélène Cixous is a feminist writer and professor at University of Paris VIII, which she founded. She is the author of numerous works, including *Inside*; *Rootprints: Memory and Life Writing*; *Stigmata: Escaping Texts*; *So Close*; and *White Ink: Interviews on Sex, Text, and Politics*.

François Colcombet is a noted French politician. He served as the cofounder and president of the Syndicat de la Magistrature from 1973 to 1974.

Comité d'Action des Prisonniers (CAP, Prisoners Action Committee) was the successor to the GIP, working for the immediate reform and ultimate abolition of both incarceration and the death penalty in France. Led entirely by former prisoners, especially Serge Livrozet, CAP published *Le Journal du CAP* from 1972 to 1980.

Comité Vérité Toul (CVT, Truth Committee of Toul) was an organization dedicated to discovering and revealing the carceral conditions at Toul Prison that led to the Toul Prison Revolt of December 1971. The group published *La Révolte de la centrale Ney*.

Daniel Defert is a sociologist and political activist. He is author of *Une vie politique* and coeditor of *Intolerable 1. Investigation into Twenty Prisons* and *Intolerable 4. Prison Suicides.* He was the long-term partner of Michel Foucault and editor of several of Foucault's works, including *Dits et écrits I* and *II* and *Lectures on the Will to Know.*

Gilles Deleuze (1925–1995) was professor of philosophy at the University of Paris, Vincennes–St. Denis. He is coauthor, with Félix Guattari, of *Anti-Oedipus* and *A Thousand Plateaus.* These works, as well as his *Cinema 1, Cinema 2, The Fold, Proust and Signs,* and others, are published in English by the University of Minnesota Press.

Jean-Marie Domenach (1922–1977) was a French intellectual, a Catholic leftist, a staunch opponent of the Algerian War, and the editor of *Esprit* (1957–76).

Michel Foucault (1926–1984) was a French philosopher who held the chair in History of Systems of Thought at the Collège de France. Among his most notable books are *History of Madness, Discipline and Punish,* and *The History of Sexuality.* The University of Minnesota Press published *Speech Begins after Death: In Conversation with Claude Bonnefoy* (2013), *Language, Madness, and Desire: On Literature* (2015), and *Disorderly Families: Infamous Letters from the Bastille Archives* (2016).

Jean Genet (1910–1986) was a writer and political activist. He is author of *Our Lady of the Flowers, The Thief's Journal,* and *Prisoner of Love* and editor of *Intolerable 3. The Assassination of George Jackson.*

Groupe d'Information sur les Prisons (GIP, Prisons Information Group) was a French prison activist organization focused on collecting and publicizing information about prison conditions and prisoner resistance efforts. It was active from 1970 until 1973.

H. M. (Gérard Grandmontagne) (1940–1972) was a prisoner who committed suicide after being placed in solitary confinement for homosexuality. His letters were published in *Intolerable 4. Prison Suicides.*

Antoine Lazarus is professor emeritus of public health and social medicine at University Paris XIII. He served as president of the Observatoire International des Prisons and vice president of the Centre Primo Levi.

Organisation des Prisonniers Politiques (OPP, Organization of Political Prisoners) was an organization formed in the wake of May '68 dedicated to defending arrested militants.

Édith Rose was a psychiatrist at Toul Prison who was ultimately fired for her courageous description of prison conditions, especially regarding prisoners with mental illness.

Paul Thibaud is a French intellectual, journalist, and activist. He served as the editor of *Esprit* from 1977 to 1989.

Kevin Thompson is professor of philosophy at DePaul University. He is the author of *Hegel's Theory of Normativity: The Systematic Foundations of the Philosophical Science of Right* and the coeditor of *Phenomenology of the Political*.

Pierre Vidal-Naquet (1930–2006) was a political activist and professor of history at the École des Hautes Études en Sciences Sociales. He is author of numerous works, including *Les Grecs, les historiens et la démocratie*; *Le monde d'Homère*; *La Torture dans la République*; *Les crimes de l'armée française Algérie 1954–1962*; and *Les Juifs, la mémoire et le présent*.

Perry Zurn is assistant professor of philosophy at American University. He is author of *Curiosity and Power: The Politics of Inquiry* (Minnesota, 2021) and coeditor of *Active Intolerance: Michel Foucault, the Prisons Information Group, and the Future of Abolition* and *Curiosity Studies: A New Ecology of Knowledge* (Minnesota, 2020).

Publication History

Daniel Defert, "The Emergence of a New Front: The Prisons" was originally published as "L'émergence d'un nouveau front: les prisons," in *Le Groupe d'information sur les prisons: Archives d'une lutte, 1970–1972,* ed. Philippe Artières, Laurent Quéro, and Michelle Zancarini-Fournel (Paris: Éditions de l'IMEC, 2003), 315–26.

Anonymous, "Declaration of Political Prisoners on Hunger Strike," was originally published as "Déclaration des emprisonnés politiques en grève de la faim," in *Le Groupe d'information sur les prisons: Archives d'une lutte 1970–1972,* ed. Philippe Artières, Laurent Quéro, and Michelle Zancarini-Fournel (Paris: Éditions de l'IMEC, 2003), 31–32.

Organisation des Prisonniers Politiques (OPP), "Report on the Prisons," is a report most likely drafted in September 1970. It was published as "Rapport sur les prisons," in *Le Groupe d'information sur les prisons: Archives d'une lutte 1970–1972,* ed. Philippe Artières, Laurent Quéro, and Michelle Zancarini-Fournel (Paris: Éditions de l'IMEC, 2003): 34–36.

Groupe d'Information sur les Prisons (GIP), "Letter Addressed to the Families of Common-Law Prisoners," is a Maoist circular written in January 1971 before the public announcement of the GIP's formation. It was published as "Lettre addressée aux familles des détenus de droit commun . . . ," in *Le Groupe d'information sur les prisons: Archives d'une lutte 1970–1972,* ed. Philippe Artières, Laurent Quéro, and Michelle Zancarini-Fournel (Paris: Éditions de l'IMEC, 2003), 42.

Groupe d'Information sur les Prisons (GIP), "GIP Manifesto," is the text of a press conference statement read aloud by Michel Foucault on February 8, 1971. It was published as "(Manifeste du G.I.P.)," in Michel Foucault, *Dits et écrits, 1954–1988,* ed. Daniel Defert and François Ewald, 4 vols. (Paris: Gallimard, 1994), 2:86, 174–75; and in Michel Foucault, *Dits et écrits,*

1954–1988, ed. Daniel Defert and François Ewald, 2 vols. (Paris: Quarto Gallimard, 2001), 1:86, 1042–43; and as "Nul de nous n'est sûr d'échapper à la prison...," in *Le Groupe d'information sur les prisons: Archives d'une lutte 1970–1972,* ed. Philippe Artières, Laurent Quéro, and Michelle Zancarini-Fournel (Paris: Éditions de l'IMEC, 2003), 43–44.

Groupe d'Information sur les Prisons (GIP), "On Prisons," was a public announcement written by Michel Foucault and originally published in *J'accuse,* no. 3 (March 15, 1971): 26. It was subsequently published as "(Sur les prisons)," in Michel Foucault, *Dits et écrits, 1954–1988,* ed. Daniel Defert and François Ewald, 4 vols. (Paris: Gallimard, 1994), 2:87, 175–76; and in Michel Foucault, *Dits et écrits, 1954–1988,* ed. Daniel Defert and François Ewald, 2 vols. (Paris: Quarto Gallimard, 2001), 1:87, 1043–44; and as "Le GIP de lancer sa première enquête . . . ," in *Le Groupe d'information sur les prisons: Archives d'une lutte 1970–1972,* ed. Philippe Artières, Laurent Quéro, and Michelle Zancarini-Fournel (Paris: Éditions de l'IMEC, 2003), 52.

Michel Foucault, "The Prison Is Everywhere," was a statement published in *Combat,* no. 8335 (May 5, 1971): 1. It was subsequently published as "La prison partout," in Michel Foucault, *Dits et écrits, 1954–1988,* ed. Daniel Defert and François Ewald, 4 vols. (Paris: Gallimard, 1994) 2:90, 193–94; and in Michel Foucault, *Dits et écrits, 1954–1988,* ed. Daniel Defert and François Ewald, 2 vols. (Paris: Quarto Gallimard, 2001), 1:90, 1061–62.

Daniel Defert, "When Information Is a Struggle," was a manifesto that originally appeared as "La Prison, enjeu d'un combat" in a combined issue of *La Cause du peuple—J'accuse* (May 25, 1971): 6–7. It was subsequently published as "Quand l'information est une lutte," in *Le Groupe d'information sur les prisons: Archives d'une lutte 1970–1972,* ed. Philippe Artières, Laurent Quéro, and Michelle Zancarini-Fournel (Paris: Éditions de l'IMEC, 2003), 69–73.

Michel Foucault, "I Perceive the Intolerable," interview with Michel Foucault conducted by Geneviève Armleder, originally appeared in *Journal de Genève: Samedi littéraire* ("cahier 135"), no. 170 (July 24–25, 1971). It was subsequently published as "Je perçois l'intolérable," in Michel Foucault, *Dits et écrits, 1954–1988,* ed. Daniel Defert and François Ewald, 4 vols. (Paris: Gallimard, 1994), 2:94, 203–5; and in Michel Foucault, *Dits et écrits, 1954–1988,* ed. Daniel Defert and François Ewald, 2 vols. (Paris: Quarto Gallimard, 2001), 1:94, 1071–73.

Michel Foucault, "The Penal System Is a Problem That Has Interested Me for Some Time," an interview with Michel Foucault conducted by Jalila Hafsia, was originally published in *La Presse de Tunisie* (August 12, 1971), 3. It was subsequently published as "Un problème m'intéresse depuis longtemps, c'est celui du système pénal," in Michel Foucault, *Dits et écrits, 1954–1988,* ed. Daniel Defert and François Ewald, 4 vols. (Paris: Gallimard, 1994), 2:95, 205–9; and in Michel Foucault, *Dits et écrits, 1954–1988,* ed. Daniel Defert and François Ewald, 2 vols. (Paris: Quarto Gallimard, 2001), 1:95, 1073–78.

Groupe d'Information sur les Prisons (GIP), "Preface to *Intolerable 1,*" was originally published in *Intolérable I: Enquête dans 20 prisons* (Paris: Éditions Champs Libre, May 28, 1971). It was published as "Préface," in Michel Foucault, *Dits et écrits, 1954–1988,* ed. Daniel Defert and François Ewald, 4 vols. (Paris: Gallimard, 1994), 2:91, 195–97; in Michel Foucault, *Dits et écrits, 1954–1988,* ed. Daniel Defert and François Ewald, 2 vols. (Paris: Quarto Gallimard, 2001), 1:91, 1063–65; as "Enquête dans 20 prisons: Introduction," in *Le Groupe d'information sur les prisons: Archives d'une lutte 1970–1972,* ed. Philippe Artières, Laurent Quéro, and Michelle Zancarini-Fournel (Paris: Éditions de l'IMEC, 2003), 81–82; and in Groupe d'Information sur les Prisons, *Intolérable,* ed. Philippe Artières (Paris: Verticales, 2013), 17–20.

Groupe d'Information sur les Prisons (GIP), "Back Cover of *Intolerable 1,*" was originally published in *Intolérable I: Enquête dans 20 prisons* (Paris: Éditions Champs Libre, May 28, 1971). It was subsequently published in Groupe d'Information sur les Prisons, *Intolérable,* ed. Philippe Artières (Paris: Verticales, 2013), 16.

Groupe d'Information sur les Prisons (GIP), "La Santé: Questionnaire and Narratives," is a selection from the GIP questionnaire, distributed early in 1971, the findings of which composed the primary content of the *Intolérable 1* booklet. It was subsequently published in Groupe d'Information sur les Prisons, *Intolérable,* ed. Philippe Artières (Paris: Verticales, 2013), 21–31, 37–42.

Michel Foucault and Pierre Vidal-Naquet, "Inquiry on Prisons: Let Us Break Down the Bars of Silence," an interview by Claude Angeli, originally appeared in *Politique-Hebdo,* no. 24 (March 18, 1971): 4–6. It was subsequently published as "Enquête sur les prisons: Brisons les barreaux du silence," in Michel Foucault, *Dits et écrits, 1954–1988,* ed. Daniel Defert and François Ewald, 4 vols. (Paris: Gallimard, 1994), 2:88, 176–82; and in

Michel Foucault, *Dits et écrits, 1954–1988,* ed. Daniel Defert and François Ewald, 2 vols. (Paris: Quarto Gallimard, 2001), 1:88, 1044–50.

Michel Foucault, "No, This Is Not an Official Inquiry . . . ," was the second part of an interview, broadcast on April 21, 1971, by the "Format France" program of Radio-Canada. It was subsequently published as "Non, ce n'est pas une enquête officielle . . . ," in *Le Groupe d'information sur les prisons: Archives d'une lutte 1970–1972,* ed. Philippe Artières, Laurent Quéro, and Michelle Zancarini-Fournel (Paris: Éditions de l'IMEC, 2003), 65–68.

Groupe d'Information sur les Prisons (GIP), "They Build New Prisons!" was originally published in *Intolérable 2: Le GIP enquête dans une prison-modèle: Fleury-Mérogis* (Éditions Champ Libre, June 7–8, 1971). It was subsequently published as "Ils bâtissent des prisons neuves!" in Groupe d'Information sur les Prisons, *Intolérable,* ed. Philippe Artières (Paris: Verticales, 2013), 94–95; and in *Le Groupe d'information sur les prisons: Archives d'une lutte 1970–1972,* ed. Philippe Artières, Laurent Quéro, and Michelle Zancarini-Fournel (Paris: Éditions de l'IMEC, 2003), 85–86.

Groupe d'Information sur les Prisons (GIP), "The Model Prison: Alone Twenty-Three out of Twenty-Four Hours," is an excerpt from *Intolérable 2: Le GIP enquête dans une prison-modèle: Fleury-Mérogis,* which appeared in *La Cause du peuple* on June 7, 1971. It was subsequently published as "La prison modèle: Seul 23 heures sur 24," in Groupe d'Information sur les Prisons, *Intolérable,* ed. Philippe Artières (Paris: Verticales, 2013), 120–22; and in *Le Groupe d'information sur les prisons: Archives d'une lutte 1970–1972,* ed. Philippe Artières, Laurent Quéro, and Michelle Zancarini-Fournel (Paris: Éditions de l'IMEC, 2003), 83–84.

Groupe d'Information sur les Prisons (GIP), "Dear Comrades, Here Are the Current Axes of the GIP's Development," was a GIP circular from spring 1971. It was subsequently published as "Chers camarades, voici les axes du développement actuel du GIP . . . ," in *Le Groupe d'information sur les prisons: Archives d'une lutte 1970–1972,* ed. Philippe Artières, Laurent Quéro, and Michelle Zancarini-Fournel (Paris: Éditions de l'IMEC, 2003), 87.

Groupe d'Information sur les Prisons (GIP), "Right to Information on the Prisons," was a GIP leaflet drafted after several of its members (including Michel Foucault and Jean-Marie Domenach) were picked up for questioning on May 1, 1971, outside the prison gates at Fresnes and La Santé, where they were launching the campaign for the abolition of criminal records. It was subsequently published as "Droit à l'information sur les prisons," in *Le Groupe d'information sur les prisons: Archives d'une lutte 1970–1972*, ed. Philippe Artières, Laurent Quéro, and Michelle Zancarini-Fournel (Paris: Éditions de l'IMEC, 2003), 88.

Groupe d'Information sur les Prisons (GIP), "The Death of George Jackson Is Not a Prison Accident," was a statement from the back cover of *Intolérable 3: L'assassinat de George Jackson*, which was published by Gallimard on November 10, 1971. It was subsequently published as "La mort de George Jackson n'est pas un accident de prison . . . ," in *Le Groupe d'information sur les prisons: Archives d'une lutte 1970–1972*, ed. Philippe Artières, Laurent Quéro, and Michelle Zancarini-Fournel (Paris: Éditions de l'IMEC, 2003), 105; and in Groupe d'Information sur les Prisons, *Intolérable*, ed. Philippe Artières (Paris: Verticales, 2013), 154.

Jean Genet, "Preface to *Intolerable 3*," was originally published in *Intolérable 3: L'assassinat de George Jackson*. It has since been republished in Jean Genet, *L'Ennemi déclaré*, ed. Albert Dichy (Paris: Gallimard, 1991), 111–17, and translated in Jean Genet, *The Declared Enemy: Texts and Interviews*, ed. Albert Dichy, trans. Jeff Fort (Palo Alto, Calif.: Stanford University Press, 2003), 91–97, and published as "Préface," in *Le Groupe d'information sur les prisons: Archives d'une lutte 1970–1972*, ed. Philippe Artières, Laurent Quéro, and Michelle Zancarini-Fournel (Paris: Éditions de l'IMEC, 2003), 107–12; and in Groupe d'Information sur les Prisons, *Intolérable*, ed. Philippe Artières (Paris: Verticales, 2013): 155–63. Copyright 1991 Éditions Gallimard. English translation copyright 2004 by the Board of Trustees of the Leland Stanford University Junior University. All rights reserved. Reprinted with permission of Stanford University Press.

Groupe d'Information sur les Prisons (GIP), "The Assassination Coverup, after the Assassination, and Jackson's Place in the Prison Movement," was originally published in *Intolérable 3: L'assassinat de George Jackson*. The original translation, "The Masked Assassin," and notes by Sirene Harb with editorial notes by Joy James, appears in *Warfare in the American Homeland: Policing and Prison in a Penal Democracy*, ed. Joy James (Durham, N.C.: Duke University Press, 2007), 140–60. The translation has been revised for this volume. It was also published as "L'assassinat camouflé, Après l'assassinat, and La place de Jackson dans le mouvement des prisons," in Groupe d'Information sur les Prisons, *Intolérable*, ed. Philippe Artières (Paris: Verticales, 2013): 192–213.

Groupe d'Information sur les Prisons (GIP), Comité d'Action des Prisonniers (CAP), and Association pour la Défense des Droits des Détenus (ADDD), "(There Have Always Been Suicides . . .)," was originally published as a prefatory tract in *Intolérable 4: Suicides de prison.* It was subsequently published as "(Il y a toujours eu des suicides . . .)," in Groupe d'Information sur les Prisons, *Intolérable,* ed. Philippe Artières (Paris: Verticales, 2013), 272.

Groupe d'Information sur les Prisons (GIP), "Letters from 'H. M.,'" was a presentation of the letters of the prisoner "H. M." (Gérard Grandmontagne), which form the centerpiece of the GIP booklet *Intolérable 4: Suicides de prison,* published in 1972. It was subsequently published as "Lettres de 'H. M.,'" in *Le Groupe d'information sur les prisons: Archives d'une lutte 1970–1972,* ed. Philippe Artières, Laurent Quéro, and Michelle Zancarini-Fournel (Paris: Éditions de l'IMEC, 2003), 277–300; and in Groupe d'Information sur les Prisons, *Intolérable,* ed. Philippe Artières (Paris: Verticales, 2013), 280–311.

Gilles Deleuze and Daniel Defert, "On the Letters of 'H. M.'" Although unsigned, this text is attributed to Gilles Deleuze and Daniel Defert. It was published as "Sur les lettres de 'H. M.,'" in *Le Groupe d'information sur les prisons: Archives d'une lutte 1970–1972,* ed. Philippe Artières, Laurent Quéro, and Michelle Zancarini-Fournel (Paris: Éditions de l'IMEC, 2003): 301–3; and in Groupe d'Information sur les Prisons, *Intolérable,* ed. Philippe Artières (Paris: Verticales, 2013): 312–15. It has been translated by Michael Taormina as "H. M.'s Letters," in *Gilles Deleuze, Desert Islands and Other Texts, 1953–1974,* ed. David Lapoujade (New York: Semiotext(e), 2004), 244–46. The translation has been revised for this volume.

Groupe d'Information sur les Prisons (GIP), "Report on an Interview with Doctor Fully," was originally published in *Intolerable 4: Prison Suicides.* It was subsequently published as "Compte rendu d'un entretien avec le docteur Fully," in *Le Groupe d'information sur les prisons: Archives d'une lutte 1970–1972,* ed. Philippe Artières, Laurent Quéro, and Michelle Zancarini-Fournel (Paris: Éditions de l'IMEC, 2003), 307–11; and in Groupe d'Information sur les Prisons, *Intolérable,* ed. Philippe Artières (Paris: Verticales, 2013), 326–34.

Groupe d'Information sur les Prisons (GIP), "The Prisoner Faces Segregation Every Day," was originally published in *La Cause du peuple.* It was subsequently published as "Le prisonnier affronte chaque jour la segregation . . . ," in *Le Groupe d'information sur les prisons: Archives d'une lutte 1970–1972,* ed. Philippe Artières, Laurent Quéro, and Michelle Zancarini-Fournel (Paris: Éditions de l'IMEC, 2003), 124.

Groupe d'Information sur les Prisons (GIP), "Violence at Fleury-Mérogis," was originally published as a GIP report on the events of September 26, 1971, at the Fleury-Mérogis prison. It was subsequently published as "Violences à Fleury-Mérogis," in *Le Groupe d'information sur les prisons: Archives d'une lutte 1970–1972,* ed. Philippe Artières, Laurent Quéro, and Michelle Zancarini-Fournel (Paris: Editions de l'IMEC, 2003), 140–43.

Groupe d'Information sur les Prisons (GIP), "A Movement of Struggle Is Developing Today . . . ," was originally published as a GIP leaflet announcing a "Prisons Meeting" at La Mutualité on November 11, 1971. It was subsequently published as "Un movement de lutte se développe aujourd'hui . . . ," in *Le Groupe d'information sur les prisons: Archives d'une lutte 1970–1972,* ed. Philippe Artières, Laurent Quéro, and Michelle Zancarini-Fournel (Paris: Éditions de l'IMEC, 2003), 125.

Daniel Defert, "On What Does the Penitentiary System Rely?" was originally the text of a speech by Daniel Defert, delivered during a meeting at La Mutualité on November 11, 1971. It was published as "Sur quoi repose le système pénitentiare?" in *Le Groupe d'information sur les prisons: Archives d'une lutte 1970–1972,* ed. Philippe Artières, Laurent Quéro, and Michelle Zancarini-Fournel (Paris: Éditions de l'IMEC, 2003), 127–31.

Groupe d'Information sur les Prisons (GIP), "Pleven Eliminates the Detainees' Christmas Packages," was originally published as a leaflet, probably drafted on the occasion of the demonstration by families on December 4, 1971, at Place Vendôme. It was subsequently published as "Pleven supprime les colis de Noël aux détenus," in *Le Groupe d'information sur les prisons: Archives d'une lutte 1970–1972,* ed. Philippe Artières, Laurent Quéro, and Michelle Zancarini-Fournel (Paris: Éditions de l'IMEC, 2003), 144.

Groupe d'Information sur les Prisons (GIP), "Declaration to the Press and the Public Authorities Coming from the Prisoners at Melun," was originally a text read during the press conference of January 17, 1972, organized by the GIP on the premises of the chancellery and then at the offices of the *Agence de presse Libération.* This document was republished in the *APL Bulletin,* no. 16 (January 18, 1972), in the *Cahiers de revendications sortis des prisons lors des récentes révoltes* in April 1972, and then in *Révolte à la prison Charles-III de Nancy* (GIP-Nancy, May 1972). It was subsequently published as "Déclaration à la presse et aux pouvoirs publics émanant des prisonniers de Melun," in *Le Groupe d'information sur les prisons: Archives d'une lutte 1970–1972,* ed. Philippe Artières, Laurent Quéro, and Michelle Zancarini-Fournel (Paris: Éditions de l'IMEC, 2003), 187–90; and in Groupe d'Information sur les Prisons, *Intolérable,* ed. Philippe Artières (Paris: Verticales, 2013), 228–33.

Groupe d'Information sur les Prisons (GIP), "Toul Prison List of Demands," is a list of demands developed by prisoners at Toul Prison and originally published in the GIP booklet *Cahiers de revendications sortis des prisons lors des récentes révoltes* in April 1972. It was subsequently published as "Liste des revendications à la centrale de Toul," in Groupe d'Information sur les Prisons, *Intolérable,* ed. Philippe Artières (Paris: Verticales, 2013), 225.

Groupe d'Information sur les Prisons (GIP), "Fresnes," is a list of demands developed by prisoners at Fresnes Prison and published in the GIP booklet *Cahiers de revendications sortis des prisons lors des récentes révoltes* in April 1972. It was subsequently published as "Fresnes," in Groupe d'Information sur les Prisons, *Intolérable,* ed. Philippe Artières (Paris: Verticales, 2013), 235.

Groupe d'Information sur les Prisons (GIP), "Tract Made and Launched by Insurgent Prisoners at Nancy," is a list of demands developed by prisoners at Nancy Prison and originally published in the GIP booklet *Cahiers de revendications sortis des prisons lors des récentes révoltes* in April 1972. It was subsequently published as "Tract fait et lancé par les prisonniers insurgés à la population de Nancy," in Groupe d'Information sur les Prisons, *Intolérable,* ed. Philippe Artières (Paris: Verticales, 2013), 234.

Groupe d'Information sur les Prisons (GIP), "The GIP Proposes a Commission of Inquiry," was originally a GIP tract, circulated on December 11, 1971. It was subsequently published as "Le GIP propose une commission d'enquête . . . ," in *Le Groupe d'information sur les prisons: Archives d'une lutte 1970–1972,* ed. Philippe Artières, Laurent Quéro, and Michelle Zancarini-Fournel (Paris: Éditions de l'IMEC, 2003), 146.

Groupe d'Information sur les Prisons (GIP), "Concerning Something New in the Prisons . . . ," was originally published as a GIP tract distributed in December 1971. It was published as "Du nouveau dans les prisons . . . ," in *Le Groupe d'information sur les prisons: Archives d'une lutte 1970–1972,* ed.

Philippe Artières, Laurent Quéro, and Michelle Zancarini-Fournel (Paris: Éditions de l'IMEC, 2003), 162.

Michel Foucault, "To Escape Their Prison," is a transcription of an unedited manuscript that Michel Foucault prepared for a Comité Vérité Toul press conference on the Toul Prison Revolt in January 1972. It was published as "Pour échapper à leur prison . . . ," in *Le Groupe d'information sur les prisons: Archives d'une lutte 1970–1972*, ed. Philippe Artières, Laurent Quéro, and Michelle Zancarini-Fournel (Paris: Éditions de l'IMEC, 2003), 151–55.

Groupe d'Information sur les Prisons (GIP) and Comité Vérité Toul (CVT), "Toul Hell," is testimonials received by the GIP and the Comité Vérité Toul (CVT) from prisoners and guards, and published first by the APL, January 9, 1972, then reprinted in *La Cause du peuple—J'accuse,* and finally reprinted again in the CVT's *La Révolte de la centrale Ney* (Paris: Gallimard, 1972). It was published as "L'enfer de Toul," in *Le Groupe d'information sur les prisons: Archives d'une lutte 1970–1972,* ed. Philippe Artières, Laurent Quéro, and Michelle Zancarini-Fournel (Paris: Éditions de l'IMEC, 2003), 158–60.

Édith Rose, "Report by Dr. Rose, Psychiatrist at Toul Prison," was sent to the penitentiary administration's inspector general, to the President of the French Republic, to the Minister of Justice, and to the National French Order of Physicians the day after the Toul Revolt. This report was read aloud by Michel Foucault during the Toul press conference on December 16 and published in *La Cause du peuple—J'accuse,* no. 15 (December 18, 1971), then in *Le Monde,* where Foucault and other public figures, including Simone Signoret, had purchased a page, and finally in *Psychiatrie d'aujourd'hui,* no. 7 (January/February 1972). It was subsequently published as "Rapport de Mme Rose, psychiatre de la Centrale de Toul," in *Le Groupe d'information sur les prisons: Archives d'une lutte 1970–1972,* ed. Philippe Artières, Laurent Quéro, and Michelle Zancarini-Fournel (Paris: Éditions de l'IMEC, 2003), 164–66.

Michel Foucault, "The Toul Speech," is a statement made by Michel Foucault during the Comité Vérité Toul press conference on January 5, 1972. This intervention was published in *Le Nouvel observateur,* no. 372, December 27, 1971–January 2, 1972, and in the *APL Bulletin,* no. 12, on January 9, 1972. It was subsequently published as "Le Discours de Toul," in *Le Groupe d'information sur les prisons: Archives d'une lutte 1970–1972,* ed.

Philippe Artières, Laurent Quéro, and Michelle Zancarini-Fournel (Paris: Éditions de l'IMEC, 2003),167–68; in Michel Foucault, *Dits et écrits, 1954–1988,* ed. Daniel Defert and François Ewald, 4 vols. (Paris: Gallimard, 1994), 2:99, 236–38; and in Michel Foucault, *Dits et écrits, 1954–1988,* ed. Daniel Defert and François Ewald, 2 vols. (Paris: Quarto Gallimard, 2001), 1:1104–6.

Gilles Deleuze, "Concerning Psychiatrists in the Prisons," is a statement made by Gilles Deleuze during the Comité Vérité Toul press conference on January 5, 1972. This address regarding the reception of Dr. Édith Rose's report among psychiatrists was published in the *APL Bulletin,* no. 12, on January 9, 1972. It was subsequently published as "À propos des psychiatres dans les prisons," in *Le Groupe d'information sur les prisons: Archives d'une lutte 1970–1972,* ed. Philippe Artières, Laurent Quéro, and Michelle Zancarini-Fournel (Paris: Éditions de l'IMEC, 2003), 156.

Groupe d'Information sur les Prisons (GIP), "I Would Like, on Behalf of the GIP, to Dispel a Misunderstanding . . . ," is a GIP communiqué, unsigned but likely written by Michel Foucault in January 1972. It was published as "Je voudrais au nom du GIP dissiper un malentendu . . . ," in *Le Groupe d'information sur les prisons: Archives d'une lutte 1970–1972,* ed. Philippe Artières, Laurent Quéro, and Michelle Zancarini-Fournel (Paris: Éditions de l'IMEC, 2003), 193.

Gilles Deleuze, "What the Prisoners Expect from Us . . . ," is an opinion piece by Gilles Deleuze, speaking for the GIP, published in *Le Nouvel observateur,* January 31, 1972, 24. It was subsequently published as "Ce que les prisonniers attendent de nous . . . ," in *Le Groupe d'information sur les prisons: Archives d'une lutte 1970–1972,* ed. Philippe Artières, Laurent Quéro, and Michelle Zancarini-Fournel (Paris: Éditions de l'IMEC, 2003), 194. The English translation by Michael Taormina was published as "What Our Prisoners Want from Us . . . ," in *Gilles Deleuze, Desert Islands and Other Texts, 1953–1974,* ed. David Lapoujade (New York: Semiotext(e), 2004), 204–5. The translation has been revised for this volume.

Michel Foucault, "It Was about a Year Ago," is Foucault's statement on the Nancy Prison Revolt from the GIP press conference of January 17, 1972. It was published in the *APL Bulletin,* no. 16 (January 18, 1972). It was subsequently published as "Il y a un an à peu près . . . ," in *Le Groupe d'information sur les prisons: Archives d'une lutte 1970–1972,* ed. Philippe Artières, Laurent Quéro, and Michelle Zancarini-Fournel (Paris: Éditions de l'IMEC, 2003), 195–99.

Michel Foucault, "The Great Confinement," is an interview conducted by Niklaus Meienberg. It originally appeared under the title "Die grosse Einsperrung," in *Tages Anzeiger Magazin*, no. 12 (March 25, 1972): 15, 17, 20, and 37. It was subsequently published as "Le grand enfermement," in Michel Foucault, *Dits et écrits, 1954–1988*, ed. Daniel Defert and François Ewald, 4 vols. (Paris: Gallimard, 1994), 2:105, 296–306; and in Michel Foucault, *Dits et écrits, 1954–1988*, ed. Daniel Defert and François Ewald, 2 vols. (Paris: Quarto Gallimard, 2001), 1:105, 1164–74.

Michel Foucault and Gilles Deleuze, "Intellectuals and Power," is a discussion between Michel Foucault and Gilles Deleuze recorded on March 4, 1972. It was published in *L'Arc*, no. 49: Gilles Deleuze (2d trimester 1972): 3–10. It was subsequently published as "Les intellectuels et le pouvoir," in Michel Foucault, *Dits et écrits, 1954–1988*, ed. Daniel Defert and François Ewald, 4 vols. (Paris: Gallimard, 1994), 2:106, 306–15; and in Michel Foucault, *Dits et écrits, 1954–1988*, ed. Daniel Defert and François Ewald, 2 vols. (Paris: Quarto Gallimard, 2001), 1:106, 1174–83. Reprinted from Michel Foucault, *Language, Counter-Memory, Practice: Selected Essays and Interviews*, ed. Donald F. Bouchard. Copyright 1977 by Cornell University. Reprinted by permission of Cornell University Press. The translation by Donald F. Bouchard and Sherry Simon has been revised for this volume.

Michel Foucault, "On Attica," is an interview with Michel Foucault conducted in Buffalo, New York, on April 21, 1972, by John Simon after their tour of the Attica Correctional Facility, the site of a major revolt in September 1971. It was translated by John Simon and appeared in *Telos* 19 (1974): 154–61. The translation was subsequently published in *Foucault Live: Collected Interviews, 1961–1984*, ed. Sylvère Lotringer (New York: Semiotext(e), 1996), 113–21. It was published in French as "À propos de la prison d'Attica," in Michel Foucault, *Dits et écrits, 1954–1988*, ed. Daniel Defert and François Ewald, 4 vols. (Paris: Gallimard, 1994), 2:137, 525–36; and in Michel Foucault, *Dits et écrits, 1954–1988*, ed. Daniel Defert and François Ewald, 2 vols. (Paris: Quarto Gallimard, 2001), 1:137, 1393–1404. The translation has been revised for this volume and reprinted with the permission of *Telos*.

Michel Foucault, "Pompidou's Two Deaths," originally appeared in *Le Nouvel observateur* 421 (1972): 56–57. It was subsequently published as "Les deux morts de Pompidou," in Michel Foucault, *Dits et écrits, 1954–1988*, ed. Daniel Defert and François Ewald, 4 vols. (Paris: Gallimard, 1994), 2:114, 386–89; and in Michel Foucault, *Dits et écrits, 1954–1988*, ed. Daniel Defert and François Ewald, 2 vols. (Paris: Quarto Gallimard, 2001), 1:114, 1254–57. It was translated by Robert Hurley and published in *Power,* ed. James Faubion (New York: New Press, 2000), 418–22. Excerpt from *Power: Essential Works of Foucault, 1954–1984.* Copyright 1994 by Éditions Gallimard. Compilation, introduction, and new translations copyright 2000 by The New Press. Reprinted by permission of The New Press.

Michel Foucault, "Prisons and Revolts in Prisons," is an interview with Michel Foucault conducted by Bodo Morawe. It originally appeared under the title "Gefängnisse und Gefängnisrevolten," in *Dokumente: Zeitschrift für übernationale Zusammenarbeit,* no. 2 (June 1973): 133–37. It was published as "Prisons et révoltes dans les prisons," in Michel Foucault, *Dits et écrits, 1954–1988,* ed. Daniel Defert and François Ewald, 4 vols. (Paris: Gallimard, 1994), 2:125, 425–32; and in Michel Foucault, *Dits et écrits, 1954–1988,* ed. Daniel Defert and François Ewald, 2 vols. (Paris: Quarto Gallimard, 2001), 1:125, 1293–1300.

Groupe d'Information sur les Prisons (GIP), "Forms of Mobilization and Axes of Struggle," is an unsigned, internal GIP document that dates from April 1972. It was published as "Formes de mobilisation et axes de luttes," in *Le Groupe d'information sur les prisons: Archives d'une lutte 1970–1972,* ed. Philippe Artières, Laurent Quéro, and Michelle Zancarini-Fournel (Paris: Éditions de l'IMEC, 2003), 231–32.

Groupe d'Information sur les Prisons (GIP), "The Second Front (The Neighborhoods)," is an unsigned, internal GIP document. It was published as "Deuxième front (Les quartiers)," in *Le Groupe d'information sur les prisons: Archives d'une lutte 1970–1972,* ed. Philippe Artières, Laurent Quéro, and Michelle Zancarini-Fournel (Paris: Éditions de l'IMEC, 2003), 233.

Jean-Marie Domenach, "To Have Done with the Prisons," was published in *Esprit,* no. 415 (July–August 1972). It was subsequently published as "En finir avec les prisons," in *Le Groupe d'information sur les prisons: Archives d'une lutte 1970–1972,* ed. Philippe Artières, Laurent Quéro, and Michelle Zancarini-Fournel (Paris: Éditions de l'IMEC, 2003), 258–67. Reprinted with permission of *Esprit.*

Michel Foucault, "Preface to Serge Livrozet's *De la prison à la révolte,*" was originally published in Serge Livrozet's *De la prison à la révolte* (Paris: Mercure de France, 1973), 7–14. It was subsequently published as "Préface," in Michel Foucault, *Dits et écrits, 1954–1988,* ed. Daniel Defert and François Ewald, 4 vols. (Paris: Gallimard, 1994), 2:116, 394–99; and in Michel Foucault, *Dits et écrits, 1954–1988,* ed. Daniel Defert and François Ewald, 2 vols. (Paris: Quarto Gallimard, 2001), 1:116, 1262–67.

Michel Foucault, "Preface to Bruce Jackson's *In the Life: Versions of the Criminal Experience,*" was published in *Leurs prisons: Autobiographies de prisonniers américains* (Paris: Plon, 1975), i–vi. Originally published in English as Bruce Jackson, *In the Life: Versions of the Criminal Experience* (New York: Holt, Rinehart, and Winston, 1972). It was subsequently published as "Préface," in Michel Foucault, *Dits et écrits, 1954–1988,* ed. Daniel Defert and François Ewald, 4 vols. (Paris: Gallimard, 1994), 2:144, 687–91; and in Michel Foucault, *Dits et écrits, 1954–1988,* ed. Daniel Defert and François Ewald, 2 vols. (Paris: Quarto Gallimard, 2001), 1:144, 1555–59.

François Colcombet, Antoine Lazarus, and Louis Appert, "Struggles around the Prisons," is the text of a roundtable discussion that took place in 1979. It was published in *Esprit,* no. 11: "Toujours les prisons" (November 1979): 102–11. It was subsequently published as "Luttes autour des prisons," in Michel Foucault, *Dits et écrits, 1954–1988,* ed. Daniel Defert and François Ewald, 4 vols. (Paris: Gallimard, 1994), 3:273, 806–18; and in Michel Foucault, *Dits et écrits, 1954–1988,* ed. Daniel Defert and François Ewald, 2 vols. (Paris: Quarto Gallimard, 2001), 2:273, 806–18. Reprinted with permission of *Esprit.*

Jean-Marie Domenach, Michel Foucault, and Paul Thibaud, "Still Prisons," is a series of letters exchanged between Michel Foucault, Jean-Marie Domenach, and Paul Thibaud that originally appeared in the correspondence section of *Esprit,* 37.1 (January 1980): 184–86. It was subsequently published as "Toujours les prisons," in Michel Foucault, *Dits et écrits, 1954–1988,* ed. Daniel Defert and François Ewald, 4 vols. (Paris: Gallimard, 1994), 4:282, 96–99; and in Michel Foucault, *Dits et écrits, 1954–1988,* ed. Daniel Defert and François Ewald, 2 vols. (Paris: Quarto Gallimard, 2001), 2:282, 915–18. Reprinted with permission of *Esprit.*

Gilles Deleuze, "Foucault and Prisons," is an interview with Gilles Deleuze conducted by Paul Rabinow and Keith Gandal on May 25, 1985, that was originally published in translation by Paul Rabinow as "The Intellectual and Politics: Foucault and the Prison," *History of the Present* 2 (1986): 1–2, 20–21. A French version, based on a transcription of the original recording, was published in *Deux régimes des fous,* ed. David Lapoujade (Paris: Minuit, 2003), and this version (which differs from the first English version) was included in a translation by Ames Hodges and Mike Taormina in *Two Regimes of Madness,* rev. ed., ed. David Lapoujade (New York: Semiotext(e), 2007), 277–86. Reprinted by permission of Les Éditions de Minuit and English translation from Semiotext(e). The translation has been revised for this volume.

Index

NOTE: *The letter* f *following a page number indicates figure.*